MISSION COLLEGE
LEARNING RESOURCE SERVICE

D0216269

DATE DUE

MAR 1 3 2003			

Demco, Inc. 38-293

3 1215 00094 6902

MISSION COLLEGE
LEARNING RESOURCE SERVICES

OPEN SYSTEMS STANDARDIZATION

OPEN SYSTEMS STANDARDIZATION
A Business Approach

Carl F. Cargill

To join a Prentice Hall PTR internet mailing list, point to:
http://www.prenhall.com/register

Prentice Hall PTR
Upper Saddle River, NJ 07458
http://www.prenhall.com

Library of Congress Cataloging-in-Publication Data

Cargill, Carl F.
   Open systems standardization : a business approach /
 Carl F. Cargill.
     p.   cm.
   Includes index.
   ISBN 0–13–268319–9
    1. Electronic data processing—Standards.   2. Information
technology—Standards.   I. Title.
   QA76.9.S8C37   1997
   004′.0218—dc20   96-28601
                                                CIP

Acquisitions editor: Michael E. Meehan
Cover designer: Scott Weiss
Cover design director: Jerry Votta
Manufacturing manager: Alexis R. Heydt
Compositor/Production services: Pine Tree Composition, Inc.

© 1997 Paladin Consulting Inc.

 Published by Prentice Hall PTR
Prentice-Hall, Inc.
A Simon & Schuster Company
Upper Saddle River, New Jersey 07458

The publisher offers discounts on this book when ordered in
bulk quantities. For more information contact:

> Corporate Sales Department
> Prentice Hall PTR
> One Lake Street
> Upper Saddle River, New Jersey 07458
> Phone: 800–382–3419
> Fax: 201–236–7141
> email: corpsales@prenhall.com

All rights reserved. No part of this book may be reproduced,
in any form or by any means, without permission in writing
from the publisher.

Printed in the United States of America
10 9 8 7 6 5 4 3 2 1

ISBN 0-13-268319-9

Prentice-Hall International (UK) Limited, *London*
Prentice-Hall of Australia Pty. Limited, *Sydney*
Prentice-Hall Canada Inc., *Toronto*
Prentice-Hall Hispanoamericana, S.A., *Mexico*
Prentice-Hall of India Private Limited, *New Delhi*
Prentice-Hall of Japan, Inc., *Tokyo*
Simon & Schuster Asia Pte. Ltd., *Singapore*
Editora Prentice-Hall do Brasil, Ltda., *Rio de Janeiro*

To Gary Robinson, my friend
To Dorothy Cerni, my teacher
To Catherine Kachurik, my inspiration

This book is gratefully dedicated.

Contents

Chapter 10   The Internal Standardization
                        Organization: Creation and Management   **131**

Chapter 11   Topics and Methods
                        of Standardization   **139**

Chapter 12   The Formal Standards Process   **159**

Chapter 13   Standards and Business   **168**

Chapter 14   The Future of Consensus
                        Standards   **180**

Chapter 18   The National Standards
Organization   242

Chapter 19   The Internet   255

Chapter 20   The Working Standards Developing
Organization   262

Chapter 21   The Model Consortia   275

Chapter 22   Governmental and Other Accredited
Standards Bodies   288

Preface

This book is a follow-up to my earlier book *Information Technology Standardization: Theory, Process, and Organizations*. It represents a maturing of the ideas that were contained in the first book, and is my best attempt to merge many of the thoughts that I've had, many of the conversations that I've heard, and many of the papers that I've read in the ensuing six years. Above all, it represents a look at standardization in "open systems"—not just computing and Information Technology, but the entire spectrum of activities that these disciplines impact.

The industry situation since I wrote the first book has changed tremendously, but, as most things, the more that it has changed, the more it has stayed the same. The entire field of Information Technology has changed; the appearance of the World Wide Web and the global nature of the Internet has been made possible by standardization. The very nature of how and where standardization occurs has changed; consortia have become significant, alliances have appeared, the formal process has weakened—and yet, the need for standards and standardization continues to grow at a frantic pace to support even more frantic growth. Computing has become ubiquitous; users expect standards—and yet the industry continues to have trouble finding a coherent method of expressing its needs. Each new movement seems to have the need to create its own methodology of standardization. Each rejects the past, and attempts to create anew a viable process. In many circumstances, what was before is no longer suitable for what is coming. But in all circumstances, the fundamentals are the same: a group of individuals or organizations who band together in an attempt to provide a common area for competition. One of the first responsibilities of standardization is to ensure that past experiences are not forgotten, but rather saved and made available to follow-up activities, thus lessening the amount of re-invention necessary.

This book is written in the hope that I can make explicit these implicit fundamental principles, and, by so doing, make any necessary re-invention easier and faster. Additionally, by describing what I feel to be the core theories and practices of standardization, I hope to provide a basis for beginning the more formal understanding of the standardization process. This formal understanding, or the creation of a "discipline of standardization," should serve the high technology industry as well as those industries which are beginning to see standardization as a method of dealing with change and the high rate of change. Finally, by expanding some of the ideas of standardization, I hope to provide a basis for beginning to understand how standardization is a component of the modern "open and virtual" organization.

As with the last book, this book can be viewed as a series of interconnected parts. Section 1 is, again, the section that contains the theoretical and philosophical underpinning. Section 2 is focused on the "how to do standardization" type of section. Finally, Section 3 looks at the organizations that are major players in the Open Systems arena. With the appearance of the World Wide Web, I have been less concerned with providing the minutiae of the standardization groups, such as the rules for operation and organizational structure, as with my observations on their viability and roles. I have provided, in Appendix C, a listing of some of the Universal Resource Locators (URLs) for the major standardization organizations, which should allow the WWW-enabled reader to find the most current references. I have also provided a list (in Appendix B) of addresses for major Standards Developing Organizations.

This book, as with the last one, owes much to the people with whom I was fortunate enough to meet over the course of nearly two decades in standardization, as well as to people who encouraged me in my sometimes solitary and weird pursuit of standardization. The dedication of the book is recognition to the three people with whom I have worked who had a significant impact upon me and the way that I've tried to "do standardization." Their influence on me, and upon the industry in general, cannot be overstated.

Throughout this book there are references to *StandardView,* a publication of the Association for Computing Machinery. This periodical was the result of an idea by Joseph DeBlasi, the Executive Director of the ACM, who believed that a business/technical focus on standardization would be accepted. Joe asked me to be Editor-in-Chief, and, despite my original misgivings, *StandardView* has succeeded, growing in circulation and influence. The industry owes much to this remarkable man.

In a similar vein, I would like to recognize the contributions to standardization by another industry pioneer, Kenneth Olsen, the former CEO of Digital Equipment Corporation. Ken, more than any other IT leader, recognized the value and fundamental characteristics of standardization long before it was popular to do so. His understanding and support of the discipline was a major reason that standardization has succeeded.

Finally, I would like to also recognize the impact that Don Cragun of Sun Microsystems and Henry Lowe of OSF have had on me. Don and Henry are both quiet and unassuming professionals who are past masters at doing what is morally and technically right, both in standardization and engineering. It is only after I'd worked with both of them for several years that I realized the depth and breadth of their influence, both on me and on the industry.

There are numerous other people who have helped with this book and the ideas behind it. Michael Spring and Martin Weiss at the University of Pittsburgh, who have led the movement to study standards as a discipline; Andrew Updegrove, who has struggled to create a legal underpinning for consortia; Stanley Warshaw, who directly or indirectly focused attention on standardization as an economic force; my editors at (and contributors to) *StandardView,* who provide constant feedback and help, especially my Associate Editor, Wendy Reid; the members of UniForum New Zealand, who regularly listen to me and provide insightful (and sometimes inflammatory) feedback on the latest theories; D. Linda Garcia, formerly of the Office of Technology Assessment, for her belief in standardization and for having the courage to publish controversial, but logically rigorous, studies; Stephen Walli, who continues to be a critic and a friend, as well as a contributor to the discipline; Patricia Kopp, whose untiring efforts to keep me involved in Z1 are succeeding; Graham Bird, of The Open Group, who has had the dubious pleasure of working with me when I'm on a tear; David Schell and Kurt Buehler or OGC, for their willingness to trust me with their ideas; and finally, to Richard Straub, of Digital Equipment Corporation, a gentleman and leader in standardization marketing. There are numerous others, and to them I owe thanks as well.

On the personal side, my thanks to my children, Adam and Helen (despite the fact that their father is "Standards Man"), and to Anne Buzbee, who has provided feedback and encouragement during the long, dark period that preceded my being able to face the task of creating again. And finally, to my mother and sisters, who continue to believe in me, even though they question the wisdom of entrusting me with important things.

As always, while success is shared, omissions and errors are mine, and mine alone. The book contains a fair share of my personality, and many will find it opinionated and possibly wrong-headed. If this is the case, I invite those that feel this way to write a description of "the right way," or an alternative way, and send it to me at *StandardView,* where it will be considered for publication so that the discipline can grow. Standardization is about sharing and increasing knowledge, and making things better. This is also the intent of this book.

Carl F. Cargill
Mountain View, California

OPEN SYSTEMS STANDARDIZATION

Prologue

"Sound, sound the clarion, fill the fife!
To all the sensual world proclaim,
One crowded hour of glorious life
Is worth an age without a name."

—Sir Walter Scott, *Old Mortality*

IN DEFENSE OF STANDARDIZATION

In the first edition of this book, the emphasis was on the standards-developing organizations that populated the world and the processes that they used to come to consensus. There was a focus on the "business" aspect of standardization, in which the rationale for standards activities was traced back to a pragmatic wish to make a "better product" by the participants. The term "better" was left to the discretion of the participants, whether they were provider, user, or "other."

In the time since the publication of that first work, the world of standardization has changed substantially. The commercial aspect of standardization has moved to the forefront, surprising and upsetting the participants in the older, more technologically derived process. Simultaneously, there was a growth in participation. These new participants—some well intentioned, some not—substituted bravado for knowledge, and forced the somewhat stolid and staid world of standardization to irrevocably change. However, these newly arrived participants sowed the seeds of their own undoing. They are being replaced by a new and different participant who has taken the time to understand the rationale for standardization—and how to use it in a new, more dynamic, and market-driven environment. This book begins at that point.

The organizations in standardization are legion; the United States alone has over 550 formal organizations actively "doing standardization." New organizations appear on a weekly basis, and older ones "revector" or "reengineer" or just disappear. The old discrete disciplinary boundaries between the organizations and the technical disciplines are disappearing; groups devoted to the multiple disciplines of telecommunication and computing are becoming common. Mergers of previously separate concepts are no longer unthinkable, and if they are unthinkable now, someone will think of them in the future and will propose something. And soon afterward, someone will propose an organization to "standardize it"; whatever "it" is and whatever "standardize" means.

Because of this proliferation of organizations, the character of the book has changed from looking at discrete organizational structures to more generalized organizational structure, and tracing some of the problems and opportunities that are found in these generalized structures. Companies that wish to engage in standardization face significant, but not insurmountable, challenges. Organizations created to "create standards" also face challenges that have a higher "surmountable" factor; not impossible, but dealing with quite a few more variables than a single organization. All of these organizations can and should interoperate; part of the focus of this book is trying to expedite this cooperation by characterizing the various types of organizations and what their various strengths and weaknesses are.

Additionally, there is an increased emphasis on the theory of standardization in business and other public and private sector organizations. There is no organization that is not touched by some aspect of standardization today; the impact of standardization will only grow over time, as increased interaction and interdependency become more common. The ability of an organization, or a collection of organizations, to deal with standardization, to internalize it, and to use it to benefit its activities should become a significant factor in business success. This book establishes some of the ground work in this area.

Finally, the ultimate purpose of the book is to increase the interest and utility of standardization, both in the Information Technology and other industries. Because I believe that the IT industry will be the first major industry to enter into the maelstrom of change (a maelstrom largely of its own creating), its ability to adapt its infrastructure to this environment will determine how others that follow could, or should, proceed. The genius of standardization is that it is the part of the infrastructure that is supposed to record the past and preserve that which is good, so that these things act as a guide to the future. Fundamentally, standardization that is not future focused is a failure; this is where the glory, passion, and excitement of standardization are found. Standardization is not the cataloguing of the old; it is the examination of the old, in the light of the new, to see what can be saved and what needs to be discarded. It is the process of change—both managing and being managed by the future—that is the function of standardization.

Section 1

THEORIES AND UTILITY OF STANDARDIZATION

This section looks at standards and standardization as a business tool—that is, an essential part of a manager's set of competencies, whether dealing with matters relating to Information Technology or nearly any other discipline. The history and application of standards and standardization are examined, and a broad general theory that applies standardization to the organization as a cultural and management discipline is explored. Additionally, a new theory for creating and making standardization effective is described.

Chapter 1

Standards, Standards Everywhere

"... Water, water everywhere,
Nor any drop to drink."

—Samuel T. Coleridge, *Rime of the Ancient Mariner*

INTRODUCTION

Standardization is the measure of an industrialized society. The greater the industrialization, the greater the amount of interdependence required for the elements of society to successfully interoperate. The greater the requirement for interoperation, the greater the amount of standardization necessary to manage the interactions which assure increasing industrialization and therefore, greater interdependence. This idea is not unique to information technology standardization; it is a social phenomenon. Interaction begets rules of behavior, and the formation of rules allows the advance of interaction to the point where new rules are necessary. Rules tend to regularize expectations and make life more comfortable and viable. These rules are ubiquitous. When they are mandatory, they are called laws. When they govern social interaction they are customs or manners. Within the Information Technology (IT) industry, the non-obligatory rules defining required interaction of parts of the system (open or otherwise) are called "standards." This book is about the process to create standards, called standardization.

THE GROWTH AND PROBLEMS OF STANDARDIZATION

Over the past six years (1988 to 1994), standards and standardization have moved on, off, and back on to center stage in the IT industry. There have been "standardization wars" over the look and feel of the user display (the GUI wars), skirmishes over chips, battles over operating systems, and fights about nearly everything else that could be looked at as a technical subject for standardization. Organizations have come and gone; the memory of the battles, with their attendant victories and losses, lingers. Industry is only a little wiser after all of these efforts than it was when it all began. What is apparent is that standards are necessary, and that billions of dollars have been invested in the activity by the participants. Finally, while the impact that standards appear to have on the industry can be examined and usually determined (ex post facto), each standardization effort appears to be treated as a unique enterprise that is not subject to (or possibly is exempt from) the experiences that happened to those that went before.

On the whole, the IT industry has embraced standards on principle, rather than on actually understanding why or if standardization is necessary. Standardization has been embraced as other good causes have been embraced by the industry—usually on faith and usually with conviction. The rationale for support, or for lack of support, varies from individual to individual, company to company, and industry to industry. The articles of faith for a hardware engineer employed by a large producer are substantially different from those of the MIS director who is trying desperately to fix a database problem for accounts payable. Each player in the IT industry is impacted by standardization and each, because of slightly different cultural baggage, will respond differently. The methods for achieving a common goal can vary widely.

The fundamental differences between Information Technology and telecommunications management are a case in point. The culture of telecommunications has always emphasized cooperation (unique telephones are difficult to network) while IT management has always valued change (my chip is faster than your chip). The underlying disconnect is how the two cultures view competition and winning. The separation is not the technology, but rather the application and use of that technology, which is also the driving force for nearly all standardization activities.

Another major issue within the IT industry stems from the fact that participants have never realized how heavily vested they are in standardization, nor have they realized how ubiquitous standards and standardization are. There is no company in the Information Technology industry that does not, in some way, depend upon standardization for success. From bus structure to QWERTY keyboards, from disk form-factors to object-oriented programming, the IT industry is riddled with standards and standardization. And yet, standardization is not a significant curricula item in most universities within the United States. The average New York union electrician knows more about standards than does the average graduate student in either electrical engineering or computer science union. The fundamental rationale for this is, of course, that the electrician is paid to accomplish a defined task using standards. Therefore, he or she knows the National Electrical Code backwards and forwards. The average graduate student, having spent several years learning how to do new and unique things that may or may not be applicable to any real world problem, is usually launched into a work force that is trying to solve workaday problems using solutions that are somehow related to current practice and which will not obviate all that has happened before. The marketplace uses and wants standards; the graduate engineers are forced to learn about standards from friends and from reading about them in industry periodicals. (It seems vaguely reminiscent of sex education in the 1950s.) As a result, there are substantial numbers of misconceptions about standards that abound in the industry that are part of the "folklore," which substitutes for education.

Much of the blame for the problem with standards rests in the nature of standardization itself. On a good day, standardization can be mind-deadeningly, eye-glazingly dull. Some of the fault for this lies in the nature of the discipline; there is no one who has not railed against "stupid rules" at some point in life. If correctly done, standards are an attempt to formalize the best of past practice; what is best, however, is all too often in the eyes of the beholder. (Chapter 3 discusses, in greater detail, some of the inherent contradictions that are contained in standardization within the IT arena. Chief among these is the concept of "anticipatory standardization.") To complicate things further within the IT industry, past practices are, almost by definition, suspect and therefore, by extension, so are standards.

An additional sin laid at the door of standards is that practitioners of standards tend to be perceived as boring as their discipline. This charge is, of course, spurious, at least in the view of the author. However, the basis for the argument lies in the nature of the discipline of standardization, which can be an exacting science, just as programming is an exact science. People who take great delight in describing their technical toys, people who surf the web, and people who dearly love programming ("nerds", "web-heads", and "hackers") have certain characteristics attributed to them; similarly, people who engage in standardization also have characteristics ascribed to them. Because standardization is not the act of actually creating something new, there is a tendency for the discipline to be slighted. On the other hand, standardization could be seen as a form of documentation of best practices; there are very few software people who can write software documentation that is coherent, unambiguous, and helpful, let alone know what the best practices for writing code are.

The fundamental problem with standardization is, however, its inherently contradictory nature to most technologists. Standards are seen as limiting freedom by halting innovation. On the other hand, the market (and most marketing people) prefers solutions that are not radically different from those currently in the vogue. Additionally, standards tend to appear in regulations with a startling degree of regularity. Therefore, by definition, they tend to be seen as limiting again. To complicate the problem further, when a poor standard is promulgated and users ignore it, technologists (both engineering and marketing) take this as proof that standards don't really matter. On the other hand, when a poor standard is promulgated and users accept it, the same audience takes this as proof that standards are just so much marketing hype and, "If people really knew their technology, they wouldn't . . ." It is a case of "Damned if you do, and damned if you don't." Finally, standards work in the realm of what is, not what if. Standardization does not (or should not) occur on the leading edge of a technology, for reasons that will be discussed. (When it does, the result is usually unfortunate.) However, most technical people like to play with new and emerging ideas, things, and areas. These, by their very nature, are unsuitable for standardization, yet market and marketing pressures are attempting to force standardization into these areas as they emerge.

The reason for this pressure is clear. There is tremendous economic motivation for "being the standard," since everyone will, perforce, have to follow it. This will allow one company to license the technology and give everyone large bonuses as well as recognition. The economic motivator that is implicit in standards, while never actually called out, is a power factor. And most descriptions of standardization allude to the "economic incentive for successful standardization." Most participants in the industry assume the existence of a body of literature that details the economics of standardization and which has been internalized by the industry. At many standards conventions and standards meetings, participants refer to the economic motivation for standards or to their impact on innovation or to a specific methodology for obtaining the truth about them. Yet no one can cite a convincing source—other than a series of particular instances where something has succeeded or something has failed. One of the problems with the "economic approach to standards" is that the economic model describes an attribute of the standards process and discipline, and not the thing itself.

Indeed, very few standards decisions are made from a purely rational economic viewpoint. While it is pleasant to claim that standards are the fruit of quantitative economic roots, it is also highly suspect and more than a little naive. In a similar manner, the technical-mechanistic approach to standards is less than satisfactory, since it reduces standards to something akin to rote memorization. This model sees the way to standardize something as the rationale for standardization. It mistakes the means for the end.

One of the major sources of "disinformation" in standardization is the push to "open systems." The emphasis within the standardization community of the IT industry has been on the "open" half of the equation. Nearly everything is "open"; many advertisements claim that a product is "more open" than all other competitor's products. The emphasis, of course, should be on the "system" portion of the equation. As was noted at the beginning of this chapter, the purpose of standards is to provide the basis for interoperability, not for "open." It is the "systemness" that should drive the standardization movement; it is the "systemness" that drives the successful companies in the industry. It is the need for interoperation—from a business point of view—that drives the reports of standardization in the general press. It is from the press that the IT industry gets most of its information on standards and standardization.

The Press and Standards

The term "press" is, at best, ambiguous. I use it because I cannot think of a better and more globally descriptive word. Basically, the term refers to both the popular press (magazines, newspapers, and popular books) and to the more serious press (less popular books that require thought and the serious journals). While this separation is somewhat arbitrary and probably reflects my bias, it is one that is probably valid. The distinction between the two lies more in what is said and how it is said. The popular press is a reporting function, while the "serious press" tries to both explain and posit possible new problems, and occasionally suggest solutions to the problems. Articles that appear on the Internet and the World Wide Web usually qualify as "popular press articles," since they usually (but not always) tend to focus on the immediate future or profound, but uninformed, speculation.

The popular press within the IT industry is a curious beast. The technical side specializes in articles that look at a technology or implications of developments from a technical point of view. It covers the topics that are of interest and necessary for technologists (and "wanna-be" technologists) to know. The articles on standards that appear in these publications are usually focused on a single standard or instantiation of a standard; on standards relating to a specific concept; articles about a specific discipline and the standards that affect it; and articles on the functioning and performance of standards bodies and the standards' processes.

In three of these categories, the articles do what they are supposed to do. Those articles that deal with a specific standard usually employ predefined and well-understood vocabularies within a set of reasonably clear-cut boundaries to address an audience that understands and is interested in the subject. Articles examining standards that relate to a specific concept are becoming more common, providing the readers with an understanding of the options available to them when considering the implementation of a possible technology. Articles examining standard in terms of their impact on a specific discipline alert readers to the existence of standards and often provide useful general background to a large audience not originally concerned with standards.

The articles dealing with standards bodies and the standards process are the least satisfactory. There is usually only a cursory examination of the causes that underlie the process or the rationale for participation. The articles tend to treat the standards groups as a collective monolithic entity, forgetting that these groups generally are composed of members of the industry: users, producers, developers, academics, and government who are joining in what is supposed to be a cooperative effort. Sometimes this produces a sometime valid description of a process and possible result of that process, but it is a description that is relatively sterile and without human, social, or economic context.

Another area in which mention of standardization is missing is in the "how to manage" books. Hammer and Champy in their *Reengineering the Corporation* mention the railroad as the start of bureaucracy (they neglect to mention that Alfred Chandler surfaced this argument in 1977), but fail to understand that the whole railroad success in the United States was built upon standards. Senge's *The Fifth Discipline* also overlooks standardization as part of learning organization. Morecroft and Sterman's *Modeling for Learning Organizations* discusses the complexity of systems yet makes no mention of the impact that standardization has on the ability of the organization to act and to change either its mission or its function or product. Fundamentally, all complex organizations derive some degree of stability (or rigidity) from standardization. The term "industry standard" had become widespread in the literature of most companies. Systems themselves are aggregate collections of standardized responses. The idea of industry standards (either de facto or de jure) had become accepted and was put into use by major companies, from Mercedes to DuPont to Mitsubishi, for market creation and exploitation. Nearly all of the computing is done with "open systems." And yet, the phenomena that is standardization is overlooked. While disappointing, the oversight is not surprising. As mentioned earlier, standardization can be boring, and the last thing that a "how to manage" book can afford is to be boring.

On the other hand, the serious press is becoming more and more inclined to look at the standardization phenomena. As the popular press has reported the activities of standardization, interest in these activities has grown and the serious explicators have begun to write. In many cases, the articles are written for obscure journals or as part of a larger book on other, but related issues, such as the National Information Infrastructure. However, compared to articles that were available even as little as three years ago, the current articles represent a quantum leap in understanding and discipline. The number of people who participate in standardization activities and who are willing to publish articles is growing—and many of them are willing to take unorthodox positions for publication. The net effect of this is to provide a basis for discussion and understanding.

Much of this increase in serious articles can be ascribed to the interest of the organizations that have funded the standardization activities of the industry. For the largest part, the commercially-based private sector has borne the brunt of making standardization happen. While both academic and governmental players exist, the majority of the activity has been funded by organizations that hope to turn a profit through their participation in standards. When firms that didn't participate in standardization were more successful than those that did, there was a search to determine why and what was happening. While there is a saying that "Nothing succeeds like success," within the standardization scholarship arena this saying might be modified to "Nothing succeeds like failure."

The interesting thing about this phenomena is that it has only been with the failure of standardization to deliver on its promises (larger market, greater success, interoperability, portability, user acceptance, and so on) that there has been serious consideration of why it is that the commercial sector would participate in this discipline. What fundamentally had happened was that the press, both serious and popular, was beginning to question the legitimacy of the discipline. The writers who made up the press that reflected the concerns of the industry had begun to ask hard and serious questions, to which, it turned out, there were precious few answers.

The industry—as reflected in the press—was beginning to ask the right questions about standardization. The overarching question was why there were few answers available to the industry? Given that the answers didn't exist, where was the industry to look for the fundamental research that might help determine which questions to ask and how to solve these questions? There are two obvious responses. The first is the academic community. The second, and less obvious, source is the standards organizations themselves.

Academic Involvement

Much of the research on standardization in academia has been initiated by economists. Many of the original researchers in the discipline seem to have started as economists who were looking for a new challenge to study. Many of them found it within the telecommunication standardization arena. Among the assumptions made in early studies were "perfect competition," "perfect arrival rate of orders," "perfect knowledge of costs and of competition," and so on, which were coupled with a lack of agreement on what the term "standards" actually meant. Over time, these analyses became more sophisticated, but they nonetheless continued to reflect the economists' obsession with predictive analysis. But standards activities reflect the industry of which they are a part, and it is neither perfect nor predictable: The standards process is buffeted by random, nonquantifiable, and at times irrational, behavior and variables. The economists, although associated with the high technology industry, were not part of the industry, nor had most of them the time or patience to participate in standardization.

Over the past five years, however, there has emerged another more eclectic school of academic researchers and teachers (some with a technical background and some with a social sciences bias). This group has begun to look at standardization from a perceptual and experiential bias. Instead of the formal models based upon abstract theory, the newer academicians have chosen to examine standardization as a phenomenon within the industry; trying to determine how it acts as a change agent, why volunteers participate, and what makes standardization effective or ineffective. These are, of course, questions that do not readily lend themselves to formal isolated investigation. These new academicians are actually mingling with the standards crowds, helping in the committees, and learning to "talk the talk and walk the walk" of the industry and the people in the industry. And they are making a difference. For the first time, the participants in programs have an awareness and elucidation of some of the problems that they've been facing, but which they couldn't clearly describe or analyze. Chapter 6 discusses this in more detail.

However, these initial efforts are the product of individuals, rather than the start of a formal recognition of the importance of standardization within the IT industry as a whole. There is still a lack of understanding on the part of technologists as to the role that standardization plays in their discipline. There is even less understanding by business people on how to exploit the advantages that standardization confers. I am firmly convinced that the message of the "Unique selling proposition" has been hammered into the heads of all business majors, so that uniqueness is the only attribute with which they are familiar. In this they are aided and abetted by the technologists, who, when gathered into an organization, begin to display signs of the "Not invented here" syndrome. Their education has taught them to compete, and compete they did.

At the same time that this unbridled competition was occurring, some companies were competing with standardization. By either becoming or by embracing a standard— and by allowing other companies to share their success—some organizations became exceedingly successful. The film industry without 35mm film is hard to imagine; the PC industry without a standardized disk form factor is even less likely. And yet this phenomenon of selected cooperation based on standardization came as a surprise to both the industry and to the academic camp followers who act as apologists.

In reality, that the IT industry was taken by surprise by the power of standardization is an interesting statement about the ability for self-delusion by many in management and engineering. Standards are ubiquitous; the failure to understand this phenomenon is inexplicable. I believe that academia, which is supposed to be the source of theoretical and advanced leadership to the industry, somehow failed to understand the dynamics of the market and the growth of the cooperative and standardized solution. The question is, why?

The Activities of Standardization Groups

Within the United States, over 550 groups are devoted to "doing standards." The activities range from boilers to broilers, and from fabric to fasteners. There are formally recognized and sanctioned organizations and unofficial groups of professionals who have banded together informally to help their industry. The United States is a nation in love with a standard way of doing things. Much activity centers on informing members of the standards activities within their industry. Each organization can deal with several hundred standards a year; producing them, reviewing them, recommending them for implementation, or making them obsolete. Each group usually follows its own procedures, based on what the group feels is a fair and equitable method. Each group maintains mailing lists, organizational memberships, and a series of other organizational and other administrative functions. Finally, each group acts to protect and expand its area of influence, sometimes at the expense of other standards groups, at other times in brand-new, nonstandardized, territories.

Given this scenario, the question is not so much why the standard groups have not gotten together for their common good as why they haven't managed to kill one another off yet. In a typical high-technology environment, engineering societies are developing standards, information processing bodies are writing standards, telecommunications groups are creating standards, manufacturing groups are recommending standards, quality circles are describing standards, and safety groups are mandating practices. The government put in its oar in the form of OSHA regulations, procurement standards, as well as state and local needs. On top of all of this are corporations' own internal standards, as well as customs and concepts that the companies have lived with for many years.

The philosophical and conceptual bond that ties all of this together is, at best, very weak. Standards groups have been attempting for some time to put together a rationale for standards. The attempts to study this phenomena have been weak within the formal groups. Under new leadership, the American National Standards Institute (ANSI) is just now beginning to move to trying to understand the philosophical and practical basis for participation.

CONCLUSION

Standards represent different things to groups and disciplines, to organizations and to individuals, and these meanings vary by time and context. The disconnect between the organizational and individual rationale and goals for participation in standardization is a major cause of confusion about standards and standardization in the IT industry. Just as there is no single consistent body of literature that ties the individual to the system, there is also no theoretical (or philosophical) basis for organizational development or participation. There is no unanimity on why standards are created from an individual or personal point of view, nor why people participate of their own free will in an arena that has only the most macro rationale for its existence. The common thread in the IT industry is a certain understanding of the major disciplines of the craft. If a commonality exists in standards, it appears to derive from the shared experiences and expectations of the industry, not from the innate characteristics of the standards process. I believe that this may be due, in part, to ignorance of the background of standards and their moderately rich heritage. Without an understanding of standards as a separate discipline and market in themselves (rather than a by-product of other processes) each new venture is pursued in isolation, recreating the successes and failures of the past.

Chapter 2

A History of Standards

"And from their lessons seek and find
Instruction with an humble mind."

—Robert Southey, *The Scholar*

INTRODUCTION

Standards have always been with us. Deliberately or inadvertently, they exist and have been used to control and organize much of humankind's activities. They can be a powerful tool to stabilize and then promote exchange and growth. They can also, if misused, cause a culture to stagnate and wither. As pointed out in Chapter 1, standards, in their broadest sense, represent the acceptable behavior and mores of a society and culture. In a more confined sense, a standard is

- the deliberate acceptance by an organization or group of people
- who have a common interest,
- of a quantifiable metric for comparison,
- that directly or indirectly influences the behavior and activities of a group
- by permitting (and possibly encouraging) some form of interchange.

This book rests heavily upon the idea that standards serve to encourage economic interchange; that is, people engage in standardization for many motives, but usually, because there is some form of real or perceived economic benefit. This statement can be made, incidentally, of nearly every activity in which the human animal engages, if one is to believe Thorsten Veblen. Even Veblen's theories depend in some degree upon standardization—how would someone be able to display conspicuous consumption if the conspicuously consumed article had little worth? The fundamental economic dilemma that standards solve is that of determining comparative economic worth.

IN THE BEGINNING

Imagine a group of early traders sitting in a early village. The headman (or potentially, at this time, headwoman) is faced with a problem. The hunters have returned with meat, and the potter's family wants meat. At the same time, the corn growers need pots, the fishers want some corn, and the wood gatherers want anything they can get. (Wood gathering at that time was held in low repute. They have since been replaced by another form of scavengers, known as the legal professionals.) The head of the group could set a price for corn vis-à-vis pots, meat, wood, fish, and everything else, but this then requires grading of the corn, the pots, the meat, the wood, and so on. The most convenient step would be to bind all the commodities (and later activities and services) to a common item—in this case, a standard arrowhead. From this, then, it was a step to determine that a salmon was one arrow head, herring twenty to the arrowhead, a deer was two arrowheads, and so on. (Wood was one mule load per arrowhead.) Granted, trade required converting things to arrowhead value and then coming up with a suitable trade, but this was easy compared to having the hunter learn that a decorated kiln-fired drinking mug was much harder to make than a simple serving platter.

This was one of the first standardization efforts. If you go back to the attributes described earlier, you'll see that it meets the criteria of deliberate acceptance (the leader cowed them into submission) by an organization or group of people (the tribe) who have a common interest (survival and prosperity) of a quantifiable metric for comparison (arrowheads) that directly or indirectly influences the behavior and activities of the group (trading and specialization starts) by permitting (and possibly encouraging) some form of interchange. (It would be strange if the definition and example didn't work together, since I wrote both of them.) The key to the success of standardization is that both parties could compare what they had to an abstract value ascribed to a third thing, and believe in and accept that comparison.

The next step in the saga would be to abstract this one step further and invent currency. Something rare would do well; possibly amber, gold, jewels, or salt. If you are of a cynical cast of mind, the less utility that a thing had, the more valuable it would be. This would lead to gold becoming valuable. Other than its high ductility, gold possesses no intrinsic value. But it is extremely rare, and it does look nice. This made it perfect for a medium of exchange.

Moving into the historical era, one of the first standards that meets the test of this definition would be the establishment of a guaranteed national coinage that is respected by more than a single locality. Beginning around 700 BCE, Lydian coins, with a governmentally guaranteed value, became a widely accepted and standard unit of exchange recognized throughout the Mediterranean littoral. The Lydian currency offered two advantages: one accruing to the Lydian traders and one accruing to all traders. The advantage to the Lydians was that since the standard was originally theirs, in order to trade, people only had to convert their currency to the stater. For trade in general, the standard stater allowed comparison of abstract things—such as the value of two local currencies. With this ability to compare two unknown qualities to a third and arrive at a common definition, it became easier to get on to the business of trade, since there was now a quantifiable common denominator that provided a basis for comparison and interchange. The advantage originally went to the Lydians, since it was their currency. Over time, the currency conversions became more common, and everyone could benefit.

With the practiced eye of the professional standards strategist, it would be useful to look at what drove this type of transaction. By making use of perfect hindsight (and ascribing motives where none may have existed), lessons can be drawn to support a case for the need for standardization. The key to the process was that there was a substantial economic advantage to be gained from creating and using a standard. One would like to believe that somewhere there was someone who sat down and thought this out, but it probably occurred over several generations. In any case, having a standard currency allowed a merchant to calculate value in local currency (proprietary currency) using a standard (nonproprietary) currency that was branded. Over time, the standard currency increased both the potential of trade and the area in which it was possible to transact trade. Extra risk and work were incurred in pricing to a standard (the conversion process), but the potential for profit was greater than the potential for loss. The Lydians were the first to implement this interface standard called "guaranteed national coinage." By being the first implementors, they gained initial economic advantage.

The value of the Lydian implementation of the standard (the Lydian stater) lay in the fact that it was widely accepted. The acceptance by merchants of other nations lay not so much in the fact that the currency was issued by a state but rather that there was a "brand" (that is, the state minting and striking of an identifiable coin) which was a guarantee of worth. Finally, as other nation-states accepted the concept of the interface standard, competition among them for the most accepted implementation (of the generic national coinage standard) became intense. Within fifty to a hundred years, there were several competing implementations, all of which had differing marketing pitches associated with the implementation ("A stater is as good as gold, because it is" [Lydia]; "If it's all Greek to you, the drachma will clarify it" [Athens]; "Use the a or we'll kill you" [Rome]).

Since then, practical, implemented standards never have gone out of fashion, especially in commerce. During the thousand years beginning in 500 BCE, trade grew, as did the need for standards to help make trade easier and more profitable. There was apparently little standardization of finished manufactured product; each manufacturer verified the quality of goods used, but there was nothing to indicate the quality of outgoing goods, other than the reputation of the maker. Secondarily, since there was little in the way of the concept of "interchangeable" parts, the need for product standardization was minimal. The Roman military appears to have been an exception. There is mention in Caesar of the legionnaire's spear (the "pila") having a soft metal shaft; there is also mention in later writers (Vegetius) of the "standard arms" of the legionnaire, which would either indicate that the classic legion had a high degree of standardization for the memory of it to survive 200 years, or Vegetius was an incurable romantic who remembered things as they should have been. However, in general trade, other than coinage, weights, and measures, little relating to commerce was apparently standardized. Over time, even the coinage became debased.

With the fall of the Western Roman Empire, European civilization took a gigantic step into isolationism. Commercial standards, for the next several hundred years, were lost in the Western half of the Roman Empire. In the Byzantine Roman Empire, however, internal and external standards proliferated. Usually based upon imperial decrees backed by the bureaucracy of Constantinople and the authority of the Emperor, these standards came to control nearly everything: from the weights and measures to be used to the duties and responsibilities of a craftsman. From a biased point of view, I would argue that these were the predecessor of today's regulatory standards, since they were used by the state to regulate and control the citizens and their activities. However, the regulations that did deal with trade kept the Byzantine Empire alive long after Rome collapsed—and the Byzantine Empire did provide a bulwark against Islamic expansion into the Balkans well into the current millennia.

Note that in China, standards were created and used. The reasonably rich heritage that the Chinese possess in this arena has been largely overlooked; however, there are few standardization activities that occurred in the West through 1500 that did not have an older, and more pervasive, implementation in the Chinese Empire. It was only after 1500, with the rise of capitalism and the growth of the nation-state in Europe that the uses of standardization began to diverge. The divergence is not in the creation or intent, but rather in the impact. In China, standards were generally used to stabilize society; in many cases in Europe, standards tended to act as change agents.

THE REBIRTH OF STANDARDIZATION

Meanwhile, back in Europe, commerce began to revive as agriculture grew above the subsistence level, leading to the growth of cities and rediscovery of trade. As trade grew, there also grew a requirement to regulate the products of craftsmen, based in part upon economic necessity. Cities became famous for a product or products, which became the standard against which other cities' products were judged. (Examples abound, but some of the more famous are Milanese armor, Venetian glass, and Bordeaux wines.) By establishing standards, these counties and cities could create a differentiation between their technical skill and those of competitors; and thereby increase the value of their product. So, again, trade drove the establishment of standards. However, trade was not an end in and of itself, but rather a method of increasing wealth. In medieval Europe, the craft guilds established requisite production and quality standards (as well as price), and indicated conformance to the guild standards with a guild Hallmark. Over time, the guilds became powerful. By linking themselves with the city's administration and tax base, they managed to become a significant force in urban life. Paris, by 1300, had 130 "regulated professions," from candles to medicine. The whole intent of the craft guilds was to promulgate a standard, and to force the artisans who were in the guild—as well as those in the city—to adhere to its rules. Because it was in the interest of the towns to have wealthy citizens, the local civil authority encouraged and helped to enforce guild rules. And because trade was taxable, the larger civil authorities promulgated rules to encourage its growth.

The merchants in the late medieval period valued such standards and the interchange that they permitted because they were a tool to gain wealth. The trading activities of the Hanseatic League, the prowess of the Venetian Grand Galleys, the journeys of Spanish, Portuguese, and Italian traders (including the Polo brothers) not only makes interesting reading, but provides an indication of how standards were being slowly reborn and turned into a tool of the economy. On the military front, one of the more famous standardization efforts was the Arsenal in Venice, which produced the Venetian war galleys. Apparently, for those who saw and wrote about the processes and products, it was seen as a major reason for Venice's independence and domination of the Adriatic and the northern Mediterranean littoral. Surviving records indicate that the galleys were mass produced: The size, fittings, ropes, and even oars were all standardized and interchangeable.

However, there was an additional significant change that began to occur after approximately 1500 in Europe. Max Weber, in *The Protestant Ethic and the Spirit of Capitalism,*[1] notes that the development of a regulated set of expectations was one of the factors that encouraged the growth of structured capitalism. It was the development of formal rules, among which were standards, that fostered the calculated capitalism that marked European growth beginning in the 1500s.

These formal rules were helped and aided by another phenomenon that dealt heavily with standardization; the invention of the printing press and the implications that this had for society. Gutenberg's inventions were not of the mechanism of the press; he invented a moveable metal type and ink that would adhere to the metal type, allowing mechanical printing to become practical. As is all too common with significant change agents, the actual invention was merely intended to modify and make easier an existing task: in this case, the creation of Bibles for the emerging middle class. Unfortunately, the press "got into the wrong hands," defined as those who wanted to use it for something other than Bibles and tracts supporting the state, and the explosion of information began. In 1450, there were about 100,000 manuscripts available in Europe. In 1500, there were over 9 million. There is no more telling statistic about the growth of the information era than this one, especially if you stop to realize that, in order to use these books, the general population had to become literate and an accepted grammar for national languages understood by all had to be produced.

As a sideline, imagine the printer of the period. He is trying to produce a book. Every week, a new traveling sales person arrives with a new type font, a new size of paper, or a new addition to the press that will help the printer produce an "open system" of books. One wonders if the sales pitches to which the early printers were subjected differed dramatically from the sales pitches to which today's Chief Information Officers and Management Information Systems Directors are subject. One can almost hear the cries of anguish as the printer realizes that the new type font for displaying the information requires a larger folio size than the bed of his current press can manage, while discovering that the fundamental grammar rules for plurals had once again changed and the books just finished were not comprehensible to the users. Even if it is not true, it is still fun to contemplate.

The role of standards continued to grow as the society became more integrated. Common coinage was never established (although Napoleon tried), but standards for money transfer made pan-European trade possible. This tied into the growth of trade, to the period of European colonization, and eventually, to the Industrial Revolution. During the late Industrial Revolution, the steam engine, and later the locomotive, would change forever the way the world did business.

INDUSTRIAL STANDARDIZATION

The railroad—that is, the application of the steam locomotive to transportation—marked a major social and cultural milestone and was a substantial technical achievement. With the advent of the railroad, dispersion and distance no longer were impediments to trade; rather, they became positive allies. Railroads themselves encouraged the use of standards; interchangability of specially crafted machined parts became necessary. With barges, rivers, and canals, the predecessors of the rails, there was not the need for standardization that railroading required. However, railroads, which demanded more planning and standards, could run where barges and canals could not, in turn encouraging dispersion of both supplies and product.

This characteristic has often been overlooked in standards. The impact of a dispersed market on the demand and need for standards is substantial, because there is the need to have standard products and services replicated or repaired when one is far away from the source of the product. Maintainability, duplication, and interchangability form the basis of a three part justification for standards from a consumer's viewpoint; that is, to allow manufacturers to provide a good product inexpensively that can be fixed easily.

The standardization of rail gauges in the United States is often pointed to as a major victory for standardization. Unloading and reloading rail cars each time the gauge changed was tiresome and slow. (For this reason, the gauges of rail lines in Europe changed at every border. An invading army, delayed for six to ten hours at a rail head, is an ideal target for attack, since it is usually bunched up and not formed for battle.) More and more things were standardized as the rail made possible increased industrialization. Industrialization, in turn, demanded ever more standards to maintain itself—standards in metallurgy, standards in information representation, in "work units," in fasteners, in terminology, in education, and in nearly every aspect of life.

The impact of the railroad cannot be overestimated in standardization or any other discipline. The first complex industrial systems grew out of the needs of the railroads in the 1850s to organize their activities. In the book *The Visible Hand: The Managerial Revolution in American Business,* Alfred Chandler argues that the need for dispersed management and control over an "open system" of railroads caused the creation of most modern management organizations, accounting methods, information handling and management, and the creation of a new form of professional manager. He makes a convincing argument for the U.S. railroads being the birthplace of the modern corporation.

Chandler also makes mention of standards without really calling attention to the difficulties faced by the creators. "In the 1870s and 1880s the papers and committee reports presented at these meetings were listed in the railroad press. Hardly a meeting passed without a discussion of national standardization procedures and equipment."[2] He continues:

> The 1880s and early 1890s witnessed the culmination of technologies as well as orga-
> nizational innovation and standardization. In those years, the United States railroads
> acquired a standard gauge and a standard time, moved toward standard basic equip-
> ment in the forms of automatic couplers, air brakes, and block signal systems, and
> adopted uniform accounting procedures. On the night of May 31–June 1, 1886, the re-
> maining railroads using broad gauge tracks . . . shifted simultaneously to the standard
> 4'8 1/2" gauge. On Sunday, November 18, 1883, the railroad men . . . set their watches
> to a new uniform standard time. The passage of the Railway Safety Appliance Act . . .
> [required] . . . standardized automatic couplers and air brakes. In 1887 the Interstate
> Commerce Act provided for uniform railway accounting procedures. . . . All four of
> these events resulted from two decades of constant consultation and cooperation be-
> tween railroad managers."[3]

In retrospect, the standardization activities of the United States were following the path one would have expected. Agricultural products were standardized by the area from which they came, and areas which were known to have superior products commanded superior prices.[4] This tradition continues today; Virginia ham, Maine or Idaho potatoes, and Florida orange juice are just a few of the examples of geographic standardization conferring some form of superiority for which the public is often willing to pay a premium.

Within the United States, early standardization tended to be very focused on a specific region or town. However, nonagricultural standards for more than local use had to wait for a compelling need, which, as noted, was supplied by the Industrial Revolution and fueled by the railroad and the Civil War and the Western movement of the United States. The multiple needs of lengthy distribution channels, of increased mechanization for production, and of constancy and commonality for repair forced the increasing use of mechanization upon the remaining artisans, as well as the farmers.

It was the secondary suppliers of products to make the railroads viable who most spurred the growth of voluntary standards. Screw sizes, pipe and valve fittings, and rail ties were just a few of the scores of newly standardized objects. Various interest groups coalesced within industries to ensure that each industry had its standards. The organizations were industry specific. No attempt was made to standardize across multiple industries, and no attempt was really made to act in an altruistic fashion, for the good of humanity. Standardization served to make the industry grow or to make it more profitable and/or less complex. Standardization was pushed by the growing group of technocrats, headed by the engineers: civil, metallurgical, mining, electrical. The engineers of the second half of the nineteenth century had created an open collection of scientific fact that support their activities. It was a collection that was growing and could, in their minds, be applied to anything, from humans to metallurgy. It is no accident that the American Society for Testing and Materials (ASTM) was one of the first organizations to gain prominence as a standards group in the late 1800s.[5]

The tone for the entire voluntary standards effort was set by 1890. There was the strong concentration on creating standards within specific disciplines (metallurgy, mechanical engineering, electrical engineering), an emphasis on demonstrable and reproducible facts, and an internal focus on the part of the participants—a modified siege mentality. These three attributes continue to this day. Each discipline has its standards committee, and several have quite a few. The emphasis is on creating hard products or standards that can be tested and duplicated, and each group is inwardly focused, composed of the developers and producers of the specific discipline. There is no place in the voluntary standards community for vague theories; all work must be based upon fact and be capable of being described in unambiguous terms, with an outcome that is certain.

The growth of industry-specific standardization organizations was significant in the mid to late 1800s. However, there was a need for more and definitive standards; standards that were fundamental and which were cross industry. The drivers of this effort were again the technologists because they needed certain tools to measure precisely. (While this sounds silly, metrology (the art of measurement) is still a very viable standardization activity within quality societies.) Measurement of emerging phenomena, including electricity, became critical to the rise of not only that industry, but associated industries. The government stepped in to help, and established, in 1901, the National Bureau of Standards (NBS), modeled after similar organizations in the United Kingdom and Germany. The NBS subsumed the office of Weights and Measures and became a technical resource for both the government and private industry.

At the same time, two distinct but similar phenomena occurred. In 1904, there was a leaf fire on the grounds of the NBS. The hoses that were deployed couldn't be connected because there was a difference in the hose connector threads. This, no doubt, caused some concern at NBS but was probably minor compared to the concern that was caused when seventy city blocks of Baltimore burned later that year. The problem in the Baltimore fire was that, although neighboring cities sent equipment to help, the fittings on the hydrants in Baltimore were different from those deployed on the visiting fire trucks. This spurred creation of standards in the area that dealt with public safety and lead to the recommendation by NBS that these standards be used. The National Fire Protection Association (NFPA), under whose charter "fire safety" fell, undoubtedly prospered by NBS's recommendations.[6]

However, it wasn't until World War I that the issue became critical. When America entered the war in 1917, it suddenly became apparent that standardization was essential in certain areas. When the war effort started, visionaries in the Army realized that trucks were replacing draft animals in the movement of weapons to the front. (It was noted that poison gas had little impact on trucks, but was most lethal to horses and oxen.) When the procurement for trucks was let, it was found that there were 287 types of tires available on the American market. The same was true for everything from clothes to coffins. The government set up a Commercial Economy Board of the Council of National Defense, later incorporated into the War Industries Board. Ultimately, over 30,000 articles underwent some form of standardization. Typically, however, the activities of the committee were focused on the executives of the industries, who then acted to change their industries. Differentiation for differentiation's sake came under examination, and gratuitous uniqueness fell from favor—momentarily. In a spirit of public agreement, five major standardization organizations joined to produce the American Engineering Standards Committee (AESC).[7] The standardization movement lasted until the end of the war, when providers decided to try the differentiation approach again. This lead to the "buyers strike" of 1919–1920, which forced providers back to a degree of commonality and standardization.

However, the Government, determined not to let a good deed go unpunished, created a Division of Simplified Practice in the Department of Commerce. This followed the "buyers strike" and a report entitled *Waste in Industry*.[8] Herbert Hoover (Secretary of Commerce, 1921–1928) initiated the "Crusade for Standardization" to reduce waste in industry. The effort was to be focused on the economy as a whole, and the intent was to simplify and make efficient American commerce and industry. The effort peaked before the end of the decade. However, it was during this period that the American Standards Association (ASA) published the assessment that, "Standardization has become the 'outstanding note of this century,' its influence pervading 'the remotest details of our industrial regime.'"

The ASA (the successor organization to the AESC) formed officially in 1928, after the AESC had accredited over 350 organizations to write standards.[9] In the 1960s, ASA became the American National Standards Institute (ANSI) after an abortive attempt to gain Federal recognition; since this time, ANSI has refrained from seeking official government status.

It is important to note that while all of this was occurring in the United States, formal organizations were also being created in other nations. Most of the European nations have a "governmentally recognized" standardization body. Germany's began in 1917, France's in 1918, and the United Kingdom's in 1901. These groups tend to reflect the culture and beliefs of the society; usually, they are seen as part of the political/industrial complex that makes these nations succeed. After the Second World War, the Japanese also adopted a similar approach, using standards and standardization as a method of increasing industrial strength. The United States alone preferred a "federated system," in which ANSI was the leader of the pack, where the pack could usually do whatever it pleased.

Another development in the 1980s was the growth in importance of the international standardization movement. The national organizations traditionally had been the dominant players in the standardization arena. In the mid 1980s, this began to change, driven in large part by the activities of the European Community. The "EC 92" movement increased the importance of international standards and began the slow eclipse of the national standardization movement. Simultaneously, the international movement spawned the creation of the regional movement, which further complicated the situation, as regional movements have no standing in the formal structure, but considerable clout in the regions that they represent. The power of the formal standardization lies in the fact that formal standards (that is, national or international standards) which were written using the consensus process were judged to be the most legitimate standards for governmental procurement. This leverage was a significant driver in forcing major corporate participation in national and international standards efforts. Just as with the guild hallmark symbolizing quality in the medieval period, the designation "National Standard" or "International Standard" came to have economic significance for the companies participating in the quest for governmental business. The size of this market should not be underestimated. Within the United States alone, the Federal Government procurement for IT systems and services amounts to several tens of billions of dollars. Securing a major governmental contract worth a billion dollars can spell the difference between a company's survival or disappearance. The state and local governments spend an equivalent, or greater, amount.

CONTINUED EVOLUTION

In the mid 1980s, however, a challenger arose to the established and formal Standards Developing Organizations (SDOs). This new type of standardization activity within the Information Technology community was the consortia movement. While the early 1980s saw the first tentative standardization activity within consortia, the next decade saw the flowering and growth of this counter movement. Usually funded by the same companies that provided the lion's share of funding to the formal process, consortia at first appeared to offer a quicker, easier, and more responsive standardization option to major producers. Consortia tended to start, as did many SDOs, focused on a single specific topic. However, as they began to mature, they began to look for other outlets for their energies—since they had, by the time that they finished their original proposal, a bureaucracy in place that wanted to continue. As a result, the consortia tended to expand, just as the SDOs had expanded. (Consortia are not immune to the spawn or hydra option.) As consortia have proliferated (there are now over 100 consortia in the IT industry), they are running into the same problems that formal organizations ran into in the late 1980s; how to coordinate and deploy their specifications for the greatest acceptance. Standardization continues to be an important part of the industry. Witness the following comment about the nature of competition in the IT arena over the next decade:

> The noisiest of those competitive battles will be about standards. The eyes of most sane people tend to glaze over at the very mention of technical standards. But in the computer industry, new standards can be the source of enormous wealth, or the death of corporate empires. With so much at stake, standards arouse violent passions.[10]

CONCLUSION

At the beginning of this chapter, the following conditions were set for a successful standardization effort:

- the deliberate acceptance by an organization or group of people
- who have a common interest,
- of a quantifiable metric for comparison,

- that directly or indirectly influences the behavior and activities of a group
- by permitting (and possibly encouraging) some form of interchange.

These conditions are almost always met by successful standardization activities. Where standardization activities have been unsuccessful, one of these conditions has usually been overlooked. The condition that is most often forgotten is, not surprisingly, the third: directly or indirectly influencing the behavior and activities of a group. The rationale for standards, simply put, is to create a need or to create a market for a good or service. The implementation of the standard—the embodiment of the attributes—is the payoff for any standardization effort. The purpose of voluntary standards (as opposed to mandated, or regulatory standards) is not to require change but to cause the market to prefer a standard solution to a nonstandard solution. The entire process is predicated upon the belief that standardization offers a better long-term solution to a market problem than a nonstandard solution, since a standardized solution provides an increased freedom of choice and action. There is no intrinsic benefit attached to participation or use of a standard; goodness derives from economic benefit of its deployment. The demand for these attributes is market-driven; they do not spring into being fully grown, like Athena from the head of Zeus. Still, whatever the causes, people have accepted standardization and the good that it provides. After serious reflection, few people seriously question the value of standards.

However, the problem with this approach is that it puts most participants in a role of blind acceptance of standardization; with a view that what happens is going to happen. The problems of the standardization process in the last ten years were the indirect result of this form of acceptance; by not understanding the cause and effect of standardization, strange things happen. The lack of knowledge of and participation in standardization by a majority of the IT industry opened the door to control the effort by demagogues who offered partial solutions to significant problems. While tactically significant, in the long run, they sowed the seeds of their own destruction. One of the more serious endeavors of this book is to ensure that players in the standardization arena are knowledgeable of the background and power of standardization so that the discipline can continue to evolve.

NOTES

[1]Weber, Max. *The Protestant Ethic and the Spirit of Capitalism,* Trans. Talcott Parsons. New York: Charles Scribner's Sons, 1958.
[2]Chandler, Alfred D. Jr. *The Visible Hand: The Managerial Revolution in American Business.* Cambridge, MA: Belknap Press, 1977, p. 131.
[3]Ibid, p. 130.
[4]For a discussion of this aspect of standardization, see the U.S. Congress, Office of Technology Assessment (OTA), *Global Standards: Building Blocks for the Future,* TCT-512, Washington, D.C. U.S. GPO March 1992, pp. 42–45. Linda Garcia, the program lead for this study, produced an outstanding report that is an excellent treatment of the role of the government in standardization.
[5]One thing that is often overlooked in the activities of engineers during this time is the extent to which they tried to standardize. The first major school of standardized management thought was developed under the aegis of the

American Society of Mechanical Engineers. Frederick Taylor, the "Father of Scientific Management" was a member of ASME, as were many of the other early management pioneers.

[6]Although the NFPA has published hydrant standards, there are still instances of nonconforming hydrants. Apocryphal evidence suggests that one problem that exacerbated the tragic Oakland Hills, California fires in 1991 was the inability of neighboring fire departments to use the Oakland hydrants, due to equipment mismatch. The Office of Technology Assessment (OTA) reports that the same phenomena occurred in Baltimore in the 1960s, when adjoining counties were noted requesting that hydrants did not comply with national standards be marked clearly to identify when adapters needed to be used (TCT-512, op.cit., p. 43).

[7]The naming of the AESC started two phenomena which continue to this day. The first is the penchant for standards organizations to either "spawn" or "hydra," so that the total number of standards organizations is contantly growing. The second phenomena is what I call the "vowel shift," which is a belief that standardization organizations succeed or fail by the number of vowels that they have in the acronym formed by their name. There is a corollary to the "vowel shift" rule, which states that organizations with a single consonant and a number will also succeed in direct correlation to the confusion caused by the name. Therefore, ASC X3 and the X/Open Consortia become confused and will succeed, ASC T1 will become confused with the standard/product of the same nomenclature and will succeed, and NISO (ASC Z39), having no antecedent and being vague as well, qualifies on both counts and will be very successful.

[8]This study was written by the American Academy of the Federated American Engineering Societies and released in 1920. The reported stated that more than 30% of the costs of production and labour could be eliminated, and more than $10 billion saved, if six major industries would adopt a minimum set of standards and simplification of work routine. As an interesting bit of irony, Frederick W. Taylor, the father of Scientific Management and an engineer, was the focus of Congressional hearings in the years 1911–1912, precisely because he was promoting scientific (inefficiency reducing) management. The committee that savaged Taylor was composed of organized labour representatives who had been elected to positions of responsibility. With the usual variety of unspecified and factless arguments, Congress persuaded itself that "scientific management" was evil. The impact of these activities by Congress with regard to Taylor's time and motion studies for increasing productivity continued until 1949, when the last of the time study and incentive bonus restrictions were removed from the Federal statutes.

[9]The number has continued to grow to this day. As of this writing (1995), over 550 organizations have been accredited to write standards.

[10]*Economist,* "A Survey of the Information Technology Industry," 27 February 1993, p. 11.

Chapter 3

Standardization and Regulation

"The glories of our blood and state
Are shadows, not substantial things."

—James Shirley, *The Glories of Our Blood and State*

INTRODUCTION

This chapter provides a look at the twin topics (which are often merged) of standardization and regulation. These two subjects, while related, should not be confused. Many people in industry lump both of these terms into the same general category. The vast majority of the standards that are used in the Information Technology arena are voluntary standards, and not regulations. However, two situations make the merging of these two separate concepts seem, if not inevitable, then more often the case than not.

The first situation occurs, because regulations are sometimes birthed in the voluntary standards committees, where the technology to create regulations is standardized. This leads to a bifurcated path, which tends to become philosophically complex very quickly. The other situation occurs when the government mandates standards in procurement for equipment. There is a tendency to view any requirement (product, performance, or interface) that a government (local, state, or federal) wants, which a provider cannot supply, as an "unnecessary regulation." This tendency to call even innocent and useful standards regulations is not only libelous, it is very near scandalous. (Bit of provincialism there, my apologies.) It is hard to get mad at a standard, but a regulation tends to bring out the assertively independent streak upon which most Americans pride themselves.

The chapter will begin with a quick review of some of the background behind the necessity of regulations and then flow into a look at a somewhat arbitrary, but none the less useful, typology of the terms "*de facto* standard," "*de jure* standard," "publicly available specification," and "regulation." Following this, the concept of the standards-based regulation will be examined. The chapter closes with a comparison of the "fitness for purpose" of the standardization world and the regulatory world.

PROLOGUE

For the first hundred years of the United States' existence, regulations were the right and responsibility of the individual states, which imposed them to protect the common good of the citizens. Regulations covered grist mills and gins, ferry crossings and highways, and sundry other activities necessary to the distribution of foodstuffs and to agricultural commerce in general. Few regulations were technically driven, since much of the technology, most of the products, and most practices were traditional. The advent of the steam locomotive required certain adjustments, but these regulations dealt with safety issues raised by the new technology, not with the technology itself. On the whole, regulations were imposed at a state and local level based on traditional learning, reflecting a relatively static civilization.

Following the Civil War in the United States, however, industrialization came in to its own; with it came abuse, as industry began its quest for profit power. By the mid 1870s, a fundamental change had occurred in the society of the United States. The commercial interdependence of the various sections of the country began to become more and more pronounced, and the need to sell to large distributed geographical areas became dominant. As an example, Sears and Roebuck as well as Montgomery Ward took advantage of the change in the ability of the local artisan to compete technically with mail order stores, and offered their merchandise as standards against which local merchants competed. The advent of large and integrated railroads (see Chapter 2) had a chilling effect, at times, on local farmers and led to the formation of the Grange societies.

However, this growth produced an unanticipated side effect. The concept of growth for profit's sake became increasingly popular. If big was good, large was better, and huge was spectacular. The ability of the populace to protect itself against the larger and larger concentrations of economic and technical power began to decrease. The federal government, concerned (within limits) about the safety and welfare of its citizens, began to regulate commerce and other activities within its borders. The government recognized that it could not regulate all aspects of industry, nor did it want to do so. Instead, it regulated those areas where the public and providers intersected and/or those in which the buyers could not evaluate the product that they purchased. Upton Sinclair's account of the meat-packing industry forced many changes, while Ida Tarbell's description of the Standard Oil Company did the same in an area that individuals or the various states could not control. In cosmetics or railroads, boilers or power companies, or any situation where the public good was threatened either by an unwilling ignorance or by economic power, the government felt compelled to step in and regulate for the public good.

REGULATIONS

Correctly applied, a regulation is a standard or specification that has the force of some authority behind it. The authority, through the use of this force, can legitimately compel use of the regulatory writing and exact a specified penalty for noncompliance. (The authority can be separated from the regulation; the regulation, however, constantly operates under the shadow of the legitimizing authority.) To be effective, the regulation must be founded in rationality—either for the producer or the consumer—and enforceable, even for a group that may find it onerous. If the regulation is rational only to its creators and enforcers, it will likely be difficult to enforce, which may lead to yet more regulations. Ultimately, of course, there must be some benefit to the regulated, whether this is initially apparent or not. (Societal benefit is, of course, always the ultimate justification for the activities of a government.) If the regulation confers no benefit and is opposed, it becomes not only useless but counterproductive as well, since the opposition to the regulation will require the addition of more authority for enforcement. Obviously, the more adversarial a relationship, the more regulators are needed. On the other hand, if a relationship is too friendly, enforcement of the regulation may suffer, either from lax enforcement or from uneven enforcement.

Most of the regulations imposed by the United States government were not too onerous at their inception. Minor problems were usually prevented from becoming major problems; usually, the regulation was founded upon a collective body of wisdom. State and local regulations usually preceded the national efforts, but were based upon local expectations and conditions. These regulations usually reflected the experience and knowledge of the originators, and were usually reasonable within the context and the time of creation. However, they suffered from the faults noted above and tended, over time, to become more of an obstacle to change than a positive influence on industry.

Where there are dominant safety concerns (nuclear power, air traffic), where issues are too large to be handled by a single state (environmental issues, economic issues), or where processes are too complex to be widely understood (food and drugs, some process industries), regulations must and should exist. The concept of regulation, however, is inimical to a dynamic environment in which change is an essential part of growth. The response to this situation is, all too often, to have the regulation respond by attempting to change the nature of change itself. If change is predictive and its course can be confined within guidelines, regulation can be applied intelligently. If, however, an unpredictable arena is regulated, then the very act of regulation will introduce abnormalities into the environment, making it still more unpredictable. Regulations should not be used to cause or enforce social change or perceptions; they are meant to regulate what already exists. Regulation is a poor substitute for market action in either a dynamic society or a dynamic industry: Regulation in a dynamic industry in a dynamic society can be positively destructive, for both the regulated and the regulators.

VOLUNTARY STANDARDIZATION GROUPS

Any cooperative joining to bring about the acceptance of a common thought or practice can be labeled a voluntary standards organization. However, within the context of this book, the attributes of standardization have been described (Chapter 2). The attributes of the group creating a standard are as follows:

- a voluntary organization or group of people
- who have a common interest
- who wish to produce
- a quantifiable metric for comparison
- that directly or indirectly influences the behavior and activities of a group
- by permitting (and possibly encouraging) some form of interchange
- which has some form of recognition for its efforts.

The basic tenant of standardization committees is that everyone has the right to equal treatment on the committees. Everyone has the right to a position, and the right to express that position. Additionally, everyone has the right to be heard and have their position respected. There is no guarantee that their position will necessarily prevail; that is left to the dynamics of the process, and the technical viability of their arguments and support. The difference between consortia and formal committees (also known as Standards Developing Organizations [SDOs]) is a matter of openness; SDOs must admit anyone who appears at their door while consortia have the right to request money as a prerequisite for participation.

Usually, within a standardization body, technical arguments are the basis for deciding what is contained in the specification or standard. Standards are not arrived at by deciding what provider's option serves a market segment best, but rather by deciding what technical position best serves as a response to the need that caused the committee to be created. The users cannot join to restrain change in a standard, and the providers cannot join to restrain trade or the introduction of new ideas.

One of the major fears shaping the structure and activities of the SDOs and consortia is that of anti-trust. Standards bodies—where members of the industry join to discuss how to apply technologies, now and in the future—can come perilously close to anti-trust activities. Because standardization bodies operate in a public (or quasi-public) forum with generally unrestricted access, they are provided with limited exemption from the antitrust legislation. Later chapters discuss some of the U.S. Supreme Court cases that have figured in anti-trust and standardization activities. Most consortia are also aware of the Addamax lawsuit brought against the Open Software Foundation. Addamax alleged that OSF, by choosing (apparently in a questionable fashion) a security technology that competed with Addamax's, inflicted economic harm on Addamax. The suit is reasonably convoluted, but states that OSF, using the consortia process, influenced the market against Addamax. If OSF had been a private company, it wouldn't have been sued. However, it wasn't, and the economic power that OSF represented was seen as being prejudicial. The same argument can be used against SDOs, since they represent a pool of influential decision makers. In both cases, it is a major rationale for ensuring that there are always accurate meeting minutes.

Consortia and SDOs share many other goals and processes, which are covered in Section 3. However, they produce only two things: standards and specifications. (The reality is that they also produce guides, tests, and implementations, but these are all driven by their fundamental production of the written technology specification.) The writing can take one of two forms: a publicly available specification (from consortia) or a standard (from an SDO).

The standard from an SDO has certain characteristics. It has been written by a committee composed of anyone who could attend the meetings. It has undergone public scrutiny, having been reviewed by any number of committees and having been exposed to a public review. All comments made about its technical content have been reviewed and have had responses provided. It is the product of consensus within the committee and for an industry, or at least an industry segment. When it has been through all of this, and when it has finally been published, it has the right (within the United States) to be called an American National Standard (ANS). Because it is a formal standard, it can then be used (in accordance with the Office of Management and Budget Circular A119) in government procurements.

The problem with this scenario lies in the fact that SDOs do not develop test suites or implementation suites for their standards. This is left to the tender mercy of the market, and because test suites are expensive and the people to write them scarce, they are rarely written in a timely fashion. This approach has always been assumed to be viable for the SDOs, since much of the practice and creation of standards stem not from IT software standards but from the hardware experience (which was based on the older manufacturing standards). A nut either mates with a bolt or it doesn't; if they mate, then they share a standard. If they don't, they don't.

In software, however, many things are produced with a "maybe" bit that can be set to either "on" or "off" depending upon the circumstance as dictated by the user. Unlike the days when people were doing "screw thread standards," we are now doing "fastener standards," in which one vendor talks glue, another rivets, and yet another nails, while what the user wanted was zippers. All are fasteners; it's just that there is no clearly defined implementation, since much of software is based upon cognitive psychology.

The best example of the problems that the SDO approach lead to in a standard is driven by the Open Systems Interconnect effort of the 1980s. OSI was a massive undertaking, but when it came to procurement, it lagged the use of TCP/IP protocols. This was because

> . . . OSI standards [were] developed without a requirement for reference implementations. This requires each vendor to develop the software to implement the standard. After products are developed, conformance tests are required to insure that each vendor has implemented the standard in a consistent manner, and interoperability tests demonstrate that products will function together. At no point do users evaluate the functionality or user friendliness."[1]

This is a side effect of the process, not an intent of the standard. However, because the SDOs work in a certain isolation from the market, there is a chance that the formal standard will either be nonresponsive to the market or will be too complex for the problem that the market seeks to solve.

The publicly available specifications developed by a consortium are a different case. Because consortia are different in their composition, they do include marketing people from the various companies and often have their own marketing staffs (something that most IT SDOs do not have). These groups produce publicly available specifications; that is, specifications that the consortium will usually make available to the public (meaning companies not in the consortium) to allow companies to build implementations of the specification. The member companies have several advantages in this process. Usually, they receive "snapshots" of the code as it is being developed, they get to participate in specifying and creating the code, they get to help in the creation of tests, and have early access to the test suites, and so on.

It is precisely because they are closer to the market than the SDOs that the consortia tend to get into trouble. Because consortia have the liberty to focus on a singular solution, they tend to follow one of two tracks. The first track is one in which they (the members of the consortium) develop a specification which has multiple implementations (so far, so good) that the members of the consortium want, but which the general market refuses to accept or to which the market assigns no value, because there is a perfectly acceptable "other solution" that is extant, or because the specification of the consortium does not play with other solutions in general market use.

The second problem with consortia is that they tend to be created to "polarize" the market. The idea of a "consortia standard" is a powerful marketing tool that permits members of the consortium to claim adherence to something that smacks of "open systems." If there are two consortia that provide dissimilar solutions to identical problems, the market has a magnificent opportunity to achieve a high state of "cognitive dissonance" and decide that the whole problem (not the solution) lies with the vendors. This then drives the users to either accept a third solution from one of the two offered solutions, or to sit back and wait. However, because there is usually not that luxury afforded in an IT crisis, there are usually choices made and they usually do not favor the warring solutions.

Both the *de jure* standard and the public specification solutions allow some form of public input to their process before they create the specification. They also allow multiple implementations of the specification to occur. It is with the proprietary implementations that providers make their money. The idea behind the open specification (which is fundamentally what the open process provides) is that there will be competition based upon the implementation derived from the specification.

The nice thing about the standard and the publicly available specification is that anyone (or nearly anyone) can influence and help write the specification or standard. The same is not true with a proprietary specification, or what usually becomes the *de facto* standard. The proprietary specification does not allow meaningful public review of its contents, nor does it allow a review of the specification before it is implemented as a product. The public specification and the standard both permit this.

It is with the implementation that there is a divergence among the "open" providers. The holder of intellectual property rights (IPR) contained in a standard is allowed to charge a "reasonable fee" for the rights to use the standard; this is permitted both under

ANSI and ISO rules. Needless to say, the inclusion of a "reasonable fee" covenant to standards and specifications has led some people to conclude that standards are not truly open: A company or organization could, by contributing technology to an SDO or consortium, cause a lock-in to occur and thereby make money from a standard. On the converse, proponents of the "reasonable fee" doctrine claim that the "reasonable fee" permits them to reclaim some of the money spent on developing the technology that was contributed to the standard, and that if this provision was not included, then there would be a lot less contributed to these fora. Fundamentally, "[t]he idea that appropriate standards could expand the market for, and the usefulness of, products and services led to the expansion of standards activities to include their functional aspects and to the opening up of the standards development process to include the direct participation of producers and users."[2] The question of copyright or patent is very difficult to deal with within the software industry. It has become, over the past several years, the norm to protect software by patent; the court is still out on whether or not the interfaces that are used in such patents are, in reality, protected by the overarching patent or whether they are discoverable.

The corollary to the "open specification or standard" and the "proprietary implementation" is, of course, that the organization with the best implementation will "win." This is where many companies forget the rationale for participation in standardization. The market rewards those implementations which it decides are best; sometimes irrespective of technical merit.

This is the crux of standardization within the IT industry. Its primary function, from the views of the providers and the participants, is to create new markets for the products of the organizations involved. In an analysis of standards committees, it was shown that a majority of the participants were there to achieve an objective that enabled their organization to produce or procure product.[3] Standards, within the IT industry, are used as a marketing tool to create and expand the pool of possible buyers. While Chapters 6, 7, 8, and 13 cover this topic in detail, it is a key point when distinguishing between standards and specifications and regulations.

REGULATORY STANDARDS

Regulatory standards are one of the two activities that spring from regulations, the source of which is noted above. The first of these is "traditional regulation," which aims at a singular industry and pursues a singular governmental objective (the Telecommunications Act of 1934, for example, for the telephone industry, and the Pure Food and Drug Act of 1906 at the food industry). It is usually broad and sweeping, forcing a restructuring of the industry and how it does business. It can have a dramatic impact on the industry. One only needs look at the impact that the fleet mileage regulations of the Congressionally mandated Clean Air Act had on the automotive industry to see what the outcome of this type of regulation can be. Normally, this type of regulation requires Congressional action; in the author's view, the action comes only as a result of the activities of an aroused citizenry, who demand that the legislative branch somehow earn their salaries. It does not occur too often, but when it does, it has a profound impact on the business that is in harm's way. (I do not mean to state that the activity is worth saving; I tend to believe, however, that Congress has a tendency to inflict as much unintentional damage as it seeks to do intentional good.)

On the other hand, there are regulatory standards, which have as their fundamental rationale the noneconomic governing of something—whether it is an act, a technology, or a service.[4] Regulatory standards usually cut across industry boundaries, and therefore impact all industries. These rules are usually made by administrative agencies in a process known as "rulemaking." Fundamentally, Congress delegates to certain government agencies the power to create these proposed regulatory standards. The ability of the agency to make "regulatory standards" is limited by both the leeway given them by the statute delegating the authority and the provisions of the Administrative Procedures Act of 1946. This is the act that requires that all regulatory standards be published in the Federal Register for not less than thirty days to invite comments, and that all comments be considered.

These standards are usually very focused, and provide a mandatory prescription of future behavior. Fundamentally, this is the requirement to stabilize. The goal of this stabilization is not economic, but rather to permit creation and assignment of rules and prescriptive behaviors. There was then, just as there is now, a cry for governmental help in dealing with complexities. The old phrase of *caveat emptor* ("let the buyer beware") was called forth, and usually the government responded by creating regulation where it was felt that the populace was either unable to defend itself or was at risk.[5] The fundamental issue that confronts the government is the nature of the protection that the government can and should offer.

The basic questions with which regulation must deal are listed here:

- What level of complexity can the consumer be expected to understand or what level of danger should a person be willing to accept; in other words, when is it necessary to establish regulatory guidelines to delineate the responsibilities of both parties in a transaction?

- Regulations must be enforced, which in turn creates adversarial relationships. Who is the adversary and who the object of the government's protection; that is, what client is being protected by the government?

- Regulations are ponderous; like a juggernaut, they are hard to start and steer, require vast throngs of people to keep them moving, and seem to acquire a life of their own once they get going. Once rolling, they are usually difficult to stop. How is a regulation rescinded; what are the indicators that a regulation no longer provides improved service to the citizenry?

- Regulation, by its very nature, is a specific response to a single activity or occurrence at a point in time. How, as the environment for which a regulation was crafted changes, can the universality of the regulation provide necessary protection in all, or sometimes even most, situations without also risking the potential for constant abuse and/or argument?

Following are two examples of areas that offered great potential for regulation. Both have similar aspects—yet the regulatory situation that surrounds them is vastly different.

The communications industry, as typified by the telephone, began to face regulatory pressure within thirty years of its introduction. This was due, in part, to problems caused by the necessity of creating a single nation-wide interoperating telephone system. There was a need to invest large amounts of capital because of the nature of the technology. Unlike the railroads, the telephone companies were given no land grants to sweeten their attempt to establish themselves. The only way that the successors of Alexander Graham Bell could make national service possible was to force smaller companies out of business, and then to buy them cheaply. The only way to do this lead to certain compromises in the regulatory process. Part of this compromise was to promise "universal service," by which AT&T meant "everywhere."[6] Congress picked up the concept and, with the Telecommunications Act of 1934, made the idea of "universal" service to mean "universal right to service" (everyone) and made it a social goal. This belief has survived to this day.

However, many visionaries in the IT industry believe that the telephone is "old and dead" technology, and should be replaced with the National Information Infrastructure (or the Internet, the World Wide Web, the Global Information Infrastructure, or the Galactic Information Infrastructure). The government sees the NII as crucial to enabling large productivity gains;[7] the computer industry sees it as the next wave, witness the Netscape IPO of 1995; retailers view it as a dream mechanism to capture a community with money to spend; and educators see it as the way to teach better. All of these make a compelling case for governmental regulation, yet none appears to be forthcoming. Part of the rationale for this, I believe, is that every time the government gets ready to regulate, the very nature of the beast changes; new technology is touted, and the market veers off in another direction. With telephones, there was tremendous capital expenditure necessary to create the infrastructure; the NII sits atop an already created infrastructure and looks at different ways to use it. It is much more confusing than the telephone and portends a much larger social change. However, everyone "understands it" and everyone is rushing to exploit it. It is also changing very rapidly. The appearance of "intelligent agents" and browsers on the World Wide Web is only the latest of a series of tremendous technology changes that have occurred in the last three years. Imagine the pace of change of this technology and that of the touch-tone telephone.[8]

The key to voluntary standards is that they are supposed to act as change agents. IT standards have their fundamental rationale for existence in the growth of a market by standardizing what is known and then expanding the market beyond the boundaries of the standard. For IT, a standard is a "way stop" on the way to a larger market. For a government, a regulatory standard is a boundary identifier.

SYNTHESIS AND CONCLUSION

The confusion between the use of regulations and the use of specifications or standards is not as intense as it was in the late 1980s, when industry was threatened by the activities of the European Economic Union. The U.S. use of the "EC 92" as a rallying cry (the fear was that the EU was going to use standardization as a nontariff trade barrier) was an effective ploy in gaining the attention of the Commerce Department in looking at the use of ISO 9000 quality management standards as a procurement tool by European governments. However, rather than discourage the European activity, it served merely to interest the U.S. government in the area of standards and standardization. As a result, there was a sudden retrenchment on the part of ANSI and other SDOs in the areas of regulation and standardization, coupled with an attempt to discourage governmental interest and participation. Unfortunately, since many of the major participants in IT standardization also happened to be multinational companies, the retrenchment was less than successful, since there was a need for U.S. governmental involvement. Over time, however, the quality management standards have proven to generally provide some positive benefit. If applied as they were intended, the involvement of the government in some parts of the standardization arena is not only accepted, but is considered to be a good thing.

The experience of the late 1980s and early 1990s taught industry and the government how to play together to make the playing field more level. It also brought home the power of standardization as a market influence. The government is becoming more accustomed to finding a "voluntarily created standard" such as the National Fire Protection Association's standards and using it to achieve standardization, rather than trying to write its own. This has ensured that the regulation is based upon current and accepted industry practice, with which the industry concurred. (The Occupational Safety and Health Act [OSHA] remains a monument to the government "doing its own thing," at times even to the chagrin of its creators.)

The government is increasingly using commercially available standards, rather than creating its own specifications and standards. While this was the case since the 1982 publication of the Office of Management and Budget Circular A119, the revision of A119 in the early 1990s gives more power to the consensus process—both the formal and the consortia based activities. Again, the government is learning to move with the industry, rather than fight it.

Table 3–1 lists some of the major differences between regulatory and voluntary standards. Clearly, each method has its virtues and each its vices, although which is which is a matter of personal judgment.

The voluntary method appears to be more appropriate to standards activities in volatile areas with competing technological and application solutions available, where there are intense user and provider dynamics. While the voluntary method is slower, it accommodates more input and garners a larger base of support for completed standards. It also prevents single interests from dominating the standardization effort for self-serving ends. Regulatory standards, on the other hand, are more useful when there is only a single acceptable solution to a problem that crosses industry bounds and which requires a noneconomic (social or cultural) solution. They are usually more restrictive and do not furnish alternatives, since their purpose is to regulate specific activities, rather than to encourage growth or provide options.

The significant point of this chapter is that there are differences between the types of standards and specifications available depending upon the level of freedom of input to their creation (de jure, public specification, de facto) to the amount of freedom in their use (de facto, public specification, de jure, and regulation). The proper use of any of these de-

Table 3.1   A Comparison of Regulatory and Voluntary Standards

Standard Type	Strengths	Weaknesses
Voluntary	—Industry (group) support —Market (user) driven —Originator must be skilled in understanding strategy and user needs —Opportunities to work outside of standards for new innovations	—No enforcement mechanism —Lengthy process for conflict resolution —Strategic planning more difficult —Need "common sense" interpretation which varies with application
Regulatory	—Requires that everyone adhere to clear standard —Noncompliance with standard is immediately obvious —Penalties and rewards for process compliance can be specified exactly —Implementation process for correctly written standard is clear —Centralization of process is easier —Control is more complete	—No innovative flexibility in dealing with dynamic market —Precisely written and detailed standards must cover all possible situations —Litigation is common stemming from disagreements over definitions and interpretations —Source of standard must be an expert in all potential applications of standard to avoid limiting innovation —Larger police force necessary to ensure conformity to standard —Compliance is mandatory, potentially arousing hostility in innovative groups

pends upon what is being standardized for what purpose, by whom, and for whom. Each of these components must be examined and understood if the industry is to use these tools correctly.

NOTES

[1]Johnson, Jerry L; Culp, Jim; Clyde T; Theibert, Margaret; Vidmar, Ronald E. "The Role of the Government in Standardization: Improved Service to the Citizenry," *StandardView—ACM Perspectives on Computing,* ACM, New York, Volume 1, Number 2, December 1993, p. 22.

[2]Smoot, Oliver R. "Tension and Synergism Between Standards and Intellectual Property," *StandardView—ACM Perspectives on Computing,* ACM, New York, Volume 3, Number 2, June 1995, p. 60. For a complete discussion of the Intellectual property rights dilemma, see *StandardView—ACM Perspectives on Computing,* ACM, New York, Volume 3, Number 2, June 1995, which has as its theme the IPR issues described here.

[3]Spring, Michael B.; Grisham, Cristal; O'Donnell, Jon; Skogseid, Ingjerd; Snow, Andrew; Tarr, George; Wang, Peihan. "Improving the Standardization Process," in Kahin, Brian and Abbate, Janet (eds) *Standards Policy and*

Information Infrastructure: Cambridge, MA: MIT Press, 1995. The article provides the best analysis of the role and need for good leadership in a standards committee that has been written to date. It goes a long way to solving some of the questions about how to lead an all volunteer committee doing all volunteer things in a completely voluntary setting.

[4]See Cerni, Dorothy. *Standards in Process: Foundations and Profiles of ISDN and OSI Studies:* NTIA Report 84-170, Boulder, CO; U.S. Department of Commerce, December 1984, pp 47–58. Dorothy was probably the most knowledgeable standards writer of the last several decades and many of her ideas and insights are scattered throughout this book. The cited work set the tone for most of the useable follow-on work in standardization, whether or not the authors realized their debt.

[5]The phrase "caveat emptor" is cited on many occasions to show the chicanery of providers. The entire phrase reads: *Caveat emptor quia ignorare non debuit quod jud alienum emit* (Let the buyer beware, because he should not be ignorant of the property that he is buying). The acceptance of responsibility for one's actions apparently was as much a problem historically as it is today.

[6]The original statement of "One policy, one system, universal service" was made by Theodore Vail, of AT&T in the 1910 AT&T annual report. Following Bell's semimonopolistic acquisition of smaller companies, Vail was faced with possible federal anti-trust action and the growth of state regulation. In exchange for allowing regulation by "rate of return," Vail managed to have the states recognize Bell as a regulated monopoly, thereby precluding competition. See Brock, Gerald. *The Telecommunications Industry:* 1981, pp. 158–161. New York, McMillan.

[7]See Wagner, Caroline S.; Cargill, Carl F.; Slomovic, Anna. "Open Systems in National Manufacturing: Implications for the National Information Infrastructure" in Kahin, Brian and Abbate, Janet (eds) *Standards Policy and Information Infrastructure:* Cambridge, MA: MIT Press, 1995. The article addresses some of the pitfalls that await the merger of the standardization process and the headlong technology expectation rush into the NII.

[8]For a discussion of intelligent agents that represents the state of the technology as this book was going to press, see Virdhagriswaran, Sankar; Osisek, Damian; O'Connor, Pat. "Standardizing Agent Technology," *StandardView,* Volume 3, Number 3, September 1995, pp. 96–101.

Chapter 4

The Players
and Their Products

"And all the men and women merely players:
They have their exits and their entrances;
And one man in his time plays many parts;"

—William Shakespeare, *As You Like It*

The players in standardization form a widely diverse lot. In most organizations, but especially in the information technology arena, the participants in standardization are viewed in the same light as Ben Johnson's patriotic politicians, seeking a last refuge because they are unable to contribute successfully elsewhere. This chapter looks at the participants from a slightly more sympathetic view, assuming their competence but questioning, at times, their motives. At the same time, the nature of the product that they are producing requires definition, since many participants often confuse the cause and effect of their activities.

INTRODUCTION

Within a formal Standards Developing Organization (SDO), there is usually an attempt to ensure balance on a committee by having representatives from the entire industry segment or the market. (The term "market" is meant, within the context of this book, to be an all-inclusive term for all participants in the industry. It is not meant to be a pejorative term that is used as a synonym for the term "marketing" or "sales.") The intent is to preclude any single interest from becoming too dominant in the creation of a standard that is supposed to serve the market. Consortia, by their nature, do not have to worry about balance as a matter of course, since they are bound only by the rules of their charter, rather than by the rules of unbridled openness. As a matter of fact, most consortia do seek balance since consortia realize that having "users" participate is a good way to ensure the adoption and use of their specifications. Similarly, SDOs seek user participation to validate their work, since it is the users who ultimately benefit from standardization.

There are two fundamental dilemmas in this approach. The first is that there is no clear definition of a "user" that is easily and readily applicable within the arena. The second problem is the nature of the product that these organizations produce. Standards are the product of the organizations that produce them, but gain currency only if they are themselves part of a longer chain that involves productization. These two elements—the user and the product—are fundamental questions that any participant in a marketing class learns to determine immediately. However, within the standardization arena, these two have never been completely and practically addressed.

A standardization group produces two distinct, but interrelated, products that the market finds of value. The first product, and the obvious one, is a document that describes how to do something—called the standard or the specification. The second, and less obvious product, is the process by which the standard is created. Both are valuable to the market as a whole but the value appeals to different segments and markets.

THE PROCESS

I'd like to examine the process of standards development; not as a process (this is done, lovingly and at great length, in Chapter 12), but rather as one of the value propositions of a standardization organization.

Fundamentally, a standardization organization exists to create a publicly available specification or a de jure standard. (The *de jure* standard, *de facto* standard, the publicly available specification, and regulatory standard were discussed in Chapter 3.) The benefit that the standardization organization brings to the party in the case of standardization is the widespread nature of participation in the actual setting and implementation of the standard or specification.

By definition, the SDO has the most lenient qualifications for membership. There are usually no restrictions placed upon participation except the desire to create a standard. There is a weak phrase—"materially affected"—which used to appear, but which has not, as far as I am aware, ever been used to deny someone participation in an Information Technology (IT) activity. This broad range of participation is necessary if a document is to achieve the appellation of an American National Standard. (I believe that the same general conditions apply throughout the world, although I also believe that some of the criteria for participation may be a little more rigorous in other areas. Obviously, the term "American National Standard" would not obviously apply to a standard developed, say, in France.) The idea behind this "openness" is to ensure that anyone who believes that they have something to say has the chance to be heard, have her or his positions considered, and be part of the process.

There are, of course, certain fallacies contained in this argument. First, the committees are "open to participation" by all concerned, but there is no guarantee that all concerned either know about them or, given the knowledge that they are happening, can actually get to them to participate. As an example, the meetings for the IEEE 1003 committee charged with creating POSIX were held all over the United States (including Hawaii) and they tried to hold them in Europe. The IEEE is a good choice for this example since all of its members are individual experts. The IEEE does not, as a rule, encourage group or corporate participation. For the independent programmer who lived in Kansas, there were very few meetings to which he or she could go that did not require some, and often extensive, capital outlay. However, the usual participant in these meetings was a reasonably well-paid member of an organization whose expenses were covered by this organization but who, to make the IEEE feel legitimate, represented her or himself as an "individual participant." The myth that American national standards represent the "will of the people" is exactly that. Even the majority of academics who rail against the massive participation by "corporations" in the standards process have their way paid by some organization.

So, the first real requirement for participation in an SDO is that you know when the meetings are and are wealthy enough to attend. Secondly, you have to be able to pay the fees that most SDOs charge members for participation and mailings. (The amount of these fees are not substantial if you have a large organization funding you. Recently, the SDOs have begun mailing out their minutes [to those who pay] on magnetic disks. While a keen idea, it does indicate that the new implicit fees now include the cost of a personal computer and other supporting paraphernalia.) While this sounds somewhat contradictory to the concept of "free and open," the SDOs will hasten to assure you that you can get the fees waived by a time-honored and complex process that makes it easier just to pay the fees. So, while you don't necessarily have to pay, it's just a lot less hassle if you do. Basically, if you can afford the travel expenses and pay the fees, you're in the game. As proponents of this form of organization are fond of saying, if you can afford the time and travel costs, once you get there, there's nothing to keep you from participating.

The same is not true of consortia. By and large, participation in a consortium specification creation activity is open only to those who have been invited by the consortium. The rules for being invited differ from consortium to consortium. Some require that all participants pay the same dues, while others have a graduated and variable schedule of fees, depending upon a multitude of factors. Some fees are very low (less than $500 in perpetuity) while some approach exorbitant ($1 million per year, plus costs). If the fees paid to just the three major consortia in the IT industry over the last three years were to be totaled, I believe that the amount would exceed the budget of ANSI for the last decade, and ANSI was serving the entire customer, industrial, and governmental base for the United States.[1]

The question that immediately springs to mind is why the IT industry was willing to pay—and pay handsomely—for an alternative when there already existed a system that was open and could produce nationally recognized standards that were good for use by industry or by the government. From a logical point of view, the alternative (which was substantially more expensive, having all of the costs of the SDOs as well as substantial additional costs) made no sense—unless you realize that what the participants in the consortia process were trying to buy was time. The formal SDO process takes substantial amounts of time to create a standard; there is the initial call, the meetings to discuss what is happening, the elections, the complete and, at times, nearly obsessive regard for strict process that meets both the intent and the letter of the law. All of these take time; a single public review can take up to three months. (A full multistage description of the standards life-cycle for both SDOs and consortia is contained in Chapter 11.)

A consortium is usually focused on a single problem and is looking for a single open specification that the sponsors can use as a basis for conforming implementations. It has a distinct advantage when competing with a "full spectrum SDO," since it is not too worried about ancillary problems or the process of standardization, allowing it to maintain focus. The participants are sent by sponsoring members to accomplish something within a discrete time frame, so there is usually a degree of motivation there that may be lacking in an SDO. The conforming implementations usually require test suites to verify that the specification has been implemented correctly. The consortium can also provide those. Finally, the consortium provides a "snapshot" of the status of the specification to members, allowing them to initiate productization sooner with less risk than they would find in an SDO. The apparent speed and single focus are the value adds that consortium sponsors find valuable and for which they are willing to pay extra.[2]

Another major advantage that consortia have is their funding level for "marketing related" activities. SDOs usually do not have a budget for "marketing." ANSI, which is only just beginning to understand that people and organizations do not necessarily value or even know about the standardization process, has a very small budget to fix these two perceptions (the value of standards and the value of ANSI) across all of American industry. Additionally, they must do this without substantial help from sponsoring members. Finally, in late 1995 ANSI was just beginning to evaluate what the worth of the American National Standard (ANS) designation is; previously, the leadership at ANSI held that everyone wanted this designation and was willing to participate to achieve it. The associations, such as the American Society of Testing and Materials (ASTM), have managed to live without it on many of their specifications.

The larger process problem for both consortia and SDOs is whether the market really cares about the "openness" of the process, or whether the market is willing to accept a proprietary solution as the equivalent of a standard. In many cases, the market has demonstrated a willingness to accept a nonstandardized product if it meets the business needs of the user. This phenomenon, more than anything else, is the threat to the entire process issue, and one that the standardization organizations and their supporters are just beginning to counter and consider.

THE PRODUCT

The standard or specification, which is the obvious outcome of the standardization process, is usually a document (most often hard copy) which the developing organization usually sells to the public. It is the result of intense labor on the part of a committee of volunteers (usually) who work together to create a specification which will guide the industry in some fashion, either by standardizing current practice or by postulating a new and future development that should be commonly implemented. Both of these approaches have serious and severe problems. However, there is a more mundane problem that these standards face when they are produced—and this is the problem of market demand.

Any introductory marketing book will tell you that a marketing plan has the "four Ps" (product, price, place [distribution channels], and promotion) and a section on competition. The "Four Ps" are essential for any marketing activity being considered by a commercial (either for profit or nonprofit) organization. If a standard is seen as a marketing venture, one would logically expect that these four questions could be answered by looking at the document that initiates the effort. Unfortunately, they usually can't. Very rarely does the requirement of what the market might need or want rear its ugly head in standardization activities.

Of course, this approach depends largely upon the idea that a standard is a marketing venture, a heretical supposition in many areas in the formal standardization process. However, I believe that I need merely point to a single practice that validates the proposition—that nearly all of the participants in the formal process (the SDO process) are sponsored by large corporate or governmental groups who expect to see a definite set of results emerge from the process. This definite set of results (called a standard) is then used either to create a product or to specify a product. Over the last several years, standardization committees in both Europe and the U.S. have seen a decline in total committee membership. This has been caused in part by the perception that the process is not satisfying the needs of the participants. In many companies, the decision to "de-fund" the process is caused by a lack of perceived value for the resources expended. The British Standards Institution, the American National Standards Institute, Accredited Standards Committee X3, Accredited Organization IEEE, and the ISO/IEC Joint Technical Committee 1, all major formal players, have seen membership drop significantly as major organizations (both public and private sectors) withdraw funding and participants. Some organizations, on the other hand, have either come into being or have seen membership swell. One case in point is the growth of standards that are management focused such as ISO TC 176, Quality Management and ISO TC 207, Environmental Management, and organizations that are focused on new technologies, such as TC 211, Geospatial Information Systems.

On the side of the consortia, there is an unusual, but unnerving, trend that somewhat mirrors what is happening in the formal organizations. Established consortia are feeling a pinch as sources of corporate wealth are disappearing. There are plans to restructure, plans to retrench, and in at least one case, a consortium has actually been disbanded.[3] On the other hand, new consortia are constantly being formed, sometimes overlapping current consortia, sometimes in areas that seem to be completely unready for standardization, and sometimes in areas in which standards already exist. Again, consortia, like SDOs, mirror the interests of the market and those willing to fund activities.

Returning to the central theme, that standardization organizations are marketing ventures, an underlying belief is that these organizations are usually expected and funded to produce a product that the market perceives as having value. Assuming that the organizations do produce a good standard or specification (which is usually the case), they are usually poorly equipped to publicize their products. My contention is that, within the IT arena, the major standardization organizations lack a minimal capacity for promotion of their standards or specifications as well as the benefits that these products deliver. This is because the Secretariat or central administrative unit is primarily focused on management of the process, not on management of the *product* of the process.

When organizations they do market the product, they usually market a "standard" which is either hard copy or some electronic form (usually a CD) which the user is required to purchase. Standardization groups receive a significant portion of their revenue from sales of books and other items that relate to standardization. One of the major problems in the ANSI federation of SDOs is the question of who receives the royalties. For example, when a standard created by the IEEE is published by ANSI and carries a designation of American National Standard, the standard is sold and a revenue stream initiated. The question of how much ANSI gets and how much the IEEE gets are vexing problems. The situation becomes complicated because the various groups all need money to maintain the large infrastructure that they have created.

Consortia are not immune to this problem. When X/Open published the Unified UNIX specification, the parts of the specification that were based on POSIX were judged to be royalty bearing events by the IEEE—who then came after X/Open. "Standards bodies often compete to sell standards. . . . Many of these organizations resemble publishers; they orchestrate standards setting in exchange for the right to sell standards and other standards-related services. Sales from standards, for example, account for 80 percent of the revenue of ASTM, 66 percent of the NFPA, and 28 percent of that of ANSI."[4]

This heavy reliance on publishing and selling standards and specifications places the standardization organizations in an interesting position. To begin, the desire to have a "big seller" becomes immense. At the same time, the effort to attract the "big seller" forces the administrative arms to look at each standardization effort not from the point of view of the market necessity for the standard, but rather from the point of view of whether or not this standard will be widely purchased by providers—not users—of standards. This focuses the efforts of the standardization organization inward, on itself and its survival. And this inward focus is ultimately destructive, since it impacts both the process and the product. With the intense focus on survival, at times to the exclusion of the real goal, the organizations are vaguely reminiscent of a commercial venture which, having a product no one is willing to buy, decide to become more efficient at producing it because it is easier to do that than to change the fundamental nature of the way they do business. The ultimate impact is to make these organizations look at the market for selling hard copy standards, and not the utility of the document.

These organizations are selling information, rather than a hard copy document. The information is the codification of a practice, either actual or desired, that the end users may find of help in doing business. However, the buyers of these documents are not end users, but providers of end user products. The creating groups are relying upon input from people who participate in the organizations who are biased towards doing business as usual. The market pull, then, is provided by the people who are providing the market push. In the commercial world, there are few companies who can continue to operate under these conditions, especially when the pool of true believers continues to shrink.

THE USERS

A simple first question that any researcher should ask about standardization is, "How big is the field? How much is spent, on a yearly basis, in pursuit of standardization?" This question is currently unanswerable. The estimates are that between $17 billion and $30 billion are spent each year on standardization. (What this entails or what this means is not clear; I believe that it represents the work to, for, and with standardization.) The only comprehensive study of which I am aware on organizations active in standardization was complied by Robert Toth, working under contract to the Department of Commerce.[5]

The problem that this presents, however, is significant. We do not know how big the standardization market is, nor do we know how many organizations are participating. Obviously, if there is a fundamental lack of knowledge about the organizations themselves, then it is probably safe to assume that we really don't know who the participants in the discipline are or what they want.

Based upon this, it becomes difficult to draw an accurate picture of a user, since we know neither the degree of participation nor the amount of participation. However, it is possible to examine what a user is from what we know of the industry as a whole. I am indebted to Dr. Kenji Naemura of Keio University[6] for his typology of the user, and to Gary S. Robinson of Sun Microsystems for the original idea of the "differentiated users."[7] Unlike many sections of this book, the following typology of the user is focused primarily on the IT industry. The Naemura user model makes use of another model with which all IT standardization participants should be familiar—a seven stage OSI model. Naemura comments that the layers of users are not fixed, so I've opted for a five stage model. Finally, in probably what is a major variation from the Naemura model, I've listed the layers of users as "users of standards" rather than as providers of standards. While the difference may seem slight, I believe that it represents a shift away from seeing standards as a *raison d'être* to seeing standards as a tool that helps the user perform a function.

The various levels of users appear as follows:

Level 5: The end user of computing equipment

Level 4: The Management Information Systems (MIS) director/ the Chief Information Officer/the Information Systems Consultant

Level 3: System integrators/IHVs/ISVs/middleware providers

Level 2: Functional product providers (and functional standards implementors)

Level 1: Base technology providers (and base standards creators and users)

The ultimate user of IT standards is correctly described as the end user, or the person who has a problem to solve and uses IT equipment to do so. The end user really doesn't care about the standards, or even the technology, except as it influences her or his ability to accomplish a business goal. It is this person of whom the User Alliance for Open Systems wrote, "An open system is one that allows a person access to information necessary to do one's job." The person may be aware of the technology that the equipment (both hardware and software) embodies, but, frankly, doesn't really care. To cast a stereotype, the typical user is a Chief Financial Officer, who is concerned with using a corporate database and using a spreadsheet. She or he does not really care if object-oriented programming, smoke and beads, or COBOL is used with SQL and RDBMS on a PC or mainframe. Of importance is that the information that is needed is available and capable of being manipulated. This person is the ultimate beneficiary of standardization because the information is there and useful. However, this person, because they have never been told about the value of IT standardization, is usually completely uninterested in the number of standards necessary to complete even the easiest activity, from the QWERTY keyboard through plugs to database structure. However, you can be assured that the CFO is very aware of the accounting standards used in financial reporting, and finds these of great interest.

The Management Information Systems Manager or the Chief Information Officer sits in a more difficult position. The Level 4 user acts as a bridge between the functional requirements of the computing system and the functional requirements of the Level 5 users. This person must understand the technology as it relates to the business goals of the company and the Level 5 users. At the same time, the capabilities of the Level 3 users must be understood and taken into account. The Level 4 user must understand what is being asked for by a Level 5 participant and what is being provided by a Level 3 participant, and how the other requests from other Level 5s integrate with other Level 5 requirements and other Level 3 responses. Fundamentally, the Level 4 user must be able to translate the Level 5 needs into a systematic way of viewing the world that will admit of technology implementation. In the more advanced position, the job is to translate functional requirements for "business systemness" into a manageable technological configuration, which acknowledges technology limitations and capabilities, but does not allow them to drive the business process.

To look at a real case, imagine a CIO who is looking at a security package for the Human Resource department. The security in the HR database must be adequate for legal protection, yet open enough to allow review of a file, within the constraints of the system, which changes from month to month. The HR database must also allow access to records by the financial organization since they process payroll. At the same time, the financial data must be protected against intrusion, except by the employee, for his or her record. The employee, however, may not have access to financial information beyond the immediate personal record, unless it is a financial person who needs this access, and then there must be some method of safeguarding both the HR and financial information. Finally, the various managers should have limited access to their employees' salary records and personnel records, but must not have access to unlimited records. Overlay this with the requirements of the ISO 9000 audit team for quality records and Federal OSHA requirements for safety, as well as the need to maintain individual and group computing resources, and you quickly understand why CIOs have a career life expectancy of less than two years. The Level 4 user is probably very aware of standards and wishes that there were more of them that solved the problems being faced and fewer of them that created problems.

The Level 4 Information Systems Consultant is, unlike the CIO or the MIS Director, usually a person who has another job and who dabbles in IT as a sideline to a line or other job. (I've used the term "consultant" because to use the term "dabbler" or "part-time fixer" lacks a certain panache.) He or she is the "early adapter of technology" in the office, who has a reputation for being able to "fix" people's systems when they won't run. The position—usually unofficial—starts as something simple ("How do I get it to print in landscape and not portrait mode?") and proceeds onto more complex questions ("Why won't the LAN stay up when George tries to print his slides?"). After a while, the ISC becomes sort of the court of first resort, and as such, highly influential in the circle of users whom he or she knows. The opinion of this person about a hardware or software package is influential in the buy/use decisions of the organization. Finally, this type of Level 4 resource will become very common in smaller offices and organizations as the personal computer becomes increasingly ubiquitous. And, to really make it interesting, this person will perform the same function in the neighborhood. (Think of the first person among your acquaintances who bought a Pentium© processor with Windows 95©, and who became the "expert" on this system in the eyes of the neighborhood, and to whose opinion others deferred.)

The Level 3 user is faced with translation between the user of a functional product—that is, the agglomeration of a set of technologies—and the Level 4 user who expresses needs of the business or organization. The Level 3 user must be familiar with the intricacies of a multitude of products and services and must be able to make the various pieces interact to solve what is often a poorly stated business problem. This level of user must be able to restate a business problem that the Level 4 user has defined in terms of the available hardware and software and then obtain or create the necessary additional pieces to make the solution work. This level is the first to discover that claims for "being standard" are occasionally misrepresented, or that the provider may have exaggerated a bit. This level may discover that the standard itself is valid but that it doesn't solve any problem known to humankind. This level of user is also one of the first to point out the holes and ambiguities in combining products, including specifications and standards, since they are the layer charged with assembling disparate parts into an interactive solution for the users.

The Level 2 functional product provider is more focused on technology than is the Level 3 user. The Level 2 user is usually part of the provider organization charged with creating the products from the technologies that are supplied by Level 1 providers. This is the layer that looks at what has been developed and written and asks, "How do we do that and still make the product attractive enough to sell?" This is also the layer that makes the decision on how to implement a standard in the product—since they are charged with actually productizing designs and prototypes of the Level 1 providers. While the Layer 1 providers can specify a standard, the Level 2 Functional providers have to make the decision as to whether or not the entire functional range specified in the standard is viable from a business point of view. This is the area where "trade-offs" are made.

To use an example. Assume that a Level 1 base technology provider has specified use of a standard in the prototype and built in all the options called for by the standard. When the specification for the product hits the Level 2 functional product provider—the "implementation team"—a fundamental decision on whether or not to include the full standard must be made. The classic case is the design of a communications protocol that has multiple connection options possible, which are all called out in the specification. The implementation team (based on input from marketing, sales, engineering, field service, and customers) decides which options to include, because it may be economic suicide to include them all. Conversely, it may be economically correct to include them all and then to add even more options that are proprietary, which would serve to lock the users into your way of doing things. This is the area in which the fundamental economic decisions about the product packaging (which attributes, which features, how much quality, and so on) are made. The standard or specification is considered as part of the repertoire of the product. If they help the product succeed, they will be used. If there is not a perceived market demand, they won't be used.

Finally, we arrive at the Level 1 user—the base technology providers are also the people who are usually charged with creating the fundamental product prototypes and usually with writing a standard. Within the IT industry these are usually technical people. Occasionally marketing people ("wannabe technies") fill this role, and occasionally they end up heading technical groups and committees, but usually the Level 1 provider is a technologist. They almost always are part of a provider organization, a research and development facility, a highly technical academic, or a consultant. In most cases, they are fascinated by the technology and seek to ensure that their views and ideas are heard by others in their arena. While this is somewhat stereotypical, it is, nonetheless, a reasonable description of the Level 1 user and provider of standards and specifications. (It is also, if you stop and think about it, true of the majority of human beings who are passionate about something.)

The motivation for this Level of participant in standardization is unusually difficult to define. Some participate because they have a desire to appear important, and standardization committees provide a reasonable arena for technological discussions where you can receive accolades from your peers. Others are what I call standardization groupies, or "open systems groupies," who like to travel and appear important as they flog around the world. However, a majority are reasonably hard working technologists who really believe that standardization can make a difference to them, their organizations, or to the industry as a whole. There are many more well-intentioned unsung heroes than jackanapes who participate; it's merely that the jackanapes receive better publicity for their gaffes and histrionics than do the well-intended workers.

CONCLUSION

If the "user levels" described above are a reasonable representation of reality, and if the description standardization organizations (both process and product) is correct, then the combination of the two should be capable of being matched and should illustrate that the standardization system is internally coherent. While I believe that the analysis of the two areas (participant and product) is correct, I do not believe that the two areas necessarily match to form a seamless whole. I believe that the product side is woefully out of line with the participant side, and that the gulf between the two is waxing, not waning, as time goes on.

Part of the reason for this lies in the nature of standardization within the IT industry. In the "early days," the IT industry was a reasonably tight community and the processes of the organizations were adapted for this environment. There was a body of literature that the practitioners generally understood; competition within the industry was based on technical merit (usually) and the rules for participation were reasonably clear and easy to understand.

Then came the "open systems" revolution, which continues today (see Chapter 6, "The Business of Standardization"). This opened the IT industry to all participants and greatly expanded the base from which the SDOs could draw participation. Unfortunately, the SDOs chose to retain their time-honored traditions (probably because they still looked valid) and continued to do business the way that they always had. In response to this, companies began to found consortia to achieve the same goal—that of cooperative development. Over time, the external environment changed again, and consortia, as well as SDOs, failed to anticipate the nature of the change.

This is all the more interesting because not one of the companies that was active in the standardization arena in 1980 has come through the last decade and a half unscathed and unchanged. IBM suffered from a series of losses and shed innumerable people. UNISYS was the result of a merger and has changed. DEC, once a leader in minicomputers and standards, is now a company half its size. HP has grown and shifted and grown again; Sun Microsystems didn't exist. Microsoft was only the hope of a handful of people. Netscape wasn't even a remote possibility. Database companies were nonexistent. Rightsizing was only a vague idea, and PCs were a nuisance that real IT professionals didn't take seriously. Yet, if you look at them closely, the procedures that the SDOs put in place in 1980, and which the consortia used as a model for transacting their business, remain relatively the same. Standardization organizations tend to be the structures that forgot time—and not that time forgot.

The debate between SDOs and consortia continues to rage unabated regarding the legitimacy of the process systems of the two types of organizations. SDOs tend to believe that, because they have an open process and consensus, they have a morally superior product. On the other hand, the consortia tend to believe that, because they are composed of people who are interested in accomplishing something, they have a better understanding of the market. Unfortunately, neither is completely correct. Organizations participate in both for the simple reason that there is a return on the resources invested. As the standardization organizations engage in continuous and endless acrimonious debate about which produces better product, the market is evolving as other forms of standardization begin to appear. This is based in large part around the ability of large numbers of people to communicate over the information super-highway, which will, as it evolves, allow more and more people access to the "standardized information" that these bodies are trying to produce.

If the published information becomes less critical, what are the standardization organizations left with? The answer to the question is usually given as "the process." The process, however, is not an end in and of itself, but is rather a method of ensuring that the outcome of the process has value. Yet, the practitioners of this process would be the first to cite the old computer aphorism of "GIGO" (Garbage In, Garbage Out). If what is produced is not relevant to the industry at large, then it has no value, or possibly a negative value, since it consumed valuable resources that might have been deployed elsewhere.

All of this leads to a need for a new definition of what standardization is. The old definition, as practiced within the current structure, reflects what its practitioners are familiar with and what they hope will prevail. It is somewhat akin to the old Western towns that lay astride the Chisholm trail, and which derived their revenues from the cattle drives. When the railroad expanded, and the cattle drives were truncated, the towns had two options: to change into something else, or to remain the same and bet that the railroad would fail and the cattle drives would start again. The towns that changed are viable today. Over time the others also changed and today are the storied "ghost towns" of the Southwest. As with the fortress castles that dot Europe, they're fun to visit, but no one lives there. One hopes that in the next decade, the same will not be said of today's standardization processes.

NOTES

[1]The annual dues for the Open Software Foundation are approximately $1 million per year now, with between seven and ten sponsors. When OSF was started in 1989, it had a commitment from its sponsors for approximately $121 million. X/Open's annual fees are about $600,000 per year. They have about a dozen major sponsors who pay for this, and several hundred other participants who pay lower fees. The Object Management Group charges $50,000 per year from its principal members, and claims over 500 total members, both primary and secondary.

[2]The apparent speed with which consortia develop specifications has often been held up as a major benefit of the consortia process. However, looking at the output of the major consortia, this claim is hard to substantiate. The Internet Engineering Task Force (IETF), charged with putting together the Internet, finally came into prominence in 1993, ten years after it had been initiated—and then primarily because the major UNIX vendors made the Internet the communications schema of choice. Similarly, OSF took four years to establish MOTIF within the market, and X/Open took nearly ten years to persuade its sponsors to embrace a Unified UNIX. CORBA2 has just emerged from the Object Management Group (OMG) and is just now (1996) coming into existence as a productized specification nearly six years after its inception. On the other hand, the Object Database Management Group (ODMG) did create a database specification, from initiation to completion and implementation, in less than three years.

[3]The unlucky consortium was UNIX International, a consortium formed in the late 1980s as part of the Operating Systems wars. UI was originally formed as a method of reassuring the market that AT&T, the owner of UNIX, would listen to the input from the market and would not act in an arbitrary manner in the creation of future UNIX specifications. The consortium was also created in response to the formation of the Open Software Foundation (OSF), which was created by providers unwilling to pay AT&T the requisite licensing fees to be able to implement UNIX. OSF's goal was to produce an operating system that looked and acted as UNIX was thought to act. Martin Libicki, in his book *Information Technology Standards: The Quest for the Common Byte* describes the evolution of UNIX very well.

[4]U.S. Congress, Office of Technology Assessment, Global Standards: op cit, p. 13.

[5]Toth, Robert, editor. Standards Activities of Organizations in the United States, NIST Special Publication 806, available from Global Engineering Documents as Cat #SP806. Telephone 1-800-854-7179. The document is not available from NIST.

[6]Naemura, Dr. Kenji. "User Involvement in the Life Cycles of IT and Telecommunications Standards," presented at the International Workshop on Standards, Innovation, Competitivenes and Policy, University of Sussex, 10–12 November 1993.

[7]Private conversations with Gary S. Robinson, 1983 and 1984. These conversations served as the basis for constructing a model for Digital Equipment Corporation's very successful standardization strategy in the 1985–1990 time frame. Gary was Director of Standards at Digital from 1981–1991.

Chapter 5

Toward an Expanded Definition of Consensus Standardization

"In front, the sun climbs slow, how slowly,
But westward, look, the land is bright!"

—Arthur Hugh Clough, *Say not the struggle naught availeth*

INTRODUCTION

The trouble with standards is that, because they are ubiquitous, and hence familiar, they breed contempt. In a conversation with a senior marketing director of a major computer firm, I was firmly told that, "Standards are a check off item. They really don't count in business. Users just put them down because they have to." Even if you ignore the egregious failure of logic in understanding user requirements, the comment shows a belief that many people in the Information Technology industry have about standards.

This perception of standards by IT marketing people (that is, people who claim to "do marketing" to differentiate themselves from people who "do sales") is pervasive. It is, unfortunately, shared with many engineering managers, who are really upset that they have to include standards in their product plans. And yet, these same people rely on standards and standardization to sell their products. Imagine a marketing person claiming that theirs is a "closed system," or an engineer claiming that the interface for disks is, ". . . just like SCSI, but different." The jump between an applied standard and a required standard seems to be too much of a chasm for some to leap all at once.

I believe that some of the reason for the problem lies in the fact that few of these people have ever contemplated the world outside of the computer industry. All industries have their standards; nearly all of them tie the standards into the practices that are common in their industries. There are very few accountants who are not intimately familiar with accounting standards; similarly, electricians are familiar with the National Electrical Code, and automotive engineers are familiar with the standards of the Society of Automotive Engineers. Even salespeople in hardware stores, if they're good, are aware of standards that impact lumber and fasteners, as well as local building codes.

In nearly all of these cases, the application of the standard is clear and demonstrable. However, in the IT industry, there are usually several intermediate steps between the standard and the application of the standard. Most articles on standards in the popular press (which serves as one of the primary sources of information on standards for most practitioners in the IT arena) are focused on a particular standard, or series of related standards, or some closely defined standardization activity. The terminology applied is suspect (usually) and adopted for use within a specific article. (When the Economist speaks of "standards," it may be altogether different than when *Byte Magazine* does the same thing.) This lack of a common terminology is something that is true primarily for disciplines like standardization, which seem to sit on a marketing/engineering cusp.

As an example, a byte is a byte (within limits), and other commonly used, applied, and understood terms and concepts serve as a form of shorthand. Most scientific disciplines seem to share this advantage; while disagreements can arise, a common vocabulary and experience eliminate the need to provide extensive background information in initial discussions. Standards, on the other hand, suffer from a two-fold problem.

Standardization is assumed to be a technical discipline because it is the source of innumerable volumes (called standards) that contain technical descriptions of how to do things. It is not a technical discipline. Standardization relies on someone (usually a technologist) to abstract features of an interface to standardize, and this begins the entire process based upon a subjective interpretation of the essential quality of the product or program. Obviously, these interpretations vary depending upon the object being described and the person doing the describing. When you add the requisite standardization committee, the interpretation becomes substantially more complex. Second, standards must use nonquantifiable terms for these already vague descriptions, since they are written in native language instead of precise mathematical notation. The people who write these documents, who play in the process, and who use the products are not economic ciphers, but rather real flesh and blood individuals, each with a unique set of expectations, aspirations, and background, all which must also be viewed in light of national, regional, technical, and educational background, and organizational or user affiliation.

The ambiguity and confusion caused by the use of the word "standard" to refer to all of the various types of standardized specifications, the process for creating these specifications, and the intent of the action of standardization in the market is a major source of the problem of the study of "standardization." The confusion generated by this lack of usable market definition is evident if one examines the definitions of standards offered by experts in the area.[1] These definitions are probably, in part, all correct. The danger is that these are broad definitions and, ". . . are too vague to guide analysis. Precision is sacrificed for the sake of comprehensiveness. This is clearly the case with standards definitions. They tend to be exceedingly broad, in order to cover the full range of standards found throughout society."[2] Much of the problem with standardization is that, as practitioners, we know what we're talking about—and then, because we do, we impute the same understanding to others. However, while the practitioners "understand," the clear definition has never been formalized except within terms of the discipline itself. The International Organization for Standardization (ISO) approved definition of a standard reads along the lines of, "A technical specification or other document available to the public drawn up with the cooperation and consensus or general approval of all the parties affected by it, based upon the consolidated result of science, technology, and experience, aimed at the promotion of optimum community benefits and approved by a standardization body."[3]

In this chapter I will examine the attributes of standards and standardization to permit a new definition of standardization and standards. The analysis looks at only the voluntary consensus standardization arena (ignoring the regulatory arena), and focuses on the attributes of standardization as the way to creating a definition of standards that is predicated upon an understanding of the "thing itself," rather than looking at a set of attributes of the standardization process. The typology that is created is necessarily to structure the definitions to permit handling of the multiple variables and to provide a more measured understanding of the nature and capabilities of the various types of standardization activities that are occurring throughout the industry.

TOWARD A TYPOLOGY OF CONSENSUS STANDARDIZATION

Within the current context of consensus standardization organizations, all standards, once undertaken, are believed to have equal importance to the market.[4] This has proven to be manifestly untrue, since standards can and do vary by importance to industry, user, and provider. There is a difference between the concept of an implementation standard (a standard used to implement a particular device) and a conceptual standard. Finally, there is the growing realization that some standards are process standards as opposed to product standards.

These three aspects of standards—importance, conceptual versus implementation, and process versus product—intermix to produce interesting challenges for the consensus standardization process. Removing these three aspects from their contextual settings will allow examination, definition, and validation. I propose to begin the examination with the most straightforward of the three; importance.

Importance

Within the information technology industry, the rift between users and providers has widened in the past several years, as users come to expect providers to fulfill the promises that they have made over the past decade. In many cases, expectations have been raised by the marketing of a particular solution. The notion of the "Open System," composed of interoperating and transparent system components, coupled with software that even a senior executive can operate, has been internalized by users. The use of "user-friendly" Graphical User Interfaces (GUIs) abounds, and each vendor seems to delight in making their GUI just slightly different from all other GUIs on the market. At the same time, the complexities of the systems (for system management, data access, or networked communications) seem to have become the latest target of standardization and yet there is no significant standardization effort being devoted to this activity.

From the wind planted by such campaigns (ease of use, the intelligent system, and so on), the industry is now beginning to reap the whirlwind: users are beginning to demand that the providers make good on their promises to interconnect and standardize systems. The option (purchase of a single vendor's product as the basis for a vendor standardization effort) is being seriously considered. If the vendors cannot standardize, then the users will make it clear that they will do it for them. At the same time, the industry technologists have moved ahead with some of their pet schemes, and are now proposing that everyone should be able to program (using the Internet and objects and browsers), so that even the novice user can experience the thrill of "programming" without first having to learn the subject. Finally, in the quest for greater efficiency and optimization of increasingly expensive human and computing resources, many users have turned to standards as the solution to the organizational and computing problems which are—and will continue to be—major problems for industry at large.

In both of these cases (keeping promises and resource optimization) the concept of importance, measured by a dollar impact in both the users' and providers' world, is relevant. For the users, it is the cost of time before implementation of a viable standard that meets business needs; for the providers, it is the cost of the implementation itself. This difference in metrics is becoming critical as the pace of change accelerates and the level and intensity of disagreement between and among the users and providers grows. Some providers view standards as a threat to their economic well-being, believing that the longer they have the best unique solution, the more they stand to profit. Others feel that the longer they do not have access to a specific technology contained in a proposed standard, the worse off they are economically. Users, on the other hand, may see a delay in standardization as a deliberate attempt of the providers to force single vendor solutions. Conversely, some believe that providers use standards to bring everyone down to a common level that can then be regulated by the providers. Finally, due to delays in the standardization process, many users are literally walking off the formally recognized fields (both SDO and consortia) and creating their own standards which they then expect the providers to implement. All of these divergent views and activities cannot be ignored without peril, and they cannot be changed without great effort.

Also varying from user to user and from provider to provider is the relative importance assigned to a particular activity by each distinct set of participants in the total process. Standards that are very important to a specialized industry niche may, for the majority of standards participants, be of no overwhelming importance. Similarly, a user who has bet his or her career on the success of a standardization activity (for instance, Ada or Objects) may have an entirely different perspective than an academic who wishes to "do the precisely correct thing." Yet, within an SDO, these standards are required to undergo the same process as a standard of major importance to the future of the entire industry. While a consortium has a different process, it too usually imposes rules that require some degree of inspection of the results of the consortium's work. The consensus process does factor importance into its procedure; each standard is accorded the same right to the process as any other. The rationale for this examination, of course, is largely driven by the creators of the standard, who are using the process (usually) to produce something that is commercially viable to a host of users and providers. Even so, if the proponents of the niche standard believe that their vital need is not being expedited, they will blame the bureaucratic standards process.

Figure 5.1 attempts to place some of these conditions in perspective. It is based on work originally done by Dorothy Cerni,[5] and appears deceptively simple. The two axes are "time" and "consensus," and the plot shows that fundamentally, the greater the consensus, the greater the time required. However, the corollary to "consensus" is that there are a greater number of options (and hence compromises) contained in the "consensus" axis, so the chart can also be seen to have the axes of "compromise" and "time." For the niche standardization participant, the relationship between compromise and consensus then becomes one of a tradeoff: The greater the consensus, the greater the level of compromise required in the resulting document or specification, and hence the greater the compromise in the resulting product. If the amount of time spent is important, as most organizations with a mission would claim, then the amount of compromise and degree of consensus would appear to be inversely proportional to the amount of importance, as measured by time.

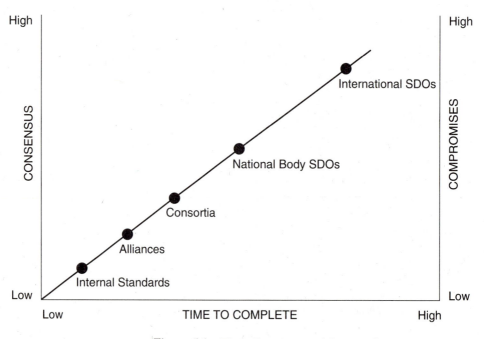

Figure 5.1   Time, Consensus, and Compromise

A great deal of importance may be assigned to a standard for the wrong reason. If a standard is required to solve a problem which users failed to anticipate, or which a corporate management ignored, the effort has a high potential for failure or, at least, for a shortened life span. Standards cannot fill a gap caused by lack of managerial or technical planning and foresight. At the same time, standards—especially those that are heavily driven by consensus—must favor longer term solutions. The logic for this statement is axiomatic, given the previous chart. Because it is known that consensus takes time, the participants in a committee must be focused on the future and future solutions. It is obvious to even the most casual observer that solving a current problem in the future is a foolish venture. Unfortunately, while this may be obvious to the casual observer, it is less obvious to many standards committees, who achieve a solution to a complex problem of the previous decade. (Two classic examples of this are the ISO JTC 1 committees completing OSI just as TCP/IP-based Internet took over the market, and the acceptance by Sun Microsystems, HP, IBM, and DEC of a GUI based on MOTIF just after it became clear that Microsoft Windows had become the market dominant GUI.) The nature of the consensus system, the nature of the problem, and the nature of collaborative work all mitigate against using standards for tactical advantage. Finally, standards created to solve present problems usually create substantial future problems by their existence.

The importance of a standards effort should be linked to some significant problem, the solution of which will enable a portion of the industry to succeed. While it sounds somewhat simplistic to say this, the easiest indicator of the importance of a standard is in the economic payback that it provides the body of users who will implement it. For some time, I have served as a "marketing angel" to the Requirements and Topics Group (RTG) for systems administration within the X/Open User Council. This group is composed of end users, software vendors (SVs), and system software vendors (SSVs). It was attempting to define a technical program for the technical managers who were involved in systems administration. (The X/Open work methodology is reasonably complicated; some might argue "unreasonably" complicated). As the resident marketing person, I began to ask that the RTG quantify the requirements being given to the X/Open Technical Managers. This effort at quantification would result in the RTG discussing the "importance," in terms of economic benefit, that a particular solution would have, rather than discussing technology and implementation details.

To give an example, there was a demand by the RTG for "software administration" which would allow a system manager to query the systems connected to a particular network to determine what software was resident on each PC. In the discussions around this proposed piece of technology, I asked why it was important and what other technical program should be abandoned, since the resources that X/Open could command from the vendors was finite. After long discussion, a simple proposal was put in place. The users would "estimate" how much having the standardized procedure was worth to them; that is, if they had this ability to determine resident software, what hard savings would accrue, and then what soft savings would accrue.

The analysis done was reasonably simple. Basically, the number of PCs was roughly determined, the amount of time installing a piece of software was calculated, the amount of new software installed each year, the amount of time taken by verifying software being extant or not, and the multiple other time critical details that impact the installation of a PC program. When the numbers were plugged in, it turned out that this piece of systems administration would save a major user (50,000 PCs or more) over $50 million per year. This allowed the RTG to go forward with a proposal to the technical side of X/Open with the benefits quantified. Unfortunately, the other requests from the other RTGs were not quantified, and the utility of a singular piece of quantified data as a comparison metric doesn't work especially well. However, the theory was good even if the larger discipline wasn't.

This is one of the problems with determining "importance." As pointed out earlier, importance varies based upon multiple dependencies, including user, provider, size of organization (this applies to both user and provider), the nature of the problem to be solved, and the willingness of the participants to do the work that is required by the standardization process. As more and more consortia and SDOs appear to work in standardization, the need for economic justification—that is, determination of the importance of the standardization activity—will become increasingly needed if the process is to survive.

EXISTING PRACTICE AND CONCEPTUAL STANDARDS

A standard, as a standard, can be envisioned as a technical plan that represents the proposed activities of the industry in dealing with an issue. No matter how the issue is viewed by the participants, the standard should represent the industry response to a real problem, providing a usable solution to that problem. There are two caveats here; the first assumes that there is a "real problem" and the second that the solution that is being proposed is usable and applicable to the problem. Neither of these are automatic; the market has a nasty habit of finding a non-technical solution to a problem much more quickly than a technical solution can be found, or by adopting a technical solution that may not be "the best," but which satisfies the market need. There are numerous apocryphal stories about this. Most failures of this sort do not make the pages of *Business Week* unless they are phenomenally bad. However, there continue to circulate, as sort of the "urban myth of MIS directors," stories of complex programs that were created to solve problems that could have been fixed by application of common sense. The same is true of standardization.

Assuming that a problem existed and that the problem was analyzed correctly, the standard should provide a valid solution. If the problem requires a sweeping solution, then the standard should provide an adequate response. On the other hand, a modest problem should not be met with the requirement that forces the entire industry to change. While this may seem obvious, solutions in "high technology" seem to be endowed with creeping elegance, which requires that additional features be constantly added until the solution neither addresses nor fixes the original problem.

However, if the idea that "a standard is the written solution to future industry problem" is accepted, then, by implication, standards committees are acting to steer the industry by changing the environment in which the industry operates.[6] There are three distinct categories into which such standards creation activities can fall: (1) Standards that plan to change the industry; (2) Standards that reinforce existing industry patterns; (3) Standards that cause change which is unplanned. Standards that plan to change the industry are usually conceptual. Standards that reinforce extant industry patterns usually relate to existing practice.[7] Standards that cause unplanned change can fall into either category.

Because the information technology industry is dynamic, solutions must evolve with the problems they solve. An existing practice standard is intended to ensure that the evolution of an answer keeps slightly ahead of the evolution of the question. An example is the COBOL standard, which changes so that COBOL remains responsive to current and future needs of the industry. While the standard is new at each revision, the solution it provides (a business oriented language that can be used widely, has stability, and is easily implemented) does not change but rather evolves to meet the changing needs of those who demanded it in the first place. Accredited Standards Committee (ASC) X3J4 (the standards committee responsible for COBOL) makes sure that changes to COBOL are implemented in a manner that is evolutionary rather than revolutionary. The intent is to reinforce the activities of the industry, not to change them.

Existing practice standards groups are not automatically noncontentious, however. The term "existing practice" refers only to the nature of the problem being considered; it does not reflect unanimity on the part of the participants in the process. As with any collection of independent people, different opinions on changes abound and are held dear. Changing people's minds can take time and energy, yet the process must proceed if the goal is to arrive at a true consensus standard that will respond to the future needs of the industry. At the same time, the participants, who are changing the standard to agree with their vision of the future, must agree on exactly what that vision of the future is. If a committee is working to make an extant standard useful to the market in several years, the participants must all agree on what the dominant technology within their area would be in the next few years. (An example is the binding of a language to a technology—such as objects—with the belief that when you've finished your standardization, objects will be the "in" technology. If the committee agrees, then things are fine; if there is a faction that believes that another technology will dominate, then there will be a fight until the view of the future is straightened out.) On the other hand, the vision of the future should probably be correct as well. There is little in life as embarrassing as arriving at the future only to find that this was not the future that was so grandly predicted.

If existing practice standards are seen as evolutionary, then conceptual standards are revolutionary; seeking to change the industry perceptions and direction, to encourage technology conversion or change, or to redefine an industry problem. Conceptual standards are usually recognized by the fact that they take a different perspective in the approach to a problem solution (usually technologically based), or take a different perspective on the problem itself. Creation of these standards, usually driven by an individual or a provider, takes an immense amount of patience, time, and effort on the part of the participants, since deliberate change is difficult to introduce.[8]

One well-known conceptual standard was the IEEE 802.3 Ethernet standard, initiated in response to a perceived market need to provide separate users access to computing facilities without degrading user performance or duplicating the centralized resources. The question of whether to distribute resources or degrade performance had been viewed as a trade-off. Distributed resources provided high performance at financial expense, and centralized resources provided low cost with degraded performance. (This, please remember, was in the days when the PDP-11/70 was the dominant minicomputer and the VAX 11/780 was just entering the market. A processor with a MIP capability was still in the $100,000 range, and a 100MB disk was considered overkill). The developers of Ethernet redefined the problem, focusing on communications between the user and the system's resources. By concentrating efforts in this area, the concept of the Local Area Network (LAN) was developed, leading to a revolution in the way that computers were conceptualized and structured. As the Ethernet standard was developed and deployed, abrupt shifts in design and use of IT equipment occurred, exceeding the original technical and market expectations of the LAN developers.[9] While the LAN could be called a natural progression of technology, it provided a starting point from which other technologies could build, allowing providers and users alike to focus their energies, efforts, and activities on providing further solutions, instead of defining and redefining the same old problem.

Any standard, once initiated, may cause unplanned change. This usually happens because someone outside the standards committee sees an opportunity to use the standard in a way that the group drafting the standard fails to see. This happened to ASC X3T9.5, which is concerned with providing a high speed interface between CPUs and their mass storage devices. The committee had originally proposed the Local Distributed Data Interchange (LDDI) as an existing practice standard to provide an elegant technical solution to a growing, but understood, problem—how to connect a CPU to mass storage or connect a CPU to CPU in the face of rising costs of interconnect and the growing need to transmit data more quickly and safely than was provided by current standards. The LDDI was an existing practice standard because it was codifying an already existing idea, and used a strategy of congruence because it was an extension of a known industry solution.[10]

ASC X3T9.5 then began work on the Fiber Distributed Data Interchange (FDDI), also as an implementation standard, which modified the work in LDDI by substituting glass for copper. The solution was partially driven by technology (fiber is newer and therefore more "fun" than copper) and partially by trying to meet the longer term needs of the industry by providing still more capacity for the transmission of data (fiber has a substantially higher transmission capability than does copper). The solution was well-suited to the problem, and would have met all of its developers expectations, except for one small problem: the committee had overlooked the fact that application of fiber was in its early stages in the IT industry. As the industry began to realize the potential in fiber optics, the expected uses for it began to multiply, and the work of the FDDI committee became responsible for changing the way people looked at interconnects. This shift was not deliberate; it just happened. The standard met the expectations of its developers. It described the necessary methods for connecting fiber optic cable to mass storage and to CPUs. The connection can do things and create markets and functions never envisioned by either the committee or the industry when the process was started.

PRODUCT AND PROCESS STANDARDS

The rate of technological change in the IT industry is increasing. This acceleration exerts two major pressures on the consensus standards process. The first of these is the collapsing life cycle of most IT products worldwide, where the product life expectancy has decreased from ten years to two years, and promises to continue to decline. The functions that the products perform are not changing; but the ever greater demands for more speed, more performance, more reliability, and less space can be met only by more and more innovative engineering, products, and applications.

The second stress derives from the nature of the consensus standards process itself. It is not a quick process, nor is it meant to be. To gain consensus, there must be a time where disputes can be resolved, not by compromise, which gives all parties a partial victory and partial defeat, but by redefining the problem in such a manner that a solution can be found that meets the needs of all participants. The process takes time and effort. When there is no one right answer, arguments can become dogmatic because of economic, personal, or regulatory need. Once a problem has been redefined, however, a new answer that can and does satisfy the participants can be worked out, but this, too, takes time. Consensus does not mean majority agreement; consensus indicates that a commonality of perception and opinions has been achieved, and this can take time to accomplish.

To mitigate the pressure of change, a new form of standard is becoming increasingly common. It is the process standard, as opposed to the product standard. A product standard describes a product or service being standardized. The product, which should have a future orientation (although this is not an absolute necessity), defines the standard in such a way that the standard merely exists to serve as a model for the product within the industry. In other words, the standard and the product/service being described are equivalent within the confines of a single discipline/structure, free of external dependencies. The standard assumes that the external interfaces to the product it described are relatively constant and consistent. Although the standard can accept a wide variability of input if the standard specifies the variability, it is more usual for the product standard to be constructed rather tightly. If a standard calls for a series of options, which can be randomly implemented, in terms of numbers, sequences, and fashions, then its purpose is defeated. Since, by definition, the consensus process must somehow include all of the opinions that are perceived as necessary, or else have a satisfactory reason for rejecting them, it is very easy for a product standard to become so generalized or so complex that it is no longer possible to consider it viable as a standard.

A model of the product standard in non-IT terms are "nut and bolt" standards. The nut and bolt must be matched; a standard that describes the pitch, the size, and the thickness pretty well describes the function for which the nut and bolt are intended. (A totally naive person would not understand, but someone with a little knowledge of industry would have little trouble understanding how to deploy the nut and bolt, how large of a hole to drill to use them, what thicknesses of materials could be attached, and so on). Fundamentally, the standard describes a product, and, in so doing, delimits an application.

The process standard focuses on the transmutation of a customer need into a customer solution, examining those things that are input and output to a system, but not concerning itself especially with the products that accomplish that transmutation. In other words, it is concerned with the ends, not means. If a process standard is intended to standardize the transmission of information, it addresses whether or not the information was transmitted and usable when it was received, and not how the transmission is achieved. This concept has substantial implications for the development of standards, because it is device-independent. Rather than specifying a certain product or service to accomplish a need, it merely describes the need, the constraints to achieving the solution, and the output necessary to allow the results of the standardized solution to interplay with solutions from other process standards.

To continue the analogy above, the process standard would describe "joining" as an output of a standard. It would not specify the manner of joining, but it would specify that when these things are joined, they will be joined such that they have certain characteristics such as the ability to withstand so much stress, so much torsion, so much compression, and so on. The method of joining (glue, rivets, nails, bolts) is left to the wishes of the implementors. This situation works well until multiple vendors provide multiple solutions, and you get glue and nails, or rivets and zippers, being mixed as part of a "joining solution."

If a standard represents a future-oriented response by industry to a perceived problem, then the process that is described in the standard must also be future oriented. Knowledge of problem definition and solution and awareness of the implications for the future that the process implies and actualizes are both vitally necessary to reach this goal. Also, process standards are the function and result of their context; that is, you cannot have an isolated problem or user need, they must somehow arrive from somewhere. It is the aspect of context that becomes most critical, and makes this aspect of the process standard the most challenging for consensus standards. The challenge danger lies not in the description of the process outcome (the systematic solution to the need) but in the accurate reading of the user need and then in the determination of the process description. An improper reading of a need can lead to a completely unsuitable process standard, and even a successful description of a need does not guarantee the successful description of the solution. Again, with the joining analogy, if the context is concrete, then zippers are inappropriate. If the context is cloth, then rivets (unless you're the Levi Corporation) are inappropriate.

For example, describing a process correctly based upon an incorrect or inaccurate understanding of the need can lead to either indifference or to confusion on the part of the market, neither of which is healthy to the consensus process. Indifference would follow the creation of a standard, under consensus, that misleads the market by causing the market to misdirect its energies, by providing a solution to a nonexistent problem, or by providing a non-solution to an existing problem.

Market confusion has even more substantial implications, which extend beyond the arena of standards. If the market is only confused, it will cast about among the alternatives available, and eventually, using some mechanism that is mysterious to rationale (to the market), select one alternative that appears to be valid: it only loses time and, sometimes, a sense of purpose. A much more serious impact can occur, however, if the industry is heavily technology driven or influenced. Improperly applied process standards can trap the industry in an obsolete technology or cause it to wander from the main course of technology. In this case, the industry must find the correct technology for its uses, redefine its purpose, and then restart to accomplish the new, or redefined, purpose. This can be made especially hard if the industry had been certain that it was doing the right thing previously, and, in fact, had been following the tenants advocated by an accepted standard. Having lost faith in itself and therefore in its own correctness of perception, the industry may turn at random, leading to multiple technologies. This sometimes causes the market to splinter and lose the coherence that sometimes adds strength to technology.

The distinctions between a product and process standards apply primarily to dynamic markets. In a static market, if the inter-relationships between products are constant, or if the pace of technological change is slow, product standards will subsume process standards. The product, in order to function, must fit into the larger process correctly; if it does not, both product and process will fail, because the desired result and the tool to produce it are not compatible. In the case of a correctly written and structured product standard that fits into the market, the process is inferable from the product. If the process described in the standard is containing steam to increase pressure and temperature and the product described is a boiler, the process and product are equivalent: one could deduce from the boiler standards the process that it is intended to carry out. (The reverse of the above argument, however, is not true.) Additionally, if the market is dynamic a product may be made obsolete by changes in the demands and requirements of the process, which do not diminish the essential validity of the process, but do affect the way it is completed.

REUNIFICATION

Of the three aspects of consensus standards that I have described, importance is a factor in all cases. Existing practice versus conceptual and Product versus process can be combined in various ways to produce several very different kinds of standards. There are four possible valid combinations: existing practice/product, existing practice/process, conceptual/product, and conceptual/process.

Most common is the existing practice/product standard. It deals with an established product or service with known rules and boundaries which is either being updated for use in a changed or changing environment or is being used to formalize a response to a known, existing, and ongoing market need. Because there is a usually a need for future orientation (postulated earlier), either the product must be capable of being modified for use in the changing environment or the requirement written to ensure the proposed standard solution will not obsolesce quickly. If the product or service being standardized is a response to a market need that is no longer valid, the standard making/codifying activities are valuable only for historical reasons, or for reasons other than those that would normally apply to standards.

The existing practice/product standard is best used in areas where there is a consensus on bounded and clearly defined user and market needs and expectations. Although the market that uses this type of standard is dynamic, I believe that it is safe to state that it has an aura of predictability. The creation of any standard can be hectic, sometimes bordering on the frenetic, but the motive behind the creation of an existing practice/product standard often is prosaic and calmly stated. These standards serve a predictable market with a predictable response.

The existing practice/process standard is more difficult to describe than the existing practice/product standard. The two adjectives seem almost incompatible as process has more future oriented global implications than does the concept of existing practice. Yet the two situations must be accommodated in situations where a well-established need, too complex or too simple to be met by a single product, requires a standard not bound to a single technology or methodology. This would be the case in the a standardization of a system with a known and expected outcome, but where the market as a whole is not especially concerned about the methods used to achieve them. Whether the market need, and the process that satisfies it, is complex or simple, the standard should describe the process of obtaining the expected result, and not the product that produces that result.

The most obvious illustration of the existing practice/process standard is the telephone system, in which users are very concerned with the user interface that they see and use (the conventional ten digits, dialing conventions, and voice transmission) but don't really care about the technology employed to achieve communication. The well-established need to communicate by voice over distance exists, and the users want this need satisfied. Methodology takes second place to results.

The conceptual/product standard is already relatively widespread in the information technology industry which is by nature dynamic with a tendency towards being product, and not process, driven. Helping the adoption of this type of standard is the widespread recognition that standardization is future-oriented and market-driven. This type of standard is appearing more and more frequently in the general population of standards, as technology forces changes in the materials use and fabrication industries. When a new technology is being implemented, a conceptual/product standard assures the market providers that their perceptions are valid. The market reaffirms its own correctness in this case. This type of standard usually relates a product or service with a technical or marketing variation about which the providers are unsure. Because safety is perceived in numbers, the call for a standard based on a future product becomes very strong.

Affirmation of a collective need (and the affirmation of the collective response to the need) is one of the more important functions of the consensus standards process. If a proposal for a standard generates no interest except among a small group of proponents, they must ask whether the future products that would result from the standard are really a valid response to a market need. If no one is interested in working to develop the standard, the odds are that the concept is of little interest to the industry at large, and that no one will endorse the resultant standard, nor will anyone use the standard in productization. This renders the need for the standard moot, since innovation for innovation's sake is not encouraged by the market, most individuals, and society in general. However imperfectly, the consensus standards process helps the market determine when innovation is frivolous and when it serves a purpose, providing a neutral arena where the impacted community as a whole can safely question, advocate, argue, and generally explore an innovative approach. The die-hard advocate risks the most in this process, since she/he must justify the change and show positive results that outweigh the cost of change. The other option, of course, is to pursue the proposal as a proprietary response to the market, choosing to believe that the proposed solution is correct and conventional wisdom foolish. Occasionally, this succeeds; more often, it fails. When it does succeed, it can pay large and impressive dividends to the visionaries, the technical term for those who succeed by capturing a market that others wish they could have foreseen.

One of the factors that is helping to increase the number of conceptual/product standards is the movement away from the use of consensus standards as a substitute for regulations. This is caused by the growing awareness that conceptual/product standards do not describe an implemented product, but rather are dealing with futures, which is inimical to regulatory use of standards. The conceptual/product standard has the potential for becoming an important part of the advanced development process as companies begin to respond to the foreshortening of the product life-cycle. Unfortunately, because only a handful of people in the industry are aware that the success of the consensus process depends on at least three general reviews, which are built into the process and which take a significant amount of time, there is an increasing pressure to quicken the pace of conceptual/product standardization.

Seeking to improve their chances of survival in an increasingly hostile market, many companies hope that their products can be standardized (read "approved by the standardization bodies so that the market will accept them") after they have exited the development cycle. The problem here, of course, is, that, within the constraints of the conceptual/product framework, the product should be offered to the market as a potential solution to a future problem, rather than as an immediate solution for a current problem. When a provider is asked to change a product or service to allow the needs of the market to be met more completely, there is the potential for conflict between the provider and standards body (composed of provider and user peers) that is asking for the change.

The conceptual/product standard provides users with a reasonably good indication of where and how the industry as a whole is moving. To ignore such a standard, no matter how valid the reason, is perilous. However, users must also realize that the standards process describes future products, which are in the state of becoming, not in the state of being. If a user has built an entire existing practice on a preliminary proposal, only to have to scrap it when a provider changes the design to conform to a request from a standards committee, the resulting feeling of betrayal can be immense and ultimately destructive.

All of this is equally applicable to the conceptual/process standard, which possesses its own unique complexities. A process standard is written to describe a set of expected events that will lead to a satisfactory set of outputs based on a specified set of inputs. A conceptual standard, however, is inherently mutable. Putting these two together yields a standard that describes an expected outcome for a future need. The risk with this type of standard is that, although the standard may meet all of the requirements for which it was originally intended, while it was being created an alternative process, which completely obsoletes the standard, may have been developed. The term "obsoletes" is used guard-edly; if the input and output are provided in an adequate fashion to solve the perceived problem, the obsolescence will come because the competing process had decided advan-tages that the market believed were worthwhile.

The conceptual/process standard is also extremely susceptible to semantic error. The process, by definition, must be somewhat vague, to allow technology and the market to change without making obsolete the standard and its future orientation.

Four general types of standards, each with a specific functionality and rationale, have been postulated and examined. With the addition of importance (or user/provider context), the clarity disappears. Imagine a typical international standards meeting working on a conceptual/process standard for the information technology industry. Assume a small meeting of approximately thirty representatives: say twelve from providers, eight from government, five from impacted users or quasi-governmental bodies, several consultants, and a couple of academics. Then consider the national, regional, and international aspects of the meeting, the needs of the providers to ensure that their processes are not compro-mised, the governmental issues such as security and national prestige and protection of in-dustry, and the academic section's insistence on a good and technologically sound solu-tion. Finally, factor in the personal characteristics of the delegates, most of whom are highly competent engineers who have been working on this type of technological problem for years and for whom this arena is a chance to air their theories to their peers. Each indi-vidual reflects and represents herself/himself, affiliated group (user/provider/govern-ment), specific discipline (hardware, software, electrical engineering, computer science, marketing, legal), national and regional positions, and the specific company or user group which funded them for the meeting. It is easy to see why tidy definitions collapse in the face of so many different interests. As an aid to understanding the influence of these inter-ests, several assumptions can be made about the participants in the process.

The most basic assumption is that everyone has a reason for participating. This does not necessarily mean that the reasons are positive. It is possible to participate in a stan-dards meeting as a spoiler, attempting to slow or neutralize a standard to allow a compet-ing technology or process to prevail.[11]

This brings up the idea of the defensive and offensive nature of standards. A partici-pant may join in a particular standards effort, even though it may rankle professional be-liefs, just to ensure that a potentially worse option is not adopted. Or, there is the motiva-tion that most standard bodies would prefer people to retain; that of getting the market to agree by means of a standard.

A second assumption is that, although the depth of belief and conviction will vary from individual to individual and from time to time, everyone who attends a meeting has an opinion about the subject under discussion and that not everyone is willing to openly express that opinion. The concept of the hidden agenda item is valid at many meetings. Various levels of strategy are being exercised, during the conference, in the meetings, din-ners, and chance encounters. This is one of the major reasons why standards meetings are so important to the consensus process: They inject the element of human interaction, in which deals are made, trades struck, and the participants come to understand the motiva-tions and obligations that impel their peers to act as they do. Such understanding will not guarantee sympathy or support for the position taken, but the exposure will provide a measure of increased knowledge.

The final assumption is that both users and providers in the industry are increasingly aware that standards are a serious business concern that can cripple or aid efforts to minimize exposure to the vagaries of the market. As this realization has grown, the composition of the standards groups has begun to change. Instead of coming from a regulatory or internal standards background, more and more representatives have a background in technical management. Perfect standards are no longer the goal; instead, the focus is on obtaining a workable and acceptable standard within a time frame that will allow it to be useful.

A DEFINITION OF STANDARDS

Most definitions of standards describe the attributes of the specific standard or standards under immediate consideration, and I certainly have provided several such lists in my rather lengthy description of the individual types of standards. However, no list, no matter how exhaustive, can truly constitute a definition. Attributes should flow from a definition, not the reverse. Thus, I propose to offer a new definition that will serve this purpose for standards. I begin with a behavioral definition of the attitudes and behaviors of the participants in the standardization process:

> Standardization is the product of a personally held belief that the market has the ability to understand and chart a valid future direction through the use of collective wisdom, to understand the impact of change on itself, and to adjust itself to that change. The specific change agents utilized in this process are collective technical descriptions of how things ought to be and function, called standards.

From the understanding of the motivation of the participant (provider or user), further attributes and definitions can be developed:

> A standard, of any form or type, represents a statement by its authors who believe that their work will be understood, accepted, and implemented by the market. This belief is tempered by the understanding that the market will act in its own best interests, even if these do not coincide with the standard. A standard is also one of the agents used by the industry process to bring about market change.

An organization will accept and use standards only if it believes that it cannot control the market directly and that standards can help it control the market. Recognition of tthe fact that the market is externally controlled determines when a firm is willing to participate in standards. This epiphany is not triggered by reaching any specified size, organizational typology, revenue, or other readily identifiable marker. The catalyst for using standards is external, residing in the mutable cultural setting in which the organization must operate.

Individuals (whether separately or collectively) accept and use standards only if they believe that standards offer a benefit. This benefit usually is not distinct or quantifiable; rather, it is a trade-off of less desirable for more desirable factors. Many of these factors are defined subjectively and unconsciously, which makes their quantification extremely difficult, if not impossible. The factor that acts as the trigger for the individual may be less difficult to isolate than the corporate trigger, but this could be proven only on a case by case examination. It is far more difficult to generalize about individual triggers, however, since they can sometimes appear to be completely illogical.

The definition relies heavily on the concept of "the market" for its legitimacy. This dependence is justifiable if the term "market" is used to mean a collection of individuals outside of the control of the particular participant. Additional definitions come into play as well. "The market" is used in the most global sense here. It is not circumscribed by location (the Wall Street market), nor by company ("our market"), nor by an individual (marketing/sales people). Rather, it denotes the large group of entities that uses some aspect of the IT industry when it needs to solve a problem. This market exists because unfilled and unanticipated needs arise, to which it responds. Its function is to provide a common ground where needs can be met and direction set.

Standardization can come into play only when there are coordination problems between two or more entities. Ensuring coordination is relevant only when the parties recognize a problem with the coordination of their activities and are willing to attempt to solve it. Without the willingness to acknowledge a potential problem in coordination, to understand the implications of the problem, and to work toward a noncontentious solution, a consensus standard process cannot work nor can a consensus standard develop.

The consensus standardization process can be considered reasonably democratic. If inequality among participants, at least in the proceedings, is encouraged, then the process must fail, since the process is based on the idea that all concerned parties will contribute and will, from these contributions, receive rewards. Contributors need not have equal expertise or resources; merely an equal right to access the process as they wish. It is true in many consensus standardization committees within the information technology industry that the position and power of the participants derives, not from their corporate or user affiliation, but rather from the perceived competence with relation to the task at hand. The locus of power will shift as the meeting progresses, depending upon what aspect of the standard is being discussed. In nearly every case all the participants are heard when they wish to voice concerns on a particular topic.

The definition is very focused on the participants in the process. The reason for this should be relatively clear: The dynamics and the attitudes that drive the standards process are heavily dependent upon the rationale for the player's participation. But it also emphasizes the importance of the user interface in a concept derived from William of Occam's Law of Parsimony: The most plausible standard will have the fewest newly invented interfaces for the user. In other words, the interface which is the most familiar to the user, in terms of user expectations and preconceptions, will probably be the most well-accepted and hence, the most successful in the market. This is equally true of existing practice (evolutionary) standards as well as conceptual (revolutionary) standards.

Testing the definition of standards against the aspects of standards used in the typology here (as well as elsewhere) creates no major problems; it even allows context to be a major factor. However, the definition is not predictive. It cannot describe when a standard is needed except by hindsight. If a standard appears and is successful then its quality and the market need for it was obvious. This failing cannot be cited as a serious flaw, however, since it is not unique to the standards environment, since it exists in all facets of business. There is no sure way to spot a winner.

NOTES

[1]Gabel, H. Landis. "Open Standards in the European Computer Industry: the Case of X/OPEN," in Gabel, H. Landis ed, *Product Standardization and Competitive Strategy,* North Holland, Amsterdam, 1987, pp. 91–116.

[2]OTA, op. cit, p. 5.

[3]ISO Guide 2 contains the official definition, which is similar to this one, but which, I believe, is worded so that there is more ambiguity.

[4]The exception to this might be the activities of the single focus consortium, which sees its activities as the key to the future of computing or as key to the success of some facet of the industry. The SDOs do not seem to be as "egocentric" as some of the consortium in this regard. Whole larger consortium (ones that are focused on multiple technologies) also seem to have a more balanced approach. The reason for this approach probably lies in the fact that when you're establishing a consortium, you have to believe completely in what you're doing, to the exclusion of other technologies that may be as important to the market. Being a fanatic helps when you're trying to create an organization that people usually don't want in the first place.

[5]Author conversations with Dorothy Cerni, 1986–1990. Dorothy and I were both employed by DEC, and we both left about the same time. However, during the four years that we worked together, we did create a tremendous amount of the current theory that still pervades the IT standardization arena.

[6]This statement is difficult to explain fully in the context in which it currently exists. What is meant is not that standards anticipate the market, but rather that a standard does change the nature of the market for which it is proposed for implementation. The nature of standardization is such that the existence of a standard changes the dynamics of the market. Participants in the market don't have to take part in the process or even use the standard or specification; its very existence has changed the way that the market operates.

[7]In the previous edition of this work, this form of standardization was referred to as an "implementation" standard. Unfortunately, the term "implementation standard" has come to refer to a de facto standard based upon an implementation of a single vendor's proprietary technology. An "implementation standard" is now contrasted with an "interface standard." To prevent confusion between industry accepted terminology and that used in this book, I have opted to change the text in the book.

[8]The standards referred to here are those which are actually trying to change the industry, and which are often created in advance of a deployed product. The term "anticipatory standardization" has been used to describe them (Cargill, Carl F. "Anticipatory Standards; The Next Wave," IEEE LCN Conference Proceedings, Minneapolis, MN, 1988). The real challenge with these standards is that they often are initiated with good intentions, but quickly end up in a fight to see which interest can dominate the standards setting body and force its will. When this happens, the committees that make up formal standardization process (the SDOs) have little recourse but to fight it out. In consortia, there tends to be somewhat less acrimony due to the fundamental narrower focus of the consortia, unless the consortium is a "general purpose" consortium, at which time the situation is similar to the SDOs.

[9]There was nothing in the original DEC-Intel-Xerox (DIX) consortium that posited the PC revolution that has occurred. DIX was merely trying to connect minicomputers and give customers an alternative to mainframe computing. What LANs evolved to over the years was unplanned. The original intent of the committee was to change the current environment, not merely modify the existing environment.

[10]The LDDI was based upon DEC's successful Computer Interconnect (CI). The committee worked for three years on defining the LLDI, only to have to withdraw the proposal after DEC would not agree to make the patented technology freely and openly available for a reasonable fee. Grant Saviers, who headed DEC's storage products division, opposed the standardization effort because he felt that the CI as a standard would open his lucrative (and captive) VAX mass storage market to the world.

[11]See Michael Spring et al. ("Improving the Standardization Process: Working with Bulldogs and Turtles," in *Standards Policy for Information Infrastructure,* Kahin and Abbate, editors, MIT Press: Cambridge, MA, 1995) for a good analysis of why people participate in standardization activities.

Chapter 6

Revolution and Evolution in Open Systems

"Yes! to this thought I hold with firm persistence
The last result of wisdom stamps it true
He only earns his freedom and existence,
Who daily conquers them anew."

—Johann Goethe, *Faust*

INTRODUCTION

If the premise of the preceding chapter is accepted and standards are accepted as change agents for the IT industry, then the perception of standards, and the model that the industry has for standards, must change. The current standardization model, especially that used by the participants in the SDOs, is fundamentally broken. The current model is based upon a myth; one that has been modified several times. This chapter examines that myth in light of the current situation and proposes a method of realigning myth with reality.

THE MYTH BEGINS

One of the enduring myths of the medieval era is that of Roland, the bravest (and possibly most arrogant) Paladin of Charlemagne. He was betrayed and killed, along with the elite rear guard of the French army, by an entire Muslim army, at the pass of Roncesvalle in northern Spain. The myth, which is part of French national folklore, is captured in the "Chanson de Roland," written in the eleventh century. The story is based upon an actual historical incident, in which a Count of the Brittany Marches named Hruotland died in Spain in the late 700s; he was probably killed by Basques who rolled rocks on to him and his rag-tag band of followers.

The purpose for the heroic poem was not to record history. When the poem was written, there was a nascent movement to make the French nation aware of its unique identity. The idea of Roland became a powerful agent in coalescing this movement for the French king. It was necessary to create such a story to ensure that there was a belief around which the French nation could rally. Roland served as an ideal for the concepts of loyalty to a king, as well as the dues and obligations of both the warriors and the king. His image somewhat codified the expectations of the nation. The person who was Roland became a convenient icon that symbolized all that was heroic and good about being French, as opposed to "foreign." The icon changed over time, but was always held up as an ideal.

In a similar manner, the concept of "Open Systems" has become a convenient icon to express all that is good about computing and the promise that computing can hold. It, too, has undergone significant shifts in its meaning, but it has always been held up as the ideal to which computing should subscribe. I would like to examine some of these shifts and show how a new iconic meaning is emerging which may play an immense role in changing the nature and direction of the disciplines that comprise open systems.

My intent is not to cause yet another revolution (or a revolting development) to occur in a field that is already crowded with "significant ideas." Rather, my discussion should be seen as a speculation on one possible (and in my opinion, highly likely) course of action and a different way of looking at the problem. The result of this discussion, I hope, will be a stronger standardization process that serves the users as well as the vendors. The reader's patience in wading through this chapter is sought, for, as Marc Bloch observed:

> No one today, I believe, would dare to say, with the orthodox positivists, that the value of a line of research is to be measured by its ability to promote action. Experience has surely taught us that it is impossible to decide in advance whether even the most abstract speculations may not prove extraordinarily helpful in practice.[1]

IN THE BEGINNING

The initial impetus for the movement I call "computer open systems" began with the "plug compatible" movement. This was an attempt to circumvent what were perceived as the onerous pricing policies of IBM in the mainframe market. The effort was intended to reduce the cost of computer equipment to the user. Because IBM was the single source vendor, and because the equipment was costly, the perception grew that IBM was gouging the users, and that a second source would break what was seen as a monopoly position by IBM.

This movement eventually wound its way through the market and the courts. Before it concluded it established several of the fundamental concepts that were to drive this particular open systems movement. To begin, the plug compatible movement set in place the most enduring mental image of the emerging open systems movement—that of the "stereo concept" of computing. Proponents argued that a component stereo audio system was a model for how Data Processing (DP) systems should be designed. The various components of a stereo system were designed to interoperate and interoperation was guaranteed by standardized interfaces. The plugs of these systems were common, and because of this, the user could create a customized system to do exactly what she or he wanted.

The "stereo model" set in place the basic set of beliefs about open systems:

- The market will become larger.
- Competition will drive down the price of the system components.
- More suppliers will enter the market and increase competition.
- The market will be more responsive to user needs.
- The users know what they want and will buy it.
- Standards enable interoperability of components.

These perceptions were (and still are) very important because they were iconic perceptions that were based on a set of beliefs about the nature of the market and the nature of the data (and later information) processing function. When the stereo model was initiated, the iconographers proposed an icon showing the concept of "plug interconnect." The problem arose when the icon was assumed to represent reality, and the underlying intent was forgotten.

This led to several myths that continue to haunt the movement today. The stereo myth states that all systems should interconnect and that this can be done easily. In the early 1970s, the components of a stereo system were the receiver and amplifier, the speakers, the record player, and the tape deck. The sole intent of a stereo was to play music: monophonic, stereophonic, or quadraphonic. It was not intended to cook, clean floors, or do windows. Similarly, the stereo model is applicable to IT only as long as the computer is a "single use" system dedicated to a singular defined function (payroll, accounting, order processing). The "stereo model" breaks down quickly when disparate applications are applied to the basic function (distribution, communications, databases), which is what happened to computers. The model is viable as far as it goes but it remains only a simple icon of plug connectability, not functional ability.

The movement's keystone, upon which all else depended, was standards. In the early 1960s the major standardization bodies for IT began with the creation of the International Organization for Standardization Technical Committee 97 (replaced by ISO/IEC JTC 1 in the late 1980s), the European Computer Manufacturer's Association (ECMA), and Accredited Standards Committee X3 in the United States. While all have undergone change over the past thirty or so years, there are few in the IT industry who are not touched by their products; from the standardized QWERTY keyboard to databases to objects. Within the United States, other groups have joined the IT standardization arena, such as the IEEE Computer Society, EIA/TIA, and NISO. In Europe and Asia, national standards bodies have created their own equivalent of X3. However, all the groups have one common thread which is the belief that the standards they are producing will lead to better IT products for the users because standards exist.

At the same time that this was happening, the nature of computing began to change. The environment impacted by computers began to grow, and more and more direct users were created. Computer Science became an accepted degree in higher education and within the IT industry. The increasing power and decreasing price of computing began to make application of IT to more mundane tasks more common. However, it is worth noting that in the non-IT literature of the day, the "computer" was increasingly seen as a hostile thing. The book *The Forbin Project* best illustrates the fears that were common during this time. The phrase, "The computer made a mistake . . ." became a standard routine for comedians, as well as a common excuse for anyone who made a clerical error. However, the users of computing began to grow, because increasingly complex organizations could not do without it.

THE FORMATIVE STAGE

With the stereo system model safely in place as the icon of choice, and with the infrastructure for standardization created, the open systems movement had the icongraphic base necessary to grow. However, there could be no real demand for open systems until the computer became more ubiquitous and touched more people. Until the late 1970s the DP department was usually housed in a separate area of the building (usually the basement) and programmers were usually given relief from normal corporate conventions, such as dress codes and a nine to five routine. The phenomena that propelled the open systems movement to the forefront began with the growing use of minicomputers, marked by the spectacular rise of Digital Equipment Corporation and Data General. The very name of "minicomputer" indicates the growing confidence level by the users. A "minicomputer" sounds much less threatening than a "mainframe computer." With the expansion of the computing needs into other arenas, the second phase of "open systems" was about to be launched.

This was the "open intercommunication" phase. Users who had received their processed information from a single source suddenly began to find out that computers did not all talk the same language. For that matter, computers not only did not talk the same language, they were largely incapable of talking to one another at all. Each vendor optimized a unique solution based upon proprietary technology. The logic for this was not hard to understand; every company in the industry competed on the basis of technology, with the watchwords being unique, faster, and more powerful. The users, who were caught up in this battle, accepted these areas of competition until it began to impact their ability to obtain computing solutions.

The frustration level increased, and in the late 1970s, the Open Systems Interconnect (OSI) model was begun. OSI focused on standardizing the communication paths between computers. Vendors had standardized on hardware interconnectability for the most part (witness the RS-232 connector and disk interface standardization movements), and the intercommunication of information became the next major arena for activity. Just as the initial open systems movement selected the stereo for their icon, the proponents of the "open systems interconnect" model selected as their icon the Plain Old Telephone Service (POTS) model.

While the icon was viable the attempt to implement the concepts represented by the icon was flawed. The analogy to the telephone was easy, convenient, simple, and ultimately, wrong. The statement was based upon the idea that if you called anywhere in the world, all it took was a series of numbers to allow you to have unique access to a specific individual. The equipment interoperated by design; the telephone system providers saw to that. These attributes were added to those of the past, and a new litany of attributes was created:

- The market will become larger for everyone.
- More suppliers will enter the market increasing competition.
- Competition will drive down the price of the system components.
- The market will be more responsive to user needs.
- The users know what they want and will buy it.
- Standards-based interoperability of components is assumed.
- Interoperability of systems is required.
- Interoperable systems are based upon standards.

The flaw in this reasoning was that the phrase, "interoperable systems are based upon standards" was predicated upon the activities of the International Telecommunication Union (the ITU), a U.N. sanctioned regulatory body. The telecommunications bodies around the world are regulated bodies. Having a unique national telephone system is embarrassing. The systems must work together. This distinction, appearing trivial, was overlooked by the open systems interconnection contributors of the POTS addition to the open systems icon. The difference may appear slight; after all, a standard is a standard. However, the telecommunication arena is a regulatory arena, and the participants in the arena can be forced to adhere to standards. The users of the phone system did not know or care what standards were in place.[2] They were not asked to differentiate and choose among technical alternatives; instead, the regulators were given these choices and acted upon them for the good of the public, which is a governmental duty.

The difference became very clear with the advent of the Open Systems Interconnect (OSI) movement. Again, the icon was accepted as reality. The reality was, however, that the IT industry, because of the underlying competitive nature of its culture, was poorly equipped to create the necessary cooperative structure underlying a "telephone system" look alike, which was the fundamental iconic representation of the OSI model. The IT industry needed a model similar to the Internet, which let anyone who met a series of simple interoperative protocols invent and add features to their heart's content—if they could prove the robustness and utility of their additions.

Because there was a need to construct the entire fabric of the OSI model without any reference implementation, JTC 1 began to create standards to satisfy the needs of the market. The OSI model required the use of "anticipatory standards." Anticipatory standards are those which standardize a technology in advance of that specific technology being available as a product in any viable commercial form.[3] As an example, the layered communication models that drove the theory of OSI are the IBM SNA and DEC DECnet protocols. While the theory of the layered model was available to the OSI standardization groups, the interface specifications needed to be written in a fashion free of any specific reference implementation (which would have been either SNA or DECnet). However, because of the lack of an underlying acceptable implementation (or even clear market definition), the standardization effort expanded to cover nearly every possible contingency. This lead to the growth of the model and the concomitant number and options of standards to support the growth. Ultimately, this caused total confusion on the part of the using public. Because of the number of options available in the standards, an OSI system provider could both comply to the OSI standards and be totally noninteroperable with another compliant system.

To solve this problem, the industry began to "invent" consortia that could test and validate the multiple profiles that were being created from the multiplicity of standards. The consortia (basically a new form of standardization organization) were nearly always the invention of vendors, who had a simple reason for founding them—they could, it was hoped, encourage use of vendor products by providing some assurance of interoperability. The major vendor contributors to the OSI model created the Corporation for Open Systems (COS), a consortium whose function it was to create test suites and profiles that would both ensure and insure interoperability. Unfortunately, COS failed in its primary mission, but did succeed in beginning a new phenomenon—the rush to create consortia to help the standardization process meet user needs.[4]

So, the addition of the "telephone interoperability" concepts to the open systems model provided the second set of assumptions that were ultimately to lead to where we are today. These assumptions included the idea that users should pick and choose the standards to which they would require their vendors to comply—and that test mechanisms would somehow exist to validate the user choices.

It is important to note a subtle shift in the open systems movement here. With the addition of the open systems interconnect model, the focus changed from replacement of hardware to interoperability of information—that is, the ability to transfer information between systems. This shift was incorporated in the next phase of the open systems evolution—again, with some subtle changes.

THE EVOLUTION CONTINUES

The next step in the ambitious program to deal with open systems derived from a commercially available product called UNIX (TM), the trademark of which is now in the keeping of an open systems consortium, X/Open. With the success and pervasiveness of UNIX (owned by AT&T at the time), a group of users coalesced to bring standards to the world that UNIX occupied.

The allure which UNIX possessed was that of a widely deployed operating system that would allow programs (applications) that were written for one family of computers (e.g., VAX running UNIX) to be successfully run on another system (e.g., 4300 running UNIX) with a minimum of rework. This desired feature was not achieved by UNIX, since there were several major, and several dozen minor, variants that precluded true portability. However, the myth was enough to start a movement in standardization to create a set of standardized calls to an operating system. This activity was picked up by the IEEE Computer Society (Technical Committee for Operating Systems [TCOS]). For the last ten years, this committee has been busily writing a series of standards called POSIX that specifies OS calls for portable systems.

POSIX was initially started as an attempt to channel the success of UNIX in several ways. UNIX had proven that there was a large and willing market of users (principally academic and non-business technical) who were pleased with the capabilities contained in UNIX. However, since UNIX was proprietary to AT&T, it was felt by some within the community that it would be better if some neutral organization (one that was not concerned with making money on UNIX) helped to define UNIX's future. POSIX was one solution to this problem, since it was to be a standard to which even UNIX would have to adhere. The other option pursued by the market was the creation of competing consortia (Open Software Foundation and UNIX International) which would supply, respectively, a competing operating system (OSF1) or a set of requirements that AT&T would follow in UNIX development.

The POSIX effort added two more major conditions to the computer open systems movement: application portability (the operating system and attendant programs performed the same on all processors) and a new one of salability (that the operating system was the same whether it was on a large or small system). Not content with having the principles implicit, POSIX created a committee (IEEE POSIX 1003.0) which produced a *Guide to the POSIX Open Systems Environment*. The definition of an open system offered by this committee (now engaging in incorporating comments into its seventeenth draft of the document) is

> . . . a system that implements sufficient open specifications for interfaces, services, and supporting formats to enable properly engineered applications software to be ported across a wide range of systems with minimal changes, to interoperate with other applications on local and remote systems, and to interact with users in a style which facilitates user portability.

It was felt that these attributes were necessary because they impacted the ability of users to access common applications across a wide series of platforms. Because the architects of the POSIX and "open UNIX" models were highly technical, there was also an unanticipated spin put on the OSI era legacy. The key focus of this group changed from information transportability to actual program transportability. The logic was that if the application program could run on a multitude of processors, then the information contained in that program would also be available on the same multitude of processors.

This was the essential feature of this phase of the open systems movement; it provided platform independence as well as application transportability. In effect, the POSIX/UNIX movement provided the final statement to the open systems movement as we currently know it. The open systems movement originally proposed movement away from a single vendor monopoly. This has been achieved by providing a theoretical system in which all vendors, from hardware to software to service, are set equal and available on a feature by feature comparison. Other technologies currently under development, such as object-oriented programming, are extensions of this basic icon that has been one of the most persistent through the history of the IT industry. A small handbook published by DEC in 1991[5] is the best description of the computer-biased concept that is available. The pamphlet describes the technical attributes of computer-based open systems, and then describes how to construct one from available technologies. It is entirely focused, as one would expect from a supplier, on ways to achieve independence from the vendors while embracing the products and theories of the vendors.

In an effort not to repeat the mistakes that had damaged the implementation of OSI, however, the vendors immediately established attendant vendor consortia such as X/Open to test the implementations of POSIX and other UNIX-like commands created by standardization committees. These consortia were to ensure the interoperability of standards-based applications. The X/Open Portability Guide (XPG) became a touchstone for the market, because of the way X/Open established branding rules. The intent of the entire scheme was to validate the basic beliefs about open systems that had their roots in the original plug compatibility concept.

When POSIX completes its task, the movement will have succeeded in setting users free to buy any mainframe or minicomputer or workstation (and even some PCs) so that they can run the same application programs easily and well. This will finally enable the icon of the 1980s to be achieved. And this is the tragedy of the computer open systems movement. When it finishes its work in the late 1990s it will have finally succeeded in answering a question first asked incorrectly in the mid-1970s and refined by the expectations of the 1980s.

The shift here is also icongraphic, but extremely difficult to characterize. Basically, the new icon is that application programs, not the information contained in them, are the deciding and driving factors in this stage of the open systems movement. The icon has become hopelessly confused. Just as the crowds in Constantinople began to worship the icon, and not the thought behind the icon, so have the computer open systems advocates focused on the representation (the application) rather than on the information itself (in philosophical terms, the "thing itself").

STANDARDIZATION IN SUPPORT OF OPEN SYSTEMS

Standardization figures prominently in all the open systems literature; without it, open systems do not exist. However, since the movement started in the early 1960s some significant changes have taken place. These need to be examined.

When the movement began, one of the key elements was that the users of the standard were also the contributors to the creation of the standard. Most current activities of formal standards developing organizations (SDOs) and consortia support this view. The industry tends to create standards so that they can be implemented in products. The standard is written to a provider model for use by the providers to allow them to "do business" in a fashion that is more salable. The problem is that the alpha and omega of IT standards are the providers, and the formal SDOs produce a product that exists only to feed, and be fed, by the providers.

By the mid 1980s, the users had been largely dispossessed in the standardization process. The problem that became significant for the industry was the lack of demand for the standards that were being produced by the formal organizations. The vendors were spending large amounts of money creating and implementing standards because it was held, as an article of faith, that users wanted them. There was no empirical data to support this proposition. The academic studies that had been done were largely in support of the theory of economics of standardization.[6]

To solve the problem of demand creation, providers began to look for ways to capitalize on their production of standards. The standards were converted to marketing tools used by the providers to prove that a product was open. (Advertisements featuring "standardization claims" began to appear in the mid 1980s, initially associated with "SCSI" compatibility.) This translated to, "just like everyone else's but better" because selling a standard product without market differentiation became difficult. As a result, there was a movement to "popularize" standards, usually in association with the open systems concept, and prove that users wanted standards. In 1986, the European Institute of Business Administration (INSEAD) held a conference entitled "Product Standardization as a Tool of Competitive Strategy." The conference proceedings are reasonably esoteric,[7] and not really applicable to business except in that the title seemed to unleash a desire by marketing managers to "use standards to prove openness."

Vendors took the most obvious route to this goal. They began to change their promotional activities to reflect how open they were and how closed their competitors were. The irony of this did not escape the users, who really wondered how one firm could be open if all of its competitors were closed. "Open" had become the operative phrase in the open systems movement. The reason the two words were paired is obvious; being the only "open" vendor is just as bad as being a completely proprietary vendor. In either case, the user has no recourse but to become locked in if there is no systemic openness. After a while, even the vendors caught on to the foolishness of these assertions and began to look for a remedy.

Within the circumstances thus far described, one of the fundamental reasons for the incredible growth of consortia is that they were vendor marketing tools, devoted to providing support for specific vendor "openness" claims. Consortia (in reality, companies acting together) began to appear. The most well known were the Open Software Foundation (OSF), UNIX International (UI), X/Open Company, Ltd., and the Object Management Group (OMG). All of these consortia were focused on providing an industry-wide standardized solution to the problem of open systems, and all were heavily funded by the providers. All the consortia initiated major campaigns to prove that they and, implicitly, their members were open because they built products which conformed to consortia generated specifications, which the users needed. (Because the need was obvious, it never required proof.)

At the same time, the SDOs (the organizations charged with creating standards under the concepts of consensus and fairness) were initiating the drive to anticipatory standardization, creating larger and larger standardization models, and never defining technologies that could be rapidly and completely implemented. Defining a technology in a committee became, rather than a technical activity, a political activity, which focused on gaining consensus at the expense of a clearly defined solution. The response to a difficult decision on a technical argument became one of "including" all solutions. This produced a fuzzy mandate and fuzzy standard at best, and left the implementors in a good deal of difficulty. To use a somewhat banal example, implementors suddenly found that the bits in a standard had a "yes, no, and maybe" setting. With the creation of the "maybe" bit, formal standards took a dive into uncharted seas. Far from discouraging innovation, formal standards now not only encouraged but legitimized multiple solutions to the same problem.

In order to compensate for the "maybe" bit confusion that was being generated by the SDOs, the consortia took up the role of creating demand and market definition. Unfortunately, to do this, the consortia had to constantly invent newer and better standardized solutions in order to justify their existence and to legitimize the open systems that they were creating. New consortia began to be created to deal with nearly every aspect of marketing, all focused on creating a clear "open system." The users, even disregarding the obvious hyperbole of these groups, suddenly found they had to decide among multiple, usually incompatible, technologies, all of which promised a brighter future and open systems.

To compound the problem, there was an explosion of standardization organizations. (Within the United States, there are over 550 formally accredited SDOs.) While only a handful of these organizations directly dealt with IT standardization (ASC X3, the IEEE, EIA/TIA, NIS0, and ASC T1), other organizations began to preempt some of the territory previously considered the domain of IT standards. The most egregious examples of this were the activities of ISO TC 176 (Quality Assurance), which published a guide to software quality as part of the highly successful ISO 9000 series on quality. (The guide was originally written by a Canadian software consultant; it was extensively modified before international acceptance.) The 9000 series was received well by users; it is the largest selling standard in the history of ISO. It appealed to a basic user need by defining a process for verifying the existence of a provider's quality system. The appearance of a guide to software quality and the entire 9000 series caught most IT providers by surprise, because they were focused on the pure technical IT standards and did not believe that there were other standards, or user expectations, that might impact or, horror of horrors, regulate their activities.

Understanding and appreciating this "computer-centric" focus is essential to understanding the "computer open systems" movement and the standardization that accompanies it. The discipline of standardization is complex and not clearly understood. There are few theoretical writings on the subject that have received widespread acceptance among the provider community. Because the providers were trying to create a discipline where none existed before, it was natural that they would continue an evolutionary course. Small modifications such as the changes between the various iterations of the open systems movement were about as daring as the IT community could accept. They could not make the leap to a different paradigm and this was required to make true open systems happen.

There was, for a while, some movement by national body IT SDOs (basically the IEEE, X3, and T1) to try to put into place some planning activities that would add structure to the process. The IT movement, led by Joseph DeBlasi (then of IBM) and Gary Robinson (then of DEC), initiated the idea that planning should be a formal committee of both X3 and the U.S. JTCl TAG. The movement thrashed about for some time, trying to determine exactly what it was planning. Ultimately, the X3 process produced a document that described standardization as more than the activities of the SDOs.[8] This was the major output of the U.S. national SDO activity. Because the committees could never divorce themselves from the problem of technology to be standardized and focus on the utility of standardization, they eventually died from lack of interest and participation on the part of the members of the SDOs.

The concept of small modifications might have been acceptable to the industry users and providers had they not lost sight of the fact that the IT industry had become ubiquitous. The very nature of the ubiquity demanded that vendors cooperate, not compete, in defining systems that were open. The standardization process tried to feed both of these dual streams. They created more and more massively open systems for the vendors to disagree upon, while telling the users that standards would be okay and that each vendor was uniquely open.

Very simply, while standardization fed the two divergent streams of the open systems movement, it satisfied neither. The vendors never agreed on common implementations, or even agreed upon what it was that they were doing. The users, after being patient for a decade, finally decided that standardization of technology, as it was being implemented, was a failure, and began to look for other, more productive, options. And this was the pathos of the standardization efforts for "computer open systems."

THE REVOLUTION BEGINS

While the evolution of open systems was progressing through the various stages of standardization, there was another movement that began in the user community. I regard this movement as revolutionary because it modified the face of the IT industry substantially, forcing (and continuing to force) a break with the past rules and governance, including that offered by standards and standardization. This movement came from an entirely different direction than did the evolutionary movement; its focus was on using computing resources. This shift from computer focus to computing focus is key to understanding the revolutionary branch of the open systems movement.

The icon of the organizational movement is the triangle signifying "hierarchy." Once you position a person, idea, or thing inside its comforting boundary, you understand the relation of that thing to all other entities in the hierarchy. Point to the top of a triangle and announce "company" and people respond "CEO." Announce "military" and people announce "general." Announce "standardization" and the response should be "ISO." As with any icon, the characterization derives from established belief. In this case, the established belief is Weberian bureaucracy, which was the result of a need to manage a complex organizational structure, having a primary attribute of stability of purpose and function. It permitted each level or individual to pass information upward to be coalesced into higher and higher abstractions, with the most senior positions in the hierarchy having the most authority and responsibility. The higher levels, in turn, acting on the increased knowledge, would send directional activity down the hierarchy. Positional authority was key to the bureaucracy.

The icon began to break in the 1960s. One of the first signs of this was the identification by Peter Drucker of the "knowledge worker." This is the individual who specialized in knowing things, as differentiated from the "blue or white collar" worker. This was the human side of the equation; the mechanization to help the knowledge worker came with the advent of the workstation and PC, agents of "information democratization." In the beginning, these mechanical aids were seen as expensive desktop helpers, much as the early calculators had been. They weren't that easy to use, but they were a badge of "specialness."

The appearance of the networked computing resource, however, changed the underlying model. The full impact which is the mark of the knowledge worker came only when the worker could get access to all information that impacted his or her position without previous filtering by upper layers of management. With access to both the information and to the managerial infrastructure, the ingredients for the change were assembled.

The key to the revolution was not "open systems" in the sense of the computer environment. Instead, there is a "general systems theory" that combines organizational structure and information usage so that the organization begins to collapse the managerial hierarchy. The highly structured Weberian bureaucracy is giving way to a situational management that is task and goal oriented, rather than structure oriented. The organizational dislocation caused by the nontraditional structure of work is politely referred to as "rightsizing"; those who have suffered through it know it as "downsizing." In many cases, the wrenching reduction is meant to make the corporation lean—but a lean hierarchy is the result, with little change in the fundamental organizational constructs. The triangle has been moving from equilateral to acute isosceles to scalene in a search for stability.

The emerging icon, however, is not a triangle, but rather a five pointed star contained in a pentagon, called Star In Pentagon (SIP) (see Figure 6.1) The SIP is basically derived from a concept in organizational psychology that describes common communications; that is, all points can communicate with all other points. This icon symbolizes the second paradigm of the open systems movement. This concept has nothing to do with computers and everything to do with the organization and computing. It is a system that allows a finite amount of information to be analyzed in an infinite number of ways, some of which had not previously been considered. The combination of information with human knowledge produces new knowledge which in turn produces a greater need for and use of information. This cycle, in turn, allows greater and greater freedom of action on the part of the participants, since knowledge is empowering. The open organization tends to grow on its successes, permitting its implementors to continue to advance knowledge and experience (the "massed SIP diagram," also part of Figure 6.1). The increased knowledge also permits the organization to grow and change and to excel in what it does best.

The standardization that the "open organization" movement requires is not standardization of the method (that is, the computers) but rather a standardization of attributes of the information system. The construct has changed from the mechanism (computers) to the goal itself (computing). In an organization that is driven by both situational computing

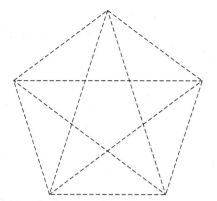

The "Star-In-Pentagon" Model of IT Networking

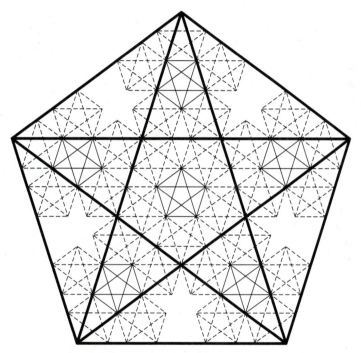

The Massed "Star-In-Pentagon" Model of IT Networking

Figure 6.1   Star-In-Pentagon Models

and by the knowledge worker, the greater knowledge of a situation does not necessarily flow up the organization, and the CEO of a corporation can, theoretically, be subordinated to a junior engineer who is situationally capable of committing large amounts of organizational resources. This is an unexpected result of open organizations; a Jacksonian leveling of the organization.

The most vocal representative of this movement was the User Alliance for Open Systems (UAOS), a loose confederation of users who attempted to create a movement that focused upon the utility, not the technology, of open systems. From this group came the definition of an open system as, "one that allows a worker access to information necessary to do one's job." While the UAOS was a reasonably short lived phenomena, it is the consortium's activity that marked the first, and possibly most significant, user revolt against the continued technological movement orchestrated by the vendors.

The theory to which the UAOS was attempting to move was expressed in the following description by Max Black. I believe that the same is valid for organizational information as well:

> . . . the following facts, which hold for every known language: (1) there is no upper limit on the length or complexity of grammatical sentences; (2) from a finite number of words (or morphemes) infinitely many grammatical sentences can be constructed; (3) a competent speaker of the language knows in advance how to understand indefinitely many sentences that he has never considered or met. To say that language has "synthetic resources" listed above is to claim that it is an 'open system.'[9]

This definition changes the nature of the equation, however. Black's use of the term "open system" indicates a system that has no boundaries. This is the key differentiator of the second wave of the open systems movement. What UAOS failed to realize, and what many of the organizations in the Open Systems arena forget, was that they were no longer dealing only with the IT resource. What the "open organization movement" is moving towards is full integration of the computing resource into the organization. A basic belief is that everyone in the organization should have the ability to access information, without prejudice. The SIP model requires that the organization think of itself as an unbounded entity subject to external information influences. A convenient historical analogy is to the growth of cities in the middle ages. As communications between the cities began to increase, commerce increased, and the set social structure of the medieval period began to collapse. (Granted, the invention of gun powder, the printing press, and improved agricultural conditions also played a part.) However, the key to the growth was the increased amount of communication which forced change to the underlying structure. Similarly, the same type of change is happening for information management in organizations. With the dissolution of the hierarchy, the underlying structure must change. This has become "chaotic" change.

Unfortunately, because there were no "boundary rules" for the construct of chaotic change, the UAOS substituted technology for the organizational redefinition. Eventually, the activity spawned by the UAOS ended up becoming the Senior Executives for Open Systems (the "SOS," composed of MIS executives from American Airlines, DuPont, GM, Kodak, McDonnell Douglas, Merck, Motorola, 3M, Northrop, and Unilever). This group published a letter to major providers (June 26, 1991) in which they explicitly called out technologies that they expected the vendors to implement. Within a year, the SOS effort and, implicitly, the USOS was dead. In some cases, the MIS directors of the companies involved did not have purchasing power; in others, there were no products that met the requirements of the specification. The first attempt of the "open organization" movement ended in failure.

SYNTHESIS

The problem of synthesis between the two streams of the open systems lies in resolving the duality of standardization which is reflected in the conflicts of the open systems movement. The standards creators (usually vendor employees) see standards as an entity in their own right. Users, on the other hand, do not see standards as a product, but rather as a bundle of attributes that they want. While both have a degree of validity, there is an unresolved conflict that the market presently does not have the ability to resolve.

The conflict can be viewed in the following manner:

1. Standards are usually created by vendors in standards committees with little user help.
2. Standards (and open specifications) are meant to describe a bundle of attributes desired by a user.
3. Standardization is the act of specifying common interfaces to which the industry can create implementations. This takes time.
4. Users specify standards in their procurement documents if the specification answers a need that they currently have.
5. Vendors create standardized implementations based on interface specifications.
6. Standardized implementations are then employed to solve a user problem if they meet business criteria.

Looking at the situation from a process point of view, the following becomes clear:

- There are no sustainable connections between the specification and the creation (points 1 and 2). This would tend to indicate the specification process is fundamentally flawed.
- There are no logical connections between 3 and 4; users and vendors have a fundamentally different time scale when dealing with standardization.
- There are no logical connections between 5 and 6. The implementation is usually done without regard to the cost of the solution to the user. The user rarely determines the economic value of a standard in a procurement situation.

These disconnects exist for a reason, and the reason lies in the dual nature of standards. The actual technical creation of standards is a skilled act and reasonably difficult. It reflects the providers trying to determine exactly how to provide a set of capabilities to the market and must be expressed in terms of a particular technological interface that allows implementations to be built.

At the same time (and this is where the providers fail to understand the full nature of standardization), the specification of standards by users falls far short of where it should because users, in many cases fail to include standardization in their plans. This is caused by both a failure of the planning process (that is, not planning with a long enough horizon) or simply not believing that a standardized product or service will be available. This makes the vendors, on the other hand, disbelieve in the process because users want standards but usually buy less expensive nonstandard products.

These trends were apparent during the "open systems" controversy. The open computer advocates of open systems tended to favor the odd numbered positions, while the open organization advocates tended to favor the even numbered items. The odds are technology focused, while the evens are solution focused.

The solution that I propose is somewhat radical within the confines of the standardization system. It is, I believe, legal, within the constructs of the current rules, and would require no changes to the U.S. system of checks and balances. It is not especially elegant and will, no doubt, offend the many purists in the process who are "standards professionals." However, it does require that users learn to cooperate and that vendors give up innovation for innovations' sake. The model is reasonably simple, but does change the way that standards are created.

The first step is to admit that the SDOs do produce a legitimate product. Standards that go through the ANSI process have an aura of moral legitimacy. To achieve the appellation of American National Standard (ANS) and be allowed into government procurements (in accordance with the Office of Management and Budget Circular A119), they must conform to certain creation rules. It is obvious that these cannot be thrown away, or chaos would result.

It is true that SDOs are poor at producing a standard in a hurry. ASC X3 claims to have reduced the cycle time for writing a standard to 18 months. This is laudable, but only part of the solution. Writing a standard is only one part of the five stages that are called out in the X3 life-cycle planning document. The other stages, from initial requirements through development and testing to user implementation and feedback, can and usually do add up to an additional four years to the cycle. There are advantages to this approach but they are tied not to standards, but rather to a general spirit of cooperation within standardization committees. (This last part is not especially true of certain committees, especially the IEEE TCOS, where there was a full time expert on Robert's Rules of Order necessary to maintain a thin veneer of civility.)

The solution to the problem of creation slowness is to provide "open specifications" for use by the SDOs. Fortunately, the idea is not as radical as it sounds; it has been used in Europe for some time by Committee for European Normalization (CEN). The specification providing group could be a technical industry consortium (Object Management Group), a consultant hired for the purpose (the CEN model), or an individual. The intent of the group (Technical Specification Group) would be to produce a specification that was a "prestandard" that represented the needs of some group that wanted a standard. The specification would be technically correct—that is, would represent implementable technology in some form. The specification would be passed to the SDO for approval, making the SDO an approval group. The SDO would not rewrite the specification, but would rather endorse it and remove, if necessary, egregious vendor bias.

Figure 6.2 represents the state of the model as described thus far. However, to be viable, the model needs a simultaneous validation. It needs the proof that product is being created that meets the standard. This work would be carried out by testing organizations such as X/Open in the IT arena, or other test houses as they come on-line and are able to test the complexities of software and hardware. I would imagine that the specification producing groups would be closely linked with such firms (called Test Organizations in Figure 6.2). After all, if the SDO is able to issue the standard in less than twelve months (which is possible, if the specification is presented on a fully written basis) then the test would have to be ready within a twelve month time-frame after the specification was completed.

To make the model succeed, two more vertical segments need to be added. These are illustrated in Figure 6.3. The left-hand column labeled "User Requirements Group" is

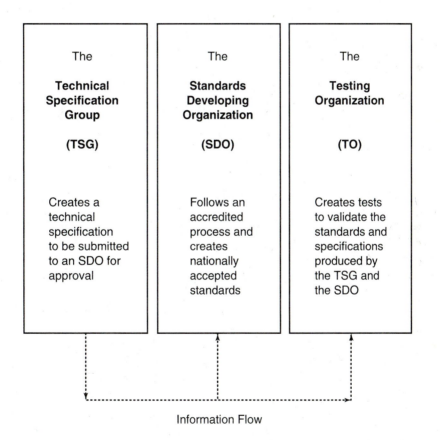

Information Flow

Figure 6.2   The Expanded Technical Model

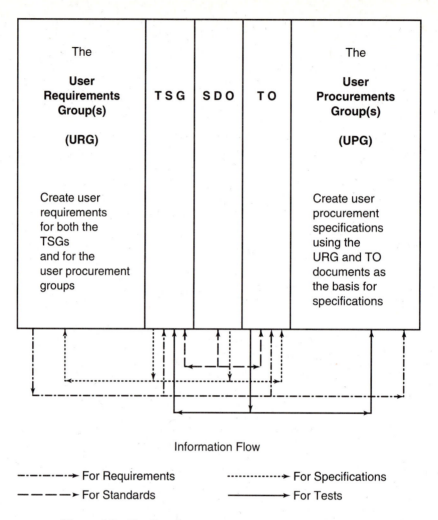

Figure 6.3   The Complete User Focused Development Model

where the users provide business requirements for the "Technical Specification Group." As noted, the problem with standards is that they are usually written by the IT industry in a somewhat confused fashion after hearing what users "sorta say" they want. In this mode, no one really is at fault if the process fails, and everyone can (and usually does) complain. (Note that in the X3 model, the section on User requirements is extremely nebulous. I was involved in creation of the original document, and the sad truth is that the Strategic Planning Group of X3 could not really say why a majority of standards projects started or who wanted them when.) This situation has resulted in vendors pushing their idea of what standards should be while users pull their idea of what standardization is.

The farthest right-hand column, labeled "User Procurement Groups," is where the user procurement of systems occurs using the tests created in the previous column.

The first question that should be asked is whether or not this approach would have solved the "open systems" wars. I believe that it would have, although there is little empirical evidence to prove this assertion. The simplest test is to examine the market, which itself is no easy task. However, a single broad trend is distinguishable. Microsoft is the dominant player in the open systems market. If you examine the five columns of the model, you will see that they followed four of the columns, excepting the SDO column. They engaged in extensive marketing to understand user needs, and then put together specifications that resulted in a product that was testable for conformance. They made the procurement cycle very easy, and made the use of their product equally easy through good human-interface engineering. Most importantly, they redefined the "open systems" question so that it was nearer to the needs of the market. The definition of "open systems" that Microsoft embraced was, "inexpensive, ubiquitous, computing." Compare this to the UAOS, "access to information to do one's job" and the similarity is much closer than, "application portability, interconnectivity, and interoperability."

The ability to move in the direction suggested by the five columns in Figure 6.3 is not lacking. Organizations such as UniForum and POSC exist as places where User Specifications can be developed. X/Open both creates specifications and test suites. X3, as well as 254 other organizations, writes standards. Companies such as MKS understand how to create and use test suites to make products conform.

To create such a system is not too difficult. To have the system work is very nearly impossible unless a new icon is established. My suggestion for this icon would be one of "competitive cooperation," although it lacks the catchiness that Roland, stereos, and telephones had. However, it is one that stresses the mutual interdependence of the activities involved in the process. Basically, "competitive cooperation" requires that groups that might normally compete must first join forces to create the activities over which they will compete. The underlying concept is that competition can take place only after cooperation has taken place to establish the market. This applies to the users, vendors, and the government, all of whom must play together to make this happen. Failure of any one group to participate cooperatively will doom the entire scheme; failure of any player to participate will doom either that player or the entire scheme. The role of standardization is reasonably simple. It will force change. Like chaos, participation is not an option any longer. The system is impacted not by participation but by existence. Organizations impact, and are impacted by, the standardization system whether they participate or not. And this, more than anything else, is the message of open systems standardization. It is no longer an option for an organization that wishes to live long and prosper.

NOTES

[1]Bloch, Marc (translator Peter Putnam). *The Historian's Craft,* Vintage Books: NY, 1953, p. 9.
[2]See Cargill, Carl F. "A Clash of Cultures: ISO/IEC and the ITU" Auerbach Report 61-10-20, 1989 for a discussion of the deeper cultural and economic differences that distinguish the telecommunication and information

technology standardization disciplines. The difference between regulatory and voluntary standardization marks a deeper cultural difference that derives from the competitive (IT) and cooperative (telecommunications) genesis of the two disciplines.

[3]See Cargill, Carl F. *Information Technology Standardization: Theory, Process, and Organizations,* Bedford, MA: Digital Press, 1989 and Weiss, Martin B. H. "Standards and Product Development Strategies: A Review of Data Modem Developments," *Computer Standards and Interfaces,* Elsevier Press, North Holland, 1990, 12, 109–121 for further discussions of the concepts of anticipatory standardization and some of the theory that is basic to the concept. The first successful use of anticipatory standardization was in the LAN activity by the IEEE 802 committee, with the establishment of the ETHERNET as a LAN of choice in the market during the 1980s. See also Chapter 5.

[4]See Weiss, Martin and Cargill, Carl. "Consortia in the Standards Development Process," *Journal of the American Society for Information Science,* September 1992, pp. 559–565 for a further description and an interesting taxonomy of consortia which still appears valid.

[5]Digital Equipment Corporation. *Open Systems Handbook: A Guide to Building Open Systems,* 1991.

[6]The works by Paul David, Joseph Farrell, Brian Arthur, and Stanley Besen, while excellent for their rigor, all tend to emphasize the more generalized and abstract economic approach to standardization, based largely on telecommunications (a regulated discipline). This made it somewhat problematic for use by the IT industry, which is largely unregulated, except by market economics (see endnote 2). Other academics, notably Garth Saloner, have done analysis of the IT arena and standardization process from an outside observer's point of view, relying on inferences and reports rather than actual participation. A newer group of academics led by Michael Spring, Martin Weiss, William Lehr, Marvin Sirbu, and Shane Greenstein (University of Pittsburgh, Columbia, Carnegie-Mellon, and Illinois) have done excellent and useful work based on actual knowledge of and participation in and with IT SDOs. However, their work was not available in the early and mid 1980s. More importantly to the field, however, is that nearly all of this last mentioned group are also educating students in the discipline of standardization.

[7]Gabel, H. Landis (editor). *Product Standardization and Competitive Strategy,* Elsevier Press, North Holland, Amsterdam, 1987.

[8]ASC X3/93-0884-L, 12 February 1993, *Standards Life Cycle.* Available from the X3 Secretariat, 1250 Eye Street, Suite 200, Washington D.C. 20010.

[9]Black, Max. *The Labyrinth of Language,* NY NY: Mentor Books, 1968, p. 65.

Chapter 7

A User Perspective on Technical Standardization

> "Here then we rest: 'The universal cause
> Acts to one end, but acts by various laws.'"
>
> —Alexander Pope, "Epistle III" *Essay on Man*

INTRODUCTION

Having examined the nature of a new model for standardization in the previous chapter, it would be useful to look at IT standardization from an organizational usage point of view. It is nesessary to look at the view of a purchasing agent or other person in business who is not in the information technology hierarchy, but who rather is in the business hierarchy. This model has been the subject of a certain amount of acrimonious debate, but I believe that it brings a valid question to the debate, "What is the value of a standard to a user?"

THE MODEL

The basis of the model is contained in the section on Users in Chapter 4. If the suppositions in this section are correct, then the users really do not participate in the standardization process on a parity level with the providers. From Chapter 6, the major input of the providers is seen as the forces that cause the providers to actually produce products that contain standards. The users are reasonably indifferent to which standard is adopted as long as the adopted standard (or standards) does not essentially dispossess them or cost them excessive money. The user's point of view is one of, ". . . we [the users] do not want to have the 'luxury' of having to manage two parallel technology solutions within our infrastructure. The argument is *not* [italics the author's] about technology issues directly; it has much more to do with the costs of procuring, deploying, and managing IT in support of our business."[1] Fundamentally, the user's interest is grounded in business, not in the technology.

THE DICHOTOMY

This approach yields the first split between the user's and provider's perspective on standardization. Users want a standard that serves a particular business need; providers need to provide standards that serve all the possible users. To phrase this in a manner that can be used in further discussion: providers tend to produce global standards to serve all of the potential users of IT products (technology-based), while users tend to implement specific standards that meet the needs of their particular business model (business-based).

PERCEPTION DEFINITION

The two sides to the model are now defined. On the provider side is the global model that describes all of the potentials that the IT industry will need to satisfy all users over a long time in nearly all situations, and that serves as a reference for all providers. This reference model, if it is correctly constructed, includes some present and future technologies, a road map function, and some of the methodologies of the thought processes that occurred when it was constructed. The time span covered is up to ten years, and the model is applicable to all technical disciplines that deal in this area. On the IT user side is a description of a solution implementation that is immediate and particular to that user's application's problems. Both providers and users have something that they call standards; the definitional gap is tremendous. But identification of the first two distinct areas of a new model has been established: the reference model and the application implementation standard.

The differences in time and complexity, however, prevent the two from having any but the slightest congruence, based as they are upon different perceptions of the role of standards. Because of this, it is necessary to provide a bridging mechanism between the two now disparate concepts. To lessen the gap, it is necessary to begin to move these standards towards a common ground. However, I do not believe that this can be accomplished with a single step.

To begin, a subset of the reference model is necessary. The qualities that the subset would contain are those of an industry consensus standard and would generally describe one set of functions or capabilities. That is, instead of a global reference model for Local Area Networks, the industry standard would describe a particular technological implementation of a Local Area Network, such as Ethernet, specific to a single industry, such as the IT industry. Basically, the industry standard is the implementation of the strategy contained in the reference model. Because it is a standard that is written primarily by the providers of the product or service, it is more focused upon a computing function; that is, how the computing function will occur, rather than what the outcome of the function will be. There is little thought given to the end use (application) here. Instead, the various providers input market data through the selection of technologies. The providers create the standard in light of what they see as possible and viable as well as needed. In the industry standard, the providers act for the users in determining the course that the standard will take. Each provider represents their users, and makes implicit and explicit assumptions as to what these collective and individual user's needs will be for the standard when it is completed.

On the other side of the model, there is a need to generalize from the very specific implementation application, which describes what a particular user wants to have in the purchased system. The next level of generalization would be the systems profile which describes what the requirements of the groups of similar users are, based upon a standardized set of needs for that group of users. As an example, a systems profile would contain a generalized description of the functionality that was being sought, along with the methodology for insuring that generality. The systems profile can be seen as an additive function from the implementation application. A group of application implementation requirements were combined to create the systems profile for a specific class or type of user.

In order to agglomerate the requirements, however, it is necessary to be able to generalize away from a specific implementation of a particular standard into a more generalized standard. In this case, user groups have been formed to write the necessary specifications that describe the standardized specifications upon which the users will base their individual implementation applications. These standardized specifications are the basis for the standards that form the systems profiles. In effect, the user group is putting together a list of requirements that providers must meet in order to be able to proceed to the implementation application; the systems profile tends to make more global the specific requirements of implementation application.

Even with the addition of these two new areas, there is still no union of the user and provider standards efforts. The industry standard is focused on the potentialities that the provider industry sees; the systems profile defines the attributes standardized by a specific user group. The bridge between these two groups comes with the addition of the functional profile. The functional profile describes a set of functions that are a subset of the industry standard, and which are extracted from the industry standard. It describes a set of needed functions for a larger class of users than is described in the more precise systems profile. Because it exists on a border between provider perceptions and user needs, it has a somewhat confused existence. Basically, it translates the potentiality of an industry's capabilities in a certain area into a set of functions from which the users can begin to construct a more specific system. It is an area of uneasy cooperation between users and providers. It is where the providers discover if they have anticipated user needs correctly, and users find out if what they need is within the scope of what the industry can provide. It is the area where I believe most conflicts will occur in the future and the area that provides the greatest ability to effect compromises. Figure 7.1 shows the full model with the five stages.

Unfortunately, the completion of the model is only the start of the attempt to deal with the complexities of the standardization process. The model presents a logical flow, but it is only a simple model. As a representation of a reality for illustration purposes, it offers a structure that will allow further investigation.

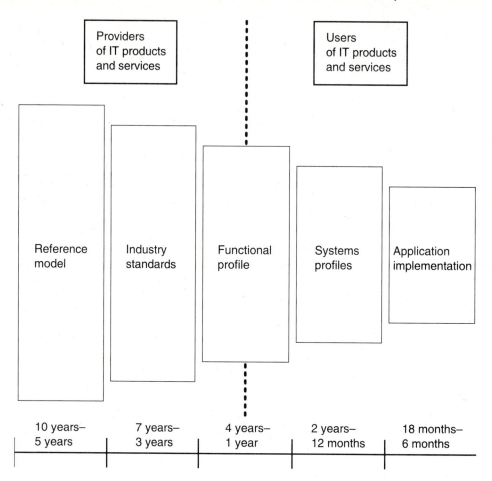

Figure 7.1   The User-Provider Standardization Planning Model

There are several key findings that have appeared. To begin, the model can be viewed as a method of describing a time/event horizon in the standards process. I have not investigated the implications of this aspect of the model and I am not sure what it implies. However, I believe that it has significance for the voluntary consensus standards process, since the event horizon of the reference model implies a ten year commitment to see a standard from conception through to implementation. If this is the case, and I believe that it is, it indicates that the reference models will become the premier planning devices for the industry, and will become the change agents for the way that IT evolves. It also says that the possibility of revolution is somewhat diminished, since revolution in a highly planned environment will be increasingly difficult. However, it does not impact the insertion of technologies, nor does it seem to restrict technical innovation, since the reference model does not describe a methodology for implementation. The growing question is, of course, the nature of the vision that drives the reference model, and whether or not it is a provider perquisite any longer.

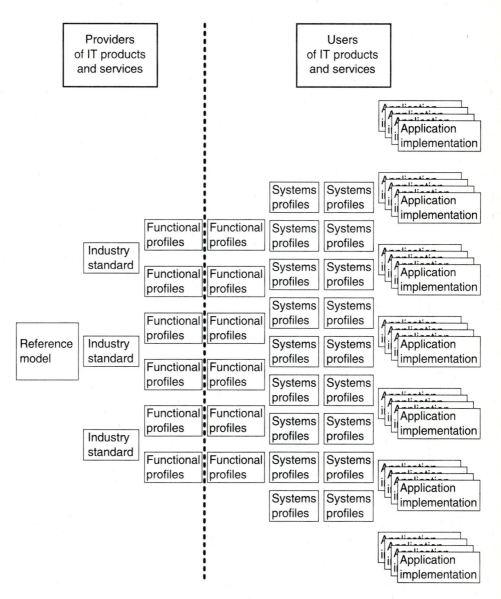

Figure 7.2   The Provider Perspective

The next interesting dilemma is the apparent linearity of the model. It is, in fact, not linear. While the assignment of a time-line and event horizon appear to make it linear, there is no proof that a reference model will precede an industry standard, or that an industry standard will precede a systems profile. While the time-line is nice for planning purposes, very few users are aware of their needs ten years in advance. In reality, all that

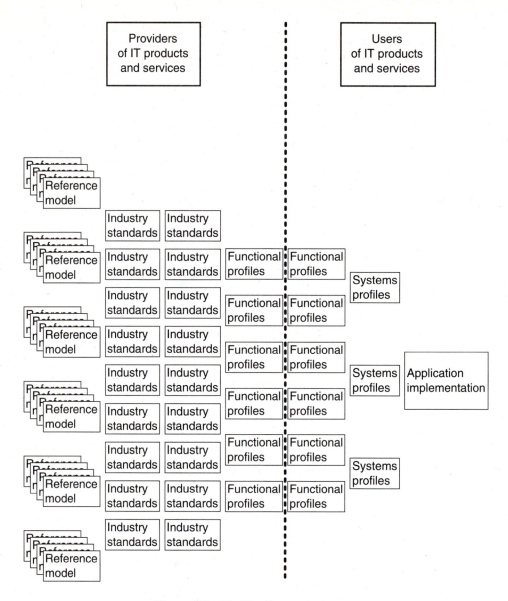

Figure 7.3   The User Perspective

can be said about the applicability of the model is that the market tends to eventually develop into the five stage model; the market does not require that the process appear in any order. This adds a level of confusion to the model, which makes it somewhat suspect as a precise tool for prognostication, but which can enhance its ability to structure and plan on a larger basis.

THE PROVIDER VIEW

Turning to a last major complication, Figure 7.2 shows the implication of the model from the view of moving from the global to the specific. The reference model can be implemented in several industry standards; each of these can be referenced in several functional profiles. Each time that this happens, however, the original feature is subsetted as it is transferred to the lower level. Each stage of the model becomes more particular. Each functional profile can be subsetted to become part of any of several systems profiles, and each of these can be further subsetted as they become an implementation application.

Normally, in a decomposition this subsetting activity is not too difficult since most decompositions are accomplished in static environments. However, in the case of standards, it becomes a major horror show very quickly. Standards are revised and updated constantly. Because standards are not monolithic any longer, but rather can have several hundred interrelated sections, the ability to determine what the revision level of the various parts and levels of the standard begins to disappear. This then eliminates the ability of the levels below the industry standard to insure that they are using the latest revision level of the industry standard in their stages. This has ramifications that extend beyond insuring that the latest technology is being used and implemented. The question that surfaces immediately is how, or even if, interoperability can be assured. The complication of the World Wide Web (WWW), browsers, and all that is electronic commerce make this a compelling and daunting question. The work that is needed here is to determine how a conformance testing model can be built for the industry if the five stage model is valid. It is an area that should not be too difficult, but would probably be too early to develop at this time based on experience.

THE USER VIEW

While this view is complex enough, it demonstrates a particular bias on the part of the provider. If the graphic is reversed, you have an entirely different but equally valid figure (see Figure 7.3). This is the view from the user's perspective. Throughout this discussion, the user's needs for standards have been dealt with in a monolithic fashion; that is, the user only needs IT standards. However, the truth of the matter is that the user is confronted by a multitude of standards, not merely those that deal with IT. The user has IT standards to consider, telecommunications standards, quality standards, governmental regulations, safety standards, service standards, and reliability standards that are all part of the application implementation. So, from the user point of view, the implementation application appears as the unitary box, with all of the other standards feeding into it.

CONCLUSION

This bit of insight, more than any other, sets the stage for the area of standards that needs to be understood. While it is acceptable to describe standards as a planning mechanism, and to describe the various types of standards that the industry is willing to supply, there are two main players in the standards arena: the user and the provider. The providers need generalized standards, based upon a reference model, which allow them to build the most generalized product set available while satisfying certain market needs. On the other hand, the users need an answer to a present or perceived problem in their application of IT products, specific to either themselves or to a class of similar users.

NOTES

[1]Coupe, Geoff. "Information Technology; Grasping at Governance," *StandardView,* Volume 3, Number 3, September 1995, p. 111. Coupe was addressing the problem of dual networked communications solutions to the Object Management Group's Common Object Requirements Broker Architecture (CORBA). Coupe's article (pp. 107–111) makes interesting reading, as it presents a user's point of view and is contrasted with the article by Geoff Lewis (Sun Microsystems), "CORBA 2.0 Universal Networked Objects," pp. 102–106 in the same edition, which argues exactly the opposite point of view.

Chapter 8

From Open Systems to an Open Organization

"On their own axis as the planets run,
Yet make at once their axis round the sun:
So two consistent motions act the soul;
One regards itself, and one the whole."

—Alexander Pope, "Epistle III" *Essay on Man*

INTRODUCTION

Because standards are ubiquitous, they are, in many cases, taken for granted. Chandler, in his book on the nature of management in the United States,[1] emphasizes how the railroad companies formed the basis of the modern corporation, and how the standards that unified the disparate rail systems were the result of and were driven by the changes in organization and management of these companies. There is no exploration of how the standards came into being: the compromises that were required by the various interests, the changes in operating procedures that were necessary, the petty and major triumphs and failures of the various nascent bureaucracies, and so on. Nor does Chandler explore how the creation of these standards imposed a structure, and at times, limitation, on the activities of the participants. By definition, the creation of a standard creates a freedom ("I don't have to worry about that any more") and a limitation ("I can't do that because it's not allowed") on the ability of management to act. This limitation can be translated into degrees of freedom very quickly and can set direction, just as technology standards can set direction of the technology that is being produced.

Much of this book has, so far, focused on how standards have changed the evolution of Information Technology. This chapter proposes to explore how Information Technology, which is subject to these standards, has changed, and will continue to change, management. This, in turn, will create a new class of management standards that will again

97

cause a revolution (or else a very rapid evolution) in management, similar to that described by Chandler. These, in turn, will lead to changes in the structure and nature of IT and the standards discipline that serves it.

IN THE BEGINNING

In the late fifteenth century, an English knight named Sir Thomas Malory wrote a series of stories about a mythical kingdom called Camelot. He described the adventures of a king named Arthur and his knights of the Round Table. These legends of King Arthur have been used for many years to illustrate a model of the medieval knight and the medieval kingdom. Unfortunately, these two phenomena (the knight and courtly life) were as dead as dodoes when Malory wrote about them. Technological change and geographic expansion had combined to make the heavily armored knight obsolete, and the growing middle class had begun to redefine the social structure of feudalism so necessary to the medieval king.

In a similar way, the structure of the multinational corporation has been forever changed by a growing technical and social revolution. The idea of "Arthurian legend," which describes how we would love things to be rather than how they are, is embodied in the creation of the Chief Information Officer, the Chief Quality Officer, and the department of Management Information Systems. Although the hierarchical model of management has been a suspect concept for about twenty years, we have insisted on continuing to embellish the model which we cannot do without; we continue to maintain the structure under which we all seem to be compelled to operate. Just as John Kennedy harked back to Camelot in the early 1960s for inspiration, we look to the hierarchical corporate structure as a source of strength and hope. We have invented euphemisms such as the "virtual corporation" and "rightsizing" to permit us to continue believing in a legend, while masking the more serious problems to which we need to seek answers.

This chapter will look at some of those problems from the perspective which says that the basic concepts driving the Information Technology (IT) industry are flawed; because a fundamental rule in standardization is that you cannot merely object, but must counterpropose, I will also provide the start of a solution based upon being able to look at and respond to the problem differently. However, since history can be instructive, I'd like to look at some parallels between what happened to change society in the 1400s (Malory) and what has happened to the corporation in the late 1900s (IT capabilities).

The structure of medieval society was a result of a technological innovation (stirrups and fighting from horseback) and external threat (raids by Vikings and others).[2] The rationale for the creation of the "knight" was that a man who could fight on horseback could almost always beat someone fighting on foot (Conan the Barbarian movies aside.) If you lived in a subsistence village and needed to be protected from Vikings and other bandits, a mounted warrior offered viable protection from professional bullies. Basically, you found the biggest, meanest warrior in the three contiguous villages and guaranteed support for him, his family, and his horse while he became experienced enough to protect you. Over time, this mounted fighter needed other things, and proceeded to take over the local protection racket. Others lost the accumulated skill of fighting (previously, everyone had been a part-time soldier), and began to default "fighting decisions" to the "knight." However, as time passed, the knight began to demand more services, money, and food—and who was in a position to deny him? As the centralized government of a king began to form, it was not the council of village elders who was looked to for information but the knight. And the knight became the source of leadership, of governance, and stability.

This development was necessary, however. It was the only practical way that society could organize itself to meet the external challenges impacting it from all sides. Central authority (the Roman Empire and the follow-on Merovingian dynasty) had collapsed. The Church was a spiritual power, not a temporal one. The Saracens and Vikings were invading, and everything had gone to pieces. It was a time of cultural, social, and economic change. The power vacuum was filled by a new form of "order bringer," based on the social need to create structure out of the chaos that occurred when the Roman Empire (and its Western successors) collapsed. The feudal hierarchy depended upon reciprocal services (vassal and liege, civil and religious, local and universal). The list of reciprocal services became increasingly complex as more and more interactions began to occur. Ultimately, because of its highly complex structure and inability to respond to new external pressures, the entire concept of the kingly fiefdom collapsed, leading to the series of destructive wars that formed the basis for modern Europe.

The keys to these relationships, and the reciprocal interactions and responsibilities, were "standards." The standards regulated interactions, specified who owed what to whom, and were generally "de facto," based upon current practice. Over time, these were codified into more formal rules, becoming "de jure" standards. (The most well known codification of the complex rules to English speaking countries was the Magna Carta, which made de facto expectations de jure law.) The rules of interaction were standardized into what could be seen as a set of standards for behavior (a king had a "divine right," a knight with a castle could fight for only sixty days a year for his liege, and so on). The use of standards was instrumental in defining how the pieces of this complex set of interactions fit together. The use of standardized responsibilities was driven by the increasing size and diversity of the ennobled class and a need to understand and manage the growing heterogeneity. With this thought, I'd like to leave this particular scenario for a moment and look at the parallels in the modern corporate structure.

THE MODERN MANAGEMENT HIERARCHY

The modern managerial hierarchy was formed in response to technological innovation (the industrial age) and external threats (massive social and economic upheaval). The entrepreneur of the late 1800s could not individually manage all aspects of a commercial enterprise (from development to production to sales to service). While some of the change was driven by simple size and geographic dispersion, the most important difference is that a large organization is not merely an inflated little organization, but one that is structurally different. This is a difference that had not been previously encountered in commercial activities.[3] The initial response to this complexity was to hire managers as owner surrogates. This lead to the vertical division of complex organizations, which was a convenient way of sizing the organization to managerial capability. It is still used today in titles such as "store manager," "district manager," and so on, and can be seen as the original "rightsizing." In this case, "rightsizing" meant the correct number of interactions for a single person to safely manage.

The solutions of the late 1800s and early 1900s, unfortunately, do not address the larger organizational issues which continue to vex the organization today: how to manage the change and evolution of the organization as it begins to impinge on its external environment, and as the external environment begins to impinge upon it. Models of how to run a complex organization that operate well in stressful and slowly changing situations did exist. (The Church and the military, especially the Prussian Army, had had them for some time.) However, in the 1800s, little had been done to codify this knowledge because everyone just knew that it worked. This situation changed in the late 1800s when Max Weber, who was trying to create a discipline called "sociology," began to investigate the sources of authority as well as how an organization's structure and efficiency related to this authority. Max Weber succeeded beyond his wildest fears.

Weber developed the concept of bureaucracy and "legal-rational" authority, in which allegiance was owed, not to a person (read the "owner of the business"), but to a position in a hierarchy (read "manager"). With this definition, organizations began the movement towards a hierarchical structure, which was vital for the nascent industries and entrepreneurs of the time. It allowed for the creation of a professional management class, trained in the management of the information necessary to do their duties, with discrete functions that constituted the division of labor necessary to permit the growth of suborganizational functions. It was based on the best suited person doing a circumscribed and clearly defined job and reporting the results of this work to a senior who takes similar work from other subordinates, reworks it, and passes it up a chain. This forms the inverted "V" that is the basis of organizational charts (see Figure 8.1). Weber's analysis of authority and its derivation formed the basis for much of later management theory and the organization structure that followed.

Returning to our technology and social change argument, what we've seen is the creation of the equivalent of the medieval kingdom. Just as a medieval knight was part of an elaborate hierarchy and was constrained by his position, so the modern executive is constrained in her or his actions by a complex web of largely unwritten but very powerful cultural rules. All of these rules devolve from a single source which is the hierarchy that has been created to ensure the successful movement of information to and from the members of the hierarchy. Much like the medieval kingdom, the glue that holds the modern corporation together is a set of usually unwritten "standards" that regulate the expectations and beliefs that people have about their roles. The amount and type of work a superior can or may request of a subordinate is clearly defined by some form of marketplace "standard," violation of which can result in a series of penalties to one or both parties. These interactions, which used to be in large part "de facto," have become, over the last decade, increasingly "de jure," as uncertainty and a desire for stability have grown. (The growth of Human Resources as a functional replacement for Personnel is no accident. It also, not coincidentally, occurred with the growth of the more heterogeneous work force.)

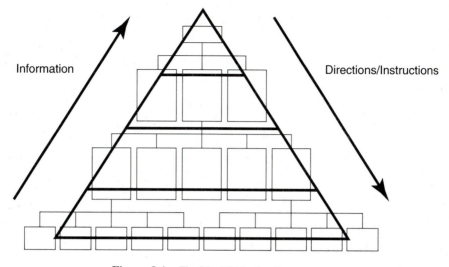

Figure 8.1   The Ideal Weberian Bureaucracy

THE HIERARCHY, STANDARDS, AND COMPLEXITY

I believe that, as heterogeneity and uncertainty grow, so do the set of rules (standards) governing behavior of the organization. This concept is critical to much of what will follow. Until the mid 1970s, the hierarchical structure served business well, but only because it was capable of managing the flow of information necessary to maintain and grow the organization. This information flow is the rationale for the organization, and its only real value added. Other attributes such as personal growth, organizational stability and so on are secondary effects of the structure that was originally created to manage information flow. The model under which most organizations operate is that the more senior the position one has, the more capability is imputed to make strategic decisions and cause action. Weber's bureaucratic model makes the reason for this clear. The higher you are, the more you know, and the better equipped you are to make a decision. This is a viable proposition—as long as the hierarchy is executing correctly. The key assumption here is that the higher in the hierarchy one is, the better one is as a synthesizer and decision giver, within a specific area of expertise. Interactions with other organizations (information flow areas) within the hierarchy and triangle must be clearly and explicitly defined and understood. The theory of "gangplank" management in which peer levels met to circumvent the long route to the top and back down (see Figure 8.2) were expedient responses to time pressure, but were accepted as part of the structure as long as rules were followed. When it was introduced, matrix management was also meant to counter the increasing time lag between start and finish of a decision cycle, but a matrix operated under even more complex rules for managing information. The hierarchy bought itself more time at the cost of imposing more and more rules.

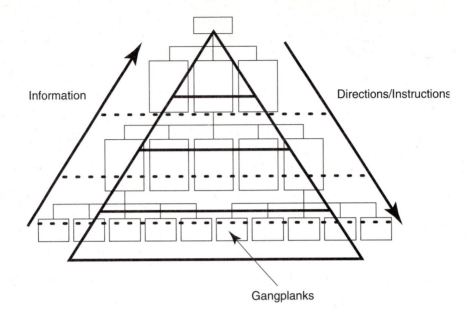

Information

Directions/Instructions

Gangplanks

Figure 8.2   The Modified (Useful) Bureaucracy

The imposition of these rules was essential to the survival of the hierarchical organization. Just as the medieval kingdom survived by becoming more and more rule bound, so did the organization survive. However, the generation of increasing numbers of rules began to create nonresolvable conflict within the organization. The place where this showed most clearly was the change in the locus of decision making power and decision making authority. The positions in the lower level of the hierarchy, as well as the decisions that proceed from these positions, are based upon technical expertise and knowledge of a particular discipline. However, as one proceeds up the hierarchy, the skill that becomes more important is the skill of synthesis which is the ability to correlate the work of more and more subordinates.[4] At some point in the hierarchy, the lines that mark a specialty (finance, marketing, engineering) become blurred, and this is where the "corporate decisions" are supposed to be made, based upon perfect knowledge transmitted up the chain from subordinate experts.

This ability to make decisions based upon combining multiple inputs from diverse sources could be referred to as "synthesis skill," and is the mark of a truly competent senior manager. However, the imposition of formal or informal "rules" changes the environment in subtle ways. The first assumption of the rule maker is that the external environment will remain stable (or at least determinable) so that the players in the organization can participate under conditions where the risk can be known. This is no longer true; the external environment is changing too rapidly. As a result, there has been an erosion of the "decision making authority" in most organizations, with decisions being made at lower and lower levels to ensure action before the environment changes again. While this can be good, two things have resulted from this shift.

The first result is that the lower level decisions rob senior managers of the ability to maneuver or to make a decision outside of very narrow prescribed limits. In effect, a senior level activity is no longer a decision, but a ratification of a series of decisions made at lower levels and surfaced for implementation. This Arthurian management myth is called "empowerment," and represents an attempt to rationalize the fact that the bureaucratic form is failing. If selected decisions were made, or if the criteria for decisions were codified (more standards), this would be surmountable. But the external environment is changing too fast for this to happen, so strategic decisions are made at a low level.

This feeds the second result, which has more serious implications for the organization as a whole. Basically, these decisions made at a lower level are usually made on the basis of a singular stream of information. The decision is made for the organization based upon a financial model that may not be acceptable to manufacturing or an engineering model that may imperil marketing. Because the decisions are made at a lower level, there is little formal structure available to create the necessary synthesis that makes the organization function as an organization, rather than as a piece part collection. As a result of the hierarchy's need for expedient fixes to the problems of information flow and "synthesis management," both of these general activities resulting from the "lower level decision making" have been ratified and now have a substantial set of rules or standards behind them and reinforcing them.

This reflects the not atypical response of using standards to continue to prop up an idea whose time might be past. It is important to note that these standards did not result from deliberate or planned activity. They resulted from situational activities, and hence suffer from the same set of problems with which the entire structure is faced. The standards, which are used to codify the activities between two or more distinct entities or classes of activities, are based, not upon a general overarching theory, but upon a particular set of "things" that happened to work at that time in that environment.

The problem with this becomes obvious as an organization grows. It forces the maintenance of the relationship and the supporting organizations as long as that standard or interaction is honored. However, if a department with a distinct function becomes extraneous, the standards that legitimize that department's interactions will cause the perpetration of that department, if only because the changes necessary to get rid of that department's activities and reports are usually a major task, for which there appears to be no time. Given this set of circumstances, what we now see is that as decisions are pushed to lower and lower levels, and the ability of senior management to modify these lower level decisions becomes increasingly difficult, unless the members of the organization are willing to both initiate and accept major restructuring changes within the organization. These "standards," which manage a particular set of responsibilities and activities among the various groups, are, to use a particularly hoary analogy, the woof of the organizational fabric, while the warp is provided by necessity to manage a particular set of responsibilities up and down the organization.

SITUATIONAL IMPLEMENTATION STANDARDS

If one were to translate what has happened to the modern organization to a more classical setting, imagine the following scenario. Much of the moral code of western civilization is based upon a set of ten standards that are referred to as the "Ten Commandments." These standards are generalized to allow them to apply to a large range of situations. According to their history, they reflect true "top down" management. However, if they were created in the situation that I've just described, the standards (or commandments) would say, initially, "Do not kill a person named Mel in the accounting department on Tuesday afternoon before the close of the quarter." There would also be another standard that would say, "Do not kill Debbi in the PR department when the ad copy carries the wrong price." There would be innumerable standards, and it would be necessary to continue to have a Mel in the Accounting department and a Debbi in PR in order to make the standards viable.

In effect, these standards for interaction specified precisely the participants and outcomes of each interaction. In so doing, they created a set of hard and stable relationships which cannot be modified without impacting other relationships. The hierarchy has made prisoners of the people who play inside of it—and disenfranchised those who do not. The standardization technique was one of "implementation standardization;" that is, standards that mandated a particular implementation of the interface. By mandating the participants (either as a group or individually), as well as the expected range of responses, the standards mandate the existence of the creating and receiving positions and organizations. (Everyone must have seen the internal standard that states something like, "Must be approved by the Group Financial manager." This presupposes that the Group Financial manager will be there, and, in effect, freezes the position and the responsibilities around that position.) The implementation standard has significant import for the future of organizations and for the future of "open organizations." It is a true situational standard that applies only to a single instance of a problem, usually because the standard maker was either not skilled enough to figure out how to generalize the solution, or because the standard writer was too hurried to spend the time trying to generalize the problem.

The approach that I refer to as "situational implementation standards" is the attempt to substitute rules for understanding by the individuals who comprise an organization. It is brought about by the fact that many people, in an organization, do not understand what their job entails; not because the job is hard, but rather because the position that they occupy is either not clearly defined or is subject to constant change (or both). The inability to understand the why and how of a job results in a need for rules, which are wonderful for a static environment. If change is seen as a series of momentarily static environments, then you can appreciate the creation of "situational implementation standards."

ADVANCED HIERARCHICAL CONSTRUCTS

The changing environment has produced some changes in the hierarchical triangle. Matrix management was one of the first experiments in this area but it has been followed by others. However, if one looks at the management triangle, it becomes apparent that it has really become a management tetrahedron (Figure 8.3). The evolution has gone relatively unnoticed but is essential to understanding the future of the organization. The management tetrahedron is multi-planar and multi-scalar. It has virtual operation; that is, at any time, it may be construed in a non-normative way. The positions in the multiple planes are not based upon the same positions or authority of the preceding or following planes. The only commonality that any of these planes have, one to the other, is that they all are attempts to counter the implementation standards and rigidly based hierarchy.

The dangerous thing here, of course, is that the information that the groups share (after all, the whole focus of the hierarchy was to share and transmit information) is derived differently in each plane. As an example, assume that one of multiple planes is an engineering plane and that the lead position (the top of the triangle) is held by a senior engineer. Part of the plane might be a management triangle as shown in Figure 8.4. However, this group will structure its engineering information in a way that it is unique to the group, because everyone in the group understands the conventions (or standards) that are being used inside the group. However, when the engineering data is moved to the next plane (the financial plane) the data will be re-interpreted in a slightly different manner and the conclusions (knowledge) of the two groups may not match. Similarly, knowledge of every functional (planar) group will vary from slightly to significantly at any given level or time. The "management tetrahedron," therefore, is a partial solution to the problem that confronts management. While it breaks the bonds of the hierarchy to achieve the necessary results, it is flawed by the fact that the source information (or data) that it needs is not available in a universal (or at least mutually understandable) format.

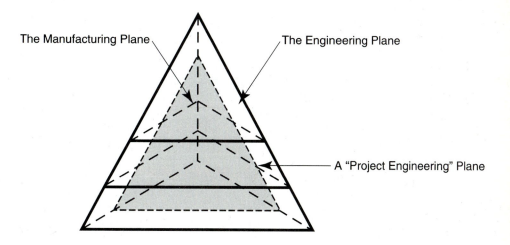

Figure 8.3   The Management Tetrahedron

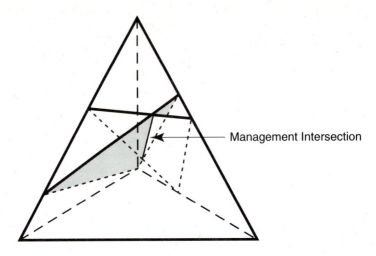

Figure 8.4   The Planar Management Structure

THE PROBLEM OF INFORMATION MANAGEMENT

There is one more aspect of the medieval kingdom/bureaucratic structure change that must be examined; that of the growth of the availability of information. At the very end of the High Middle Ages in 1450, Europe possessed an estimated 100,000 manuscripts. By 1500, there were nine million books circulating in Europe, few of which were under the control of the leaders of the feudal hierarchy. The hierarchy was not built to cope with this information expansion. Its function was to provide stability to allow the participants to exercise their duties and obligations, and not be buffeted by change. With the advent of the printing press, the hierarchy lost the ability to control change. And with this loss of control came massive social and economic change which gave rise to the society in which we presently live. However, if you examine this change more carefully, the real mover for the change came not so much from the growth of books but from the basic fundamental change created by the "openly available" information in books. What the book represented was an implementation of a new form of standard thought of as an "interface" standard. The interface was the actual information. The use of "native language" made the information in the book available to anyone who could read, without any other restriction. The book was one of the implementation methods (others were pamphlets and newspapers) of this standard. It is the interface standard that is the most successful, least recognized, and most difficult form of standard to accomplish. This form of standardization is essential to the continuation of the organization and to the economic viability of the United States, as well as the IT industry.

Regressing for a moment, the question for an organization boils down to how it manages the information becoming available. There are obviously at least two alternatives to this; one focuses on the tool for managing the resource that provides information to the organization, and the other on the nature of the organization itself. The first is open systems and the second, the open organization. Both are built upon the concept of standards and standardization. The difference between the approaches is the nature of the standards and standardization imposed. Chapter 6 discussed the evolution and revolution in open systems.

Returning to the analogy of the growth of books breaking the hegemony of the Church on writing and learning, the growth of knowledge about the potential achievable with user-driven computing (as shown by the workstation and personal computer) has forever broken the carefully constructed world of the MIS manager and implicitly, the CIO. Just as the growth of printing and the attendant mental revolution broke forever the hegemony of the church in the control of learning, so has the growth of the workstation/PC broken the control of the MIS manager over the computing environment.

As noted above, the Weberian bureaucracy was built to take advantage of specialization of skills and to ensure that all the data that impacted a particular problem affecting an organizational unit could be brought to bear. The underlying construct of Weberian bureaucracy was a paucity, rather than a surfeit, of data. The intent was constructionist, meaning to create information flow upward so that appropriate actions could be "constructed" and then flow downward. As we have seen, today's bureaucracy has a surfeit of data, which has lead to it becoming instructionist. The subordinate layers tend to select the information passed up the information channels to "instruct" their superiors, causing their superiors to endorse a particular form of action. As stated earlier, the standards that drove the Weberian constructionist bureaucracy tend to be implementation standards looking at distinct interactions, specifying distinct groups, and mandating both input and output. This severely restricts the ability of senior management to manage. The multiple planes within the management tetrahedron, with their recognition of the ability of different planes of operation and hierarchy, provide partial relief.

THE STAR IN THE PENTAGON (SIP) MODEL

However, if the hierarchy—which was an 1880's schema to show information handling—is abandoned in favor of a different construct, there is the possibility that a different form of organizational analysis can occur. If the organization is viewed from the point of view of "information processing units" (or functionally) instead of being viewed as a "power or positional structure" the appearance of the organization would look something like the "star in a pentagon" of Figure 8.5 (the SIP of Chapter 6). In this diagram, each of the points of the pentagon is a source of an input—or a destination of an output. Each of the points is connected with the other, assuring that all points have access to all other points in the communications network. Figure 8.6 shows a network of networks where the pentagons become part of a set of pentagons, composing a larger "star in a pentagon," with the smaller "star in a pentagon" as a node point. It is important to remember that, like the tetrahedron, the concept is multiplanar. Two or more of the points may be located in another "star in a pentagon" that comes off the page into the third dimension.

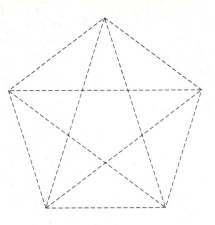

Figure 8.5 The "Star-In-Pentagon" Model of IT Networking

There are several things that make the "star in a pentagon" a better descriptive model for the organization than the tetrahedron. To begin, the "star in a pentagon" can be seen to have the characteristics of a chaos model. It has a nonlinear repeating fractal pattern (basically the "star in a pentagon" shape can be seen, but is always slightly different based upon the activities occurring). It is present in multiple scales; it can be based successfully on the individual, organization, or group of organizations. It is changed by the

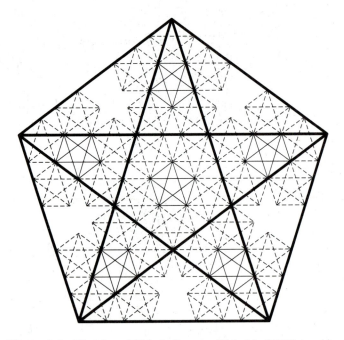

Figure 8.6 The Massed "Star-In-Pentagon" Model of IT Networking

observer even if the observer does not participate. The phrase "deterministic disorder" has been used in chaos theory; the same can be said to apply to organizational theory with the advent of the ability to share large amounts of information.

The key to remember is that this organizational theory is built upon the principle that any node can communicate with any other node in the known universe of possible nodes, and that there is always a routing mechanism that can be established. With the establishment of this new network, however, comes the creation of a new "star in a pentagon" that will overlay and complement existing paths. If the "star in a pentagon" is examined, a tentative theory can be built behind it.

In the smallest of the fractals, individuals occupy the points of the pentagon. Each individual may be part of a nearly infinite number of other "star in a pentagon" arrangements, based upon both the professional and personal interests or requirements of the person. As an example, the individual may be a financial analyst in an engineering group, may be networked into the financial analysts of the other functional groups in the company, may belong to a network of CPA candidates across the network, and may maintain contact with friends and colleagues at her or his previous company. The pentagons of which they are a part act as an information conduit for all of their relations. A similar construct can be made for each of the larger "star in a pentagon" models. A collection of individuals (a group) becomes the focal point of the larger pentagon, composed of all members of the engineering team on a specific program. The activities of this "star in a pentagon" are supported by all of the information skeins of the individual members of the various groups of the subordinate "star in a pentagon" points (Figure 8.6). In this model the concept of interface standardization reemerges. The only requirement for successful implementation of this management model is the successful creation of interface standards between the various parts of the organization and the recreation of the generalist as a part of the organization.

The key to the modern organization is that everyone is on or has access to a communications net. This could be sneaker net, telephone, the Internet, or other form of communication device. When this theory was first devised, it was in response to the management of Local Area Networks (LANs) and peer to peer communication under conditions of business uncertainty. The key to being able to participate as part of a "star in a pentagon" comes not from position, but from a competence based on the ability to provide a help. This source of authority is based upon knowledge or competence. The "star in a pentagon" participant (or the "knowledge worker") is judged by the contribution he or she can make to the task at hand (situational competence or knowledge competence). To make this virtual structure work, there are some necessary standardization dependencies.

STANDARDIZATION DEPENDENCIES

To begin, there must be a common basis for understanding; everyone must be aware of everyone else. This is a major organizational problem and has been a problem since Plato first set size limits on the ideal size of the state in the Republic. However, with the advent of "electronic highways," the ability to find information and to know one's respondents is less difficult. More difficult is the problem of using "common information." Here the concept of "open systems" fails. "Open systems" does not focus on the computing paradigm, but rather the computer paradigm. CIO and MIS managers today are preoccupied with the computer paradigm. They are focused on the technology of getting computers to interoperate. Yet the true question for the CIO or the MIS manager is not the computer but getting the computing function to be accepted and getting the users to interoperate. This form of interoperation is not currently being dealt with in organizations.

The star in the pentagon (as the actualization of the tetrahedron) can provide some of the answers to the problem of communication. This can create an open, synergistic corporation, but one that suffers from the flaw that the definition of competence is not established. The open organization model does not have the ability to discriminate that well between organizational thrashing (that is, everyone is trying to lead) and purposeful work. As a result, there is a need for a new basic construct under which groups can work in an open organization. Much of what follows is predicated upon my experience in the standards arena.

COMPETITIVE COOPERATION

There exists a type of organizational behavior which I call "cooperative competition." The concept derives from the paradox of the common, expressed in the following way. There exists a village common, which is large enough to allow every family in the village to graze three sheep. Since it is the common, no rules can really be made governing it, but there is the honored tradition of grazing only three sheep. One day, one of the families begins to graze four sheep. Soon everyone is doing it, but understanding that they are diminishing the common wealth. The traditional question asked is, "Who will remove their extra sheep first, diminishing personal gain and suffering economic harm for the common good?" The answer is usually that no one will, so the commonwealth is eventually eroded and everyone ends up poorer. Cooperative competition looks at the question differently. The question is not about who will remove the first sheep, but rather, "Can we make it possible to feed all of the sheep by increasing the grass production, common size, or some other method?" I suppose it is a matter of perspective.

One approach seeks to deal with the question within artificially imposed boundaries; that is, defining the questions within traditional restraints, and not looking at the nature of the conditions. The other approach seeks to redefine the question or to ask a different, but similar question that allows a solution. An accepted term is "paradigm shifting," but it is much simpler to refer to it as "asking the right question." Cooperative competition has an underlying belief that you cannot gain at the expense of another's potential. The idea is to redefine the question so that everyone can profit by the increase. There is no assurance that everyone will do better. However, the opportunity for growth must be presented in a manner to preclude disadvantaging any willing participant. Hopefully, the proposition can be presented in a way that everyone is advantaged, sometimes unequally, but always advantaged. Positional skills will not be enough. Positional authority will not cause the program to succeed, because positional authority relies, even in a completely democratic arena, upon some measure of threat of coercion to maintain itself.

A NEW SOURCE OF AUTHORITY

Competence authority, on the other hand, is subject to constant review and challenge. If competence authority is correctly used as a management tool, the result is synergistic. If it is improperly used, it is no worse than arbitrary positional authority and is easier to overcome. The underlying methodology which is absolutely necessary in the "star in a pentagon" environment is predicated upon gathering and using consensus. Consensus indicates that everyone has been heard and all objections considered and answered and/or implemented; it does not indicate unanimity. This is a fundamental concept: Everyone must have their chance to speak before the decision is made. If the "star in a pentagon" networks are wide enough, the network will quickly spread word about the concept, and the wider review will result in better and more complete decisions. Once an item has been agreed to and consensus reached, there should be no recourse to "revisiting the decision" by those involved in the decision. If consensus was reached by exclusion of an interested party, the decision must be revisited if contention happens, but a senior manager should not be able to skew the process because of dissatisfaction with a subordinate's work. (This forces participation in the program based upon manager-subordinate trust and commitment.) Again, this is based upon the subordinate and manager understanding the subordinate's role vis-à-vis both knowledge and positional authority. If the subordinate is unprepared to discuss substantive issues, then the network will disregard that person. If the issues are discussed, and overridden by a manager, then the network will learn not to trust the subordinate or the manager in future negotiations. This is basically a modification of the "Prisoners Dilemma" from game theory, which is a major concept for management style for the "star in a pentagon" and competitive cooperation. The assumption that guides success is that everyone will work for their own good, but that in so doing, they will follow the fundamental rule of cooperative competition: One cannot disadvantage anyone else to achieve advantage. The entire process depends upon the open and willing interchange of information.

While we have the ability to exchange data, exchange of information occurs only when data is validated. The exposure of an idea to a large group of people allows a consensus to build; comments are catalysts for the improvement process. A basic rule is that one cannot condemn without counter-proposing, and lack of response is not acceptable. The ability to share information and build consensus based on that sharing is what the nonhierarchical situational computing model is all about. As proof that this concept can work, one needs only to look at the formal standardization process for validation. While most people look askance at this process, it does provide a viable testing ground for the theories covered. The basic concept in standardization is that all players are playing because there is no way that a single player can, or should, dominate the market. The secondary theory says that by creating a standard, there is an expansion of the total market available to the implementors of the standard. While the process is justly condemned as being slow, this is the result of the lack of clear strategic planning, a failing that an organization should not have.

The skill in "open organizations" will not be management of technology, but rather management of the network of the multiple "individual information networks" that build the "star-in-the-pentagon" vision. It speaks to the empowered individual who has the right, or possibly the duty, to be informed and to express her or his views in the organization, both at work and in other places. More importantly, it puts a great deal of emphasis on the individual being able to express ideas and thoughts in a clear and coherent manner that is easily understood.

THE ROLE OF INFORMATION MANAGERS

Where does this leave the Chief Information Officer and the Management Information Systems Manager? The answer to this question is entirely dependent upon how they see their function. If their function is dealing with the care and feeding of computer and information processing equipment, then the answer is that they are, like the medieval knights, doomed. The emphasis is no longer on the gadgetry of the information processing, but rather on achieving results with and through the organization that is using the information. If the titles of these two individuals correctly reflect their responsibilities, they should be dealing with the types of issues I've described in these pages. The Chief Information Officer should be responsible for creating a new paradigm for information management within the company, not for determining the future of software or hardware. (Chapter 4, "The Players and Their Products," discusses briefly the role of the CIO and MIS director, and the types of "things" with which they should be concerned.) The CIO should concentrate on the utility of information and who needs it, how it is used, where it is used, and how an organization can be altered to use it, rather than concentrating solely on the creation of an information processing architecture. While understanding that technology is one of the responsibilities of the position, it is roughly akin to demanding that the head of an airline be a mechanic or the head of a flour company be a miller. The question is not what the mechanics of the process are, but rather what the use of the product is and will be. The CIO should be the architect and feeder of the "star-in-the-pentagon" teams for the corporation.

The requirements of this "new CIO position" include ensuring that the network of individuals is capable of using the system and that the system, as embodied by cooperative competition, is working. The CIO should have it within her or his power to stop battles in information management and information conversion, by using the process and by creating common definitions using terms that people in the larger organization understand. At the same time, the CIO/MIS manager acts as the cooperative competition champion to the hierarchy because, as we've seen, the hierarchy cannot go away. A necessary corollary is that the CIO understand the nature of "information" as it is used by the various entities in the organization. Currently, the CIO is a cross-functional entity. She or he is responsible for ensuring that the disparate parts of the organization have the capability to pass completed information back and forth. To phrase it within the paradigm I am advocating, the CIO is currently charged with managing the information feed to the separate management tetrahedrons. The CIO is, in effect, the feeder of chaotic information throughout the organization.

As noted earlier, one of the problems with the tetrahedron is that it does not have a commonality of information; the information elements of the participants are discrete to the particular discipline or to the particular circumstance. Without the context of the originating organization, the information is either suspect or completely liable to misinterpretation. The function of the CIO in nurturing the new organizational structure is to reduce the data elements (those elements which make up the feedstock of the corporation) to an atomic level. To do this, the CIO must understand the nature of the information being used. To use a parallel in current information technology, the information must be similar to the encapsulated information found in the object-oriented programming paradigm. In this concept, the information carries its context, its history, and derivation with it. The CIO must be capable of making the data elements of a corporation atomic and then ensure that the users of these elements understand how to assemble them into larger and larger groupings to effectively yield information and eventually knowledge.

However, because of the nature of the "star-in-the-pentagon" structure, the data to information to knowledge transformation must always be part of the contextual base. This places a severe burden on the CIO but makes the individual act as the Chief Information Officer, not the Chief Technologist. In this capacity, the chief function of the CIO will be planning, not the execution function. Because the flow of information is the main reason for the organization, the management of this flow among individuals, groups, interorganizations, and extraorganizations will become the hallmark of the agile corporation in the 1990s.

There is an important caveat that needs to be applied. The "star-in-the-pentagon" is highly useful for managing the information assets of a corporation and coming to closure on them. However, because of its consultative nature, it is not good at naming promotions, or doing the type of decision validation work that the current hierarchy does. The hierarchy has a definite role to play in the future organization. It is necessary to reinvent the role for this structure as well, and this role will be unique to each organization, since this is one of the areas that can offer a competitive advantage. As an example, the hierarchy may be used as the process control arm of the information group, or it may be responsible for implementing, in a coherent manner, the actions of the information processing sector. In any case, the concept of cooperative competition should also be useful here because the membership of the two functional units should be intertwined.

CONCLUSION

Where does this leave hardware and software? Basically, it makes actual equipment (from operating systems through the Net) a minor point. To use a parallel example, the technical nature of the book is usually of limited interest to the person reading the book. Few people can tell you what the type font of the book was, or how it was bound, or any of the mechanics of the book creation. What they can tell you is how much they paid for the book, the way it was distributed, its story line, and its value to them. The same will be true of the hardware and software over the next ten years. The technology, from a user's point of view, should become an enabling background activity. It will become more and more interface-standards driven. The user will see a graphical user interface (GUI) that is responsive to the needs of the user, rather than to the needs of the technology. The key to the success of any software will be its adaptability to transformation. This will, of course, lead to increasing levels of abstraction and increasing standardization. This will allow users to specify a set of interfaces that allow the system to serve the needs of the "star-in-the-pentagon" style of management which is interface rich. The function of Management Information Systems will be to correctly specify the interfaces which will allow technology providers to plug into the network to make the system useful. The components will, by definition, interoperate. Those that do not will be discarded. The MIS group will be the advocates of the users. They will understand both the needs of the users and how these users interoperate. The ubiquitous nature of the computer will give way to an ubiquitous computing environment, which focuses not on the technology but on the results of the technology. With the new organizational construct, and with the new interoperational construct, it will finally be time to give the lie to the old sorry phrase of "computer literacy." The enabling function for software in the new construct is to be "people literate," meaning that the software must act the way people do. It must move from its Aristotelian model of "from the specific to the general" to the Platonic model of "from the general to the specific." This is the challenge for both the organization and for standardization in the next millennia: to fully enable the person, both individually and as part of the integrated and interoperative system of society.

NOTES

[1]Chandler, op. cit.

[2]See Lynn White, *Medieval Technology and Social Change,* New York: Oxford University Press, 1964 for a very good description of how technology had a profound impact on the culture and history of the medieval period. While White has been criticized (Norman F. Cantor. *Inventing the Middle Ages,* New York, William Morrow and Co., 1991) for a straight line rationality, his writing reflects a willingness to look at technology and measure the results of the technology—in its blatant and subtle forms—against the social fabric of the time of the technology's appearance to see what changes occurred.

[3]Again, see Chandler's *The Visible Hand* for an excellent analysis of how the geographic dispersion of the railway created a new type of managerial class as well as initiated a new set of problems.

[4]Katz, R. L., "The Skills of an Effective Administrator," *Harvard Business Review Classic* #74509, available from Harvard University Publishing.

Section 2

THE APPLICATION OF STANDARDIZATION

This section looks at how standardization can be used and applied. It covers diverse topics such as the nature of the standards participant (helpful traits), how the process is supposed to work, and how to establish a standardization activity. It provides a rationale for the creation of a standardization activity from the perspective of how the standardization activity fits into the strategy of the company, and concludes with an analysis of where I believe that the process is going, over time.

Chapter 9

Standardization Organizations

"No man is an island, entire to himself;
But each a part of the main."

—John Donne, *No Man is an Island*

INTRODUCTION

Standardization organizations create standards and specifications. This widely accepted statement embodies the folk wisdom about standardization organizations, their standards, and their specifications. While it is widely accepted, it is one of the IT industries most enduring urban myths; it represents the way that its proponents want things to be, not the way that they are. It is just much easier to believe that standards are created and given to the industry than to believe that a portion of the industry helped (or could have helped) in their creation. Mysterious benefactors (and malefactors) have always fascinated people.

A more correct statement would be that standardization organizations are enablers of standardization and provide a structure in which standards and specifications can be created to cause industry change. Indeed, in many cases, the best that they can hope to do is to provide a forum for the proper creation of standards and to allow the possible participants to meet one another. Of course, there is always some question about what constitutes "proper." The industry as a whole may appear to know where things are going, but each segment of the industry (providers, users, and "others") usually has its own opinion. The standardization organizations were created to meld these divergent points of view.

The melding of these divergent points of view was necessary for a very important reason. The IT industry was and continues to change, and providers were becoming aware of the need to interoperate in order to satisfy user needs. Chapters 5 and 6 described the rationale and details of these changes with regard to the intent and purposes of standard-ization. The changes, however, also had an impact on the organizational structure of the standardization organizations. This impact was driven by the need of the providers for dif-ferentiation, not standardization. The need for differentiation, was, in turn, driven by the need to be both "unique, yet the same" for business reasons.

Within the IT community, more than any other, standards are a business issue. The IT industry was a bellwether industry in making standards a part of the business process by stressing that standards should be a named product attribute in the design and build phases, and then in the procurement of product. While other industries used standards as part of their product cycle, it was only in the IT industry that standards were used as a product differentiator. As early as 1986, there was an undercurrent within the industry that was focused on basing standards on business considerations. The idea surfaced in the 1988 time-frame as a new form of rationale for participation in standardization activities.[1] The idea was picked up quickly by the IT industry, which was in the midst of a looming battle over "open systems" and what they meant. The concept quickly spread throughout the IT standardization players and then spread more widely in the literature of the day. By the late 1980s, the idea was reasonably well-known in the literature on the discipline of standardization.[2]

This chapter looks at Standards Developing Organizations (SDOs), consortia, and collaborative ventures (alliances, associations, and other strangly named things) as they relate to the creation of standards and common specifications with regard to an underlying business rationale. As far as possible, the examination will try to include a generalized overview of the activities of these groups, the methods that they use to create their output, the coordination mechanism, the normal players, and so on. Specifics are reserved for the chapters on organizations in Section 3 of the book, since the exact processes tend to change somewhat more rapidly than do the general set of activities that these groups must accomplish.

STANDARDS DEVELOPING ORGANIZATIONS

SDO Functions

Viewed simply, a formal Standards Developing Organization is usually seen as having two components. The largest of these two in an SDO is the volunteer committees, consist-ing of representatives of the discipline served (Information Technology, quality, tele-phony, earth moving), who meet on a regular basis and actually write the standards that are published under the auspices of the standards organization. The standards organiza-tions themselves are the keepers of the management process and the rules for the commit-tees. These committees (also called working groups and technical committees) have their own hierarchy, and each major committee may have subgroups reporting to it, some of which do the actual technical work assigned to the committee.

The second part of the standards group is the administrative section of the group. While constant acts of administration occur in each and every committee, subcommittee, working group, and technical committee (meeting management, draft mark-up, editing, and document creation), there is usually only one centralized, professional administrative function for an industry specific standards organization. This function usually falls under the purview of a group known as the secretariat (the term has remarkably consistent usage across all standards organizations) which acts as the nonvolunteer portion of the standards group and is charged with ensuring the survival of the entire standards effort for the organization. The term "survival" is used deliberately, since the failure of the secretariat to maintain records, to ensure procedures are followed, or any of a number of other myriad details could cause the certifying organization to pull certification. The ISO derived definition of a standard in Chapter 5 states:

> A technical specification or other document available to the public drawn up with the cooperation and consensus or general approval of all the parties affected by it, based upon the consolidated result of science, technology, and experience, aimed at the promotion of optimum community benefits and approved by a standardization body.

The Secretariat is charged with the details necessary to make sure that there is "consensus or general approval of all parties," that the outcome is "available to the public," and that the process and standard is "approval by a standardization body." This is no mean feat, especially when the volunteers usually outnumber the staff by a 150 to 1 ratio.

More specifically, the secretariat monitors the initiation of work by the subsidiary committees and sees that schedules are met, that the proper work is being done, that the rules of development are followed, that rules for representation on the committees are equitable, that no prejudice is shown to any class or group, that the various members have adequate and sufficient access to the decision process, and that consensus is reached within the bounds of the process. Some secretariats also are charged with publishing the standards that are created, insuring that the standards are available for a moderate fee to anyone who wants them, keeping track of the myriad standards that are published, and causing them to be updated on an as needed or regular basis (or causing them to be deleted). Finally, through liaison, some secretariats also keep track of what is happening in other standards organizations throughout the world, to ensure that there is a minimal duplication of effort.

If these were the only functions of standards organizations, it would be relatively simple to categorize them. Information technology standards organizations, telephony standards organizations, ferro-concrete standards organizations, and so on could be grouped into nice, neat, and discrete packages. However, life, people, and organizations being what they are, there are a multiplicity of standards organizations for each discipline.

For example, each major country has special requirements or expectations that mirror the needs of that country; whether these needs are rooted in the national ethic, the national economic welfare, or simply a desire to be different is immaterial. At times, the country will use a standards organization to justify the setting of these requirements. The classic case in regard to this was the blatant attempt by the Japanese to disregard the international standards for skis by insisting that Japan had "different snow." It was a case of absolute misuse of standards, and the Japanese backed down very quickly. The case, however, illustrates in a humorous fashion the fact that sometimes, there is no rhyme or reason for an action outside the needs of an organization, whether it is an individual, company, government, or nation.

The use of a standard as a method of national market control is contrary to the concept of voluntary consensus standards and falls into the category of regulation. If consensus standards are a true expression of market will and direction, the country that imposes artificial standards will find itself in one of two situations: Either it will force the market to change to its will (if it has economic importance to the market), or it increasingly will find itself isolated from the mainstream of products within the market and generally unable to share in the benefits that consensus standards provide, including technology transfer. In the long run, if it is true that standards are market driven, this situation will correct itself, and the inappropriate standards gradually will disappear as the market finds ways to circumvent them. In the short term, however, technical and economic disruption may occur, either in the industry or throughout the country.

When a country realizes that it does not have sufficient economic clout to force its concepts of standards on the market, it may choose to join a regional organization, which then has the interest of the region at heart. The same conditions apply to this group as did to the country group, except that there is now the power of the region behind the standards organization. If there is sufficient economic presence to force the market to accept the hoped for change, then the standards group succeeds. Unlike the country organization, a regional group must compromise some of its members' interests over the longer run to preserve the whole. The question is which country will sacrifice or at least modify national interests in order to insure the good of the larger group? The answer depends on where the national entity feels that it can find the greatest good, and goes back to the question of the common good and cooperative competition posed in Chapter 8.

Standards groups are not limited to country organizations, however. Although consensus standards groups are legitimized by their national organizations, many groups may sometimes represent the same discipline. This phenomenon occurs during the high growth phase of an industry's life, when the discipline is rapidly expanding and new knowledge is always being created. The creation of this new knowledge in turn causes continued expansion, which in turn causes the formation of new expert groups. As the expansion slows, the previously separate disciplines will continue to grow since growth is all that they know, and increased interaction (also known as "turf wars") may result. Ultimately, the groups will begin a process of consolidation, until they become very much like one another except for artificially assigned jurisdictional boundaries.

These boundaries continue to be valid only as long as they are accepted by the members of the various standards groups. If a group feels that its survival is at stake, it may attempt to expand its jurisdiction, either by taking on a new technology or by seizing an extant technology and giving it a new nomenclature and set of attributes that fall under its charter. On the other hand, an established group, already loaded with responsibilities, may consider a new technology a mere duplication of what already exists. If some other body is willing to take a new technology under its wing and nurture it, then this often results in the default creation of a new expert group. If the new technology succeeds, this new expert group becomes the authority and then begins to look for ways to expand its importance and power within the standardization arena. Eventually, of course, two previously separate groups may end up doing the same activity with different technologies. It is at this point where the potential for conflict and destructive behavior becomes high, since each group has proponents for its way of doing things and, one assumes, each group a certain amount of actual or potential market share.

In all cases, the function of the standards organization is to represent the particular needs of its users. Standards organizations are composed of individuals who participate because they believe that these organizations can use their collective economic power to change and influence the direction of the market which is something that they, as individuals, cannot do. This function of the standards organization has often been ignored, but it is central to understanding them. In some cases, the clients have a multiplicity of needs that the organization must fill, while in others, the groups focus sharply on a single need and market requirement, but all have a clientele to whom they provide an opportunity to express a collective voice. The success and longevity of the standards organization is in direct proportion to its ability to convince its members that it has the power and ability to move the market in a direction that the members feel is correct.

One recently occurring development in the high technology arena is the growing lack of differentiation between technologies and ultimately, the participants in the various differentiated organizations. IT is becoming very similar to telephony in some of its applications. The users of standards are identifying the base technology with the application technology, and this lack of discrimination on the part of the users (natural because of the change in the nature of standards) is beginning to complicate the life of standards organizations tremendously. The client bases are no longer discrete; as the systems standards become more prevalent, the interrelationships between standards organizations will become more complex, and the management of the secretariat, key to any standards organization, will become increasingly difficult.

SDO Administration

Henri Fayol, a French managerial theorist at the turn of the century, ascribed the functions of planning, controlling, organizing, coordinating, and commanding to administration.[3] I feel that this list, which I've ordered according to the importance of each function to the standards community, accurately describes the duties that the standards organizations administrative groups should attempt to fill; although many of them, unfortunately, do not succeed in doing so.

For Fayol, control was the aspect of administration that was concerned with ensuring that the other administrative functions were observed and carried out and that rules were followed. Because of the strict demands of the consensus approach to standards setting, distinct rules for ensuring consensus have evolved over time. Most secretariats of standards organizations are very good at making sure that these rules are followed. It is a time consuming and thankless job.

It is in this area that the administrators receive the most praise and condemnation. The rules, while important, often appear to be petty and pointless, more aimed at satisfying a bureaucratic requirement than at doing real standards work, yet they validate the entire process and assure that consensus standards are produced. At the same time, however, they should not be the ends in and of themselves. Their ultimate purpose is to produce, in a fair and timely manner, standards that meet market needs and requirements. If the rules inhibit this activity, then they, and their enforcement or interpretation by the administrators, have become counterproductive. There is a fine line between anarchy and totalitarianism in the standards world.

Of all of the administrative functions, planning is probably the most important and, at the same time, it is the most difficult. (Fayol's use of the term *prévoyance* for "planning" emphasized the forward looking and strategic nature of the planning function.) This difficulty derives from the nature of the administrative group; it cannot demand action from its members, since members are all volunteers, joined by a common belief in standards and the standards process. Moreover, the secretariat is nearly a pure staff organization; they have no line authority, except in the interpretation of the rules. Even here, they are always open to challenge by members of the committees as well as by senior national and international committees. As a result, the secretariats rely upon the members to accomplish the strategic planning function, which usually is delegated to a group that reviews and approves standards proposals. This group, because it is composed of members of the industry (producers, users, and general interest groups), is a bit more able to impose its will, but even so, all of its decisions are subject to an open and complete review at any time.

In any environment where there is no strong or congruent belief about the future, there is difficulty in planning. For standards organizations, not only are there disparate views about the future, but each member has an interest in guaranteeing that his or her view of the future is actualized. In many instances, the planning function of the secretariat consists of ensuring that the organization's perception of the future is broad enough to include the needs of all of the members while not penalizing the industry.

Organizing generally is part of the charter of the standards committee. Each committee organizes itself in a fashion that appears best to accomplish its perceived role and that mirrors the beliefs and desires of its members. While the senior standards organizations may provide general rules for membership, voting, and other functions, the independence of each committee in interpreting these rules is substantial.

There is a managerial concept that says that organizational form should mirror the strategy/belief of the organization. This concept is very important to standards committees that exist in a dynamic environment. If the organization or structure of such a committee is rigid and devoted to a singular end, the committee may become obsolete as the environment changes around it, since it will be tied into an organizational form ideal for activity that is no longer valid. The administrative function here is to ensure that the organizational aspects of the group are flexible and that there is a continuing inflow of members who can help the organization adapt to the changes in the environment. Again, the skill with which this administrative function is carried out is a major determinant in the success of the standards committee.

Coordinating is concerned with maintaining harmony in the organization and with keeping the organization moving toward its goals. It is not an unusual or especially difficult activity in a company or in most other enterprises. However, the secretariat must coordinate the activities of a group of volunteers who have separate agendas, concepts, needs, and goals. It also must coordinate the needs of the specific standards committee with the activities of other standards committees in different areas. Again, the problem lies in accomplishing this role of coordination without the actual or implicit power to do so. The personnel of the secretariat must keep everyone satisfied, or at least not too irritated, while pursuing a set of goals and objectives that reflect the wishes of the committee, which are also fuzzy. The role of the committee administrators is not so much to perform this function themselves as it is to encourage the members to do so. It requires patience, tact, and understanding, as well as a ruthless determination.

Finally, we come to the concept of command, best described as the leadership ability and quality. The other functions need to be actuated by the secretariat. Command is that intangible, unteachable ability to succeed in the management environment. It causes the other functions to be carried out. How well they are carried out is the utility derived from command. However, the metrics for predicting success are not clear; the definition of success is usually applied after the completion of an arduous task, or over the passage of time. If standards are produced that mirror what the industry wants and needs, if they are produced in a timely manner, if there is little contention in the organization, if there is a willingness to undertake new challenges, if . . . success is a judgmental call, and can be applied only in retrospect.

The burden of these five functions is tremendous, since the administration must manage them with little or no real power and authority but a great deal of responsibility. It is accountable to a host of people for all of its activities and operates in a spotlight. While a poor administration function will not paralyze the working groups or standards committees with any particular action, a good administration is essential to the continued success of the standards organization, since it provides continuity and serves as the organizational glue by keeping volunteers informed and interested and participating. Without this interest on the part of the volunteers, there are no consensus standards.

SDO Working Groups

The working groups (technical committees, task groups, subcommittees, and so forth) are composed of volunteers representing all facets of the affected industry. It includes providers, the users, government, academia, interested or involved groups, and individual experts. It is in the working groups that the industry reaches consensus, that technical details are debated and resolved, and that actual standards are created.

There are usually no requirements involved in being a part of the standards process, other than having an interest in the standard under consideration and a desire to participate in its development. Membership dues are imposed, but these dues are intended to pay the administrative costs of the committee, not to impose an economic barrier. They can be waived by the committee if they are legitimately onerous and prevent participation. In general, however, all expenses associated with standard creation, from the mailing costs (sometimes assumed by the working group chair or secretary) to the payment of dues, are the responsibility of each individual. Most organizations impose strict requirements for attendance at working group meetings. However, because the working groups meet relatively infrequently, attendance is one of the more observed points of etiquette. Each working group establishes its own administration (usually a chairperson, assistant chair, and secretary), decides its own meeting schedules and locations, and defines its own task within the charter that the standards committee has granted it, as well as within its area of expertise. Once this definition of intent is resolved, the group can put together its organization, set a proposed timetable, and begin its deliberations to complete the standard. To ensure fairness, there are fundamental rules intended to maintain equity in the structure.

A working group's deliberations should be relatively simple, since everyone is like-minded and working for the common good. Unfortunately, as I have pointed out before, the term "common good" not only is unclear at best, it is virtually meaningless in this context. When a working group begins its creative function, there is no guarantee as to what will emerge from the standards process: The common good is a complete unknown. It is the process of consensus which is the interaction among members, the compromises and confrontations, and the ability to reframe questions so that they admit of a common answer, that leads the successful standards working group to its goal.

When a standard is completed, accepted, and becomes implemented, a working group either can dissolve or it can press on and take on the next challenge in its area of expertise. Its membership can change from meeting to meeting, or it can remain stable with a constant membership. Everything depends on the nature of the beast, and the beast is protean.

CONSORTIA

Within the industry, the first goal of many companies is to create a *de facto* standard. The *de facto* standard promises a single implementation of a specification (which ensures interoperability) and spreads the acceptance and dissemination of the technology, leading to market dominance and the economic payback that this provides. There are several ways to do this. One of the most successful is to provide the industry with a technology that is needed and to put the technology in the public domain, or make it easily available. If the technology is really needed, it will be adopted by other providers and become the "de facto standard." The payback, of course, comes from the unique (usually proprietary) additions to the standard that this then permits the original provider to sell. The other method which is to create a product that embodies a technology that is successful in its own right and then dominate the market, is a little more difficult, but it still can be done. There have been many attempts to accomplish this and most of them have been highly unsuccessful. Of the ones that did succeed, however, the economic payback has been spectacular. The maintenance and growth of a *de facto* standard, however, is difficult and requires tremendous concentration on the dynamics of the market. Organizations that succeed with *de facto* standards over the long term are usually very competent marketing firms with a good technical capability.

If the players in an organization can't cause a *de facto* standard to emerge, the second drive is to get a standardized specification out faster than the SDOs could—hence the consortia. The idea that SDOs are slow springs from two roots. The first reason, of course, is the process which most standards organizations use to create standards which I refer to as the "multi-stage model." It is described in Chapter 11. The model is lengthy and is largely concerned with the starting of the process, since asking the right question is essential. However, because some of the rules necessary for openness and consensus are unwieldy, things tend not to move as fast as they might have in another form of organization. Additionally, SDOs tried to produce "anticipatory standards," or to design, in committee, future technologies. This was a guaranteed recipe for failure, since details could be argued for years and usually were. Both of these became part of the reason for consortia's rapid rise.

The larger more compelling reason, however, rests with the failure of the SDOs to convince anyone that they had done anything. Within the IT arena, SDOs are notoriously bad at marketing. The Secretariat's usually do not have a budget for it, and, even if they did, they would still have to get the marketing plan through the SDO itself.[4] A consortium, on the other hand, usually has a marketing group within the organization. Whether or not the consortia do the marketing is another question; however, they have (usually) the wherewithal to market their goods and products which is something that most SDOs forget to do.

The consortium is a collection of like-minded companies who are devoted to doing something using the same basic technology. They believe that, if they could get a common technology out, they could all compete using this common technology. The birth of this idea was not substantially different from that of an SDO except that the consortium was focused on (usually) a single instantiation of a technology and its application to a particular market problem. The benefit of the consortium over the SDO is not, as many suppose, in the laxity of its rules.[5] Rather, the benefit of the consortia is that all the players are like-minded, and that the quest for consensus does not take as long. In many cases, the technology that is under consideration by a consortium is based on the specification of one of the participants and the intent of the other consortium participants is not so much to "correct the specification" as it is to get a product based upon the specification out into the market where it could be sold.

Within the IT industry, consortia tend to be focused in the software industry, or within the software side of the hardware components. The reason for this is driven by the fact that the hardware business is usually more stable than the software business, and the stable environment allows the use of the more formal and structured environment of the SDOs. (A computer mouse is a mouse, and a keyboard is a keyboard.) Within the software industry, however, the intended use of an Application Portability Interface (API) is somewhat nebulous; the API may be used to control whatever the software writer can conceive and occasionally, what he or she cannot conceive. The application of the interface by the user is nondeterminant, in that there is absolutely no way that the designer can really know how the user will employ the software. (A spreadsheet is a spreadsheet, but the use that it will be put to, the demands made upon it, and the data that it will be asked to transmute are up to the user.) At the same time, the market at which the software standardizers is aiming is not the end user (who usually does not care about software APIs) but is rather the application developer, who writes the application programs that the end users buy. This introduction of a two tier demand systems for standardization is also im-

portant in considering consortia since a single consortium might be appealing to a very select class of software writers. This is allowed in the consortium rules, while an SDO does
not have this luxury.

The "two-tiered user" structure is important. The IT industry writes standards not
for the end user, but for an intermediate layer of application providers and manufacturers.
However, the attributes promised by the standards (commonality of information, the ability to intercommunicate) are what the end user (or the ultimate consumer) wants; the
mechanisms to achieve these goals are provided at the discretion of the intermediate layer
of providers. The IT industry, with its multiple layers of suppliers and differentiated users,
is no different from many other industries. The complicating factor is, however, that the
use and knowledge of IT is ubiquitous; at some point in time, nearly everyone has fancied
her or himself a programmer and has used a personal computer to solve a problem or to
lose information. Because of this ubiquity, the standards proposed for the industry to
drive itself are part of the active consciousness of the end users, who may not understand
them, but who do, at times, demand them.

It is because of this ability to target a specific need among like-minded entities that
consortia have their greatest appeal. The consortia can create specifications in isolation
from other standardization efforts without pressure, except from their sponsors, to include
other work items that may be deemed necessary by the larger market. While consortium
sponsors used to claim that consortia can act more quickly than SDOs, this is not the real
justification. What the consortium provides is a formalized structure (mimicking the
SDOs) to which organizations can send people to accomplish a set task within a defined
time frame. The key differentiators are **set task** and **defined time frame**.[6]

Within the SDO, there is no mechanism that mandates a schedule. All Task Forces
or Working Groups or Sub-Committees file an "expected calendar" when they begin, and
all routinely violate their schedules. While this may occur within a consortium, it is usually less likely. Since the players who participate know one another through common interests (or else they would not have paid the entrance fees to get in), the various management structures can be brought to bear on recalcitrant individuals or on recalcitrant
organizations to meet schedule and to meet consensus. While the same bickering that occurs in SDOs may occur in a consortium, there is almost always a quick end to the problem because the players have a vested interest in success at multiple levels in the corporation.

This situation must be contrasted with that of the SDO, where there is not the level
of commitment by the participants to create on time. There is no guarantee of the depth of
"common purpose"; rather, there is only a guarantee of "interested participants." The
SDOs, by opening their doors to everyone, guarantee that they will be somewhat ineffi-
cient. In trade for this inefficiency, however, they are supposed to produce a superior
product. Experience has proven that this is not the case. The marginal benefit of permitting anyone who has the desire to participate does not outweigh the benefit of schedule
and fixity of purpose.

Let me cite an example of this. In a recent meeting of a consortium that I chaired, I
managed to gather experts from six of the world's leading database companies for a discussion of a possible standard. I designed a process that we would use, received a quick

approval for the process, defined the technology, and then set to work. It took us approximately three months to come to a business based decision on inclusion of a technology. We conducted only one vote (the final one) and held two meetings. Had I had to reach the same decision within an SDO, I would have had to advertise the meetings to all interested parties, run the meetings with a process that was originally created for a different purpose, and then have made sure that all opinions were considered, and so on and so on. I believe that the final decision would have been the same. The difference is that, under the rules of the consortia, I was allowed to gather subject matter experts and come to an informed and final decision with them. The marginal benefits that would have accrued from having another constituency represented would not have substantially changed the decision of the group, nor made the technology better.

Another function that consortia have is the ability to create and run tests for implementations of their specifications. The ability to create test suites from the specifications and to enforce adherence to the specifications by anyone who wants to claim conformance is a powerful tool in the consortium's arsenal. Because many consortia have the contractual ability to compel their participants to use the consortium's specification in preference to another specification, the consortium specification can be adopted and implemented more quickly than an SDOs standard, which usually comes out lacking these features. This ability to add the test and conformance mechanisms to the specification provides an added level of user safety; since the guarantee of conformance to a specification (and specific redress if the conformance fails) is a powerful incentive to a manager who is seeking a guaranteed heterogeneous solution. Additionally, within the IT industry, this type of conformity guarantee is seen as the last step in solving the interoperability problem. The solution offered by many consortia is a "**complete solution**."

The idea of the complete solution is not as common in other industries as it is in the IT industries. The reason for the testing and verification of the implementation rests in the nature of the IT standards and specifications produced. In many cases, the specification or standard has options, and the implementation of these options is left to the discretion of the provider. In many cases, the options are mutually exclusive options such as "connection-based service" or "connectionless service." If one provider selects a series of options (labeled A) and another provider selects a series of options (labeled B), both may be conforming but not interoperable, destroying the fundamental rationale for standardization.[7] Conformance testing, to a specific profile, is the answer; however, test writing is an art, not a science, and the creation of tests is as expensive and time consuming as the creation of the standards themselves. Even worse, the two disciplines are different. Standards creation requires one type of technologist; test creation a technologist with an entirely different mindset. So, when consortia offer a specification and the tests to validate implementation, they provide a higher level of service and meet more requirements than do SDOs.

In conclusion, the fundamental rationale for consortia is not, as many people have assumed, a laxness of rules and a possible speed of creation. Rather, it is a common fixity of purpose, the ability to make and adhere to a schedule, and the delivery of a complete specification (from business rationale to testing and conformance guarantee). Basically, the consortium is seen as a full service organization which provides better return on invested resources than does an SDO.

ALLIANCES: THE RATIONALE

Consortia came into their own in the late 1980s, and, within the IT industry, there were several significant ventures. The Corporation for Open Systems (COS) was started by the providers of Open Systems Interconnect (OSI) standards and products to provide interoperability testing. This was followed by the Manufacturing Automation Protocol (MAP), driven by GM to create a profile for a Local Area Network. Technical Office Profile (TOP) was driven by Boeing to create an office profile. Other consortia began to spring up, driven by the promises of success that COS, MAP, and TOP were delivering.[8] These promises were followed by other promises, and by continuing growth in the consortia industry. At one time in the 1990s, consortia were appearing at the rate of two per month, with a major consortium (with fees of $50,000 or more per year) appearing once a quarter. However, the progress that many of the consortia made was not enough to satisfy many of the participants in the IT provider arena.

This lead to the most recent phenomena of alliances, which are seen as places in which vendors can collaborate on technology to provide a single interface specification that is used on multiple products. While alliances had existed before, the action that marketed the serious start of alliances was the creation of the Common Open Systems Environment (COSE), which was initiated in March of 1993. In the COSE announcement, the major systems firms in the UNIX arena announced that they would cooperate in the creation of a common desktop Graphical User Interface and a common UNIX-based operating system, as well as starting activity to bring other technical activities under the same roof. The Common Desktop Environment (CDE) and the Unified UNIX operating system that emerged from this alliance were given to the X/Open, Ltd. consortia to both manage and to create the necessary test suites. The birth of COSE marked the end of the UNIX wars and the start of the Alliance wars.

The rationale for the alliance is that it can create a core specification very quickly; the Unified UNIX specification was created very quickly (but was tied up in external legal wrangling for nearly a year). The alliance, not being a long-lived body, tends to seek a place to position its work and will nearly always select a consortium, since the members of an alliance tend to favor consortia. The bias of alliances towards consortia over the SDO lies in the consortium's ability to provide those things that make the specification useful, such as tests, branding, and marketing. If the consortium is successful in convincing a large part of the market to accept the work of the alliance and the consortium, then there is a final step called the Publicly Available Specification (PAS), in which a publicly available and implemented specification is given to an SDO for acceptance as a formal *de jure* standard. The PAS goes through some of the hurdles of a formal standard; it is subject to widespread review and comment, but not, as a matter of practice, subject to change.[9]

The alliance is a strange beast, however. Because it operates under somewhat unusual rules (decided at inception by the sponsors) there is very little that can be said in a general fashion about its shortcomings or successes. What can be said is that it represents the latest wave in IT standardization's attempt to make specifications happen more quickly and in a more cooperative fashion.

CONCLUSION

This chapter has tried to provide information about what a standards organization does, or is supposed to do, from an organizational perspective, and why there are at least three different models for these organizations. As with any generalizations, there are things that I have probably omitted that are of vital importance to some of the organizations (at least from their participants' point of view). However, most organizations function roughly as I have described them. The structure may vary (within certain constraints), but the essential task of each standardization group is to create something that is viable, both economically and technically, and acceptable to its constituents. While this last goal is often overlooked, it is also the reason that there are multiple ways to create a standardized specification or a standard. Each group represents the bias of its creators. However, this bias offers an advantage. The specification or standard, when created, will mirror the needs and desires of the industry segment that it serves and probably will not lead its clientele down a costly and potentially destructive proprietary dead end.

NOTES

[1]Cargill, Carl F. "A Modest Proposal for Business Based Standards," *Computer Standards Evolution: Impact and Imperatives. Computer Standards Conference Proceedings,* 1988. Washington, D.C.: IEEE, pp. 60–64.

[2]See, for example, Gabel, H. Landis (editor), *Product Standardization and Competitive Strategy,* North Holland, Amsterdam, 1987, Cargill, Carl F. *Information Technology Standardization: Theory, Process, and Organizations,* Digital Press: Bedford, MA 1989, and Toth, Robert (editor), *Handbook for Profits:* ANSI: New York, 1990. Gable's edition is a collection of pieces that has a heavy academic economic overtone, but nonetheless looks at standardization as an economic activity. Cargill's book is a combination of theory and experience in standardization in the Information Technology industry. Toth's edition (published by ANSI) is a collection of pieces that provide an overview of how standardization fits into a company and how it can be leveraged for profitability.

[3]Fayol, Henri (Trans, Constance Storrs). *General and Industrial Management,* Sir Issac Pitman's and Sons: London, 1946.

[4]There is a tinge of bitterness in this comment. When I worked for DEC and was the Vice Chair of X3's Strategic Planning Committee, I wrote a four page marketing brochure aimed at explaining the standards process to senior corporate management. I sent the document to the Secretariat and then lost track of the effort. *Five* years later the document emerged from the X3 hierarchy (the volunteers who made up the management committees) because it took that long to get "consensus" on what to tell companies about standards. While I will grant that my prose may have been difficult, it wasn't *that* bad.

[5]See Updegrove, Andy, "Consortia," *StandardView,* Volume 3, Number 3, September 1995, for an analysis from both a legal and procedural point of view about the rigor of a consortium in enforcing rules and process.

[6]An important distinction must be made here. A consortium is not necessarily a consortium. In an article in the September 1992 *Journal of the American Society for Information Science,* Martin Weiss and Carl Cargill argue, in a piece entitled "Consortia in the Standards Development Process," that there are three types of consortia. Of these three types (proof of concept, implementation, and application) the type that is being discussed is a hybrid "implementation" consortium. The three types correspond to the nature of the work being done. Proof of concept focuses on proving that a technical concept can be brought into existence. An implementation consortium focuses on creating a successful implementation from a known standard or specification, while the application consortium tends to focus on creating a specification to favor a specific group of companies. In the time since the article was published, application consortium have been largely overtaken by events, but some of their attributes—such as creation of specifications that serve the market—have been picked up by implementation consor-

tium, who are looking at creating a specification that is capable of being implemented and having proof that the implementation corresponds to the specification.

[7]Interoperability testing was not considered essential when the first major standardization efforts that required it began. It was not until the vendors had poured hundreds of millions of dollars of effort into Open Systems Interconnect (OSI) standardization that it became apparent that interoperability tests were needed. Since the late 1980s, nearly all IT standards have mandated that test points be inserted in standards to facilitate the completion of tests.

[8]In the larger scheme of things, and in relation to major currents in the IT industry, these three organizations delivered mainly hopes. Because they were user-driven technical consortia, they became detached from the mainstream of computing technology, which was driven by the providers. As Ken Olsen, the CEO of Digital, is once supposed to have remarked about GM's MAP effort, "Digital doesn't build cars; GM shouldn't build computers."

[9]The rationale for the unspoken rule restricting change to a Publicly Available Specification is very simple. If the PAS does represent the installed market base, a standard that was "sort of the same but different" would be largely useless, since the market would not change from current practice merely to be "standard." The rationale for the PAS is to bring specifications into standards, not to make the market change to embrace standards.

Chapter 10

The Internal Standardization Organization: Creation and Management

> "Myself when young did eagerly frequent
> Doctor and Saint, and heard great Argument,
> About it and about; but ever more
> Came out by the same Door as in I went."
>
> —Edward Fitzgerald, *Rubaiyat of Omar Khayyam*

INTRODUCTION

There are no hard and fast rules for creating a standards group and placing it in an organizational structure. Beside having all of the problems of a normal organization, the standards group is usually suspect because of its heavy external focus as an industry change agent. Furthermore, as with any market discipline, its actual contributions to a success are vague although its relations to a failure often are explicit. As a change agent, however, the standards group must work through other organizational groups and needs the willing help of the organization to succeed. What follows is an overview of issues that should be considered when attempting to establish a program that will allow an organization to participate successfully in an external consensus standards program.

INTERNAL PLACEMENT AND JUSTIFICATION

Why would a company, in the business of doing business, embrace standards? The arguments against the use of standards are, at times, overwhelming. If you have a truly unique solution, for example, why share it with your competitors who don't have your abilities?

There is the argument that standards decrease a company's ability to innovate and to meet changing market requirements and, at times, even prevent change by increasing market inertia. On the other hand, if you are a "fast follower," standards may serve to hinder your ability to get to the market quickly with a follower product that has some added value. Finally, many claim intelligent providers will offer solutions as the market demands them, regardless of whether standards exist or not.

Complicating the equation even further is the fact that standards are not an all or nothing approach. A company can use standards in some areas, and reject them totally in others. A company producing a brilliant proprietary solution may, and usually does, demand from its suppliers parts that meet some form of standard, whether of quality, performance, or size. The company will use standardized metrics to test itself against the market. It will make use of standard formulas to avoid being preyed upon illegally by competitors. If it produces parts that have electrical components, it will meet certain test-house standards that ensure the safety of its products, and will rely upon the national electrical codes to see to it that its appliances are provided with adequate and correct power. The list can be continued to the point of distraction; the point is that all firms impose, and expect to have available, certain standards.

A more appropriate question then is: Which standards does a company/association/ firm choose to uphold and which does it wish to avoid, and how are these decisions made? Logically, it is safe to assume that a firm will support standards that help it and will ignore or refuse to support standards that are irrelevant or inimical to its interests. This does not answer the question, however, it merely casts it in a different way. The answer, I believe, lies in the firm's perception of itself and the market in which it is involved.

A firm can be described as risk neutral, risk adverse, or risk seeking. Further, each aspect of the firm has its own risk-acceptance or risk-avoidance characteristics. The more a firm is risk adverse, the greater will be its reliance on regulations and standards as a possible hedge against risk and potential failure. A firm that is risk neutral will tend to view standards dispassionately, using them when and as necessary. Risk taking firms will tend not to use standards, seeing them as limiting factors in their pursuit of business. Some firms are willing to accept a different risk by attempting to grow and then lead the market with a standardized product.

An organization can be seen as a collection of individuals and as a reflection of their ideas and activities. This seems to indicate that the definition has come full circle; individuals who believe in standards will use standards, while individuals who do not believe in standards will not use standards.

As Max Weber was searching for a reason for why "rational capitalism" was a distinctly Western phenomena, he came to the conclusion that one of the primary reasons for the phenomena was the rational structure of law and administration. Without this rational structure, Weber reasoned, it was impossible to predict, with any degree of certainty, the returns that were available to the investor capitalist. Without these calculations, there was no incentive to engage in a rational capitalism.

Additionally, Weber points out that Western capitalism is strongly influenced by technology; for that matter, it is technology driven. The development of the technology did not necessarily occur in the West (witness the borrowing of algebra, the decimal, and various and sundry other technology). What did occur in the West was the application of these technologies as solutions to problems that appear, at first, unrelated to the solution.

Weber's comments on capitalism provide insight into why standards, especially voluntary consensus standards, function as well as they do. The earlier definition of standards has as a basic tenet the belief in the essential rationality of the market. The use of standards adds a degree of rationality to the market and provides another of the rational incentives for investment in a market. Standards can permit some quantification of the market prior to actually engaging the market; that is, standards can give a perspective on the market which, when joined with other indicators, can provide a method of anticipating and measuring the market. This added rationality may take several forms, serving to indicate a common acceptable path, indicating an absolutely unique and therefore extremely valuable solution, or acting as a test/proving ground for a product concept. It is another tool for a rational manager to use.

When a firm claims to reject standards, it is in fact rejecting the use of standards in its marketing process. "We don't use standards," really means, "We choose not to produce products according to what conventional market wisdom states that the market presently needs and will demand." This choice is usually predicated upon a firm's belief that it can provide a solution superior to that which the "market" has endorsed. While this approach may be justified, with the advent of standards that describe systems of products and services, changing the market with a proprietary solution is less and less viable, unless the solution is a quantum improvement over competing alternatives.

HOW TO START A PROGRAM

Too often, the standards program is initiated without regard to the consequences of this activity on both the standards participants and the organization with its multiple interdependencies, yet planning and thinking of the long-term rationale and interplay that the group responsible for the program must have, constitutes a challenge that should never be avoided. It is easy to decide to whom and where a group should report; determining what will be done with the ideas that such a group exports (or imports) is a far more difficult task.

Once the rationale for the existence of a program is established and the responsibilities of the standards group have been considered, it is necessary to place the group in the organization. I would recommend placing the standardization function in a department that meets two basic criteria: It is sure enough of itself not to need the function but is capable of using the function to effect positive change on the larger organization. Standards are only guides, and any organization must know how to use them if they are to serve any purpose. Because there are so many standards (and so many standards developing organizations), a department that does not have a strong internal belief system and ability to make its own decisions will tend to be driven by standards rather than drive and use them. Such strength will also allow the department to accept and implement external ideas without feeling that its own competence is being threatened. (Both self-assurance and self-awareness are necessary, but, if a choice must be made, I believe that self-assurance is the more important of the two. Self-awareness can follow from self-assurance; the reverse is not usually true.) Of course, if the standardization function is placed in a self-assured, self-aware, but essentially powerless department, the impact of standards on the organization will be substantially diminished. The department that owns the function of standardization must be able to influence the business planning of the organization, since standards are ultimately an economic activity. Within the IT industry, the standards function is most commonly placed in the engineering or the marketing activities, depending upon which function has the role of driving the organization's response to the external environment.

The next problem will be one of deciding how to staff the standards group. Again, this is not a trivial task. The type of standards representative will depend upon the rationale for the creation of the group. If the standards group is supposed to exert a major influence on the activities of the organization, then it should be composed of individuals who are viewed by the organization as having the necessary understanding and competence to effect that change. For example, if the locus of power in a company is the engineering, and standards will be used to impact the engineering cycle, then the engineers must be able to respect the standards delegates. The standards representatives must also have a talent for dealing with people, as well as being competent in their technical discipline, since they will be required to sell the goodness of the standards inward and the goodness of their organization outward. Finally, will the standardization group consist of a few professional standards people, who will matrix manage a large organization of standards volunteers, will it consist of a large centralized staff that alone has responsibility for standardization within the parent organization, or will it fall somewhere between these two extremes?

Deciding on the structure of the standardization group also can be interesting. If there is an accepted model for the group within the larger organization, there is no problem. If no such model exists, two factors will largely decide what the group's structure will be: the type and nature of the people involved and the type and nature of the function that the group is expected to accomplish. If the group contains brilliant iconoclasts, no structure will serve well or long, especially one that is highly centralized. However, if the standardization group is expected to impose its activities on the larger organization, a highly centralized organization probably would be most efficient. While I tend to believe that form follows function, in this case, it must accommodate the idiosyncrasies of the people involved and the role that these people have in the larger organization. Finally, the interfaces that the group must have should be specified. Knowing when and with whom to talk is a key ingredient in consensus standards.

While a manager who has time and discretion may be able to take advantage of these guidelines, what happens to the ordinary manager who suddenly is confronted with the need to participate in consensus standards activity? The usual approach is to graft the external group onto the internal group. Economical in terms of time, complexity, and people, it seems like an easy solution to a complex problem. In fact, it is usually completely disastrous, since the two types of standards have only their name in common. Where the internal group tends toward enforcement and regulation, the external standards group must favor conciliation and consensus. One is charged with immediacy, the other with planning. The two groups have fundamentally different philosophies and operating constraints. If the two are merged, they should be separated by some nearly impermeable membrane that will allow the flow of ideas but not of restrictions and problems. The operation will only work under the supervision of a reasonably competent manager and subordinates, who realize all of the complexities.

HOW THE PROGRAM SHOULD FUNCTION

To begin, the larger organization must decide the nature of its involvement in external standards. While the standards developing organizations (SDOs) encourage participation and minimize the cost to the delegates in their fee structure, the requisite travel and participation are expensive. Meetings vary in length and location, from one day planning meetings in Washington D.C. to three week Plenaries in Sydney. Each delegate is responsible for paying her or his own way. Each organization must decide where and to what extent it wishes to participate. If an organization has an outstanding interest in a single field it may choose to participate only on those committees directly related to that interest. It may escalate its involvement and become active either vertically (in the parent committee) or horizontally (in more standards-committees). It may decide to become involved in the administrative arenas (nearly all of the administrative committees have open membership) or perhaps in the national organization. The depth and level of participation will depend on what the parent organization sees as the payback of the standards group and how far it can support the group's activities.

The effectiveness of a standards delegate derives in some extent from the credibility of the sponsoring organization. If a delegate represents an organization which has always denigrated standards, the delegate will have a more difficult time than would someone representing an organization that has encouraged standards. Additionally, the sins of the parent are visited upon the children; that is, a delegate from a suspect organization will likely be credited with the same aspirations as the parent. Vacillation in participation can be seen as a lack of commitment, which can lead to disaster, since the level of respect and the concomitant influence that a delegate can expect in the committee will be based in large part on her or his competence and commitment. If the delegate's commitment is deemed lacking by association, the value of participation will decline.

This type of perceptual bias is never static because the participants are engaged in a dynamic business, where alliances change with business and political considerations. Politics, whether positive, neutral, or negative, are never far from the surface. While the individual delegates are primarily responsible for these undercurrents, the company, the committee, the committee chair, the national body, or any of a dozen other influences can combine to create the political atmosphere in which both the committee and the delegate operate.

Once the producer understands the structure of the committees and the implications of their work, the problem arises of how to participate. There is the "observer" participant, in which the participant observes and reports to the company. (The use that the company will make of the report, ranging from filing it away to using it as the basis for the next product or system design, should have been decided at an earlier time.) There is the "participating" participant, who takes an active role in the proceedings, shares knowledge, and supports or opposes particular developments. And then there is the "contributing" participant, who advocates a solution or technology which has been contributed by their sponsoring organization, or who badly wants a particular technology to be accepted to permit expansion of influence. All of these particular observations apply to users as well; producers have no lock on the advocacy role in standards organizations.

Once the delegate understands what the goal of the sponsoring organization is and how the committee helps or hinders that goal, the delegate begins to function as part of the committee and part of the standards process. The enabling process becomes important here. If participation is critical to the survival of the sponsoring organization (in either a positive or negative sense), then the delegate must have the complete support of the sponsoring organization. If a delegate does not know where compromise is possible and where it is impractical, then she or he is already crippled, and participation can turn into a fiasco. Also, if a delegate does not understand the consensus standards process, or the parliamentary procedure of the process, then the potential for success becomes even less likely. Another benefit of enabling the delegate is that he or she can funnel quantities of information back into the sponsoring organization: competitive information (the positions that other organizations took), technical information (the industry seems to believe that this is the correct technical way to proceed); marketing information (the committee, composed of industry representatives, believes that this will occur in x years). In other words, the standards delegate can provide much more technical information and positions if she or he knows that the organization wants or needs it. Conversely, if there is no clear enabling mechanism, or if the standards process is not understood clearly, then the delegate will not be able to contribute nearly as much.

Obviously, enabling the delegate within the sponsoring organization is critical. Because the delegates to standards meetings are all volunteers, there is no formal structure to ensure that the committee work will proceed in any particular fashion. If the delegates know why they are attending, and each hopes to gain a benefit for the sponsor, there is some motivation to move the process along. If the delegate is not sure of the sponsor's reasons for participation, the motivation becomes questionable and the direction fuzzy; moreover, the delegate may unknowingly approve of a committee action counter to the sponsor's interests.

HOW TO FUND THE PROGRAM

Funding should be tied to the concept of return. A modified zero base budgeting concept can be applied. What would happen if an organization chose not to participate in the standards process? In many cases, nothing would happen. Most IT companies are well-served by standards and adhere to them when they need to or must. Lack of active participation is acceptable if a company does not need standards (because it produces a unique nonstandard product) or if it is a follower in a standardized area. Lack of participation, however, means that an organization cannot impact the process and must, therefore, follow it willy-nilly.

When an organization begins to participate, each time it increases that involvement, each step should be analyzed in terms of what the organization will gain from this participation and from the position of what would it lose if it did not participate? At times, participation may only confirm a worst suspicion, but such confirmation can be valuable. On the other hand, if there is no participation, the organization may miss a potential opportunity to influence a standard to make the market served by the standard more friendly. This analysis is difficult. Lost opportunity cost is highly subjective, especially in standards, where the outcome is never certain. (Participation in the national administrative committees and organizations is the most difficult to justify. The national organization is supposed to serve the interests of the industry as a whole; the organization must feel convinced that the national programs and the entire standardization effort are necessary to the future of the industry to commit to this level of activity.) In many cases, a manager can make the analysis and then justify the choice only after the fact. However, the rationale and evaluation are important, since they provide the metric by which the success of the standards group can be judged and future actions taken.

One of the chief characteristics of standards in commercial industry is that they can be seen as an enabling activity by an organization about to undertake something. In the past, producers often overlooked this function of standards, either from lack of knowledge or lack of need, while users ignored it because they preferred to deal directly with the producers, rather than the industry as a whole. Now, more and more, providers recognize how standards enable an enterprise to begin forming part of the functional (market) plan (a proactive process used to permit a product to come into being). The users see standards as a prerequisite at times and consider them to be an incremental, but positive, activity. By contrast, the governmental use of standards seems to be more devoted to cost constraint or cost lessening. Lack of standards, in a governmental environment, is a disabling activity.

In the end, however, money must come from somewhere to do something. The something that standards do is dependent on the organization's structure and belief in the role that it wants to play. The somewhere that the money comes from, however, should depend on one major consideration: Who benefits from the activity of the standards group? If marketing is receiving all of the benefit but engineering is footing the bill, standards is highly unlikely to survive a budget crunch. While requiring those that benefit to pay seems obvious, it is not a one time exercise; it is advisable, every now and then, to check who is helping to pay the bill and whether they are getting results equal to or greater than the amount that they are contributing.

STANDARDS AS A DISCIPLINE

Considering the practice of standards as a discipline in its own right will be difficult for many people who think of standards as an extension of regulations, where the main responsibility of the participant is to understand the technology of her/his industry well enough to be able to explain it to people who are considering regulating it and to elucidate why things are done the way that they were without using the phrase, "We've always done it that way." This point of view is common among participants in today's standards activities within the information technology industry in which the criteria for participation often seems to be limited to extreme technical competence and ability to be a persuasive advocate for their particular technical solution.

Certainly, standards is a very technical discipline that requires a great expertise in the area under consideration. Because the use of standards seems to be concentrated in disciplines that are more technically driven (that is, more capable of being described in precise metrics with established interrelations), there will continue to be a demand for highly competent technical people to formulate and write the standards. The emphasis will change slightly from a product to a systems orientation, and the technical expertise demanded may be used to describe future systems instead of present products. But the necessary talent will continue to be the ability to translate abstract technologies into written descriptions that are applicable and useful in a technical and business arena.

CONCLUSION

With this need firmly established, a new participant in the form of the "technical engineering/business manager" will slowly be brought into the standards arena. This somewhat awkward title reflects the bundle of attributes with which the participant must be endowed. In effect, the person must understand both the technical and business needs of the particular company or group represented, the purpose of the proposed standard and its relations to other existing and proposed standards, the methodology of the consensus standards process, and the needs of the standards committee. The manager must possess the ability to plan and coordinate all of these simultaneously and to reframe problems and to unruffle feathers, as needed. The term "business," as it is used here, refers to all of business, not merely the financial aspects. This concept, in which the organization rather than the balance sheet is central, is essential to standardization and the activities of the standardization process.

These technical engineering/business managers, representing the best that the industry has to offer, will become the actual managers of the standards process within the standards communities, serving primarily to practice what I refer to as "intersectional management." Intersectional managers do not manage in the traditional sense of the word. They manage the potential areas of conflict (the intersections between the various competing individuals, factions, groups, segments, and theories) to ensure that conflict does not occur or that, if it does, its impact on the process is minimal. In addition, they must manage the various groups that will move them toward and finally achieve a goal. Finally, the goal itself must be managed, since it may change with changes in the environment.

The intersectional manager is vitally necessary to the long-term success of the consensus standards effort. But one of the prerequisites for this style of management is competence on the part of the members of the committees. Such competence is assured only if the industry, or the significant players, are committed and convinced that the consensus standards process is valuable. Without this understanding, commitment, and belief, the process and the discipline of standardization will fail.

Chapter 11

Topics and Methods
of Standardization

"A little learning is a dang'rous thing;
Drink deep, or taste not the Pierian spring"

—Alexander Pope, *Essay on Criticism*

INTRODUCTION

This chapter looks at the discipline of standardization in terms of practical internal and external standardization activities and attempts to draw some generalized rules about what and how to pursue standardization activities. There is a bias in this chapter. Because the book focuses largely on the IT arena, there is a focus on the activities of the high technology, highly fluid organization, confronted with a dynamic and constantly accelerating change in both the creation and application of its products. While I do not believe that the bias changes some of the fundamental principles, I do believe that there is a possibility that some of the examples and principles might be a little skewed in favor of this environment.

INTERNAL STANDARDIZATION

Internal standardization, that is, standardization within an organization, is usually the creation of a process, based upon either a new or an existing practice, to enhance the use of company resources. It is increasingly complex, increasingly difficult, and increasingly overlooked as a method of ensuring not only survival but also success in the current business environment. An internal standards program is one of the more difficult corporate functions to manage and make effective. In any company, numerous things can be standardized, from paperwork routines through personnel policies to design processes. Standardizing a process in these areas requires an understanding of the company, its management, its operating structures and strictures, and its culture. It must be done without compromising innovation yet must be implemented completely enough for it to offer substantial benefit. The standardization strategist, the standards creator, the implementing group, and the standardization management must be competent in both the processes being standardized as well as the process of standardization to maintain credibility within the organization.

Ultimately, the decision for or against standardization must be measured in the amount of resources that are required to provide a solution to a specific problem. Indeed, an internal standard can be viewed as an attempt to describe a method of using a scarce resource (usually labor, sometimes capital, now more increasingly, intellectual property) in such a way that it is utilized more effectively in pursuit of the goals of the organization. Obviously, the perfect standard would allow resources to be used in the most effective fashion possible, but the determination of what constitutes the ideal depends on how an organization views its resources. If a company prides itself on engineering, and skilled engineering labor is limited, then engineering may receive the brunt of attention. Similarly, a company that stresses its manufacturing expertise may use standards to strengthen its manufacturing processes. But if a standardized solution favors a particular resource at the expense of other, scarcer resources, its economic value is doubtful.[1]

Why and how would or should an organization standardize its internal procedures? The answer will depend largely upon the nature and value of the return from the standardization program. The nature and benefit of this return, however, can only be judged from the base of an organizational culture at a particular place and point in time. Because standards span an organization, from engineering design, to marketing (and sales), to manufacturing, and finally to field service, the application, as well as the method of application, varies and derives from varying culturally based moral precepts. Application of a standard in one company may spell success. Application of the same standard in another company may spell disaster.

The major initial effort in a campaign for internal standardization must be to establish which internal competency or internal resource is perceived as the most valuable by the company and then to determine if this resource is also the most scarce. This effort alone may produce a series of surprises for the organization; the resource perceived as the most valuable may not be the one which is the most critical or most necessary to the organization. If it is not, some form of education, at the least, will be necessary to concentrate the standardization effort in the area that will produce the most benefit. Furthermore, there is the need to factor in organizational behavior. At times, the imposition of a standardized methodology may be completely counterproductive or, if it is chosen and attempted, may turn out to be impossible. Some areas in an organization admit of standardization easily, because it is "intuitively obvious" that standardization would help. However, there are the times when intuition fails, and attempting to standardize the "intuitively obvious" candidate will either consume tremendous resources or will produce a great deal of noise but little result. One of the things that standardization attempts should be aware of is that standardization can produce some extremely irrational behavior on the part of the standardizing or standardized group. Merely because it is "correct" does not, in many cases, mean that it is "right."

Once the decision to standardize is made, another question arises on the nature of the enabling power for the standards program within the organization. Without this enabling function, and the legitimization it brings, the entire standards effort is probably condemned to either quick failure, or, more painfully, a lingering death. A standards group should begin by determining what its purpose will be. While this necessity is so obvious as to be axiomatic, it is a neglected by many internal standards groups. If the standards group exists to codify repetitious and simple procedures, its focus and staffing needs will be different from those of a group attempting to standardize an esoteric technology so that it needs to be created only once. If the group's purpose is to free a scarce resource so that it can be used for more important things, this should be stated. If the group is going to standardize other aspects of the company to make the scarce resource more available, this, too, should be indicated.[2] In effect, the group must identify how it plans to operate, what its area of expertise is, and who its clients are, and then should create a charter that can be used to inform interested or impacted (or both) groups, within and without the organization, of its intentions.

A major consideration in the creation of an internal group or effort is that standardization usually will cross organizational or suborganizational lines and will, on occasion, have as much impact on an ancillary organization as it does on the target organization. If a process undergoing standardization in manufacturing requires input from accounting, the two departments may have different goals for both the process and the information that makes up the organization.[3] To be effective, the standardization group must recognize the potential conflict and find a way to mediate between disparate needs and requirements of the various groups. This must be accomplished. The failure to act as the impartial mediator will lead only to the eventual erosion of the moral authority of the standardization function. Since standardization groups fundamentally operate in the area of moral suasion, the loss of this moral highground can be dangerous. Going back to Chapter 7, if standards are viewed as a change agent, then the change agent becomes the standardization group, which must be viewed in a positive light. So, it is usually necessary to help create the underlying rationale, structure, and activities that support the process, as well as the standardized activity that the standardization group is attempting to accomplish. If the group creates a standard without this agreement, it will sabotage is own efforts since the impacted groups may be forced to expend their resources, which are already in demand, to repair the damage caused by the misguided standard.

With the decision to move forward on standardization made and the charter of the group established, the next step is to determine where the program should begin. Most standards departments are born of a company's need to ensure that its products are free of legal liabilities; that is, they won't kill, maim, or injure someone, or, in service companies, they will not create/delete user systems and information. Meeting this aim may not determine where standards will help the most and which resource is most valuable, but it serves the very pragmatic purpose of protecting the survival of the company against liability lawsuits. In some instances, the legal department (or "Department of Suing") can be seen as a standardization group, since they are usually one of the lines of defense in this area.

Ensuring that internal mechanisms conform to external expectations is probably as far as most companies go when they first institute a deliberate standards program. Other standards are added on an as needed, as written, or as desired basis, usually very haphazardly. Because the planning range of many companies is so short (usually less than three years), internal standardization is usually an afterthought in the product development process. It is invoked only after the market requirements are listed, the product has been specified, and the design engineering cycle has begun. Yet, when standards are used in this way, it is usually too late to effectively use the benefits that standardization can provide. If a company, in completing a product design, has ignored a market need/requirement, the product may not sell well. Retrofitting it normally requires a great deal of effort, as well as causing a great amount of frustration, and is sometimes highly ineffective, since the product may have missed its window of opportunity in the market while it was being improved (fixed). Likewise, any need (internal or external) expressed by a standard should be stated explicitly prior to any major commitment. The phrase, "Do it right the first time," while trite, is very valid for standards.

A standard is a planning tool, meant for use during conceptualization, and to help eliminate the need for someone to re-do, or to correct, or for some resource to be expended in a reconstruction, rather than in creation. Unfortunately, there is no handy guide to indicate when internal standards should be invoked; too early, and creativity is stifled; too late, and the product/process loses the benefit that caused the standards to be created in the first place. Deciding what to standardize is equally troublesome, because it can lead to acrimonious debates between the proponents and opponents of standardization. The dispute is over the border between legitimate innovation and frivolous re-invention. Take the wheel, for example, since it usually completes the cliché. Standardization proponents would argue that the correct implementation of a standards program would allow the creation of better chassis but would keep the design of the wheel the same. Opponents of standardization would argue that if this were the case, wheels would still be constructed of stone, which would limit the remainder of the design. This problem is not resolved by choosing sides, but by determining the purpose of the standardization program. In this illustration, the program should not altogether disallow the improvement of the wheel; however, it should be focused upon the concept of the wheel as the primary form of transportation. It should disallow the creation of legs, but encourage the development of pneumatic rolling devices. It is a matter of asking the correct question which is one of the most challenging of all activities in business, not because of insoluble problems, but because of the difficulties of definition and understanding.

If decisions had to be made about only one standard, one product, or one person, they would be reasonably easy. However, usually quite a few standards will be invoked at once; in some cases, they are contradictory or their use may imperil other goals such as profitability. The most dangerous plan that a company can follow is to blindly set a course and to move on that path, modeling a program after someone else's successes. In the end, the internal standards program must suit the corporate strategic plan. A standards program must be directed by an understanding of what the corporation's strategic direction is, rather than by tactical considerations.

If an organization decides that it needs a standard, it must remember that even blessed and sanctioned internal standards have limitations. Frank Feigin, a senior standards engineer at Digital Equipment Corporation, expressed it best when, in a fit of outrage, he informed an engineering group that, "... no matter how well a standard was written, it could not contravene the basic laws of physics."

The next question for the organization is "how to standardize." There appear to be three distinct methods by which a company can bring about internal standardization. Usually, a firm will pursue variants of all three, depending upon the company, program, time, and any of a host of other variables.

The first method is to use a regulatory style, which assumes that a standard can be written explicitly and definitively, and the use of which will usually will be mandatory. The regulatory style is most suited to a mature, evolved industry, or at least to the portion of such an industry that is least susceptible to change. For matters that are based upon externally imposed regulations or mandated by the nature of the business (for example, product safety or something similar to nuclear regulatory activity), the regulatory style is ideal. Additionally, this style may also be found in low-tolerance manufacturing processes, where definite processes and procedures are required to ensure that a product is produced that meets the design needs and goals.[4] As with any rule-based systems, this approach is only as strong as the imagination of the original rule writers. Rapid change will obsolete rules and cause the group to spend all of its time writing new rules, which in turn will become obsolete quickly. Finally, it is necessary to ensure that the use of this approach does not quell helpful innovation.

Standards imposed by a regulatory style have a nasty habit of turning into substitutes for planning. With the arrival of regulation, and the necessary enforcement of these standards, this style of internal standardization can easily cause the standard to become an end in itself. This leads to it becoming a "silly rule" type of standard; that is, one that is enforced long after the rationale or the justification for it is remembered. As people forget why it was imposed in the first place (because the situation that caused it was transient or because the standard really succeeded in eliminating a problem), people begin to devote as much energy to getting around it as to following it, especially if the standards program has managed to eliminate its "group memory," which remembers why things are/were done a certain way. This eventually will require an organizational police force; the full-time attention of an enforcer. Since the primary goal of standards is supposed to save resources, this method appears to be self-defeating. After all, bucking the standard should be allowed if it allows the organization to use resources more effectively. (The purpose, again, is not standards for standards sake, but standards because there is a reason that makes money.) However, the regulatory style sometimes is pursued with single-minded and tremendous vigor, since it seems safe. It also panders to a fundamental desire of bureaucracies to fall back on rules rather than having to make an independent or unusual decision.

The second style can be described as laissez faire, or the absence of a program that has meaning. In effect, it allows the developer to ignore or to omit the use of standards.

There is a major difference between an existing standards program that is not utilized and a standards program that merely does not exist. Where there is no standards program, there is the possibility of developing a meaningful one. Where a standards program exists and is ignored, the program has no meaning and little chance of acquiring any. This situation, closely related to anarchy, can serve a viable function in an environment of reasonably narrow, noninterrelated product lines. The lack of standardization where and when necessary, especially if some people use it and some do not, can have a dramatic impact on the functioning in an organization, since the absence of expected commonality causes the users to both expend resources in training and to curse while doing so. It is, for a standardization program, one of the worst of all possible worlds, since, at best, it consumes resources and accomplishes little, while at worst is counterproductive and expensive.

The final style combines aspects of both the regulatory and laissez faire methods. It is probably the most difficult to exercise, since it requires that every potential standard be evaluated for return and impact on the company and customers. If standardizing a particular process, product, or activity is critical to the company's survival, the decision must be made to standardize and then to enforce that standard. If a standard is not especially necessary, then the decision must be made to ensure nonstandardization. Difficulties arise, of course, when there is a need for standardization and an equal need for innovation and speed. In these cases, standardization becomes very complex. Ultimately, however, management must make the decision actively, since default decisions have a way of setting unfortunate precedents that return to haunt the defaulter or the defaulter's successor. It is on these rare occasions that the standards management of a company proves its worth.

Looking at the three types, it is clear that each has a place in an organization. The decision on which to use and when to use it will depend in large measure on the organization itself.

The nature of the organization, especially in the high technology arena, can run the gamut from laissez faire to tyrannical. In his book, *Strategies for Cultural Change,*[5] Paul Bate identified a characteristic that he calls "strong culture companies," which exert control based not upon externalities to the company, but rather because there is an implicit control system based upon internalized meanings and values. The "strong culture" approach, which is found in many high technology organizations, appears to be the ideal type of organization for implementing internal standards, but only if the management is convinced that standardization has value. If management (which ultimately determines the nature of the culture as a control tool) decides that standardization is not valuable, then no amount of rational arguments or pleading can help. The danger here is that the management will become so enamored of its beliefs that it will neglect the externalitites that impact, or should impact, its decisions.

A company can gain the most by standardizing on products, processes, and methods that require a great deal of expertise to create (such as an internal bus scheme or complex software, a manufacturing process, or a quality program) and which provide the basis of differentiation or unfair advantage in the external market. The company should focus on its strengths and reinforce them through the use of standardization. The decision to proceed in this effort is the domain of the company management, since in many cases, the "things" that are possible candidates for standardization are the core competencies of an organization. These decisions, however, always seem to be left either to chance or to a lower level of management, where this type of decision does not really belong. One can argue that this lack of knowledge is the fault of the senior management; however, if they are unaware of the nature or import of their decision, then I would argue that the standardization staff is also guilty for not making the import of the decisions clear. Wherever the decision is made, however, the successful standardization of any of these organizational competencies is hard enough without the initial decision having been made either by default or in error.

Rather than take on the challenge of standardizing in complex areas, people often turn to things that should not be standardized at all (usually those processes that are the easiest to quantify and adapt so well to the quantifiable processes of standardization). Typically, these are ancillary processes that serve to enhance products, development processes that require maximal flexibility and responses, or any process that can adjust to deal with an uncontrollable external or environmental influence. These processes are poor cases for standardization since by their very nature, they are either exception cases to a larger process or "one-time-special good deals."

It is equally dangerous for a manager to seek a proven solution to a difficult problem, instead of attempting to determine the problem's real nature. Often, a standardized solution will be seized upon, based on historical precedence and safety or because it once worked in the past: Innovation and thinking are displaced by the safe rule-based answer. Reliance upon standardization to solve difficult problems, not the presence of standardized specifications and standards, stifles innovation and creativity. Correctly written, standards are applicable to many situations; they are not, however, a panacea. Blind adherence to standards, or the substitution of standards for the real understanding and solution of a problem, is the most serious blunder that an internal standards group can commit. In fact, it can be fatal to a company if it becomes endemic and prevents the adoption of new procedures or technology essential to survival. Obviously, the final responsibility for guarding against this type of error is management's, for it is management that sanctions the actions of the standards group in the first place. Again, this is where management, knowledgeable of the capabilities and problems of standardization, is critical.

This is also the place where internal standards management should or must be made responsible for proposing valid areas for standardization to senior corporate or organization management. Each specification or proposed standard should be examined from the point of view of its impact on the organization across the broad front. If a single standard acts as a gate to a host of other activities or areas of expertise, or serves as the common thread, it had better be a very good and carefully crafted standard. Unfortunately, it usually isn't.

Another error crops up when a standards group attempts to standardize two similar but competing processes. It is easy, especially in any high change, high technology area, to lose sight of where all the processes that need to be standardized are headed. Occasionally, apparently competing processes are intended to achieve the same goal. This sets the stage for some internal bickering and forces the standards department to retract one or both of the standards. This can be very embarrassing and occasionally fatal to the organization's reputation, if not the organization's standardization management. A variation of the theme involves the refusal to standardize two or more processes that appear to have a common starting point, since it is intuitively obvious that they accomplish the same thing. If the hope is to standardize only one of the processes, it is necessary to ensure that they accomplish the same thing in the same manner, or that the processes are the same. If they end at different points, they obviously are not the same although one may be a valid subset of the other. If they end at the same place, they may have used different processes to get there and if this is the case, then an understanding of why the different processes were used is essential. In some cases, the processes are used for checks and balances; in others, they test reality at different points and so complement each other. Of course, sometimes they duplicate one another.

The most common error of the type described in the above paragraphs occur when the internal standardization group selects a "product design process or methodology" for use across the organization (this is where the high technology, high change bias enters). In cases that I've seen, the organization (especially software development) will select a process that meets the goal for one specific component of software such as, for example, development of an operating system or the creation of a new user interface. The initial success of a product (since the successful product has many parents) will be ascribed to the "process" used to create it by some, who conveniently forget that the same process produced several failures on the way to success. The process is then enshrined as the "standard," which is all well and good as long as the external variables and internal variables remain constant, and as long as the same thing (OS, application, GUI) is produced. When variations begin, however, the process is usually not equipped to handle them and eventually the process sinks of its own weight.

The standards group must carry out the planning and execution cycles responsibly, taking the time to review, revise, and even reject its proposals before passing them on to management. It is a staff function and should advise, not mandate, appropriate courses of action. At this point, management must assume its load of responsibility and work to understand the validity of the proposals. There are usually no criteria by which to judge these proposals. Because so little management theory exists that covers the qualifiable aspects of standards as an aid to the planning and management function, most decisions are made on a wing and a prayer and the hope that things turn out for the best. However, the most common decision is to waffle and hope that someone else makes the decision first.

EXTERNAL STANDARDIZATION

External standardization covers standards activities outside the realm of the company. Where internal standardization is relatively closed to anyone except the producer, external standardization suffers from no such constraints, and the full panoply of standardization activities, and participants are active.

From a producer's point of view, external standards are all too often seen as a necessary evil. The best of all possible worlds for a provider would be one in which there would be a widely accepted proprietary product for which the market could find no substitutes, which filled a market need that was real and of vital importance to a growing segment of the population, and for which there was no possibility that competitors might leapfrog and create a different response to an expanded problem. As long as this is an ideal scenario, the provider would be able to meet the demand generated by the expanding market on a "just in time" basis, so that over production or under supply did not occur.

From a user's point of view, an entirely different scenario appears. A user would prefer multiple sources of supply, competition among providers, and a reasonable degree of commoditization so that there are multiple possible sources of supply that can be pitted against one another to gain a lower cost of goods. At the same time, the producers who are supplying would be varied enough so that they would form a natural second (or multiple) source of goods. And, as long as this is the ideal world, the products offered would be on the cutting edge (or at least close to the leading edge) of technology that provides the greatest cost benefit.

In the real world, however, the IT market emphasizes change, technological innovation, uneven market growth, occasional single source provider, multiple options that are "sort of" the same, and occasional production or demand constraints—and, at times, some downright lying about things. All of these combine to make standardization a viable management tool to deal with change because these are the types of market attributes that can fall under the aegis of standardization.

The ability to participate in external standards is less a function of technical ability than it is of endurance. However, because many managers (both engineering and marketing) tend to be driven by demonstrable short-term goals, many people find the standardization process too lengthy, too convoluted, and too cumbersome.[6] The key to understanding and using external standardization is to consider it a strategic planning mechanism, that is slightly more difficult to deal with than internal standards. By the earlier definition, standardization is an attempt to bring a bit of order to a chaotic market or to provide structure to an unstructured activity. This makes the rationale for external standardization a little bit more understandable. Finally, if the totality of the market is seen as a system containing a great deal of momentum, a standard can be seen as an effort to direct that momentum. The larger the change, the greater the energy required. It is not a trivial task.

External standardization is a lengthy process. There are three paths that external standardization can take based upon whether the organization wants to use the formal SDO process, the consortia process, or the alliance process. The three are not necessarily exclusive; parts of one can appear in another or one can serve as prelude to another. I propose to examine them jointly, calling out differences where they exist.

A MULTISTAGE MODEL OF STANDARDIZATION[7]

This description is a description of what the process is (or should be) about, rather than being about the "rules of the process." Long before a standard is even envisioned I believe that the process can first be seen in the attempts in the market by people who would change the market and the nature of the market. The process is described as a series of stages. Each must be completed before the next stage can be entered. Additionally, each stage anticipates the following stage, telegraphing the intent of the process so that there is an anticipation of future activity.

From the participant's point of view, the standardization process can be divided into a "before" and "after" stage. The "before" stage is the one that precedes the actual process in all three paths to standardization. I refer to it as the "preconceptualization" stage, and it takes one to five years to complete. The next three stages—conceptualization (up to a year), discussion (the same), writing (up to three years)—are usually under the control of the formal organizations in the process (the SDO) and they take between two and five years, as noted above, depending on the amount of discussion and controversy that the proposal has generated. There is also a dependency on technology in this arena, which can stretch the cycle slightly. The final stage (implementation) can take approximately forever.

Preconceptualization

Preconceptualization does not occur in any standardization group at the present time. It is, to use the phrase of economists, an "externality" to the formal system. This is the stage in which the market is examined to determine if there is a legitimate need for a standard. The need must exist, either in reality or in the market's perception, which will cause reality to be assumed. The idea for the standard must be applicable to the market in general, must be widespread enough to be accepted by a substantial clientele, and yet must be contained enough to be created or adapted/adopted. Ideally, a standardized solution should "bring something to the table" that cannot be supplied by the existing products or other solutions and/or markets. If the need does not exist because the market is not ready for the standard or for the concept, the originator may wish to try to drive the market in a correct direction, where "correct" is a relative term. It is here that fanaticism comes into play, since only someone with a mission will be willing to take on this usually thankless task.[8]

As noted earlier, the preconceptualization stage is common to all three of paths that a standardization effort can take. It also exists in the *de facto* standardization model, as the stage that the de facto product goes through as it attempts to gain hegemony. Preconceptualization could also be referred to as the "strategic marketing stage" in which the market is analyzed to see if the solution that someone is proposing (or is implementing) does, in fact, satisfy a market requirement or want.

Once the market need is determined or created, it must be examined to see if it can or should be met with a standardization solution. While this step may be patently obvious, there is much room for abuse here. Occasionally, standardized solutions are created to satisfy a provider's spurious need or want, stemming from the limitations of current technology, a misunderstanding of the problem, or a desire to disadvantage another provider or group of providers. In effect, a standard is being used to solve a nonstandard problem. It is the equivalent of using software to solve a hardware problem or using hardware to solve a software problem. In either of these cases, a solution has been found to solve the problem. The question that is usually not asked is whether the solution is appropriate to the problem, or whether there is a larger and more complex problem that might be being masked by the obvious problem. The following example, while it deals with an application of a standard to a problem, can be generalized to illustrate the problem of trying to create and use a standard because the wrong question was asked or answered.

The problem began with the mandated use of a commonly accepted (standardized) language (COBOL) for programming a cash register—a function for which COBOL was absolutely the wrong choice. The logic of a decision such as this is not hard to understand; COBOL is a business language and retail terminals are business tools; therefore, they should be programmed in a COBOL since both are built around serving business. One fatal flaw in this argument is, among others, that COBOL is entirely unsuited to handling the nature of transactions that a retail terminal provides.[9] The flaws in the logic here can be extrapolated to the creation of a standard to mask management flaws—such as, "Isn't there a way to get better programs out?" This can be done with a new programming language, better training, more efficient programming techniques, threats to the programmers, better business process understanding, or quality standards for software, or a combination of all of them. But a new standard is easier, because it removes the management burden by shifting it to a technology problem, for which management can disavow any responsibility.

Similarly, cosmetic proposals that seek to utilize standards to cover a design flaw or a marketing error also may appear to be valid at first glance, but will prove false on deeper inspection. The case here is the touting of a standard as proof that the product is mainstream, when the standard is either not used or not germane to the issue at hand. The most egregious examples of this were the "disk interface requirements" levied by the government in the mid 1980s, known as the FIPS 60 series for disk I/O. These standards were based around a proprietary IBM technology that even IBM objected to being standardized. Ultimately, all large disks sold to the government came with this channel interface supplied, but never used. There were about four competing technologies that were better and more useful—as well as more used—at the time. However, the government had made an error in their specification process, so all providers either obtained waivers or provided essentially a useless interface to their products.

The most common failing of standards participants is to attempt to standardize items that should not be standardized; a technical architecture, for example. By definition, a standard is reasonably unchanging; therefore, the only time that an architecture should be standardized is when it is no longer subject to change. When an architecture is no longer subject to change, it is dead. (Architecture here is meant to denote a particular family of computer systems; it is not meant to imply a global view of computing.) The skill of standardization for a producer lies in standardizing only enough of those things that the user needs to permit constancy in the user's operation. Anything that should and must change to take advantage of changes in technology or conceptualization, and anything that remains hidden from general knowledge and access (and therefore from practical usage) should not be standardized.

The users shoulder a large responsibility in standardization. The implementation of a standardized solution usually costs the producer some resource, and the provider will pass those costs along to the ultimate user. Over time, the economies of scale, a larger user base, a greater understanding of the developmental process, and more acceptance by more markets should allow the provider either to decrease price or increase performance (or both), which is of benefit to the user. This scenario, however, is based upon the user being willing to accept and pay for standards, which brings up an interesting point. If the standard is built to solve an industry problem, should the users consider this a feature (goodness added) or a fix (a problem corrected)? Features have value; fixes are expected. The key to this dilemma is user-based standardization (see Chapter 7), in which users specify the nature of the product attributes (including standards) for which they're willing to pay. If there is a discrepancy between what a consumer wants and what a provider is providing, the providers may have just added an expensive, nondesired feature. To punish providers who violate their expectations, the market tends to vote with their dollars.

When a real problem and a valid potential solution are found to exist simultaneously, the preconceptualization stage is nearly over. The only problem left is finding an appropriate standardization association to initiate the solution.

Within the formal organizations, an SDO is the obvious answer. This effort, in and of itself, can be very difficult. The standards submitter will find either a plethora of potential standardization committees, or will be unable to find any at all. In nearly all cases, it is best to start with the national forum within the United States, this would be the American National Standards Institute (ANSI) which can usually direct a visionary towards a society or committee that can handle the problem. This can take some time however, standardization is not an exercise for the impatient. Once the organization is found, the conceptualization stage can start for the SDO track.

For the consortia approach, there are three options available at this stage. The first is to contribute the technology to an organization of which the sponsor is a member. The second is to find an organization that is currently involved in the work and submit the proposal to this group. The third option is to create your own consortium. (For the government, consortia are probably not a viable option, since the government generally can't belong to them, although there are exceptions to this rule.) Contribution to an existing and sympathetic group (to which you belong) is usually the easiest option. Creation of your own consortium is the most fun. In all cases, the next stage is the conceptualization stage.

For alliances, the preconceptualization stage is the dominant stage. At the completion of this stage, most of the work is done, since you will have achieved the goal of getting other possible participants to join in the ideas for standardization that are being espoused. The question for the alliance at this stage is whether or not to pursue the SDO or consortia approach. Largely, (almost invariably, really) the decision here is made to submit to a consortium once the alliance has announced that the members are venturing into a new area of standardization. However, the alliance can continue discussion into the conceptualization phase and then submit the more completed description to either the SDO or consortia route.

Conceptualization

Once the proposal has been submitted to a standardization body, the initial phase of the formal standards process begins. Conceptualization is a recognized part of the standardization process, although it is only described vaguely in many organizations' operating procedures.

Within the SDO arena, the standards organization with jurisdiction over the program will review it for technical feasibility, with an eye to preventing the initiation of a standard that requires a major breakthrough in engineering for success. A standard, after all, is supposed to be something that can be used by the general public and not just a few practitioners of an esoteric art.

If the proposal is found to be technically feasible, it is reviewed for economic feasibility—justification of the need. This is usually no more than a symbolic review although it may, in the future, become increasingly significant as standards begin to increase in their interrelationships.

After passing these reviews, the proposal is advertised in a standards bulletin or similar organ to attract individuals interested in participating in its development. When enough participants have been found, the standard is assigned to an existing or to a newly created committee, the officers of the committee are appointed, and the committee commences work. In some cases, however, the standard never generates enough interest to permit the formation of a committee. It is then up to the sponsor (or the fanatic) to arouse the necessary industry interest or to withdraw the proposal. Trumpeting the proposal in the popular and trade press seems to work fairly effectively. Also effective, but requiring more effort, is gaining the interest of the government or of a legislator, who then provides free publicity. Finally, the originator can set about converting people to the cause individually. While this approach takes much longer, it usually is the most effective. Both the popular press and the trade press are constantly filled with standards ideas of varying validity, and legislators are fickle at times.

For the consortia approach, the process is usually a bit more streamlined. Most consortia know what they are doing because the task is specifically derived from their charter and it is the thing for which their members pay them. The proposal either fits within the charter and interest of the sponsors or it doesn't make it into the consortium. Additionally, the call for participation is greatly reduced, since participants can assign members of their organization directly to the activity, since it usually has more management visibility than the activities of an SDO.

The alliance activity here is, of necessity, the last stage of the alliance, since they now *must hand the proposal off* to the organizations that are focused on specification creation. The idea coming out of this phase for an alliance should be very clear since the discussions will have focused the expectations, the timeframe, and the market wants and needs to a wonderful degree. If it hasn't, the proposal is doomed. The most classic "alliance" that failed in this regard was the short-lived but immensely destructive Advanced Computing Environment (ACE), a fiasco from start to finish.[10]

Discussion

Within the formal SDO process, the committee begins by determining the scope and nature of work facing them, gaining an idea of the impact of the standard on which they will be working, estimating the kinds and amount of resources that they will need, and the time that it will take to complete the process. The chairperson of the committee can initiate the discussion phase. Interestingly, this phase is not mentioned in the description of the operating procedure, and usually everyone roundly condemns it as a waste of time and resources. However, it is vitally necessary to the success of the consensus standards process. The discussion phase is where most SDO standardization efforts begin to fail.

First, the discussion phase allows the committee to decide exactly what is being standardized. It allows alternative technical and philosophical views to be worked out in a nonhostile, nonbinding environment. The exact definition of the scope of work for the standard can be considered, and the methods presented in the proposal for solving the problem can be reviewed. It is at this stage that the originator of the proposal oftentimes loses control of the standard. The originator usually has a specific solution and has found a problem for which that solution is applicable and so tends to be blind to alternative solutions. There is a potential for extreme divisiveness during this stage, and with the nature of the problem that the committee is trying to solve always in mind, the chairperson must resort to a high level of skill and cunning to ensure that the committee does not self-destruct.

As the committee decides exactly what the conceptual basis for the standard is, work also can proceed on the technical issues that the committee faces: the choice of the technology that will be employed; the sophistication that is necessary; the reliability of the components; and a host of other topics that must be considered before work on the standard can proceed with any degree of consistency. Again, it is up to the committee chair to insure that these issues are at least placed before the members, not for a final decision, but at least to make them aware of some of the decisions that must be made eventually.

During this stage, the parties who will be impacted by the standard have the right to join the committee and comment on the proposal. Users, providers, and the government use this period to lobby their needs into the standard. It makes for organized chaos in the committee but a chaos that is very productive. Interested parties have a chance to exchange views, perhaps giving each participant a wider understanding of the issues. This is an important step toward the consensus that is so important in the later stages of the standards process. Additionally, the turbulent discussions spark an excitement that notifies the market that a standard is coming. Market acceptance of the standard begins with these discussions on the committee structure, concepts, and technical analysis. In effect, the discussion stage places a marker in the market, reserving a space for the future standard.

Over the past five to seven years, the discussion phase has taken on a life of its own—based upon two phenomena. The first of these is the person who attends with no intention of causing or allowing anything but her or his solution to be adopted. Usually this person acts not from a motive inspired by the market but rather inspired by his or her employing organization. This person will insist on acceptance of their solution until the committee goes away. During this time, the market waits for a solution, and waits and waits. An unnatural complement to this person is the expansionist; that is, the person who takes a problem and keeps expanding it to find the megasolution. Of course, no solution is quite adequate for all instantiations of the problem, so ever larger problem definitions and problem solutions are found. Typical of this type of activity are the committees that ISO/IEC Joint Technical Committee 1 had on Open Document Format (or Office Document Format), depending upon with whom you spoke. It was an attempt to standardize all formats and typology for all documents, everywhere. The attempt was ambitious, and may still be ongoing.

The other type of individual who appeared was the "standards politician"; the person who used process and procedures to ostensibly "protect the consensus process" while ensuring that the committee produced a weak or compromised document. This person was known by the constant reference to *Robert's Rules of Order*, which was used to ensure that the committee managed to get to a consensus on nothing. It was not the use of the *Rules of Order* that was wrong, but that a committee, supposedly gathered to come to a common conclusion on something that they all believed in, needed to be governed by strict rules originally meant to run contentious town meetings. It was this approach to standardization in the late 1980s and early 1990s—primarily the IEEE POSIX Committees—that resulted in much of the disarray in standardization that occurs today. The POSIX committees argued about everything, and the rules of order were used as a weapon by the leadership, who really didn't understand how to work to consensus with a group. While I have singled out the POSIX committees as the most egregious example of this type of activity, ASC X3 certainly had its share of it as well.

Either of these two activities—the Every Contentious/Ever Expanding Ploy Makers and the Point of Orderer's—will doom the discussion section, never allowing it to coalesce on what it is that the committee really should do.[11] And because SDOs don't have a distinct accountability to anyone, these two camps continue to flourish.

The consortia approach has an easier time of it in the discussion phase. A consortium proposal does not have to cater to a large and unknown group of individuals who are working together for the first time. Basically, all the members of a consortium are aware of the activities of the other members and why they are there. Management of the sponsors is expecting something to emerge, and there is pressure on the consortium management to expedite the process. Usually, the output of a consortium is anticipated by the product side of the sponsors. This causes a commitment of resources by the sponsors to the consortium activities. Finally, with the resource commitment comes the accountability that is usually lacking in SDOs; if the Every Contentious/Ever Expanding Ploy Makers and the Point of Orderer's appear, other participants will usually have recourse to their management, who then can act to ensure that the group makes progress (if that is what the management of the organization wishes to happen).

It is this potential that has earned the consortia their "bad reputation" among non-consortia participants, since there is the possibility for abuse of the system here. Because there is the possibility that a manager can quash a participant's objections, the claim of "individual expertise" and "doing the right thing as an individual professional" is held to be threatened. However, my contention is that the same possibility exists for most SDO participants, who do not pay their own way and who are there representing an organization. I suppose it depends upon whether you participate in an organization or not that makes it appear evil or benign.

Writing

Finally, with any luck, the committee reaches the phase in the standardization process with which everyone is familiar, and in which the technical merits of many participants shine. Now the concept is crystallized and translated into reality, yet the transformation can be exceedingly boring.

The purpose of writing a standard or consortium specification is to turn ideas and concepts into repeatable, understandable, and concise language. Unfortunately, language is inherently imprecise, and since some words gain their meaning from context, there is a high potential for misinterpretation to occur. A standard must be written clearly, with a very precise choice of words. Fuzzy, pejorative, and highly emotive words routinely are avoided. However, no matter how carefully it has been composed, the original wording, while clear to the author, can be vague or confusing to the uninitiated reader who, after all, is the standards consumer.

The standards writers must guard against making implicit assumptions or using terms and language that only the experienced will understand. The language should allow only one interpretation of the intent of the language. If the standard permits to more than one implementation of interpretation, this can be designed into the standard; however, it should be absolutely clear that only the implementations (not the interpretation) are several. (The cynical reader might enjoy the idea of two dozen brilliant engineers sitting in a room wordsmithing a document into clear and easily understood English, given the questionable ability of many engineers to write a coherent English sentence on a simple subject, let alone a complex one.)

The consensus process becomes important, since it is here that the checks and balances begin to take hold; insuring that there is consensus, but with the potential side effect of slowing the process down. The drafts are reviewed by the committee, by the larger committee, by all interested parties, and then the process is reviewed to ensure that it has been followed correctly. Comments are answered, more changes made, and the momentum begins to build. While all of this is occurring, the standard is receiving notice from the market. The marker placed in the earlier phases is getting ready to be called. When it is, technical expertise gives way to marketing competence.

The claim to complete and open review is one of the SDOs strong suits and the basis, for U.S. produced standards, for the claim of American National Standard. Within the United States, the standard is advertised in the *ANSI Standards Bearer*. In other countries, there are similar mechanisms to alert the general public to comment on a proposed standard. While this is all well and good, I would suggest that the "general public," at whom this process is aimed, really doesn't care a fig about the process or the review or much else. The people who review the standards are pretty much the same people who write the standards and who receive the mailings about the appearance of the standard as it goes through its review and other steps. The "public review" is really a review by the members of the public who are focused on the process and who stand to be financially impacted by the creation or noncreation of a standard. While this procedure probably makes sense, the claim by SDO proponents that this ennobles the SDO process is somewhat self-serving.

Within the consortia process, the review is less demanding, since the participants are usually more closely aligned with their product organizations and the consortium normally does not submit the specification to a larger audience. As a result, the review cycle is also quicker.

Sample Implementation

Some consortia produce a sample implementation of their specification to prove that the specification can, in fact, be implemented. SDOs do not do this. The sample implementation can be considered as "proof of concept."

Industry Implementation

This is a major problem within the formal process, and a looming problem for the consortia, because there is no foolproof method for causing standards implementation within the IT industry. Although the ultimate purpose of a standard is to make the market more efficient, to permit users to have a common metric, and to allow the sale of additional features above and beyond the standard, there is little market pull for standards which would indicate that users are aware of the standards, that they know how to demand them, that they understand the implications of standardization.

For the formal SDOs, the outstanding problem stems from the fact that there is no good way to make the users aware of the value of standardization, let alone make the users aware that a particular standard is available. Normally, in the United States, this is the responsibility of the national standards body, which publishes and sells these standards. However, since a single IT standard rarely will be pushed by the national organization which is responsible for standards from all industries, it is up to the specialized standards group to publicize the standard. In the United States, the Accredited Standards Committee for Information Processing Systems (ASC X3) is one of the primary channels through which new standards information is disseminated. Although this is not one of X3's official functions, its numerous committees, which work on nearly all major IT standards, provide a forum where members can meet to discuss standards activities. Although it is devoted exclusively to IT standards, X3 and its committees have a demonstrated inability to convince users that the standards they produce are germane to the market. As a result, the people most familiar with the standards are unable to convince users (who are the ultimate source of standards demand) about the market need that the standard meets.

Within the consortia, there is a better understanding of marketing but a similar ability to increase user understanding of the value of the consortia specifications and their implementations. The primary method for disseminating standards information continues to be vendor and or consortia or association campaigns. Vendors include information about standards in their advertising and product brochures, consultants sell consulting services that are predicated upon standards, and the industry goes out of its way to convince users that standardized products are superior.

Users, however, have not moved to assigning value to standards. While they refer to them in procurements with phrases such as, "must meet POSIX" or "must have XPG4 brand," there usually is no monetary value ascribed to conformance. If a sales person offers a discount to the purchasing agent if a standard is not present, the purchasing agent has no ability to judge whether she or he is being offered a great deal or merely red herring. Until users understand how to put a value on standardization the discipline will continue to have problems. It is in this area that much work remains to be done, and it is here that providers have the least leverage.

Testing, Conformance, and Branding

These are not found in the SDO process, since the SDO is in the business of producing standards. However, these functions are necessary to ensure compliance of products to standardized specifications. This arena is where more and more consortia are beginning to concentrate their efforts, since this service is lucrative if done correctly. However, it involves significant effort, since the tests must be written, a testing program put in place, and a method of selling the value of the test established. If the conformance to a specification has no perceived value to an end user it is very difficult to produce a test that ensures that providers have provided something of little or no value in the market.

CONCLUSION

There is no clear conclusion to this chapter. It could go on indefinitely with cautions and warnings, tales from experience, and case studies. The purpose of the chapter initially was to survey methodology and topics for standardization. However, I continue to believe very deeply that each program of standardization is unique to the group that wishes to standardize. Programs vary with organizational behavior, expectations, needs, perceptions, place, and time. If there are any constants, they are based on an organization being able to isolate the variables that it believes are essential to its success, to understand the nature of a standards program, and then to tie the variables to the program.

Earlier in the chapter I referred to Paul Bates' book on organizational structure and made the comment that no amount of rational facts or pleading could change the mind of a culture and management that did not believe in standardization. As proof of this (and at the conclusion of this chapter) I offer Apple Computer as an example of an organization that did not, as a matter or principle, believe in standards or standardization. Apple, which decided at its inception to permit neither its hardware nor its operating system to be standardized, decided that its unique solution was the best and that the market (or the users) would come to realize this fact if they just understood the better ergonomic design (both hardware and software) of the Macintosh computer. In the 1980s, Apple was an impressive performer, but the "IBM compatibles" began to own the market. While Apple had (and, as of this writing, still has) the largest share of the market for any single provider, it has less than a 15 percent share of market when the various coalitions of computers are analyzed. The Microsoft-Intel combination has about a 80 percent share of the market. I do not believe that Apple ever understood that people saw the technology and ergonomics not as the reason for the PC, but rather as a "hygienic factor"; something that was nice after the essential function of the PC was delivered. That essential function was the ability to have a reasonably common (read standard) operating system that was ubiquitous and inexpensive. Because Apple bore all of the costs of unique product development (including drivers, peripherals, printers, memory, the operating system, and so on), it could not compete with Intel, who did chips, Microsoft who did only the OS and applications, Compaq, who designed boxes and packaging, and so on. If there was ever a case study about the producer benefits of an open system (or about standardization), it was Apple Computer, who believed that it held the truth.[12]

And it is this point that should be carried away from this chapter. Management of standards should not be taken lightly; standards can turn quickly and create more havoc than existed before their creation. On the other hand, they are ignored at the peril of those who chose not to consider them. Fundamentally, standards are powerful tools, and should receive the same degree of management interest and concern as any other staff planning function or tool.

NOTES

[1]The use of intellectual property as a basis for standardization has gained more attention over the last several years. The issue of IPR as a competitive tool—through sole possession and use—has changed to the idea of licensing technology to others. Standardization is an ideal way of allowing proprietary technologies into the market with a degree of control over the nature of the specification development.

[2]Within the IT industry, an increasingly common function of a standardization group is to act as an intermediary between the organization and the external standardization groups. The reason for this is two-fold, but both are derived from the concept of specialization and complexity management. As the stakes for IT companies in the standardization process have grown, so has the necessity of having a specialized organization that knows how to operate in the increasingly rule driven and formal standardization process. Secondly, the organizations tend to try to use expensive technical people to do "technical things," rather than use them to do both "technical things" and to manage a standardization process and interaction.

[3]An example of this would be the standardization across the multiple star-in-pentagons (SIPS) mentioned in Chapter 9. The information that is used by the various layers of the organization may be, and usually are, derived from different data bases or data warehouses. The fundamental nature of the data isn't different, but the way that it is manipulated and stored and then modified tends to ultimately cause the data to become disparate and change.

[4]In the first edition of this work, I used the concept of quality here. Following an uncomfortable amount of comment, I was convinced of the error of my initial description by some members of ISO TC 207 and the U.S. ASC Z1 committees. As they clearly pointed out, quality is a continuing state activity that permeates the organization. It is not a discrete attribute or isolatable "quality" of a product or service.

[5]Bate, Paul. *Strategies for Cultural Change,* Butterworth Heinemann Ltd.: Oxford, 1994.

[6]These are the same people who believe that Microsoft's market success occurred overnight—or over a two year span. These are also the people who did not see Apple's fall from grace, the growth of UNIX as a viable operating system, or a host of other things that seem to have suddenly emerged. The latest of these is the "appearance" of the Internet and the World Wide Web, which they firmly believe appeared only yesterday.

[7]Cargill, Carl F. "A Five Stage Conceptual Model for Information Technology Standards," 31 October 1988, unpublished and unnumbered paper submitted to the X3 Strategic Planning Committee. The basis of the paper was a conversation with Gary S. Robinson, then Director of Standards at Digital Equipment Corporation, now Director of Standards at Sun Microsystems. Gary and I were trying to understand why some standardization efforts never seemed to come to closure, why some came to closure slowly, and why some coalesced very quickly. The paper was the result of analyzing the process from a group psychology, rather than technical standardization, point of view. It has been expanded for the book to include consortia and alliances.

[8]In presentations on the model, I have often referred to this as the "martyr" stage, since the proponent usually ends up getting martyred by the industry, and someone else either makes money or receives the credit. It is unfair, but it is the way that the system seems to work.

[9]While this decision appears ludicrous, it did, in fact, happen at NCR while I was employed there in the late 1970s. The decision was rescinded after several months of silliness by the developers, who knew perfectly well that the edict was foolish, but who could only convice their reasonably nontechnical management by demonstrating that the idea didn't work. It was a classic "Dilbert scenario" (with compliments to Scott Adams).

[10]ACE was one of the notorious consortia that appeared as the IT industry was trying to counter the successful growth of the Reduced Instruction Set Computer (RISC) chips that were making their weight felt at this time. The original intent was to create an indefinite group of companies who had little in common except stopping something and then weild them into a positive force to stop the encroachment of the RISC chip on the CISC chip vendors. As the ink was drying on the agreements, the participants began to realize that they had nothing positive in common, and the agreement began to collapse. It was the victim of its own pomposity, size, and, from a standardization point of view, unskilled set of managers who did not know how to run a large complex voluntary organization.

[11]See Michael Spring et al. in "Improving the Standardization Process: Working with Bulldogs and Turtles" in Kahin and Abbate's *Standards Policy for Information Infrastructure* (op. cit.) for a more lucid and more critical understanding of the nature of the participants in the process.

[12]In a series of advertisements that appeared when Microsoft's Windows 95 appeared, Apple tweaked Microsoft for finally almost reaching the GUI level that Apple had achieved in 1987. What Apple failed to comprehend was that Windows 95 reached first year sales that Apple never achieved in its history. The difference between the companies was that Apple was selling what they knew users would want if only the users were smart, while Microsoft was selling a standardized product that users bought.

Chapter 12

The Formal Standards Process

"Imagine the whole, then execute the parts—
Fancy the fabric
Quite, ere you build, ere steel strike fire from quartz,
Ere mortar dab brick!"

—Robert Browning, *A Grammarian's Funeral Shortly
After the Revival of Learning in Europe*

INTRODUCTION

This chapter will look at the theoretical mechanics of consensus standards creation in the United States. In some cases, it will employ the exact terminology of the American National Standards Institute: In others, the discussion will be flavored with my impressions and views, and may not mirror precisely the intent of the ANSI language. At the end of the chapter, certain of the fallacies that are inherent in the theory will be examined, and a critique of the theory as it is currently being applied in SDOs will be presented.

METHODS OF STANDARDS CREATION

While many other countries have a single organization dedicated to the creation of standards, the United States, under ANSI procedures, has three types of organizations that can create a standard: the Accredited Sponsor using the canvass method, the Accredited Organization (AO) method, and the Accredited Standards Committee (ASC). Each of these organizations use methods that have their own proponents and detractors. An examination of each will clarify the reasons for their creation. Much of the rationale derives from the culture of the United States and the essentially individualistic, competitive nature of business.

Accredited Sponsor Using the Canvass Method

This method of standardization is based on the idea that a given organization has an interest in seeing the creation of a particular standard, which has an interest group that is larger than the organization's constituency. The organization, which must be an approved (or at least recognized) entity, thus sponsors a drive for standardization and begins the canvass method of standardization by inviting comments on the standard that they are proposing from anyone who cares or may be materially affected by it. The assumption is that a consensus on the proposed standard is extant; what is being sought is confirmation of consensus of impacted parties, and a demonstration of honest interest and intent in the standard. When the due process has been completed (and the due process provisions apply to and all other methods that produce standards) the standard is submitted for approval and eventual publication as a standard developed under the auspices of ANSI.

The benefits of the method are substantial. It moves relatively quickly (as the standard's world goes), it identifies the working and concerned parties interested in the arena, and it provides the community a chance to coalesce and help itself. However, the canvass method is appropriate only when substantial agreement on the thing to be standardized already exists. If there are multiple opinions on the need, solution, methodology, concept, and rationale for a standard, the canvass method breaks down very quickly, becoming largely ineffective. Thus, the canvass has been proven effective in the creation of noncontentious software standards, such as Ada. (There was contention about Ada as Ada, not Ada as a standard.) It would not have been successful in areas such as the COBOL revision, which was marked by substantial divergence of opinion and numerous comments on the content of the standard.

In effect, participants in the canvass method can be compared to a group of people who assemble for a party. They share a commonality of purpose and a certain familiarity with the activities expected, and, when the party is over, everyone goes home feeling satisfied. The intent is not to form a new concept but to reaffirm commonality and friendship.

The Accredited Organization (AO) Method

In the Accredited Organization (AO) method, an already existent group completes a standard in an area in which it has direct and material interest and a perceived expertise. Usually an industry trade group or association of industry experts or participants, the AO often has extant standards that are based upon the methodologies of its profession or discipline.

The AO method begins with an accredited organization indicating to ANSI that it wishes to become certified as a standards creating/writing body. To receive such certification, the AO must demonstrate its competence in the area of interest and its willingness to use an ANSI approved consensus methodology to create standards. While these criteria do not appear to be burdensome, they can become a major point of contention. The consensus approach encourages anyone with a direct or materially affected interest to participate in the process of standards creation. If the organization is a professional society or a trade group, it must accept participation by those whose perceptions of the discipline is liable to be different from that of most members. In many AOs, the development of standards may have proceeded much more smoothly prior to the acceptance of the burden of the consensus approach. Once accredited by ANSI, however, an AO can produce standards that become American National Standards.

There are two major questions in this method of standards formation. The first is whether the group really possesses the necessary expertise. The second problem, more difficult to resolve, is to establish whether the group is operating in the best interests of the industry as a whole or merely attempting to maintain or increase its influence and power base. This extremely sensitive issue is addressed in part by the checks and balances of the standards systems. It is assumed that, because of the honesty of the majority of the membership, an attempt to create a standard that precludes another's interest will not succeed. I believe that this usually will be the case; in this age, the specter of the evil conspiracy tends to be raised by interest groups trying to account for their inability to gain special treatment. However, the potential use of standards to protect the status quo is a constant worry with which the AO standards development group must live. There is a great temptation to standardize only upon things that are familiar to the majority of the members who, in the main, share similar educational and philosophical backgrounds. Ideas that come from outside the "circle of expertise" can be looked at with jaundice.

In general, however, the AO usually produces standards that have merit for the industry. This is especially true for the more mature, stable industries, where the knowledge is shared and is reasonably static. In more fluid environments, the ability of an AO to accommodate change while continuing to create meaningful standards is likely to become somewhat diluted.

The AO method is more complex than the canvass method. However, AOs accept this complexity because they generally exist for some purpose other than to write standards. Standards are a sideline; usually, the exchange of professional ideas, industry knowledge, and shared experience is the ultimate goal of the AO.

To continue the analogy of the previous section, an AO's standards creating group is comparable to a company bowling team. The bowling team is an off-shoot of the commonality of the workplace. Without the underlying bond, the team probably would not have formed; if the team is dissolved, the commonality of shared work experience will remain. It is similar with the AO; without standards, the commonality of the shared professional discipline would remain; without the shared discipline or professional society standards would not be sufficient to hold the group together.

The Accredited Standards Committee Method

The Accredited Standards Committee (ASC) is formed for the specific purpose of creating standards in a contentious environment. It is, like today's corporation, a fictional creation that exists because it has to, not because it makes any real sense. The most sophisticated and most contradictory form of standards organization, the ASC takes groups and factions with diverse and even antagonistic viewpoints and melds them into a semicohesive whole. They aim to engineer a solution that encompasses all of the diversity while maintaining the benefits of individuality.

The key to the ASC is the secretariat. The secretariat is held by a sponsoring organization, whose function is to provide the legal, administrative, and financial backing. The secretariat functions as the point of contact for ANSI and acts as the collective memory for the ASC, as well as managing the administrative details of the ASC. Without the secretariats, the ASCs would become bogged down in administrative nightmares, and ANSI would be unable to cope with the multitude of contending committees.

The ASC usually has a committee structure and an existence in which control and anarchy are kept in precarious balance. The creation of standards takes place in the committees; the administration of the committees (with concomitant rules) is the responsibility of their officers, who must observe the doctrine of consensus while maintaining their professional ethics and judgment. Normally, each committee is accountable to its senior committee, and the senior ASC officer (usually a chairperson) is responsible to ANSI, through the secretariat.

The ASC normally decides how it wants to operate, what its charter encompasses, and within reasonable limits, what its area of expertise is. It also decides how to structure itself in order to complete the necessary standards that lie within the scope of its charter and expertise, which should match. In effect, the ASC is the ultimate master of its own expectations, capabilities, and direction.

The areas to be standardized are publicized, and a call is goes out for volunteers to staff the committees. When the committees are assembled, the development of standards begins. During the actual work, consensus is observed, and all those who wish to participate are heard. When the committee finishes its work, it creates a draft standard, which is forwarded to the secretariat for action. The remainder of the consensus process is invoked, and, ultimately, a standard results.

The strength of an ASC standard is that it is the work of a cross-section of all interested parties. One of the main activities of the secretariat is to ensure that no one group holds an overwhelming edge that might adversely influence the fairness of the standards produced. In theory, the standards are egalitarian; composed to favor all participants. However, I believe that it was Voltaire who pointed out that the laws of France were applied equally, forbidding both the rich and the poor from sleeping under bridges. A similar observation can be made about the ASC process, and here lies its chief flaw. Standards work is time consuming and therefore is expensive in terms of that human resource. Additionally, it costs money to travel to standards meetings and to participate in the formal and informal dialogue that shapes standards. So, while the ASC process is open to both the rich and the poor, the rich have easier access to it. And, while the standards process is not as onerous as sleeping under bridges, being rich does make it less grueling.

CHECKS AND BALANCES

Central to an effective system of checks and balances is an understanding of the ultimate object for which one is attempting to gain equality and balance. If the purpose is to ensure that all parties have an opportunity to be heard, to comment, and to see the results of their comment and criticism, there usually is little problem. One designs a system in which every action is open to scrutiny, review, reaction, and contradiction. These characteristics usually are attributed to anarchy, yet they come reasonably close to defining the check-and-balance system in the consensus standards process.

This check-and-balance system is predicated on two major assumptions: more than one person or group shares a desire to standardize something and their concern will translate into action. If these two assumptions are valid, the design of the system can be accomplished with a minimum of effort. If they are not valid, then the system cannot possibly work.

The initial premise of the consensus process is openness. All activities concerned with the standard are open to public participation and comment. Rules for participation are available to anyone who cares to participate. The standard does not become final until all comments and objections are answered fairly and objectively within the process. Finally, because the process is voluntary, users, manufacturers, and the industry as a whole are not required to use the standard.

The secondary premise is that the standards developers understand that they are participating in an activity that may transcend individual or corporate needs and goals. If the participants are involved only to espouse their own causes, at the expense of the common good, the system will not work. Usually however, a single individual or corporation does not make the move to increase the common good; rather, there is a sense that movement must occur, and when a leader appears and asks if a new consensus can be achieved, this focuses the group momentum to produce a shift. Whether catalyzed by informal discussion, conversations, common sense, or a feeling of desperation, the shift occurs, prompted by the need to gain consensus, and to achieve something that can be used by everyone. After all, this is the purpose of a standard.

In addition, standards groups usually are structured to strike a balance between the standards process matters (achievement of consensus, equality, and fairness) and the technical content of the standard (usability, completeness, and applicability). Generally, the organization that validates process is different from the organization that validates technical content. This ensures that the need for technical implementation and validity does not interfere with the larger need for consensus. If the standard is valid but does not represent consensus, it is not really a standard, but instead an imposition of a solution. More commonly, the technical solution is correct, and the technical validation is intended to verify that the committee answered the question that was asked of it. This review, however unusual, frequently provides interesting, and occasionally dismaying, insight to the developers.

The standard is subject to appeal and review at all stages of development. Reviews are the responsibility of panels that become increasingly more process oriented and less technically oriented as the work proceeds. Initially, a review examines a proposal for technical merit. If the proposal is challenged and the challenge rejected, the protester has the right to appeal. At each stage of objection appeal, the appellant has the right to increase the level of review until the claim reaches some form of ultimate appeals board. If a valid case for violated process is made at this level, the standard will be rejected and reworked. If the process is found to have been correctly followed, the proposed standard will be made an official standard.

The success of the entire process hinges on the existence of committed participants. If concern is lacking in the industry, the process may produce some interesting standards, but these may or may not be valid. The ultimate check and balance is an enlightened industry self-interest. The industry cannot afford to ignore the process; the greater its involvement, the more useful the checks-and-balances system. Apathy, not conspiracy, is most to be feared.

TIME REQUIREMENTS AND EXPECTATIONS

The time required for the creation of a standard is in direct proportion to the interest that the standard has created in the industry. Creation time also is directly proportional to the number of delegates on the committees. And, finally, the degree of need in the market may be inversely proportional to the speed with which the standard is developed. These truisms conceal much of the rationale for why things appear to happen so slowly in standards.

To begin with, the type of standards committee that is creating the standard greatly affects the speed of creation. A committee formed under the AO method would probably move the most quickly, since it have would have the available expertise to create a standard easily. The canvass method would probably be the next most time-efficient, since it presupposes of consensus. Finally, an ASC would be the least time-efficient, since ASCs are supposed to deal with the contentious issues.

Industry interest, reflected in the number of delegates who attend the meetings, is the next consideration. The ASC normally handles standards that attract the interest and participation of everyone in the industry. For high interest standards that are more specific to a discipline, the AO would be better. And, finally, for a single common and understood subject, the canvass method would be best.

If the topic to be standardized is easily defined, the standardization process can be completed in a reasonable period of time. A technically bounded standard dealing with a simple issue can take as little as eighteen months to complete. If the subject is complex, and has multiple interpretations, or large-scale economic consequences, development is likely to require substantially more time.

A complete complex standard on a highly contentious issue that involves a great deal of industry participation can and should take at least five years to come into being. A standard is rarely completed in less than a year; approximately four years should be the average.

In these estimates, the term "should" is used advisedly. It carries a double meaning indicating that this is the typical time, and suggesting that it is desirable for a standard to take this long. The problem, of course, is the industry's ability to deal with rapid change. If standards are a change agent for the industry in which the entire industry can compete, measured and rational change is essential. At the same time, standards are a marketing tool, which can and should be used by providers as a means to gain a market advantage. These two goals are not mutually incompatible, but they do lend an aura of tension to an already complex forum. Standards should be part of a midrange strategic plan in most corporations in the United States. As was stated in an earlier chapter, standards are not a quick fix to correct lack of planning. The process is difficult to manage as a solution to an immediate corporate problem. It does not respond well to frenzied cries of desperate marketing people; rather, it emphasizes and rewards careful planning and strategy.

Finally, and possibly most importantly for the success of the standard, the nature of the program being undertaken should be matched with the potential of the organization chosen. Ada was probably a good match for a Canvass method activity but, for the ultimate success of Ada as a language, it may have been wiser to have used an ASC. Ada failed in its first interation because it was not commercialized; there was no demand for it in the commercial sector, nor were there compliers developed for it with any alacrity. This resulted in Ada languishing and ultimately being disparaged as a U.S. Department of Defense only language. Had the sponsors gone through an ASC, the language may have had fewer strong constructs (due to the nature of the compromises necessary for ASC standardization), but it may have had a wider audience to implement and productize it commercially. The committee choice should be made not only upon what is technically wanted, but also upon what is economically wise. This, of course, requires that standardization participants understand the nature of the organizations as well as the nature of the technology.[1]

CRITIQUE OF THE THEORY

When I originally wrote this theoretical analysis of the standardization groups, I was describing standardization when it was the province of a reasonably small set of committed technocrats who were focused on "doing standards" and understanding the process in which they participated. These technocrats were usually part of the technology group of the organization—and were capable of taking the time to understand one another's positions and to work to a consensus position. The operative phrase was "work", since standardization, if done correctly, is difficult. Operating inside a company is much easier; the internal environment, while stressful, operates under a common culture (unless the organization is completely dysfunctional). The same cannot be said of the external standardization arena, in which everyone can participate.

During the first half of the nineties, however, standards seemed to have acquired a glamour and been the resting place for what I call "Open Systems Groupies." These were technologists and marketing people who had a good grasp of the obvious and knew that they were better at the process than the "stogy old fools" who were "in the way of the new standards thinking." This group of self-professed experts arrived and began to achieve quick results, much to the chagrin of the "older generation" of practitioners. However, the quick successes were not followed by continued successes. The "Open Systems Groupies" began to meet the same problems in the running of standardization organizations that the older practitioners had encountered, whether the organizations were SDOs or consortia. The fundamental problem that confronts any standardization organization is that consensus takes time; it takes time inside a company and takes more time outside a company. In many cases, the newer managers didn't have the necessary interpersonal skills to cause consensus to form. They had grown up and been trained in the art of contention, rather than in cooperation. In many cases, table pounding, yelling, flaming E-mails, and threats of legal action (as well as grandiose posturing) marked the actions of these newer participants. Over time, the good ones came to understand that things didn't happen quickly and learned how to manage the newer organizations. They did bring good ideas and good actions. Even ANSI is trying to determine how to deal with consortia and other standardization organizations that are not part of the process. ANSI is looking at how to make the process less painful and more responsive. It has even created a method of accepting non-SDO contributions (Publicly Available Specifications) as the basis for standards.

The changes that are occurring in the process of IT standardization are necessary, and are happening (very slowly) due in part to the severe pounding that standardization took at the hands of the "barbarians." (I wouldn't want any prejudice to show here.) However, the IT industry is no longer the leader in the application of standardization as a change agency for an industry. The Europeans and the Pacific Rim countries have begun to use formal standards as the basis for regulations (a recurring theme in the history of standardization). The European Telecommunications Standards Institute (ETSI) IPR undertaking[2] was an attempt to apply standardization to a fundamental business problem and change the entire telecommunications industry; the use of ISO 9000-3 (Guide to Software Quality) may force a fundamental way that software is created. The use of the Internet as a storage and retrieval device for information, the free distribution of software over the Internet, and so on all will be based on nontraditional standardization models. People and groups outside the IT industry who are not subject to the cynicism of the last decade of standardization wars will use standardization as a powerful economic and social tool. It is this use of standardization for which the IT arena is poorly prepared, because we have lost much of the expertise that we had. The awareness of the new implications of standardization is just beginning to filter through to many executives, who are beginning to wonder if they've been well-served by their existing philosophies and practitioners. I believe that, like Belshazzar, many of the current practitioners will be found wanting and will suffer the same fate that he did.

CONCLUSION

The standards process is not found in many strategic plans. Many businesses are unaware of the consensus standards organizations that provide standards for their industry and the opportunities to participate in the process. As with other methods of achieving an economic advantage, the standards process requires some discipline, calculated thought, and analysis of the variables that will be encountered. Part of the analysis should include an effort to understand the process, with its strengths and weaknesses. This chapter covered some of the variables of the system that are independent of the goodness or validity of the proposed standard. Because standards are created in the human arena, there is a large potential for random occurrences to determine the success or failure of a proposal. The process, with its multitude of implicit and explicit checks and balances, can be confusing.

Ultimately, however, a proposal's success will be decided by how well it meets market requirements and needs. The process cannot insure success for a standard, nor can it guarantee that bad standards will not exist. All the process can do, and all that it is supposed to do, is to ensure that the standard is created in the public eye, and that the solution does not provide an automatic disadvantage to anyone. Everything else depends upon the willingness of the public to participate and use the process. As was noted earlier, the enemy of standardization is not too much participation or conspiracy: It is apathy. The same can be said for any form of voluntary governance.

NOTES

[1]It would be wise to insert here that the formal process may not be the correct process at all, and that the standardization may well want to take place in a consortia or as a *de facto* standard. However, this chapter is focused on the formal process rather than on a comparison of the various available processes.

[2]See Mark Shurmer and Gary Lea. "Telecommunications Standardization and Intellectual Property Rights: A Fundamental Dilemma?" in *StandardView,* Volume 3, Number 2, June 1995, pp. 50–59.

Chapter 13

Standards and Business

"Cursed, ill-devised properties,
With envy, avarice,
And fraud, those fiends that spoiled ev'n paradise
Were not the object of mine eyes;"

—Thomas Traherne, *Wonder*

INTRODUCTION

One of the nice things about writing about business and standards is that both terms cover a myriad of definitions. According to my Oxford English Dictionary, the term "business" appeared in about 1000 C.E. as a reference to one's position or to one's activities, but it did not receive a commercial implication until the late 1400s. By the 1700s, a commercial sense had become associated with the term. (One would expect this, as the growth and respectability of the commercial enterprise began to occur in this time in England.) Since that time, the term "business" has come to mean any activity in which people engage for some form of remuneration: from the business of government to the business of religion to the business of child care and so on and so on. As Calvin Coolidge remarked, "The chief business of the American people is business."[1] With this helpful definition, it's reasonable to expect that everyone knows what business is all about, and that's why we have so many people teaching it and writing about it. We don't really know how to define it (as evinced by the plethora of economists who don't agree), how to measure it (we sort of take a wild whack at it), nor how to do it consistently. However, most of us admit that we take part in it.

The same problem exists in standards. They are everywhere, everyone uses them, but no one can really tell you how they came into being. And this for a technically based discipline that is supposed to be one of the major supports of the industrialized world's

168

ability to interact and interoperate. It is a testament to the success of the entire movement that the great majority of people just expect standards to exist.

I used to puzzle about this until I ran across an interesting article about time and the regularizing of this commodity. The author, Martin Bruegel, maintains that it was distribution of mass produced time pieces that changed the nature of the Hudson Valley from a somewhat bucolic agricultural setting to a time conscious economy that began to be outwardly focused.[2] The contemplation of this helped to understand the problem with standards; they are a background activity that do not interest anyone except when they fail. And when they fail, people are too busy trying to fix the problem to consider the nature of the entire phenomena. (This perspective would account for the activities and attitudes of the "standards managers of the 1990s" mentioned in Chapter 12.) Like time, the consideration and practices of standardization do change. While the process and outcome are resilient to directed change, they are not absolutely immutable. This chapter looks at some of the ways that standards are used in business to change things, and then examines a theory of standardization that appeared, indirectly, in Europe and which has tremendous implications for the nature of business and standardization.

One of the major problem areas with standards and standardization is the lack of precise definition of terms; there are nearly as many definitions for the term "standards" as there are standards available. This has, as might be expected, lead to a certain amount of confusion in the industry. Standards, using the ISO definition in Chapter 5, tended to be focused upon a product or a salable thing, whose attributes are described by standards. They describe something that was already known and tangible; something from which the specifications could be empirically derived. The standard can have a major impact on the business of business, as pointed out in much of the remainder of Chapter 5. The proposed definition that standardization is a change agency and that standards are change agents, recognizes that standards have become a significant "change agent" in the information technology industry.

MARKET CREATION

The term "change agent" however, is somewhat ambiguous. Normal usage of this term means that the agent is actively the cause of change. It is an active ingredient in the change. Standards can assume this form, as they did in the Local Area Network (LAN) arena. In the early 1980s, the technology necessary to create LANs existed and was well-known. However, there was no consensus in the industry as to what LAN scheme would succeed, nor was there clear definition as to why anyone would use a LAN, except in a specialized environment. General office workers were not expected to use the more expensive connections and wiring. Finally, there were about fifty potential and actual proposed LAN schema that completely complicated the picture.[3] The effort was initiated in the IEEE after it was rejected by X3 as being too radical.

By the end of the standardization effort, there were three primary LAN schemata and topologies accepted and actually worked on in committee. The first, CSMA/CD, was sponsored by DEC, Intel, and Xerox (DIX group); the second was the IBM token ring approach, and the third was the Manufacturing Automation Protocol sponsored by GM and other users. While the standard was being hacked out in committee, the press and marketing began to both comment on it and speculate on how to use it. Other providers (such as connection makers) began to see a market and began to build to the market, and users began to become interested in it. By the time that the LAN standards were finished, there was a multibillion dollar market that had been created around the standardized versions.

This was market creation at its best. The entire market for LANs was created by the activities of the committee; it was the standardized LAN approach that succeeded. For those who do still doubt, consider the fate of two good but proprietary technologies of WangNet© and ARCNet©. Neither is really around today but WangNet©, which was a broadband technology, touted as being technically better and ARCNet© originally was much more widely deployed, since it didn't have to go through the "silly standards process." Both would now be a good subject for a computer trivia quiz.

However, standards can also serve as a catalyst that cause change because of their presence, but do not actively get involved in the change. The best example here is the change in the market that occurred because of the failure of the Open Systems Interconnect (OSI) model. In this case, the actual OSI standards were a misguided effort (either inadvertently or deliberately) by many of the participants in the market. I believe that much of the misunderstanding was because the standards were designed by engineers who were given poor advice by their marketing people, who were enamored of technology and who failed to listen to what the users were saying about what the market could and would accept. OSI was meant to interconnect networks of mainframe and minicomputers. It was complex and filled with compromises. Many of the developers suffered from an arrogance born of "having done things right" before, and of belonging to large companies that had tremendous resources. Smaller companies that did not possess similar resources developed an alternative, with the U.S. Federal Government's help. While OSI (as a standard in the process of coming into being) helped to set market directions and expectations, these expectations took off in an unforeseen direction by the OSI creators and backers, leading to confusion in the market, the success of the Internet, and the failure of OSI. (I predicted the standardization of LANs somewhat correctly; if you have a copy of the previous edition of this book, you can see that I missed the OSI story completely.)

THE LIFE CYCLE AND STANDARDIZATION

I'd like to look at using standardization to revitalize the product life cycle or at least, to slow its collapse. The idea that standardization can compensate for the shortened life cycle is one of the reasons that helps to explain why standardization continues to exist in the IT arena in multiple forms today.

Figure 13.1 shows the standard life cycle curve that is taught to any marketing class in any and every school. There are four phases: introduction, growth, maturity, and, finally, decline. Traditional marketing states that the expenses are incurred in the introduction and growth phases, where the provider is attempting to convince the market of the goodness of the offering. The market maturity phase is where money is made. The decline

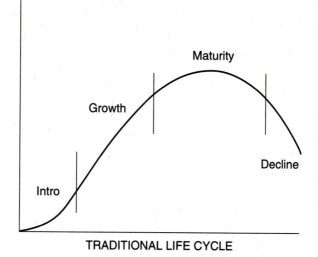

TRADITIONAL LIFE CYCLE

Figure 13.1

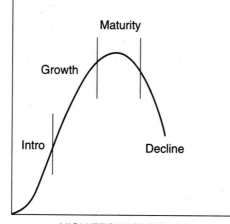

HIGH TECHNOLOGY LIFE CYCLE

Figure 13.2

stage is where resources are committed to other things and the product or service acts as sort of a source of revenue. There are all sorts of advanced and abstruse theories that detail how to modify the use of the theory by participants (mid-life kickers, tag-a-long, fast-followers, and so on) but very little has been written about the use of standards as modifiers to the life cycle.[4]

Within high technology, the life cycle has changed to the illustration shown in Figure 13.2. The introduction and growth phases have been compressed so that they do not occur over as long a time as they did previously. Additionally, it is not clear whether or not they rise to the same heights that they did previously. In either case, they lead to a compressed maturity curve, which is followed by a more precipitous decline curve. This is an altogether depressing pattern, caused in large part by the obsolescence of technology and its associated byproducts.[5]

However, if the principles of the "multistage model" of standardization described in Chapter 11 are applied to the shortened life cycle model, the model can be partially, if not completely, lengthened.

If the preconceptualization and the conceptualization phases are conceded to be part of the introduction phase, the standardized solution can be presented to the market (in true anticipatory marketing activity) up to two years prior to an actual product introduction. (While you may be able to go longer than that, it is probably not good for either the product or the standardization activity.) By announcing that standardization is beginning, or that a consortium is initiating work, or that an alliance has formed to do something, the market can be alerted to the potential. The caution here is, however, that the "thing" that is to be done must both be capable of being done and must be needed. (Both of these are preconditions of the two stages under consideration, incidentally.)

If the market is alerted to the activity in a standardization committee, technical pundits and other hacks in the standardization arena will begin to notice what is happening and may begin to comment on it.[6] Once this happens, it is up to the participants in the activity to ensure that they both meet schedule and expectations. Standardization committees, unfortunately, have a reputation for doing neither. The ability to hold a schedule is vitally necessary for the standardization arena or else, setting the correct time expectations is.

In either case, the participants will have covered the introduction phase with the conceptualization and discussion phases of the standards life cycle. Additionally, if the organizations that are participating in the standardization effort help to publicize the activity, there will be an increased awareness of the capabilities of the products when they are finally released.

The writing and implementation phases can map to the "growth phase" of the product life cycle. It is in these two stages that the producers actually begin to write and test their implementations against the reality of the market. Again, if the standardization organizations can maintain schedule, the participants will find that they will be more successful in their pursuit of profits when the product built to the standards finally makes it to market. While too long is definitely worse than too early, too early will cause a provider or a group of providers to begin to use some very strange marketing tactics to succeed in the growth stage.

One of my favorites claims in this arena is to be "more open" than the competition. The idea is that open is like a door. At least one of the major vendors has used the analogy in its advertisements. While this makes sense in a "numbers game sort of way" for the number of interfaces built to standards (that is, a company with 100 standardized interfaces has more standardized interfaces that a company with ten), it was meant to convey the impression that interfaces can be "sort of standardized," and that the organization that ran these advertisements was more standards conformant, and hence compatible, than its competition. Compatibility, when talking about screw sizes and other physical properties, is fine. Compatibility, when discussing data transmission and sharing, is quite another.

The definition of what compatibility is and what compatibility implies needs to be discussed. If the definition of "existing in harmony" is accepted, then standards do provide a measure of "harmony" to disparate systems. However, if compatibility is interpreted to mean interoperation, then the "more open" example is useless, since you either get the information from the system or you don't. What these advertisements seem to say is that, "We're not really standard, but we're not as bad as them." I suppose that it is like giving a thirsty man an empty glass and saying that you have provided half a drink, since you gave him a container.

However, if the organizations structure their marketing campaigns correctly, the providers of a standardized platform will be rewarded. Another interesting thing in dealing with standardization is that most high technology firms rush to be "first" with a standardized product. The question that they don't stop to ask themselves is, "So what?" Being the only standardized product is exactly the same as being a proprietary product. It is only when over half the participants in a market become standardized that it has any value to the users since it fills the fundamental requirements of competitive and comparable multiple sources of supply.[7]

The use of standards and standardization fills another role in the life cycle. It allows a firm to mitigate some of the product development and introduction risk. Because of the rate of change in technologies, many organizations find that collaborative ventures can reduce the amount of risk in the form of resources committed to a program. By combining technologies and by gathering a group of experts from multiple organizations, the possibility of all the organizations failing to see a paradigm shift or failing to be able to solve a problem is substantially lessened.

As a final comment on the use of standardization in the life cycle, If an organization has a "great idea" and asks others to collaborate in its development, and no one responds, then something is definitely wrong. The organization can view itself in one of two lights: either it is a visionary firm that can exploit a wonderful piece of new technology, or it has a dog of an idea that probably has been tried by everyone else and rejected. In either case, it is free to make a business decision based upon more information than it previously had.

Basically, joining in a standardization effort provides the participants (both users and providers) with a form of insurance that they will not make an independent wrong decision (although there is still the possibility that users and providers may be wrong en masse), and indicates to providers that there is a market for a "standardized widget," and thereby encourages production of widgets by many competitors. With increased production come economies of scale, which in turn allows the price of the product to drop. (This sounds like economic theory; in this instance, I would tend to believe that it is fear of getting locked out of market that drives the price reductions, not a lowered cost to produce.)

At the same time, it allows the technical specifications of a widget to be known to the market, providing other firms an ability to enter the market, by either supplying widgets or widget accessories. Additionally, there are potential widget certification and widget test facilities, widget consultants, and so on. The implicit acceptance of the widget standard—and hence widgets—by the market has spawned an entire industry that revolves around widgets.

STANDARDIZATION AS INFRATECHOLOGIES

There is a danger with the success of standardization (either de jure or de facto) in driving and controlling a market. As was noted earlier, the standardization process has been receiving increasing interest from providers, governments, and users because it can lead a market. The potential for using the standardization process to gain or assert market (not technological) control has increased dramatically over the past five years. The capability of a single participant to influence a single standard has not changed; it is the capability of a single participant to influence the direction of multiple standards that has changed dramatically.

For example, if a participant in the process (call it ABC Corporation) has delegates on five committees who are working on standards in the connection arena, and all five delegates are working towards a common purpose as defined by the ABC Corporation, there is a high level of possibility that some form of synergy will take place, and the five committees will begin to move towards a common set of beliefs or practices that favor the ABC Corporation.

This is, of course, not illegal, nor is it even unethical. To the outside observer, it would appear that ABC Corporation is prejudicing the market in its favor. This may be true if one assumes that ABC's competitors are all dunces and incapable of participating in standards in a coherent fashion. Any competitor of ABC has a myriad of options to invoke. The first is, of course, whether or not to compete in the standardized interface market or to rush a competitive design to market to establish a de facto standard. This can be done and can be lucrative. Second, the competitor can opt to participate in standards to make one or all the standards technically compatible with what is being offered by competition. This provides the famous "level playing field" of standards, where each participant gets to field a team. It has always struck me that everyone worries about the playing field; no one ever worries about the size of the field or even what game is being played on the field. If you come prepared for soccer, and the opposition field is a polo team, you're probably going to lose, and in this case, the level playing field would work to your disadvantage. There are numerous other options, including embracing another (and possibly competing) standard, being the first to market the standard implementation, being a niche provider, and so on.

The mere existence of a standard provides no benefit to ABC Corporation. Implementation, productizing, and use of the standard is of value. It is in this arena that understanding what the market wants and needs is important. If ABC is better at understanding what the market wants than its competitors, it would have won anyhow. By committing to develop technology, and by sharing that technology with the industry, the organization has benefited the entire industry, including (usually) the users and the other providers. This is the key to the matter. In a free market environment, the more capable firm will probably succeed; the use of standards, as any other marketing tool, will be employed when they provide a perceived competitive advantage.

However, there is another form of standard that the market depends upon. This is the non-product based standardized technology which is the basic building block of a technical society. Gregory Tassey describes these standards as infratechnologies, and points out that these standards have a high level of public good in them.[8] Tassey's claim of 40,000 of this type of standards, which describe things from weight and distance measurements to wavelength measurement, is an endorsement of the success of the fundamental nature of standards made earlier (that no one realizes that they are there). However, two interesting things spring from Tassey's description that are worth watching in the IT community at large. The first is a derivation from the concept of "infratechnology" applied at a microlevel to an organization; something that Tassey does not actually mention in his writings.[9] The second looks at the concept of "infratechnology" as it applies to some of the developments in IT standardization today.

The first question is how an organization deals with standards and standardization within the organization. Any organization that engages in standardization needs to have both a "doing" and a "planning" function associated with these internal standardization activities. The "doing" deals with the actual participation in external standardization activities and the creation of products and services that meet the needs of the organization. The participant here is usually the skilled and topic knowledgeable participant; the network engineer for the IETF, the quality specialist for the quality committees, and so on. These participants, however, need some form of infrastructure support to ensure that their efforts, internally and externally, are not misdirected. This is the second activity which deals with the creation of the standardization infratecheologies, that is, those things that permit the effective participation of the "doing" element. This is not the "administrative" function which many organizations provide; rather, it is the professional who acts as the coordinator and problem solver for the standards function in the organization. Just as the management of the internal standards group is supposed to manage the activities of the group within the company and provide an outward strategic focus, the infratechnologist of the standards group should be able to answer questions about what and how much to standardize, the problems that may or may not be encountered and how to deal with them, the benefits of standardization in a particular organization, and so on.

Just as any discipline has its own set of rules gained by experience, standardization also has its own set of rules, nuances, and interpretations. There is a specialist skill for standardization just as there is for law, medicine, health, safety, or any of a hundred other disciplines. Unfortunately, because everyone has "done standards," the specialist skill is unusually hard to define or to quantify. The lack of specialist skill, however, is a leading cause of the current poor state of many standardization efforts in many companies. Choices are often predicated upon absurd reasoning such as, "Let's use the formal process. Bob knows the chair of a subcommittee in the IEEE," or of a consortium because, "Richard is known as an expert by the Jim-Bob Group," or, my favorite, "Let's not standardize. Kate did that once with her product and it didn't work at all." Not one of these people who would hesitate to call a lawyer on a legal matter; they certainly do not self-prescribe prescription medication (mostly); and nearly all of them call in field service to straighten out their computers after they have miss-installed software. They persist in believing that they understand standardization.

The problem derives from the nature of standardization. It is nonlinear, and most practitioners are linear thinkers. They have been trained to this discipline; scientific thought is predicated upon cause and effect thinking. "Even at its most lucid, [the] discourse [of computing] is inescapably linear, doling out scraps of meaning in a fragile thread. But significant thought is seldom linear; cross references and overlapping relationships must be left for the good reader to tease out by himself. Much, also, must be 'read between the lines.' The disparity between linear verbal form and nonlinear conceptual structure is as true of mathematics [and standards] as it is of literature. Both—indeed all forms of discourse—need the services of an art of explication."[10] The "standards infratechnologist" is the explicator for the process; it is her or his job to know how to make standardization succeed, beginning with the derivation of the business question through the completion of the standards effort and productization of the standardized product.

The second issue of Tassey's "infratechnology" deals with the basic nature of the nonproprietary infratechnologies that are available in the public domain and which carry what Tassey describes as a "high public good" content. The original "Internet" was, and is, such a standard. While the Internet Engineering Task Force (IETF) has now been charged with crafting the specifications that manage the Internet, and commercial providers are the fundamental source of funding, the original concept and much of the original funding and care came from the governmental side. The "infratechnology" under consideration here was one that the private sector could not have established on its own. The government's participation was absolutely necessary to make the Internet come into being.

This raises a controversial question for standardization and for the Internet as the first instantiation of an "infratechnology" that is not just national in its scope and application. The problem deals with the idea of the right to limit usage of something that contains, or affects, the "public good." In Chapter 3, there was mention made of the ability of the government to foster regulations of the public good; the question that surfaces now is the nature of this "good."

Currently, the government is proceeding with the National Information Infrastructure (NII). The Global Information Infrastructure (GII) is also being discussed in ISO and in national and regional bodies, as well as consortia such as X/Open, The World Wide Web Consortium, the Internet Engineering Task Force, all of whom want a piece of the action. The first of these initiatives (the NII) transcends the state boundaries in the United States; the second (the GII) transcends the national boundaries. The standardization organizations come in all shapes and sizes. They represent a full spectrum of activities, a full range of private and public organizations, and they are all basically too late.

In December 1995 and early 1996, German authorities informed CompuServe, a major provider of on-line-service, that they were violating Bavarian obscenity laws. CompuServe, in an effort to stay legal, closed down the access to the offending news groups for everyone for whom they provided service, affecting all of their subscribers worldwide. In January, the national PTT of Germany blocked access to another service web site which was publishing neo-Nazi materials, again stopping access to the Internet. In both cases, the bodies were responding to national laws which required them to act in certain ways.[11]

This, of course, outraged the cowboys and cowgirls of the electronic frontier who said, "Cyberspace can't be censored; it's about the freedom of expression." However, what all of these protesters forget is that the fundamental premise of any cooperative venture such as the Internet or NII or such is based upon the cooperative activities of a large host of entities, all of who are subject to the laws and customs of their various national states. The Internet is a "public good;" it was established with the use of standardization, and, as such, represents a national resource. The underlying theory for this argument is contained in the idea that standards are not infinite but are a limited good, and must be managed for the good of the general population. There is only one entity that can manage (or should manage) a resource of this nature, and this is the government.

The other option, of course, is the "free market" forces. This is the claim by those who do not want governmental interference both on the right and the left. On one hand, "free market forces" are the ones that provide cable with sixty channels of home shopping videos and reruns of TV shows long dead, because business cannot figure out how to make a profit selling something like educational TV or "culture." These same people who would not trust business to cut a tree down are willing to give up control of the premier information distribution and dissemination to these business focused "self aggrandizers." Apparently, regulation is acceptable if it panders to a preconceived prejudice.

Conversely, the business community would love to be able to use the Internet to "do business" without the hassle of governmental regulations. The claims that I've heard seem to say that the Internet is not a "limited public good" which is also a valuable resource. Rather, the Internet is posited as a commercial venture that really does not need regulation, since the market forces will act as the regulatory mechanism. I believe that the same was said about cable television just before it was deregulated, and again before it was reregulated.

In both cases, there is a lack of "looking at the public good." On one side, there is a claim for unlimited freedoms; on the other, the claim for unlimited rights. While the government may not be the ideal possessor of the rights of the Internet, it does have a particular claim to hegemony since it does provide the infrastructure that created the net and, in many cases around the world, still controls national and international communications capability. The proof of this is the International Telecommunication Union (the ITU), which is a United Nations Treaty organization. It sets policies and standards for national and international telecommunications and telegraphy. The representatives to this body are not corporations nor are they public spirited citizens; they are governments, who have an abiding interest in what their citizens are told.

CONCLUSION

The nature of the "infratechnology" and the rights of the government and the citizenry does not admit of easy definition. If a standard is a control agent that enables or inhibits a certain class of actions on the part of the public by its existence, then there is a rationale for regarding it as a public good and part of the techno-infrastruture of a state or country. If to this is added the idea that it is a limited public good—meaning there are only a small number of such things (standards) available and which impact the general good then there appears to be a reasonable case for giving the government oversight of standards. However, if they are a marketing tool that is used to structure commercial ventures, then the only oversight that the government legitimately has lies in its right to prevent fraud and other evil commercial things.

I tend to feel that the decision (as with so many other things in standardization) is not subject to an overarching definition, but rather is based upon individual actions. As an example, if a disk interface standard is one of five in the market, and if there are competing technologies to the disks, then the standard seems to fall in the "commercial activity" arena. On the other hand, it there is a single standardized schema for communications, the government has the right and duty to ensure that the standard, whether private or public, is governed for the good of the majority of its citizens.

Ultimately, it comes down to the fact that standards and standardization are not a mechanism for social good or social evil, or for business good or business evil. They are merely one of the more common catalytic agents that allow these mechanisms for good or evil to become widely dispersed and used, and which forces society in general, and business in particular, to examine itself. When you stop and think about it, this isn't too bad.

NOTES

[1]Yes, I know that's not how it's usually quoted, but this is the correct quote. The quote, "The business of America is business," is incorrect; My source is Platt, Suzy ed. *Respectfully Quoted: A Dictionary of Quotations From the Library of Congress,* Congressional Quarterly, Washington, D.C., 1992.

[2]Bruegel, Martin. "'Time That Can Be Relied Upon' The Evolution of Time Consciousness in the Mid-Hudson Valley, 1790–1860," *Journal of Social History,* Spring 1995, Carnegie Mellon University.

[3]This information was from a private conversation with Gary Robinson, Sun Microsystems, who was one of the major drivers of the IEEE 802 committees which were charged with LAN standardization, and with Don Loughry, of Hewlett Packard, who helped Gary. Don and I were discussing this topic in the X3 Strategic Planning Committee and Don volunteered this bit of information in response to my guess that there might have been "up to twenty competing ideas." Gary later clarified the actual number.

[4]I am sure that I will be contradicted in this point by the legions of marketing professors who will read this book with intense interest. I am sure that they will point to a class of activities called "*.*" to prove me wrong and will affirm that they knew about this phenomenon all along. Unfortunately, none of their students have, so I am awaiting with bated breath their clever rationalization on this point as well.

[5]For those who are familiar with this phenomena, and how it can impact profitability, Intel's Pentium© chip set and its placement in PCs in 1995 is interesting. According to press accounts, Packard Bell, a leading supplier of PCs for the home, bet that users would be satisfied with the 75 Mhz Pentium. When they made this decision, the 75 MHz Pentium was head and shoulders above the 486 chip that it was replacing. Within six months, however, it became clear that users wanted the 90 MHz and higher versions of the Pentium. Even the popular cultural icon Doonesbury specified a 133 MHz Pentium PC in the December 1995 strip. The life cycle of the 75 MHz PC was short and rather brutal and a classic case of life cycle failure.

[6]The terms "pundit" and "hack" do not, of course, apply to the current author and others of his ilk, all of whom are hard working and diligent artists of inestimable veracity and integrity.

[7]The experience of the X/Open UNIX providers was illustrative of this problem. When the specification was announced in February of 1995, the first question from the analysts was, "Who's going to brand to the specifica-

tion first?" What the analysts did not seem to realize was that the vendors had to cooperate on completing the test suite and upon building new Operating Systems Interfaces to meet the stringent requirements set forth by X/Open for the brand. Since nearly all the participants in the development of the 1170 APIs for the Unified UNIX specification had about a two year product revision/rebuild cycle, it was not a matter of who would be first, but rather who would be last that was important.

[8]Tassey, Gregory. "The Role of Standards as Technology Infrastructure," Presented at the International Workshop on Standards, Competitiveness and Policy, University of Sussex, 10–12 November 1993.

[9]I provide this because I am not sure that Tassey's original concept would support my usage of his idea in the organizational context. However, I feel that the concept that he has introduced does have applicability. Fundamentally, I would like to absolve him of blame but still provide him the credit for having the idea in the first place.

[10]Black, Max. *The Labyrinth of Language,* Mentor Books: New York, 1969, p. 26.

[11]The Germans, who are more thorough than most and probably more sensitized than most, are, I believe, the harbingers of things to come. That the German state is highly competent in technology, coupled with a dedication of their civil and social organizations to maintaining and upholding the law, provides a reason for why the Germans would figure in the first cases of this kind. However, I feel that they merely have a two year lead on everyone else; it is not something that relates to the German culture, as many commentators have so devoutly wished.

Chapter 14

The Future
of Consensus Standards

"They reckon ill who leave me out;
When me they fly, I am the wings;
I am the doubter and the doubt;
I am the hymn the Brahmin sings."

—Ralph Waldo Emerson, *Brahma*

INTRODUCTION

This chapter looks at the future of consensus-based standardization organizations. It opens with an examination of what constitutes success for these organizations; that is, what must they do to be adjudged successful. This is followed by series of problems that militate against their success. Some captious critics might say that the list of problems is overwhelming, and that the whole idea of consensus standardization is either morally bankrupt or hopelessly outdated or both. I would argue, however, that the concept is viable. It has, however, been misapplied by those who have taken neither the time nor effort to learn about the discipline. This flaw applies not only to standardization. It can be generally applied to much in business, from rightsizing (a morally bankrupt statement) to junk bonds to politics. It's just that there are few apologists for standardization.

SUCCESS METRICS

The first problem that should be considered is one of determining what constitutes success for the open processes by which standards are produced. This phrasing is very important; the success of standards (whether de jure or de facto) in the IT market is assured. There is no longer the danger that was faced in the early 1980s of the camps of proprietary computing arguing and fighting to maintain hegemony. It is now reasonably agreed that no provider can produce something without embracing some, or many, standards. Fundamental interoperability is assumed. Products that are completely proprietary are no longer offered. Even Microsoft, the current "evil empire" of the standardization world, participates in standardization organizations and really does implement standards when they serve its business needs. Being "not standard" means ending up, over time, isolated and alone.

What is questionable is the consensus process of standardization. What constitutes success for an effort of this type? Too often, the functional goodness of a standardization group is measured by the amount of paper it produces, its ability to create new and improved specifications and brands, or by the count and amount of members and dues. I am reminded of Emily Dickinson's lines:

> Success is counted sweetest,
> By those who ne'er succeed.
> To comprehend a nectar
> Requires sorest need.[1]

In the worst case, the SDO or consortium is formed for the express purpose of stopping something. The something is usually the success of a competitor. Gladstone phrased it best with the comment that, "To be engaged in opposing wrong affords but a slender guarantee for being right." Organizations that succeed in making an opponent fail by using standardization have shown the depth of their intellectual and technical honesty; it is easy to destroy something. Building takes less time and patience than thinking, that hardest of all human activities.

Ideally, each standardization organization should be driven by the same goal of the continuation and growth of the information technology industry in some form, shape, or way. The goal may be to increase confidence by improving quality, increase performance by increasing speed, or to provide any of a hundred or more attributes to the market that it may need. A deliberate non-goal of consensus organizations should be the creation of standards. If a standardization group never creates a single standard, but provides a common forum for the industry/discipline it represents, makes available useful standards developed by other groups, and interacts freely and constructively with other organizations, then that group has succeeded. Success, therefore, appears to rest heavily on the ability of a group to cause something to happen that helps the industry grow and helps users do what it is that they wish to do better, faster, and cheaper (or, less expensively) in both the long and short term. Determining what is good for the industry, and what is meant by good, is the responsibility of each participant in the process.

Market share and growth, profit, and satisfied customers, singly or in combination, are all priorities that vary from company to company, discipline to discipline, and industry to industry. Each standards group must recognize the diversity of goals and interests that confront it and learn to manage that diversity. All too often the groups are more interested in the creation of standards and the continuation of the organization than in the service that they render to their ultimate clients, the end users. A viable definition of "good" might be standards that have a larger audience within the industry and help the industry as a whole.

Most of the major SDOs in the world were creatures of the first half of the 1900s, although they keep appearing, although more slowly. Most of the consortia were created after 1980, in response to perceived weaknesses in the IT SDO arenas.[2] However, nearly all of them have at least a hierarchical structure, or slightly modified version thereof, as their basic organizational and management template. This structure has a splendid history of success in heavy industry, where there is a long tradition of slow predictable change and the functions of each position are known and well-defined. The preconditions for success of regularity and constancy are noticeably lacking in IT standards work. Suggestions for standards can arrive from anyone, anywhere, at any time. This is one of the major strengths of the consensus standardization process. The nature of the IT business changes constantly, depending upon what technology is hot and what problem the users are trying to solve. Additionally, the industry is very mobile, so that people who start in one organization can move to another with diametrically opposed views and continue to participate in the standardization groups.

Standardization organizations have responded to this change by adding layers and layers of management and coordinating committees to ensure that their hierarchical structure continues to function. This has slowed the pace of change with which these groups have had to deal, since proposals for some form of action are now relegated to a committee to examine the activities and to ensure that they are in consonance with another, as of yet undefined, plan. Eventually, the proposals are placed in a committee or move slowly through several layers of management. (If you keep extending the pipeline, nothing will ever emerge from the open end.) The price for this control is very high. Standards now take an average of four years to complete; much more, if they are controversial. The majority of end users, the ultimate consumers of the standards, as well as a large number of participant users, are beginning to question the usefulness of the standards that are being produced, since the fragmentation of the groups has led to multiple and redundant standards and specifications.

The revolt of these disaffected groups, however, is itself interesting. The participants who have dropped out did so because they objected to the practices and activities of standardization organizations; yet, the form in which they chose to express this revolt was identical to the one to which they were objecting. In other words, the creation of similar organizations is a revolt not against the concept of consensus standards, but against the managerial and organizational template of the standards groups that create them. What this says is that the underlying principle is healthy, but the application is flawed. The perception has surfaced that a set of users is unable to impact the standards process in a timely manner. Whether or not the feeling is correct is immaterial. In some cases, the users feel that the consensus standards process, which is supposed to represent all interested parties, is failing. It is this perceived lack of responsiveness, or sense of systemic failure, that is driving the activities of the new standards bodies, the governments, and the industry.

Can the consensus standards organizations regain their ability to satisfy their customers needs and wants? I believe that it will depend on improvement in two areas: forecasting the social and economic needs of the users and decreasing the elapsed time between standards proposal and standards creation. Both of these are managerial problems and both are capable of solution. Both require that the standards groups initiate a planning function, but of a nontraditional nature. It will also require that the groups remember that they exist only to plan and make things better for the society and industry who fund them and under whose aegis they operate.

PROBLEMS

Charter Conflicts

At the present time, SDOs and consortia have broad global charters that are increasingly in conflict as the external environment changes and interdependence among disciplines becomes commonplace. For these problems to be addressed, decisions must be made about which organization or technology or activity or national body has hegemony, based on the success of the group in satisfying its users (both immediate and final end users). For the common good, it will be necessary for each standards group to take a little less than it is claiming as its area of responsibility and sacred trust. It also will be necessary for each group to recognize that, if each separate group claims less, the entire process will function more efficiently and increase the absolute potentiality for everyone. The question becomes, "Which group is willing to make the first sacrifice for the good of the common-wealth?" Whichever group volunteers must be rewarded for its selflessness by the users. Its sponsors must be able to somehow gain some reward for their activities. However, in real life, it will probably be punished, and other standardization groups will move in to take advantage of the perceived weakness.

The solution is reasonably simple and is beginning to be implemented. People are no longer joining organizations; in fact, many organizations are seeing declining membership. This does not solve the immediate problem of conflicting charters, but over time, will delete those organizations that do not really produce something that the participants find valuable. While it is not as selective as one would hope, it is effective.

Consensus Organization Management

As more and more parts of the IT industry become interconnected and interdependent, the participation in the various organizations should become more common, and the resolution of conflicts between participants will span more than a single organization. Participants, technically competent and politically astute, are beginning to move into the standardization process to represent the interests of their sponsoring organizations. These professionals will belong to more than one organization; their interests will be present in more than a single nation or region. These interlocking interests will pose the greatest challenge to standards organizations over the next decade, who will have to dedicate time and resources to the development of a new managerial theory that takes into account the volunteer nature of the cross-organizational membership, the ability of each new professional to move and to switch loyalties, and to act in whatever manner seems best in the specific situation at any given moment, all while remembering that the purpose of standards is to increase commerce. It is true situational management of the most complex nature.

Most delegates represent personal, professional, national, discipline, and industry goals, all because of their participation in the consensus standards process. Moreover, delegates must act in a manner that is consistent with the expectations of the committee of which they are members. If a delegate is good, he or she may influence the process positively by participation, by reassurance, or by the very act of being there. By extension, however, if the participant is not good, or is not backed sufficiently by his or her sponsor, damage can occur to the individual, to the support or funding organization, and to the entire process itself.

Finally, there is the positioning of standardization within the various high technology organizations themselves. Normally, participation in standards work is viewed as a career limiting move. It is this aspect of participation that must be overcome, and it is largely the role of the standardization organizations to do this. A dull product, no matter how good for the industry, is still a dull product. Unless the SDOs and consortia can somehow show that their products make a difference to the industry at large, they will remain in a backwater, and delegates will continue to suffer within their own organizations. This applies not only to the technical level, but also to the managerial level as well; CEOs very rarely care, choosing to delegate responsibility to the Vice President of Making Weird Deals and Standards or to the Director of Processes and Standards or to the Standards Group. In nearly all cases, the official in charge of standardization is not as powerful as his peers, and has standards as an afterthought. There are some companies that have moved standardization to the forefront, but they largely are the minority.

Also of importance for the managerial efforts of these standardization organizations will be the changing nature of the companies that participate in these groups. There is nothing to preclude a company or other organization from having representation on multiple committees in multiple arenas (SDO, consortium, alliance) all of which are struggling to standardize the same—or very much the same—thing. The question of how to ensure that all of these groups are aware of one another and work together is going to be a major challenge over the next five years.

Internal Structure

The most basic component of the consensus standardization groups, working groups, technical committees, what have you must be examined for its continued applicability to the job at hand. In nearly all organizations, the work is assigned to a subgroup. The membership on the subgroup is predicted upon willingness to pay or the willingness to participate (which is another form of payment). The typical meeting is a committee of the whole who discuss the situation at hand. About 20 percent of the delegates do all the work and the other 80 percent ratify the decision of the most vocal or most persuasive participant. The meetings have become places where procedure is discussed endlessly; the only thing that allows the process to continue is the activity of the minority away from the meetings.

The solution is, of course, to clean up the basic operating procedures of these "working groups" so that they retain consensus while encouraging (or demanding) that people work. This will be more difficult in the SDOs in the U.S. who are terribly afraid of legal action, but much less so in consortia and alliances. The pressure to change must come for the members of the organizations, and this has proven to be substantially difficult to manage since the members in many of the organizations tend to view their positions as sinecures—they've earned it and no one is going to change the procedure just as they've gotten comfortable with it. It can be done, but it must either be done slowly by persuasion or brutally by blatant use of power. In either case, it must be done because the current standardization regime is failing.

THE NATURE OF STANDARDIZATION

There are portions of the Information Technology industry where the market is growing explosively and is dynamic to the point of instability. Internal relationships are unclear and there are no guarantees that tomorrow's market will be based on today's activities. In this atmosphere, planning is impossible; it is a speculator's market. No standards can be written for this type of environment: Standards are postulated on a recognized growth path and a certain continuity of progress. In a high-growth, highly dynamic market there is nothing but discontinuity. If standards, voluntary or otherwise, are introduced into this environment, they will fail, since standards act to stabilize a market and the explosive market does not need or want standardization.

Conversely, in a market where growth largely has ceased and where the internal dynamics are regularized, there is little opportunity for standards to make a contribution. When the industry relationships are known and the attributes of the market are clear, the market has already attained the stability that standards might have offered. In these instances, standards serve only to clarify the attributes of both the industry and market and tend to slow the market dynamics even more. It is here that "perfect" standards are written. In effect, the industry is proclaiming its fatigue by having rules substitute for originality and order substitute for growth.

In both of these markets, standards are unnecessary, because they cannot or will not fill the function for which they are best suited. Standards need a setting in which they can provide some stability without becoming moribund. This is tied to the growth of the standards activities in an industry itself.

Portions of the information processing industry have reached this "in-between stage," where this is still phenomenal growth, but the growth has been channeled into a general matrix of possibilities and impossibilities. (Technically, there probably are not any impossibilities, but these are things within the realm of possibility but outside the realm of probability.) The dynamic nature of this market, coupled with the start of stability, makes the standardization necessary. It has become too expensive to support random growth, and the growing interdependence of the various portions of the market act as a further inducement for standards, which do provide a direction. Additionally, standardization provides a stable launch platform for future attempts to improve products or concepts. The use of standards furnishes the market with a free lengthening of the product life cycle. They also provide an essential gestation period for products under development, when ideas and products can be evaluated and tested, corrected if necessary, or offered without change depending upon the response of one's peers in the standards community.

THE NATURE OF THE STANDARDIZATION MODEL

The current standardization model in the high technology industry is predicated upon what I call the "systems vendor's model of standardization." The model shows the operating system component, the storage component, the communications component, and the applications component, and so on. Each component is clearly delineated (which is not that clear in reality), but which does figure significantly in the design of these components. Additionally, it is the way that standardization committees work. Languages go here, the OS goes there, storage there, databases somewhere else.

This model works for the systems vendors because they can cross-subsidize standardization efforts. If they standardize something in the OS domain, they can compensate for the Intellectual Property Rights (IPR) release by adding a proprietary feature, or by extending the OS in a different direction into the storage area, and so on. Finally, systems vendors can afford to standardize a component if it will sell more of another type of component for which they can become the single source supplier.

The middleware vendors (the group of companies who are moving to the forefront as the vendors of prominence in the late 1990s) cannot cross-subsidize based on the releases of intellectual property to standardization organizations. The reason for this is not hard to see. The IPR that makes up many of their internal interfaces that would have to be standardized to make a difference exists throughout all of their products and designs. To give up even a small piece to a standardization organization may have unexpected consequences for their entire product portfolio. The minimal gain from standardization is not worth the damage that could occur if the IPR position was compromised.

As of this writing, there is no new model of standardization for middleware vendors, nor do I know of any organizations that are working on solving the standardization problem that these organizations face. It is an area that needs work but one that will require a cultural mind shift on the part of the systems vendors and standardization groups.

INTELLECTUAL PROPERTY RIGHTS AND STANDARDS

The question of who owns the copyright on standards, while not of concern to most people, is of very high concern to standardization organizations. Most SDOs (and to a lesser extent, consortia) gain appreciable revenue based on publication of documents. In Chapter 4 there was a description of the revenues that accrue to the various SDOs based on publishing (up to 80 percent in some organizations).

Yet, if the whole idea of a standard is to make the technology available as widely and as freely as possible, would it not make sense to put standards that people need on the Internet? This is not "rocket science." Companies put their specifications, product brochures, and any other information that they want the market to use on the Internet and the Web. Yet SDOs have been reluctant to do this because it will deny them publishing revenues. How lucrative the market is can be shown by the fact that some SDOs charge phenomenal prices for their documents. ISO charges nearly $1000 for the ISO 10646 standard that describes the Universal character sets, and the ISO 9000 series is also phenomenally expensive in comparison to what is delivered. Since there are no authoring costs for these documents, the price becomes even more inexplicable, until you consider that the organizations are keeping themselves alive and paying their employees with the proceeds from these sales.

The question of IPR then surfaces. If the organizations have no real "sweat equity" in their publications, what can they copyright? Well, apparently they can copyright the look and feel of the document, and the look and feel is the first thing to go if you pull text off the Internet. Each SDO has publishing conventions that are rigorously enforced (down to paper size, margin constraints, and so on, let alone type font and paragraph heading). The rationale for this level of control is revision control; the bound document that you receive from the SDO or Standard provider is "guaranteed" to be the current one. SDOs claim that there is no universal browsing system that would allow everyone access without imposing economic penalty—so that the printed format is equitable and controls revisions and is immensely profitable.

There is a growing user anger with this approach. If standards are meant to be usable, then they should be on-line; every other major engineering requirement is. The IT industry is turning into an electronic medium. The failure of the SDOs to provide technical specifications on-line is a major stumbling block in their use. This strikes to the heart of the problem. If the SDOs had searched for a way to make things more complicated, they would have had to go some to find a more contentious and silly issue. But they have done it and their failure to respond to a user need that everyone else seems to have overcome could result in large-scale damage to the IT SDOs at first and then to the system as a whole over time.

SPENDING ON STANDARDIZATION

How much does the U.S. IT industry spend on standardization activities? How much does industry as a whole spend? How much does a single standard (any standard or specification) cost?

Right now, people assume that standards are free or at least, minimally expensive. There is no research that I've found over the last fifteen years that provides any clue to how much anyone spends in this area. Most companies do not know. The government does not know how much MilStds cost it from any point of view; from creation of the standards to lost opportunity cost because of their use or such. The IT industry does not know how much the OSI standards suites cost. I have put the amount at up to $2 billion— and received precious little disagreement.[3]

If this is a serious discipline as I claim, it would be logical to assume that somewhere there is an interest in this. There are academics willing to work on the problem— but they need the funding to do this. It is beyond the ability of a graduate student to research and complete; I've watched several of them try to come to grips with the problem and have to, in the end, admit defeat. And yet, without this information, there is no real hope of making the discipline better, since we don't know where we are or what we pay, nor do we know what it is we get for the money that we spend.

CONCLUSION

The industry growth thus has proved to be a mixed blessing. It got the standards groups out from under their tamarind tree and made them necessary and vital, but it is also forcing them to confront their interdependence. While I sincerely doubt that consensus standards have the power to cause fundamental changes in the way that capitalism and the governments interrelate, I do feel that the information technology industry is a major social and cultural force within society. Because consensus standards are part of the IT industry, their failure and its concomitant impact on the IT industry probably will ripple throughout society as a whole. A failure of the consensus standards program to achieve internal coordination of its own activities will result in its own removal; it will be replaced by a more efficient and workable method of setting industry and market standards. I have a certain fondness for the present method, I would prefer to see it survive. Certainly, I believe that standards and standards organizations will continue and will prosper. There will always be someone or something creating standards in the world. At the same time, there will always be someone or something that objects to current standards, standards organizations, and standards processes and structure, and will fight to change or improve them. The question is, what form this objection will take? Ultimately, it boils down to whether the change in standards, standards organizations, and their processes will be evolutionary or revolutionary.

I believe that, as time passes, the national organizations, the SDOs, consortia, and alliances will become more and more focused on international standardization activities and international audiences and will attempt to increase their ability to impact, either for better or for worse, international standardization activities. There will be a gradual evolutionary movement away from the consensus system as it appears today, perhaps towards greater participation in single larger national forums, either privately or governmentally driven. The speed of decision making will not increase substantially. Planning and consideration of standards activities long before they are actual, however, will increase.

NOTES

[1]Emily Dickinson, "Success Is Counted Sweetest."

[2]The IT industry seems to attract more than its share of consortia. I tend to believe that this is because it does have the characteristic of rapid change but also because it has a history of "two men and a garage" creating something that the industry needs, and then having someone form a consortium to promote the idea. With low costs to start a technology, the consortium serves, in some cases, to make possible the publicity necessary to gain mind share in the market. Also, computer companies have money.

[3]After I wrote this, I received a paper from Dr. Michael Spring in which he claims that the total spending on OSI may have amounted to $500 million. Unfortunately, I do not know how Michael derived his costs, nor do I remember how I derived my costs. In a recent conversation with Michael Hoynes of the ANSI staff, I asked for his help in qualifying the moneys that are spent on creation of standards, since ANSI does retain records (or can gain access to records) that have the necessary details for this type of research. See: Spring, Michael; Rutkowski, Anthony; O'Donnell, Jon; Oksala, Steven; "The Structure of IT Standardization," March 1996 *StandardView,* Volume 4, Number 1.

Section 3

THE ORGANIZATIONS

This section of the book looks at the organizations that actually do standardization. The section includes descriptions of the Standards Developing Organizations, the consortia that are active in the IT arena, and the alliances, which are by nature transient, but which have a tendency to remain in the public mind's eye long after they have ceased to exist.

The section does not attempt to be all-inclusive. I have listed those groups that met the dual qualifications of filling what I believe to be an important role and of which I was aware. For these organizations, I will attempt to follow a generalized structure that has three primary sections. The first section will generally cover the committee, how it works (if there are any surprises), and what it was supposed to do. The second area that I will try to cover includes what the organization does, what it currently thinks its mission is, and what its claims to glory are. The final section examines what I feel to be the weaknesses and some suggestions as to what is needed to make things better. The third section represents my point of view and represents some of my biases. One of the comments about the predecessor work was that I often failed to include more than apocryphal stories to support some of my views. I believe that, for the larger part, I've overcome some of that criticism in the earlier chapters of the current book. However, I will honestly say that the "Futures Section" of these chapters represent a best guess of what I feel will happen to these groups. (I feel like Scrooge interrogating the "Spirit of Christmas Future" in Dickens' *A Christmas Carol*. I am not sure if these are the "shadows of things that *might* come" or the "shadows of things that *will* come.") Where possible, I've tried to relate the problems and activities of the organization and what has been written earlier in the book about general theory and practice.

Where I was unaware of an organization, or where I just did not believe that an organization was germane, I have omitted it. This brings up an interesting problem, however. I am currently the standards strategist for a Fortune 100 company, involved in nearly every aspect of IT, either directly or by reference. I make my livelihood in this milieu. If I am unaware of a burgeoning standardization organization, how is an Information Technology user, an end user, or, even, in the worst case, a political leader making decisions on something like the Telecommunications Bill, supposed to find out about these organizations, let alone find out about how they work? Consortia appear at the rate of about one every two weeks; significant consortia (those with dues of over $50,000) appear at the rate of about one every quarter. SDOs are not blameless in this arena either; ISO is up to at least Technical Committee 211 as of this writing. The difference with ISO is that the committees are at least required to register and become known. Some consortium appear like a wraith from a low budget horror movie; one's first inclination is to laugh. Only later do you realize the danger that these groups pose to you and to other living organizations.

However, despite my occasional despair at dealing with all of them, the organizations that keep popping up do display one thing; the fundamental belief in the IT industry that standardization does play a role in the industry, and that the whole concept of standardization is important. After all, if there were no new organizations appearing, the discipline would either be static or dying. And this is not the case. IT standardization is as alive and vibrant as the industry it serves.

Where possible, I have included a pointer to the Web page of the organization in Appendix 3, and have not attempted to duplicate too much of what is on the various Web pages. However, when I thought that it was important to know a particular bit of information, I've included it in this book. I have also included, where possible, the addresses of the organizations so that the book does not require Internet access to serve as a source of information.[1]

NOTES

[1]For those with Internet access, the best entries that I've found are maintained by Markus Kuhn, a Computer Science student at the University of Erlangen, who for several years has maintained an excellent source for obtaining information about the ITU, IEC, and ISO. I usually start information searches from his site, since he covers a broad area well. He also updates it constantly, and has a large range of interests. Unlike the party line that the organizations will provide, Markus tends to permit and encourage dialogue.
Internet Mail: <mskuhn@cip.informatik.uni-erlangen.de>-Germany
WWW Home: <http://wwwcip.informatik.uni-erlangen.de/user/mskuhn>

Chapter 15

International Standardization Bodies

"By me, the hemispheres rounded and tied
The unknown to the known."

—Walt Whitman, *Prayer of Columbus*

INTRODUCTION

The three major international Standards Developing Organizations that impact the information technology field will be examined as part of this chapter. These organizations are the International Organization for Standardization (ISO), the International Electrotechnical Commission (IEC), and the International Telecommunication Union (ITU). Each of these organizations produces standards or recommendations using a form of voluntary process, and each has an area of expertise which it believes is its alone. These areas change since the external world does evolve, producing sometimes overlapping areas of interest and standardization activity. However, they do manage to usually sort things out, occasionally to everyone's satisfaction.

While there are several consortia that must be mentioned in the international context, since their operations do span the globe, and they do have an international influence, I've opted to put them into the following chapter, not because they are of less importance, but merely because its easier to look at like problems and like solutions. The SDOs have a different set of problems than do the Consortia. To alert you, I have classed the Open Software Foundation and the X/Open Consortium, Ltd. (in the process of merging as this book goes to press) and the Object Management Group (which has just finished reorganizing), as major consortia. The Internet Society, which is another international consortium, has its own chapter.

All of these organizations are trying to create common specifications that can be used by the industry to create information and knowledge. Many of these consortia have SDOs working on the same topics. However, in many cases, the SDOs have not made the progress necessary to keep industry as an active participant. When this happens, the consortium and SDO have a most interesting time trying to sort out who is going to do what to whom and when. It provides a nice dynamic tension in the system. Interestingly, it is almost always the consortium that has reached towards its SDO counterpart and not the other way.

While the emphasis in this chapter is on the standardization committees that produce IT standards, there is a larger world of standards that impacts the nature and the functioning of the IT market, as well as the business of the users of IT products and services. Some of these committees (Quality and Environmental Management, and Service Sector Standardization) will be examined as well for their impact on the IT industry as well as the impact that these standards will have as they arrive from the standardization bodies. This topic will also be examined in the section that looks at the future of the organization, especially with regard to the tendency of well-meaning governments to make mandatory requirements from these standards.

THE INTERNATIONAL ORGANIZATION
FOR STANDARDIZATION (ISO)

The Charter, Intent, and Functions

The International Organization for Standardization (ISO), established in 1946, is the leading standards organization in the world.[1] Unlike the other organizations discussed in this chapter, ISO is not concerned with a single discipline, but rather deals with "industrial standards." This term covers areas ranging from mica (Technical Committee 56, but now inactive), to boilers and pressure vessels (Technical Committee 11), to information processing systems (ISO/IEC Joint Technical Committee 1). My favorite committee is TC 196, which is concerned with the standardization of Natural Stone (really called the Ornamental Garden Rock Committee). It is this broad range of interests and concerns that qualify ISO as the premier standards organization.[2]

The purpose of ISO is to facilitate the international interchange of goods and services, and to encourage cooperation in economic, intellectual, technological, and scientific endeavors. Belonging to ISO is a voluntary decision; the organization is the result of free and open agreement among nations to recognize the hegemony of a single standardization organization and to attempt to coordinate standardization efforts to encourage lessening of national prejudices. The creation of ISO reflects the post World War II view of the victors of the war that nations should cooperate economically, rather than compete, since the major result of competition had been shown to be reasonably destructive wars. When it was created, the intent was to encourage trade, and move away from the protectionist policies that had been so damaging to the world before the great depression. The 1930 Smoot Hawley tariff is the archetypal occurrence that the diplomats hoped to preclude with the creation of ISO and other organizations, including the United Nations. The degree of success that these organizations achieved in this arena is not clear; however, the creation of ISO did help the standardization movement tremendously by providing a central focus for standardization activities on a global scale. As for the economic cooperation, the topic of free and open trade figured very heavily in the Uruguay round of General Agreement on Trade and Tariffs, where the realization that standardization could be used as a nontariff trade barrier became a concern. The nations participating in Uruguay GATT went to great lengths to make sure that they obviated most opportunities of most governments to use standardization in this way.[3]

ISO's range of interests is as broad as it is because of the membership that composes it. It is composed of the national organizations believed to be the "most representative" standards organization of the country that they represent. (This created an interesting problem when the former Soviet Union broke up. The question of who owned GOST [the USSR's standardization organization] was a minor issue. The larger question was who was lucky enough to start from scratch, and were they better off because they did?) Because representation at ISO is by nation, each nation selects a single organization that acts as its representative to ISO, thus avoiding representational battles both at ISO and within the country. This national body organization represents all of the country interests, not merely those of a specific discipline or area. As originally envisaged, I believe that this was not a bad idea. The world of standards moved rather slowly, and the single central organization in a nation was probably aware of all of the players that needed to be contacted and who could make a significant contribution. However, the choice of the "single standardization entity" seems a little arcane today, when the standardization of heavy earth moving equipment, Information Technology, and management standards all use the same rules for standardization. The appearance and disappearance of individuals, organizations, and companies are continuing its accelerated pace, while the growth of multinationals (something not really foreseen in the 1940s) has also acted to confuse the systems even further.

ISO does not have "standards authority" in two important areas; telecommunications belong to the ITU, and electrical and electronic engineering standards are the preserve of the IEC. As IT became more and more intertwined with electronic engineering, the differences between some of the standards efforts of the IEC and ISO became blurred. As a result, and at the urging of the Untied States, ISO and IEC joined to create the ISO/IEC Joint Technical Committee. By merging the ISO and IEC technical committees that were charged with dealing with standardization of information technology systems, the two organizations took a brave first attempt in making ISO and the IEC responsive to the needs of users. They have not done so since. While the ITU cooperates more closely with ISO, the ITU is a UN treaty organization, rather than a voluntary consensus group.

ISO: Membership and Organization

ISO membership is open to any recognized standardization authority from a national body. There are two types of membership associated with ISO. The first is the "member body," which is the organization that is most representative of standardization within its

country. In this form of membership, the organization (and hence its nation) may participate in any ISO technical committee, has full voting rights in any technical committees
and subcommittees, is eligible for Council membership, and has the right to be seated in
the General Assembly. Of the ninety members of ISO, eighty are member bodies. It
should be noted that over 70 percent of member bodies are governmental institutions or
organizations that are incorporated under public law. In nearly every case, the member
bodies have close ties with an organization that is perceived as representing the national
interest. The member bodies themselves usually vote, or are viewed as voting, as the "national will" indicates.

The second form of membership is the "correspondent member," which is usually a
governmental organization of a developing country. In this case, the country has no standardization organization, but sends a governmental group to insure that they keep track of
the activities of ISO. Correspondent members do not take an active part in the technical
groups, nor do they have the right to vote in the General Assembly, although they may attend the General Assembly as observers.

ISO has recently established a third category of membership, called the subscriber
membership, for countries with "very small" economies. Fundamentally, the intent of the
subscriber membership allows these countries to "subscribe" to the information of ISO, to
encourage them to become part of the international standardization arena when they become wealthier. The subscriber members pay reduced membership fees.

National participants are charged with the following duties:

- Informing potentially interested parties in their country of relevant international
  standardization opportunities and initiatives,
- Organizing so that a concerted view of the country's interests is presented during
  international negotiations leading to standards agreements,
- Ensuring that a secretariat is provided for those ISO technical committees and sub-
  committees in which the country has an interest,
- Providing their country's share of financial support for the central operations of
  ISO, through payment of membership dues.[4]

From a U.S. point of view, the system of "federated organizations" militates against
the success of an organization with the above goals, unless all parties interested in standardization are somehow supposed to be represented in the singular national organization.
The problem for ISO is that there are so many divergent points of view in the IT industry
in the U.S., where central government involvement with standardization is much weaker
than elsewhere in the world.

The glue that holds all of this activity together is the Central Secretariat of ISO. The
Central Secretariat, located in Geneva, is composed of approximately 150 people, and is
responsible for insuring that the activities of ISO make sense, that the technical committees do not interfere with one another, that the ninety member nations are aware of what is
happening, and that the mini-UN that ISO is survives and prospers. However, since the
basic function of a standards organization is to cause standards to be produced, the Cen-

tral Secretariat must also respond to the needs of the Secretariats of the Technical Committees which are the groups that are responsible for managing the volunteers who write the standards.

The Central Secretariat is paid for by the sale of publications (30%) and the subscriptions of its member bodies (70%). Each member body pays according to a sliding scale calculated upon the GNP and the value of imports and exports; reinforcing the basic concept that standards are a trade tool, and that standardization is an economic issue. (If the whole idea was based on technology, it might make more sense to base the subscription on something like patents, Nobel prizes in science, or such.) Contributions to fund the central Secretariat came to about 27 million Swiss francs in 1994, leading one to conclude that publications netted about 11.6 million Swiss francs. Additionally, member bodies pay for the care and feeding of the various secretariats that they own, since each nation vies for a Secretariat that it wishes to influence. The total cost of all of the Secretariats (Central and Country) in 1994 came to about 135 million Swiss francs.

It is interesting to note the following (again taken from ISO documentation):

> To that [the costs of the secretariats], one must also add the value of the voluntary contributions of some 30,000 experts in terms of time, travel, and organization of meetings. While no precise calculation has ever been made to assess in figures this contribution of fundamental knowledge to the work of ISO, it is nevertheless certain that this expenditure amounts to several hundred million Swiss francs each year.

One would assume that an organization that has been around since 1947 would have a very good handle on the costs that are associated with its operation. A business is reasonably expected to be able to report on the number of users, the value of its installed base, and the amount of sunk and continuing costs. If it could not, it would probably be severely criticized. Yet the statement here is so brazen as to enthrall by its very effrontery. It shows a fine disregard for the idea of standardization as a business tool, but a sincere belief that standardization is a "special discipline" that is a lofty combination of technology and economics. It is a tune that is being less and less sung by participants.

The Technical Committee (TC) is the key to the standardization success of ISO. Each major topic for standardization is examined to see if it applies to a current committee. If it can be assigned, it is. If it cannot be assigned to a current committee, and there is sufficient interest in the topic to warrant creation of a new committee, then a new committee will be formed. The committees are assigned a number upon creation. The numbers, assigned in sequence, provide a chronological order for the committees; that is, TC 25 must antedate TC 26. TC 1, begun in 1947, dealt with Screw Threads.[5]

Each Technical Committee has a Secretariat assigned from one of the member bodies. (The member body must volunteer to sponsor the Secretariat; as noted above, they are somewhat expensive to maintain.) The TC Secretariat is responsible to the Central Secretariat of ISO for ensuring that all the necessary checks and balances of the consensus standards methodology are followed, and that the activities of their TC proceed smoothly. Each TC can have Sub-Committees (SC) which must have Secretariats (again, from member bodies, and again, carrying an administrative cost borne by the member body) that are responsible for their subcommittee activities. Finally, each TC and SC can have Working Groups (WG). The WGs do not have Secretariats, using conveners (who must belong to a member body) instead. Each TC Secretariat is responsible for maintaining a liaison with other TCs that might be impacted by its work. There are currently slightly over 2700 of these groups, and over 30,000 people working on ISO standards throughout the year.

Representation on a TC carries with it a commitment to participation in the activities of the TC. Any member body of ISO can request representation on any TC, SC, or WG. The representation can come in either of two forms: participant (P-Member) or observer (O-Member). Members who elect observer status are kept informed of the work of TC, SC, or WG. Members who opt for the participant status must take an active part in the creation of the standard by attending meetings and voting on the standard issues. Furthermore, only a P-Member may serve as a secretariat of a TC or an SC.

Finally, there are two types of liaisons between an ISO committee or subcommittee and outside organization. These are the infamous Category A and Category B type liaisons. Category A liaisons are for those organizations which can or do make an effective contribution to the work of the technical committee or subcommittee. The Category A liaisons are provided with copies of all relevant documentation and are invited to meetings by senior management at ISO. Category B liaisons are what one would call "information only" groups. They are sent documents from the committee. Category B is good if the other organization is in a monitor mode; Category A is best if the outside organization wants to participate in the debate.

ISO: Procedures

The policies regarding international standardization have changed over the years since the last edition of this book was published. While the primary function of the TC or subcommittee continues to be to develop and maintain standards, there have been a few interesting additions to the process.

To begin, each committee has to prepare a "strategic policy statement" that looks at the business environment into which it is to cast its standard, the nature of the standardization activities in the area (expanding, shrinking, static), at the amount of revision work that will be needed, and finally, at the emerging needs of the area. While there is still a very heavy focus on the standardization aspect of the work, this stage appears to dovetail to the "conceptualization phase" that was mentioned earlier in Chapter 11.

The formal stages are listed here:

Stage 1: Proposal stage

Stage 2: Preparatory stage

Stage 3: Committee stage

Stage 4: Enquiry stage

Stage 5: Approval stage

Stage 6: Publication stage

The first stage seems to complete the requirements of the "conceptual stage," and the "Discussion Phase and Writing" sections of Chapter 11 seem to be subtended by the activities of Stage 2, 3, 4 and 5. Stage 6 can arguably be said to be the equivalent of the implementation activities of the multi-stage model. It is interesting to note that ISO takes no thought for the stages that I've ascribed to the consortia earlier, such as testing, branding, or market analysis (preconceptualization).

Stage 1: Proposal Stage.   The first formal stage of the ISO process is called the "New Work Item Proposal Stage," yielding a New Work Item Proposal (NP). This step is supposed to confirm that a standard is needed and that there is a responsible set of participants willing to work on it. Responsible is defined as at least five P-members who are willing to work on it, and a majority of the P-Members of a TC or SC vote in favor of the NP.

Stage 2: Preparatory Stage.   With the appointment of a leader, the group sets to work to create draft standards, or Working Drafts (WD). The group continues to work until they feel that they've got it right, at which time they pass the WD to the parent committee for the consensus-building phase.

Stage 3: Committee Stage.   The parent committee receives the draft, and it is immediately registered by the ISO Central Secretariat as a Committee Draft (CD). The document is sent out for comments until consensus is reached that the document is satisfactory. Once consensus has been attained, the text is finalized for submission as a Draft International Standard (DIS).

Stage 4: Enquiry Stage.   The Draft International Standard (DIS) is circulated to all ISO member bodies by the ISO Central Secretariat for five months. It moves out of DIS status to Final Draft International Standard (FDIS) if a two-thirds majority of the P-members of the TC/SC are in favor, and not more than one-quarter of the total number of votes cast are negative. (If it does not meet success criteria, it is recycled until it is "right.")

Stage 5: Approval Stage.   When the DIS becomes an FDIS, it is circulated to all ISO member bodies for two months by the ISO Central Secretariat for a final Yes/No vote. Technical objections are overlooked here; they're registered for the next version. If a two-thirds majority of the P-members of the TC/SC are in favor and not more than one-quarter of the total number of votes cast are negative, the text is approved as an International Standard.

Stage 6: Publication Stage.   Once a Final Draft International Standard has been approved, the final text is sent to the ISO Central Secretariat for publication as an International Standard. To date, ISO's work has resulted in 9,300 International Standards, representing some 170,700 pages in English and French.

Fast Track Procedures

If a document that has a "certain maturity" is submitted, it may be allowed to enter the process at the Stage 4 level. If another SDO is submitting the document, it may be admitted at the Stage 5 level. Of course, the success of the fast track is dependent upon the sponsor of the proposal having all of its ducks in a row, since objection in the Fast track can cause the proposal to begin as a Stage 1 proposal.

ISO has attempted to create some guidelines for making the programs work a little more quickly. Ideal deadlines are

Working draft within six months
Committee draft within two years
Final Draft International Standard within three years.

However, it appears to be reasonably easy to get extensions of these proposed guidelines, since the volunteers who are trying to obtain a standard can always go to a consortium to complete the standard. This is something of which ISO is aware.

ISO COMMITTEES OF IMPORTANCE

ISO-IEC Joint Technical Committee 1 (JTC 1)

Many of ISO's Technical Committees are involved in some way with information technology. However, only one committee has the charter to deal primarily with Information Technology: Joint Technical Committee 1. As of 1996, JTC 1 had twenty-five P-Members and twelve O-Members, sixteen SCs (and their Secretariats), sixty-two WGs, nine ISO TCs with which liaison was maintained, and seven IEC TCs which also required liaison.

JTC 1 was formed in 1987. It was created from an amalgam of ISO Technical Committee 97 (ISO's IT Technical Committee) and two IEC Committees (TC 47B and TC 83) which were also concerned with IT standardization. Since most of the activity within JTC 1 is based on activity formerly in TC 97, a look at what used to be TC 97 will give a review of JTC 1 in a contextual setting.

TC 97 was created in 1960 partly in response to the proposed creation of ASC X3. It was formed to standardize "computers and information processing." The Secretariat of the committee was offered to ANSI, which accepted with alacrity. The committee's charter was written and expanded so that TC 97 dealt with computers, peripherals, and computer systems. Slightly earlier in the same year, TC 95 had been formed to deal with office machines, which were still relatively distinct from computers at the time, or at least there was a perceived difference. By 1981, however, this distinction had blurred, and TC 95, which had accomplished a majority of what it had been chartered to do in 1961, was merged into TC 97, becoming one of the twenty-eight "missing" committee numbers. In 1983, further integration occurred when two of the TC 97 Sub-Committees (SC 8, Numerical Control of Machines, and SC 9, Programming Languages for Numerical Control) were spun off to create a new ISO Technical Committee: TC 184, Industrial Automation Systems.

In 1984, TC 97 was reorganized to make it more responsive to the needs of the information technology industry. The scope of the committee was changed to read, "Standardization, including terminology, in the field of information processing systems including, but not limited to, personal computers and office equipment." The various committees in TC 97 were modified, and an effort was made to compartmentalize (or at least group) like activities through the creation of three vice-chairpersons each of whom was responsible for coordinating the activities of a group of SCs with similar interests. The three groups were the Application Elements, composed of SC 1, SC 7, SC 14, and SC 22, Equipment and Media (SC 10, SC 11, SC 13, SC 15, SC 17, SC 19, and SC 23), and Systems (SC 2, SC 6, SC 18, SC 20, and SC 21). As this reorganization was taking place, there was a shift in the internal make up of the SCs, with the phasing out of SC 16 (Open Systems Interconnection), SC 5 (Programming Languages), and SC 12 (Instrumentation Magnetic Tape), and the creation of SC 21 (Information Retrieval, Transfer, and Management for Open Systems Interconnection), SC 22 (Application Systems Environments and Programming Languages), and SC 23 (Optical Digital Data Disks).

In 1987, after several years of discussions, meetings, and conferences, ISO and IEC agreed to create a joint technical committee that would be responsible for standards in the IT area. The force that drove the compromise was the fact that both international organizations were moving to a merge point in their standardization activities in IT, and the overlap had the potential for producing incompatible standards for the same device or product. At the same time, the volunteers who served on the committees creating the standards were pressing both organizations to come to a compromise for the good of the industry. This led to the establishment of the Joint Technical Committee 1 of ISO/IEC, with the scope of, "standardization in the field of Information Technology."

The Secretariat of the committee was offered to the United States (ANSI). After some discussion within ANSI on the benefits that this valuable (if expensive) Secretariat conferred upon the United States, a majority of ANSI's membership came to realize that having the Secretariat in the United States would be of major importance to the national standards effort and well worth the cost to the U.S. national standards associations and members. Current SCs are as follows:

SC 1: Vocabulary

SC 2: Coded character sets

SC 6: Telecommunications and information exchange between systems

SC 7: Software engineering

SC 11: Flexible magnetic media for digital data interchange

SC 14: Data element principles

SC 15: Volume and file structure

SC 17: Identification cards and related devices

SC 18: Document processing and related communication

SC 21: Open systems interconnection, data management, and open distributed processing

SC 22: Programming languages, their environments and system software interfaces

SC 23: Optical disk cartridges for information interchange

SC 24: Computer graphics and image processing

SC 25: Interconnection of information technology equipment

SC 26: Microprocessor systems

SC 27: IT Security techniques

SC 28: Office equipment

SC 29: Coding of audio, picture, multimedia, and hypermedia information

SC 30: Open electronic data interchange

This list has been stable for several years; since 1986, only three groups (SCs 28, 29, and 30) have been added.

The purpose of JTC 1 is to see that an international vehicle is available to aid in the standardization of information processing systems. Its existence is predicated upon the participants understanding of what a standard is expected to provide, and to whom it will provide a benefit. It all turns on the thesis that a standard is a workable piece of technology. It is a solution that may not be technically superior but an acceptable solution for the technical and business problems that caused its creation. JTC 1 has a mandated international focus; each delegate has a national focus, representing her or his country in the international forum. This representation is expensive for all delegates pay all of their expenses. Meetings are held from Tokyo to Brighton to New York, and a delegate must either be personally wealthy or else have a sponsor with deep pockets. (Again, attendance at meetings is necessary if one is a P-member of the committee.) The need to be at the meeting is not required by the by-laws of JTC 1, but by the need to understand what is happening and thereby represent the national interests of the delegate. The dynamics of any meeting are vital to an understanding of the activities and positions that are taken by the various delegates. Because attendance is as costly as it is worthwhile, it is usually logical to send the "best" delegate (technically, politically, organizationally) that one has available to insure a return on expenses. Most delegates to JTC 1, in fact, are standards professionals who understand the intricacies and complexities of standards development. This leads to the problem of what it is that these participants are really representing, and how effective they are within their own organization. As noted earlier in the book, participation in standardization is all too often seen as a "kiss of death" to a good engineer, and the good standardization representative must be competent in her or his discipline, as well as having organizational and political skills.

Additionally, there are three fundamental viewpoints that each JTC1 representative should possess. The first perspective is a bias toward the national government whom they represent at JTC 1. While the delegates should all be skilled professionals who speak the same language of the IT industry and standards, they all represent their nation and are seated with national delegations at JTC1 meetings. Second, representatives all incline towards the point of view of the IT industry; that is, one of the most fundamental concerns of the delegates is the Information Technology industry and the growth of that industry. Finally, a majority of the members represent sponsors and so look at the activity in standards from a very pragmatic point of view, since they are ultimately charged by their sponsor to provide a return on the investment occasioned by their participation in the standards process. It should be noted that the nature of the sponsorship itself can impact this bias. Although a preponderance of members do come from companies within the industry, the standards professional can be sponsored by an organization, such as a school or a government, with an interest in seeing something done in a particular way, in which case the bias involves advocacy of a national interest or to a technical methodology peculiar to a school. In the end, from a member viewpoint, JTC 1 can be said to look at standards first from a national viewpoint, then from a viewpoint of the standards profession (and all that this implies), and then ultimately arrives at an international perspective.

The problem that even JTC 1 management is aware of is that all the "good things" are going somewhere else: either to consortia or to the *de facto* model. Middleware is not arriving at JTC 1. As pointed out earlier (Chapter 14, page 186) the standardization model for middleware is not particularly suited for formal standardization. Middleware, if it does go for standardization, is going to consortium. It is interesting to note that the effort that JTC 1 (and attendant organizations) made to accommodate the consortium model was only introduced in 1994, after the consortia had been in business for nearly seven years.

The Publicly Available Specification (PAS) process is very rigorous. It requires that an organization that wishes to have its work reviewed to complete a reasonably lengthy questionnaire that examines the goodness of the providing organization with respect to its openness, its willingness to work with ISO or ANSI or whomever to meet the requirements of consensus, and so on. If the requesting organization passes all of these tests, it can submit its technology for consideration at the Stage 4 (Enquiry) level, so that the work can be progressed upward for completion and consideration as a formal standard (Stages 4, 5, and 6) after consensus across the industry is ensured. This is what it took JTC 1 seven years to finally propose.

During those seven years, the consortia have created a new GUI, overwhelmed the POSIX model of standardization with UNIX, designed a communications schema that is far and away more successful than OSI will ever be, created a series of interoperability tests, modified international character set standards so that they can be used by real operating systems, modified standards so that they can be used by engineers building products, and taken poorly written standards and provided test suites and sample implementations to permit the standards to be globally implemented. They have also espoused a theory of "open systems" that the market has bought into, and they have managed to ensure that organizations continue to support both the informal and formal process by their urgings. This is not to say that the consortia have not had failures; they have had more failures than not. But, when they fail, everyone is very aware of it. When an SDO fails, it tends to bury its mistakes or merely not produce anything. Basically, JTC 1 still does not get the picture that standardization is not merely the SDOs. Consortia technologists are just as good, and consortia members are also members of organizations that fund the formal process.

By continuing to emphasize the difference between formal and informal standards, and by claiming moral hegemony for formal standards, JTC 1 is merely exacerbating an already hostile solution. The consortia have tried to extend an olive branch; JTC 1 must somehow do more if it is to remain even a part of the evolving information age.

Technical Committee 176: Quality Management and Quality Assurance

TC 176 is a committee that does not directly impact information technology except for its infamous ISO 9000 series of standards that relate to the *management* of a quality system. All too often, ISO 9000 is taken to be a "quality standard" that describes how to achieve quality. It is not, nor is it a cookbook on quality methods and standards. Rather, it is a re-tread of an old U.S. Military standard on quality management and quality assurance from the 1960s that was rewritten by the British and then sold to ISO as the first of a series of "management standards."[6] The idea wasn't bad, but the execution, especially within the United States, was poor.

The actual 9000 program does carry benefits; it is not a great quality program, but it does provide a company that has only a vague idea about quality a starting point from which to build. It is based upon a common standard (which is unfortunately, subject to interpretation in places), and is not really too difficult to begin in a company. The major stumbling block to ISO 9000's acceptance has been the reliance on third party inspection, and the emphasis in the United States on "registration" and certificates as preconditions to purchase. The registration and certification produced a firestorm of objections to the program in the United States, with vague threats of nontariff trade barrier violations and the start of a "Fortress Europe" mentality brought about by EC 92. None of this was real, of course, but it did cause a delay in the acceptance of 9000 within the U.S. Fortunately, there are consultants who, realizing that the program was a virtual gold mine, jumped right on the 9000 bandwagon and began selling "ISO 9000 made simple" courses and certification preparation and all sorts of other things. There are even programs available for your PC that tell you how to become 9000 registered. You can buy these programs for as little as $99.99, using your credit card, of course.

Sarcasm aside, the 9000 program does offer a set of benefits that a company can use to start a quality program. It doesn't produce quality; if you have a really well-administered program that produces trashy goods, you still will have a good program and no quality. But the intent was, and continues to be, the creation of a base level program that makes the management and workers aware of the aspects of quality in their day to day jobs.

Technical Committee 207: Environmental Management

TC 207 is the same as ISO 9000, except that it is a management program for establishing an environmental management scheme. Basically, the new series of standards are called the 14000 series, and they are being implemented in 1996. Like the 9000 series, they are based upon a management systems approach. Like 9000, they require certification and some form of mark to indicate compliance. And like the 9000 series, they have the consultants and test houses slavering in anticipation of another certification gold mine.

Fundamentally, the British standardizers, driven by the success of the 9000 series, are attempting to duplicate the success by convincing everyone that the world would be a better place if only management of these complex entities was regularized and made harmonious. The concept is not new. It worked with the British Empire, when Britain exported Victorian morality and structure into a changing world, and they feel there is the need to do it again. Aided and abetted by the French standardizers, who also wish for a place in the sun, they are making their way across the world providing the benefit of their management experience and skill. However, if one accepts any of the organizational or management ideas contained in Chapters 6 or 8 of this book, it becomes apparent that the classical structure of the organization, for which these ideas are intended, breaks down. For large, stable, successful, and coherent organizations such as the large car makers of France or the coal mines of Britain, the ideas contained in 14000 may apply. However, for the dispersed manufacturer of electronics who buys disks from Taiwan, mother boards from China, chips from Macao, with cases assembled in Mexico using Brazilian cables and Korean monitors for transshipment to Europe, the idea of a 14000 certification and registration program is somewhat ludicrous. It is merely another penalty for companies who have a large base of installed capital goods in countries where 14000 is considered a prerequisite of doing business.

Service Sector Standardization

Because the growth of the service sector of the economy is expanding more rapidly than the manufacturing sector in most (and especially European countries), standardization of services has become the newest and hottest area of potential standardization. However, we must ask the question of how one justifies involvement in the service arena?

The ISO Council Committee on Consumer Policy (COPOLCO) came up with a solution. It found a new avenue to justify intervention. To quote from one of the articles in the ISO Bulletin: "The relationship was complex between provider and consumer: The latter was wary because it was difficult to assess for quality and for performance prior to service, and he or she was often not even sure what the service entailed or what he or she would get."[7] According to COPOLCO, consumers wanted quality of service, transparency of service, and reliability of service.

The term "service" can be taken to mean your relationship with your bank, your dentist, your psychologist, your travel agent, your advertising agency, and your telephone company, as well as anyone in the retail or hospitality business. It also includes the software business. Again, citing ISO's monthly publication, service standards are ". . . needed and could be developed before the technology actually even exists." As an example, the Stiftung Warentest (Consumers Testing Organization) tested numbers of mobile phones and found that the phones (hardware) were generally acceptable, but that the quality of service was radically different. Speech quality needed to be improved; some phones sounded muffled and many were not loud enough for use in a car. But things such as dialing and using the memory features could have been designed to be "far more practical."[8]

Even more instructive was the fact that the different prices, the different features, and the different conditions of the service made it difficult for the consumer to know which one to choose for his or her condition. It was obvious to COPOLCO that service standards were the answer to this confusing morass presented by high technology. Unfortunately, consumers in the U.S. have been dealing with these phenomena for years, without the need to be helped by standards. The arrogance of the standards developers boggles the mind. As an example, COPOLO is looking at the standardization of "hotel accommodations." The Australians and the Europeans worry that the term "five star" hotel may mean different things in Perth than it does in Brindsi or in Kabul. A visitor might find that the appellation "first class" may mean different things, and it was apparent that a standard was needed to prevent the traveler from having to find this out the hard way. As a result, it is being proposed that a certification service (surprise!) be made available to judge the world's hotels to a common standard. If these people weren't serious, one could almost regard this as a Monty Python comedy sketch.

The impact of this on the software consulting and application development business would be interesting to observe. How would one rate the quality of software consulting? How would one rate the nature of a software package that did your taxes? Is it on the final result of lowered taxes, ease of use, convenience of purchase, clarity of interactions, or price? Or on a combination of all of these and the attendant weighting?

To continue, COPOLCO came up with the idea of "horizontal standards"; that is, standards that cut across all service industries. As an example, they cited the need for a common complaint resolution standard, a common method of guaranteeing users the right to be heard, and the right of a user to have essential needs satisfied. Also identified was the concept of a "family" of standards; that is, banking satisfaction depends upon telecommunications, and telecommunications depends upon software. Therefore, it might be necessary to build up families of standards that might have complex interconnections. The interesting thing to consider is that COPOLCO came up with this idea during the time that the users of the Internet and the Web were struggling to make the Internet financial transactions secure without benefit of ISO standards and responding, in near real-time, to the needs of the market.

Why ISO Survives

ISO survives, simply, because there is a need for an organization to do what it does. If ISO was not there, it would be necessary to invent something like it. Because of the complexities surrounding modern industrialized life, an organization that is charged with co-ordinating the activities of the various groups creating standards (which, often provide the "techno-infrastructure" of IT) is needed. The question may be not so much one of "Is the organization needed," but rather one of "Is ISO that organization?"

What ISO provides, in response to the first half of the question, is a place where people who are standardizing can meet to discuss their collective efforts and come to some sort of agreement on how these things can be achieved and completed. ISO has the ability to invoke and maintain a camaraderie among those involved in the discipline and the publication of a set of rules that, while subject to abuse, do guarantee that honest organizations that take them to heart will have a better product than those that do not. The second half of the question, "Does it have to be ISO" is looked at in the section on futures.

The reason that ISO stays alive is very simple: No one has come up with a more viable replacement for it as of this time. While there is a level of satisfaction for it in the non-IT sector, there are very few in the IT sector who can be said to truly make ISO one of their major concerns. While ISO has the capability to influence legislation in non-IT areas such as the environment or in quality or in areas of management, the larger ability of ISO to influence the direction and future of the IT industry, as a positive force for change, appears to be minimal.

The Future for ISO

ISO has major challenges to overcome if it is to survive as a viable entity in the Information Technology Standardization arena. The challenges revolve around ISO's ability to be responsive to a different market than existed when ISO was created.

In 1947, the existence of the multinational corporation was really not considered. ISO was built around the idea that a nation's industrial might would be reasonably concentrated inside the national borders of a single nation state, and that nation state would manage the standardization activities for those countries. The environment has changed, and the fundamental assumption that drove the creation of ISO the way that it was has changed substantially. In the IT arena, companies are literally "everywhere." The corporate headquarters may be inside the United States, but the corporation may be the largest single employer in a province or town or country in Europe or the third world. This can, and has, influenced the vote of a smaller nation's national body. Looking at it simply, a member of the U.S. Technical Advisory Group to ISO/IEC JTC1 has one of approximately forty votes in the U.S. TAG. In the Irish body national TAG, the level may be one in ten, or in Morocco, one in two. The ability of an organization to lengthen its influence is substantial, given the nature of the multinationals. The problem comes in when a multinational uses its power to stop, slow, or limit activities that would cause it economic pain by using these delegates from these nations.

At the same time, these multinationals combine into organizations that are not limited by national boundaries. The nature of alliances in which U.S., German, Japanese, and Korean computer manufacturers combine to create a new program or joint effort, are far beyond the efforts that the national bodies can mount. The nature of the effort is one that involves only those manufacturers and not the remainder of the industry. It is focused on production of a mutually acceptable and implementable specification. The specification neither wants nor needs approval of *all* of a nation's providers; it merely wants the sponsors to give it a chance to succeed. In this case, the all-inclusive system is too burdensome.

The rules under which ISO operates are also somewhat arcane. While they are superior for established industries which are making slow, but evolutionary progress, they fail with an industry that is trying to create and deploy products (not specifications) within a six month period. As was noted earlier, programs that are in a high flux state are poor candidates for standardization, and much of the industry is currently in flux, especially in the software arenas. Of the six stages in the procedures, four are concerned with voting and process rules, not the drafting or creation of a specification. At any point in time, a strong national body protest could send the proposed standard back for more review or rework. If you are trying to deploy a new language on the Internet, the last thing that you want or need is a bunch of technologists telling you that what you have is contrary to what their nation needs or wants and that you have violated any of a number of stages of a process model of which you were not aware.

Finally, and probably of most concern, is that ISO seems to believe that it is owed its existence. This statement hinges on my interpretation of two distinct elements that make up part of what I have described above.

Firstly, ISO proudly proposes that it is focused on international trade and increasing economic activity. So are most major corporations today, so the claim is not especially significant. It can claim that it does represent more than just a single entity but, as anyone who has studied a multinational can point out, so does a multinational. It claims that it represents a broad cross-section of the society yet, I would venture to guess, would soon be clear of members and participants if the major corporations in the world stopped participating.

The arrogance necessary to claim that it has no idea how much the participants spend, and yet say that there are 30,000 active participants in the process, shows a casual indifference to the reality of the business world. There is not a major corporation in the world that has not gone through some wrenching times in the last ten years. In many cases, there have been layoffs and re-engineering. New clients have been added, new ways of doing things established, and cherished traditions abandoned. Yet, over the last ten years, ISO has made no major changes to a process that was already under stress in 1986. Within the IT industry, JTC 1 is more ignored than used. The lack of new significant programs and of new significant activities is telling. JTC 1 is still working on Open Systems Interconnect standardization; OSI is commercially dead. It has not been a serious contender for commercial viability for six years, yet JTC 1 continues to pass standards that relate to it.

ISO, on the other hand, continues to irritate its mainline membership by embracing ever more esoteric schemes from COPOLOCO and CASCO (Committee on Conformity Assessment) to figure out new ways to register and accredit organizations. The height of the foolishness is the statement that, "these organizations have contributed much, through their documentation, to the success of world trade." Basically, I feel that COPOLOCO and CASCO, through their sycophant relationships with ISO and the certifications organizations, have created a vast wasteland of unnecessary certification and conformance schema, and continue to do so with the tacit acceptance of ISO, primarily because the testing and certification schemes generate revenue, which in turn sells documents, which in turn make up 30% of ISO's budget. Unfortunately, the testing and certification schemes are proving to be a hindrance to the development and competitiveness of European industry. However, the schemes continue, since clearly if only everyone would merely certify and comply the world would be a much better place. Chapter 2 describes the activities of the medieval guilds whose function was to force artisans to meet standards imposed by the guilds. That system broke under the press of capitalism. If ISO does not change, it too will break under the press of the information age and the Internet and Web.

When ISO was the exclusive coordinator of international technology, it could afford to be deliberative and focused on the past. Unfortunately, it is no longer the only coordinator or even a little exclusive. Rather, it resembles nothing so much as the outraged shopkeeper who, having determined that competition is difficult, proposes legislation aimed at stopping efficient competition from large chain stores because his method of retailing is the only right one, having been handed down, as it was, from his father. And, failing to find a new and better way to compete, ISO will suffer the same fate.

THE INTERNATIONAL ELECTROTECHNICAL COMMISSION (IEC)

As noted in the previous section, the International Electrotechnical Commission (IEC), stands on equal footing with ISO. While it works with ISO, it reached an agreement with ISO in 1976 that defined the responsibilities of the IEC as the field of electrical and electronic engineering, with everything else being ISO's bailiwick. Formed in 1906 as a result of a resolution passed at the International Electrical Congress in St. Louis in 1904, the IEC was a response to a real and perceived need to standardize in the electric and electronic fields, specifically the increasing divergence of the European and North American electric power requirements (220 and 115 volts). Although the IEC was created too late to stem this rift, it has become a force in preventing similar situations, or minimizing their economic impact if they do occur.

The IEC focuses on the technical aspects of electricity such as measurement, testing, utilization, and safety. It is concerned with producing "specification standards" which detail the minimum set of acceptable features to which each product must conform or be tested against. (The product may exceed the minimum standards and remain acceptable.) These standards provide a criterion for value. If a product does conform to a standard, it is recognized as having a distinct set of features that quantify its value. This quantification allows the users and manufacturers to understand what they have, to understand that the designs and safety features are proven (or at least tested), and a common methodology may be used to accomplish a technical electrical task.

IEC: Membership and Organization

The IEC, like ISO, is a voluntary organization, composed of national members who represent the interest of their countries, but who also represent the users, manufacturers, trade associations, government, and academic associations within that country. The commission has forty-nine national committees.

The IEC has a reasonably complex committee structure, similar to that of ISO, with Committees of Action, Advisory Committees, and various other helping and advising groups. However, the fundamental job of the IEC is to write standards, and for this it turns to its technical committees. Currently, there are eighty-six TCs,[9] each of which can have Sub-Committees. The Sub-Committees can also have Working Groups if they believe it necessary. Each Technical Committee has a Secretariat, as does each Sub-Committee. In 1996, there were over 200 TCs and SCs in IEC. A major difference between ISO and the IEC is the nature of the representation on the TCs. In the IEC, each member nation belongs to every TC, whether or not they have any interest or concern. As a result, each member nation has a stake in an emerging standard and is requested to ballot on the acceptance or rejection of every proposed standard submitted by the TCs.

IEC: Procedures.   The standards creation process is the same as that of ISO, although there are nomenclature differences in the various stages. A draft standard coming out of a TC is circulated to all members, who then vote on acceptance, rejection, or change. Unreturned and "No response" ballots are taken to indicate a positive response, since IEC operates under the assumption that if something bothers someone, they will respond. If 20 percent of the votes are found to be negative upon completion of the balloting, the proposed standard can be modified to incorporate changes and the draft recirculated, or the entire effort can begin again.

The members of the IEC have a bias (or perspective) similar to that of JTC 1 in that there is very heavy manufacturer representation. IEC standards are focused upon the manufacturer of the product and are intended to ensure interoperability by providing a comparison metric, rather than an interconnection performance metric. This perspective is valid for the IEC. There is a need for everyone in the industry to attach a similar definition to the terms "ohm," "amp," or "volt." IEC standards can be considered as groundwork standards for ISO; with these IEC standards, the common vocabulary, upon which systems understanding is built, would not exist. The IEC bias, then, is nearly the same as that of JTC 1, except that its second most important perspective is that of industry and company, followed by standards and international interests.

Liaisons.   The most important liaison of the IEC, other than that to ISO, is with the committee known as CENELEC, (the European Committee for Electrotechnical Standardization), with which IEC shares eighteen members that are primarily the industrialized nations of Europe.

Why the IEC is Still Alive

The IEC fills a role that others are not willing to play. It is reasonably specialized, and some of the standards that it writes tend to become regulations, especially in the fire safety arena. If you look over its committee listing, you will see that some of the topics are, for the IT arena, mind-numbingly dull. SC 24, for example, has as its charter "electrical accessories." Sub-Committees include switches for appliances, plugs, sockets, and switches, circuit breakers for household use, and so on. Yet, if the IEC was not there to standardize these items, they would either all be unique to each provider or they would be delegated to some quasi-official government agency in each of the countries, which would make the shipping of products nearly impossible. (Everyone should have some level of experience trying to plug a power cord into a socket in England and then in Italy. If you do not have the necessary adapter set, you are basically out of luck.) To convert the UK to a different plug than the one they currently use would cost about $6 billion; I can't imagine the English being willing to pay that much "merely to help the French plug in their mustache curlers," as was so graciously expressed to me by a proper old English gentleman.

The Future

I believe that the IEC, among the three major International SDOs, is in the best shape, because it knows what it is doing and seems to be concentrating on what it does best. I do not believe that it will become a major player in the IT industry, but it will continue to grow marginally over the next several years. There are no, or very few, consortia that will bother it. Fundamental electrical engineering is really a boring subject for a consortium, and is usually best left to people who enjoy it. It is one of the absolute providers of infra-technology standardization, and, as such, will retain a position that makes it valuable and permits it to survive, as long as it stays focused on that role.

THE INTERNATIONAL TELECOMMUNICATION UNION (ITU)

The International Telecommunication Union (ITU), one of the few organizations covered in this book that is not a voluntary standards group, is a formal treaty organization, organized and run under the auspices of the United Nations. As a treaty organization, the ITU has the right and duty to set international regulatory standards, which are administered by governments rather than industries. If a government, as a national entity, accepts the positions of the ITU, it then proposes regulations, backed by both positive and negative sanctions, to enforce the regulations within its jurisdiction. The seriousness with which the regulations are regarded can be judged by the mechanisms that are employed by the national government to enforce them. The area of jurisdiction of the ITU, simply stated, is all telecommunications usage—planning, regulating, coordinating, and standardizing.

The ITU Convention recognizes three purposes for the organization: to maintain and extend cooperation in the development and use of telecommunications between present members (and to help developing nations); to promote the development of technical facilities to help improve the efficiency of telecommunications; to harmonize the actions of nations to attain these two goals. To meet these aims, the ITU allocates radio frequencies, coordinates efforts to eliminate radio interference between nations, helps developing nations use telecommunications technology, helps members set rates so that they remain fiscally viable while serving their communities, looks at safety of life issues as they relate to telecommunications, and undertakes studies, makes regulations, adopts resolutions, and collects and publishes information on telecommunications matters.

History

The ITU was born in 1865, when twenty European nations signed the first agreement setting up the International Telegraph Union. The intent of the union was to attempt to guarantee standardized and general interconnection, uniform operating instructions, and common international tariff and accounting rules. On a smaller scale, they faced the same problem that Chandler described for the railroads during the following decade. The difference was that, in Europe, there was the fear that transborder transmission of data would result in the passing of military secrets and political activities from one country to another. The same holds true today except that the medium now is the Internet and the countries are complaining about strange (either politically or morally corrupt) ideas being *imported* via telecommunications.

Telephony was added to the ITU in 1885; radiotelegraphy in 1905. By 1927, it was controlling the allocation of radio frequency bands, testing and measurement. Finally, in 1934, it became the International Telecommunication Union. In 1956, the International Radio Consultative Committee (CCIR) and the International Telephone and Telegraph Consultative Committee (CCITT) were established, and became active in telephony and telecommunications. This structure became well established with the dawn of the computer age and, in the U.S., was held as an ideal by members of the RBOCs when AT&T was broken up and the telecommunications standards participants joined ISO/IEC JTC1 and the national IT standardization bodies. Every four years, the CCITT would publish a set of books, known by their colored covers, that constituted the standardization activities planned for the next four years.[10] The ITU Recommendations were always coordinated, one with the other, with a regularity to the cycle.

The problem with this idea, of course, was that the market didn't wait. By 1988, the CCITT Recommendations were dreadfully behind the merger of the IT and telecommunications market; gamely designing interfaces that had been overtaken by technology several years before. In 1989, the ITU established a group to examine what to do. By 1992, the report, and attendant restructuring of the ITU, was put into place.

ITU: Membership and Organization

The ITU consists of 164 nations, and each nation signs the ITU Convention at the Plenipotentiary Conference, held every four years. The Plenipotentiary Conference, like the ISO General Assembly, sets broad policy and objectives, called the Constitution and Convention of the ITU. Because the ITU is a specialized agency of the U.N., it is therefore a treaty organization, and member nations are usually represented by an agency of the government. In the United States, that agency is the State Department. In most other countries, it is the national Postal Telegraph and Telephone (PTT) organization, or, with privatization, the government agency in charge of the telecommunications sector.

The new organization has the usual trappings: the Plenipotentiary Conference (the highest and largest authority); the Council (the working subset of the Plenipotentiary Conference); an authority on telecommunications standardization (referred to as ITU-T, and replacing the old CCITT); an authority on radio frequency issue (called the ITU-R, and replacing the old International Radio Consultative Committee [CCIR] and the International Frequency Registration Board [IFBR]), a telecommunications development sector (ITU-D, replacing the Telecommunications Development Bureau [BDT]). There are also World Conferences on International Telecommunications, held at the behest of the Plenipotentiary Conference, which are charged with revising telecommunications standards. Participation in these conferences is limited to the members of the ITU-T and selected other international agencies of diplomatic standing, such as UN groups, regional telecommunications organizations, and multi-government satellite groups.

The budget for the ITU is over 150 million Swiss francs and the staff amounts to about 750 people. Fees to the ITU are based upon the choice of the country and agreed to by some obscure formula with is not evident. The countries paying the highest fees include France, Germany, Russia, Japan, and the United States.

Normally, Telecommunications Standardization Conferences (TSCs) are held every four years. At these conferences, the participants set the course for the next four years, establish direction, and approve or disapprove of the creation of committees, as well as accept or reject "Recommendations," so called because they are "voluntary." Recommendations offer technical and operational standards, tariffs, administrative directives, and terminology statements. These Recommendations are exactly that—recommendations—and are not binding, but are usually used as the basis for any negotiations and agreements. Additionally, the technical Recommendations have a way of becoming international de-facto standards, since they provide technical insight on how to connect to the international telecommunications system. The attendees of the TSCs are those members of the ITU-T (governments), members of the U.N., authorized operators, scientific groups, international and regional standardization groups, international and regional telecommunications organizations, and so on. However, participation in the Technical Standardization Study Groups (TSSG) is open to all interested parties, and over 200 private sector companies and over forty organizations participate. Fundamentally, the standards directions are set by any and all committees or groups who can prove that they have a stake in the established hierarchy.

Of course, the problem with the four year cycle was not fixed by the reorganization. There was a problem of how to deal with the issue, and I believe that the following extract from an ITU Public Relations document says it best:

> In order not to lapse into inefficiency and be outstripped by other national or regional standardization forums, the ITU reassessed its method of work. What was at stake was the ability to meet the demands of industry and the economy by maintaining the preeminent role of ITU international standards-setting activities so as to prevent the creation of *de facto* fragmented markets. If the technical and economic enclaves were allowed to develop, a large number of activities like finance, which are global in nature, would be curbed and the world's economic foundations could be affected. It would be almost a return to the pre-1865 era. . . . If the ITU is to retain its preeminent role in the field of standardization to ensure global interconnectivity and interoperability of telecommunications systems, it has to respond dynamically to the competition and challenges of regional standards-setting bodies [Author's note: read here European Telecommunications Standardization Institute (ETSI)] and industrial groups and produce Recommendations (i.e., standards) fast enough to prevent regional or proprietary standards to take precedence thus safeguarding the benefits of global standards.[11]

What the ITU Really Does

This description of why the ITU-T has gone to an "as needed" approach to standardization is very informative. In this statement, the ITU-T is fundamentally saying that if it does not lead, and heretofore control, the international standardization movement in telecommunications (and by logical extension, Information Technology), then there will be a regression to the trauma that existed before the American Civil War. While I can appreciate some of the puffery that is necessary in a marketing piece, the implicit threat that is being waved about is that, if the ITU-T is not dominant, then there might be a regional or possibly even an industry lead sector that takes over creating internationally accepted and used standards. I believe that the fundamental truth is that the market would accept whatever standards it needed regardless of the source from which the standards were derived. While there might be a time of confusion as new technologies were implemented and change occurred, it would appear that moving back to the "old days" in which governments tried to control information access by standardization (or by lack of it) is reasonably well-eclipsed by the current age of information technology, which embodies telecommunication as one of its attributes.

Basically, the ITU-T is trying to catch a moving target in IT, but it is providing some of the technological infrastructure that telecommunications providers need. Its recommendations include X.400, X.500. X.25, v32bis (modem) and lots and lots of OSI and ISDN standardization.

The Future

The primary concern and responsibility of the ITU-T continues to be telecommunications. This occupation with a singular discipline, coupled with the nature of the full members (governmental administrations and service providers, which, in many countries, are one and the same), gives the ITU-T its perspective. Simply put, the ITU-T perceives the nature of telecommunications standardization as an entity in and of itself, rather than as a subsystem component of information technology implementation and deployment.

Of all of the organizations discussed in this chapter, I believe that the ITU-T is in most danger of losing any mandate that it retains. The fundamental problem that it must confront is the change in the fundamental nature of the telecommunications arena. While there are service providers, and there will always be necessary changes to the infrastructure and infratechnology that keeps telecommunications functioning well, the nature of what the infrastructure supports has changed, and this is what is driving the standardization of telecommunications. The ability to use the telecommunications as the basis for things that were not even thought of three years ago (the Oracle corporation's $500 browser-based terminal), the appearance of mobile modems to support gypsy computing, mobile telephony, and electronic commerce will drive the world of telecommunications, not the rules and regulations of the ITU.

Until the ITU realizes that it supports change and industry rather than being the driving force, it will be in peril of failure. And the failure that it will sustain will be most difficult of all to survive. The organization will not go away; rather, it will become a relic of what it could have been, and exist in the shadow of its former importance. This is the cruelest existence of all.

SUMMARY AND CONCLUSION

The groups described in this chapter all use essentially similar methods and structures to create standards or recommendations. All three of these organizations go to great pains to avoid making unilateral decisions, which, after all, could cause a loss of membership and the creation of alternate standards bodies. At the same time, the inability to make timely decisions, that is, decisions that are created within the timeframe needed by the market, has largely crippled the ITU and ISO. The IEC has survived this problem because it does make decisions as they are needed.

It is this aspect of the formal organizations that creates their greatest danger. The decisions that the IEC must make usually have to do with things that receive little publicity; battles are fought and won, standards are produced, and the market accepts them. The users, systems creators, and systems integrators are not really going to get too excited about "terminal markings" (TC 16) or "degrees of protection by enclosures" (TC 70). There is no need on the part of vendors to "implement them yesterday" because of critical market pressures. Finally, many of them relate to hardware, which tends to be somewhat less volatile than software.

The ITU, however, is sitting on one of the most explosive markets that exists today. By way of illustrating a point, one of the favorite topics for academic study in standardization was the telecommunications market. I once asked a reasonably well-known economist why this was. His response was, "Because they have the ability to pay for our research, and because they are regulated, so we have a good paper trail." The regulated nature of the business is largely gone. There is a growing and increasingly sharp competition for new and existing markets as all the telecommunications providers find it necessary for survival. The industry itself is suffering massive dislocation with layoffs, rightsizing, dismemberment, and competition, always unceasing competition. The new players do not know the old rules, nor do they care to. "They" make their own rules; sometimes with the help of the government, sometimes despite the government. "They" are no longer working on systems solutions, but rather are looking for niches or enclaves that they can own and from which they can expand. The scary thing is that the "they" are organizations whose roots are neither in computing nor in telecommunications, but rather on the cusp of both. The providers of these services, such as Sun Microsystems with its "Java" language, or Netscape, the browser company, or a host of other companies are all beginning to occupy areas of prominence in the ITU's traditional space. The Internet Society, with its ubiquitous Internet, is a dominant player in the services arena that people see.

The ITU will continue to do a good job in the infrastructure role providing the fundamental basic rules that define how to "do telecommunications." But in the application arena, they are out of their depth because they must drag with them the complex and time-consuming process of consensus standardization, which they must carry with them because they are a U.N. treaty organization. What their strength has proven, as of this juncture, is that it is their fundamental weaknesses as well.

The same can be said of JTC 1. The newer competitors do not play in the standardization arena. The old, mainline systems vendors provide the lion's share of the participants, and they provide them to areas in which the newer, more aggressive companies have already carved out niches and markets. IBM, DEC, and AT&T continued to fund OSI development long after it was apparent that the TCP/IP schema had succeeded and that OSI was a losing proposition. The main line systems vendors cannot conceive of their hegemony being over, but all of them (or at least the ones that are left) have been through wrenching changes in the last five years. The new and the agile companies are those that have not embraced the SDOs.

The thing that the organizations forget is not how long (in absolute time) that it takes to develop a standard. The key thing is how long it takes to develop a standard with respect to how long the market is willing to wait for a technology to be deployed. If the market is willing to wait for six months, then a standards development time of two years, while laudable by other standardization metrics, is just as bad as a standard that takes five years.

Finally, I believe that the slow collapse of JTC 1 is a harbinger of things to come for ISO. Just as the pace of change has been accelerated in information technology, so will it begin to accelerate in other areas and these other areas will have to be dealt with as well. I do not believe that ISO can recapture the IT market, barring a collapse of the speed of change, but it can change to retain its strength in other markets. Unlike the ITU, its processes are mutable. Its tragic flaw, however, is its belief in the fundamental goodness and purity of its process, and its unwillingness to change that process to match changes in its environment.

NOTES

[1]A bit of trivia might help explain the use of the acronym "ISO," which, as ISO points out, really isn't an acronym, but rather a play on the Greek word root "iso," meaning "equal," which was then seen to be the equivalent of the term "standard." Is this suitably confusing for an organization that is supposed to make things clear?

[2]A list of all ISO committees, as of 1996 is contained in Appendix A of this book.

[3]The Agreement on Technical Barriers to Trade, drawn up under the General Agreement on Tariffs and Trade (GATT), calls upon its signatories to establish in each country an enquiry point capable of anwering questions about the standards, technical regulations, and certification systems in force in that country.

[4]Extracted from the ISO home page, dated January 1996.

[5]When a technical committee is dissolved its number is not allocated to another technical committee. The following 28 technical committees have been dissolved: 7, 9, 13, 15, 16, 32, 40, 49, 53, 62, 64, 66, 73, 75, 78, 80, 88, 90, 95, 97, 103, 124, 139, 140, 141, 143, 151, and 169. The TC count is now up to 212.

[6]The most lucid description of ISO 9000 that I have received came from Robert Kennedy, formerly of DEC. Bob and I sat on the ASC Z1 and U.S. TAG to TC 176, and I had heard most of the 9000 series proponents go on at length. After discussing my irritation, Bob looked at me and explained that it was Margaret Thatcher's way of trying to get the several hundreds of thousands of small British firms ready to compete in the commerce of the Unified Europe and then in the international arena. He pointed out that many small European firms who were soon to have to play in an expanded market, had no idea what quality was nationally or internationally, nor how to achieve it. ISO 9000, or its British predecessor, was the attempt to remedy this problem by introducing the concept of management of the quality program; that is, if the leaders believe in it, then everyone else will because the leaders lead. The theory worked well in the U.S. military, from which the British adopted the standards that formed the basis of the 9000 series.

[7]ISO Bulletin, September 1995 (no publication information given, but I suppose it is Geneva) p. 8.

[8]Ibid., p. 10.

[9]Listed in Appendix A.

[10]The color of their bindings were, in chronological order: 1960 red, 1964 blue, 1968 white, 1972 green, 1976 orange, 1980 yellow, 1984 red, 1988 blue, 1992 white. The 1992 collection marks the end of an era; after 1992, all Recommendations will be published separately, as they are completed.

[11]*The International Telecommunication Union—An Overview,* 1993, Geneva, pp. 18, 19, distributed as ISO/IEC JTC1 N 2461, 1993-04-05.

Chapter 16

The Major Consortia

"Look on my works, ye Mighty, and despair!
Nothing beside remains. Round the decay
Of that colossal wreck, boundless and bare
The lone and level sands stretch far away."

—Percy Bysshe Shelley, *Ozymandias*

INTRODUCTION

This chapter looks at the major consortia that have shaped the modern IT industry. Inclusion is not a statement of success, necessarily, nor is exclusion a mark of failure. The consortia that are included are those which have played (or do play) a significant role in the IT arena over the past five to seven years. "Major" is used to describe consortia that have (or had) the ability to change market direction in multiple areas, not merely in the area in which they were focused. As an example, UNIX International, while failing in its goal to unify the UNIX market behind SVR4, did succeed in causing fundamental changes in the way that consortium and SDOs were viewed. Its interplay with other groups was a part of the milieu in the early 1990s. On the other hand, a consortium such as the Unicode Consortia finished its work in its domain and then went on to something else. While what it did was significant, it did not really impact other disciplines as much as UI or X/Open.

When I originally wrote the book in the late 1980s, I compared the consortia to the Political Action Committee (PAC) special interest groups in the U.S. that effectively lobbied with legislatures and legislators to obtain favorable laws. PACs, by gathering enough constituents and enough financial backing, could make the legislative branches aware of the power they could wield. My contention was that standards consortia seem to have come into existence for the same purpose.

At that time, these groups were usually user and provider driven; they were focused on ensuring that standards were developed and implemented in a fashion that fit the special needs of the consortia members (the application consortia). The Manufacturing Automation Protocol (MAP), the Technical Office Protocol (TOP), and the Corporation for Open Systems (COS) represent the first generation of standards consortia, and were examined in some detail.

In looking at MAP and TOP, I drew the conclusion that members of these organizations established a solution to a specific problem by freezing a technology, and in both cases, technical developments overtook the efforts of the technologies chosen. This resulted in constant revisions and conflictual reports from the committees and participants, which, at the time, I reported as having the potential for splintering activities. The question in my mind, became one of whether an organization could expand its role while maintaining its original focus of creating a tailored standard. Neither MAP nor TOP survived as a viable entity. MAP was subsumed into the Ethernet LAN camp although it did enjoy a few years of gradually diminishing success. TOP just disappeared.

Then there was the Corporation for Open Systems (COS), an industry group that was funded by organizations interested in participating in and exploiting the Open Systems Interconnect series of communications standards. OSI was developed in ISO/IEC JTC 1, and nearly every national standards body organization participated in its creation. The original purpose of COS was to rally support to the standard by promoting the use of the OSI standards. Ultimately, however, COS moved into the certification and conformance testing arena, creating the test suites that would be used to validate providers' offerings in meeting International Standardized Profiles. If the provider passed the test suite, a "COS mark" would be awarded to indicate that the product/service had passed the test suite. Because of the complexity of the OSI concept, and the enormity of the standards effort, OSI never became salable. At the same time, the testing and branding proved to be much more complex than had originally been forecast, and the suites were never developed. This caused the National Institute for Standards and Technology (NIST) to lose substantial faith in OSI, which they had made into a federally required Federal Information Processing Standard (FIPS 146) based on the assurances from industry that conformance tests were coming. COS is still alive, having been through many instantiations as all sorts of things. It is now COS-Network Management Forum, an amalgam of two consortia that have both been overtaken by events but which have continued to survive. However, if you remember the comment in Chapter 4 about the ability to kill a consortium or SDO, you will understand why the continued existence of a COS-like organization is possible.

My original statement in 1987 was that I felt that the original intent of consortia was to allow user/provider forums to influence standards. I then pointed out that I felt that they had shifted their intent to how to "do standards." I predicted that they were going to have trouble fulfilling this promise. I was wrong. The ability of the consortia to "do standards" in a way acceptable to the market has been proven. They have proven more resilient and more adaptable than I imagined that they could be, and they have added a level of interest and excitement to the standardization arena.

THE OPEN SOFTWARE FOUNDATION (OSF)

OSF is included here for historical reasons, since it was merged into the Open Group with X/Open on Valentine's Day, 1996. However, since the nature of this merger is not at all clear as this is being written, a description of the component of the Open Group is necessary so that those reading about the Open Group can understand the history of one of its major components.

Background

In 1988, the computing industry was taken by surprise when Sun Microsystems (a leading UNIX workstation vendor) and American Telephone and Telegraph (the UNIX supplier) reached agreement on a tightly coupled business arrangement in which Sun would abandon work on its highly popular Berkeley Systems Division (BSD) UNIX (Sun OS 4), and instead, develop its operating system on the similar, but incompatible, UNIX System 5, Release 4 (SVR4).

The leading non-UNIX systems suppliers, including DEC, HP, and IBM, having tried to license UNIX from AT&T only to find the licensing clauses too restrictive or too expensive, decided instead to create their own scaleable and portable operating system that would work on all of their hardware, as well as support software for distributed computing.

To support this initiative, seven major companies agreed to create and fund the Open Software Foundation, or OSF. Members of these companies constituted the Board of Directors, who, since they were the major stockholders and providers of funding, legitimately felt that they were entitled to disproportionate governance rights. (The ideal of oligarchy lives.) OSF's funding was approximately $121 million over four years, after which it was to become self-supporting through the sale and licensing of the software that it would develop. This software included a portable operating system (OSF 1®), a common Graphical User Interface (Motif®), a distributed computing environment containing an accepted Remote Procedure Call (Distributed Computing Environment, or DCE®), and finally, a solution to the problem of managing the complexities of networked computing (Distributed Management Environment, or DME). With the launch of this program, OSF was under way.

The initial publicity was very good. OSF made headlines in the trade press. The fact that big vendors could work together to use a consortium to make a series of products was seen as a sign that the cooperative spirit was not dead and so on and so on. The fact that these same group of vendors could not agree on common efforts in the standardization arena was overlooked, but as was mentioned in Chapter 1, when a writer has only twenty-one inches of column space to tout a "miracle of cooperation," he or she probably won't get into too much detail about the real problems facing an opportunity.

The vendors who funded OSF saw its charter as helping in the creation and delivery of "vendor-neutral" software source code, emphasizing scalability, portability, usability, and interoperability of systems, software and information, and people. (If this sounds a little like the Open Systems definition from POSIX 1003.0, it is because POSIX was strongly influenced by the founders of OSF.)

One of the first standardization battles in which OSF engaged was the fight with Sun and its allies in the IEEE Technical Committee for Operation Systems (TCOS) over which GUI would be chosen for preeminence. (TCOS also was in charge of POSIX.) Sun had a large installed base with its GUI, while OSF, backed by its sponsors, had magnificent marketing clout and the start of a deployable GUI based on MIT's Project Athena. The two hostile camps met in the standardization arena, where they fought the battle over the merits of their respective GUIs not on technology, but in the press. There were the "Robert's Rules of Orderers," the "delayers," the "angry shouters," and the "we'll bring the lawyers" participants on both sides. The groups fought for nearly five years; every six months, one side would declare that the other side was incompetent or evil or cheating, and then there would be renewed interest in the market in this arena.

The GUI war continued as did the DCE war. DCE was a technology that was built to solve complex systems problems, but it was up against a rival communications architecture that was built (you guessed it) by Sun Microsystems, called ONC. The wars started; the two systems were again incompatible. While DCE was better technology, ONC was widely deployed. OSF made a concerted effort to influence procurements. Sun made a concerted effort to influence its base.

At the same time, to alleviate the fears of the market, AT&T created an independent operating subsidiary called UNIX Systems Laboratory, which was to develop the future follow-ons to SVR4 that did not necessarily favor AT&T. To make the subsidiary more believable, it sold equity positions in USL to eleven other companies. USL formed a consortium called UNIX International (UI). UI was to advise USL on the future customer wants for UNIX. UI and OSF became bitter rivals, and further exacerbated the "UNIX wars" that were occurring. (UI is covered later in the chapter.)

In the meantime, OSF 1 was failing. The portable operating system was turning out to be a lot harder to make than was originally expected, and the major supporters began to abandon it. Finally, only DEC was left supporting OSF. The other vendors had, in a fit of cooperation, solved the problems of the GUI wars and the DCE wars.

By 1993, OSF was in interesting shape financially. Only Motif was a commercial success. DCE was beginning to be deployed, but there was a question of the various vendor's implementations interoperating. OSF-1 was not a money maker, and DME had been abandoned. Finally, Microsoft was getting ready to announce NT, and the confusion in the UNIX market place was beginning to hurt everyone. To finally end the wars, the major UNIX vendors (HP, IBM, Sun, Novell, and SCO) announced on St. Patrick's Day, 1993, the formation of the Common Open Software Environment (COSE), which was focused on solving these problems. A new GUI (that would combine technology from all major companies) was announced, which would be Common Desktop Environment for the new UNIX operating system, which was to be based on Spec 1170. This specification contained the 1170 most popular APIs of the most popular application programs that ran on all the UNIX variants available to the market. All of the major vendors agreed to build products that complied to Spec 1170. Additionally, all vendors would sell ONC and DCE. To really complicate things, the announcement was made at UniForum (sponsored by the

UniForum Consortium) and the 1170 program (now called UNIFIED UNIX) was given to X/Open to manage. Finally, in one of those strange twists of fate, Sun Microsystems joined the Open Software Foundation's Board of Directors.

What it is Supposed to do Today

As part of the reconstituting of OSF, the mission of OSF changed. OSF adopted an industry-wide, collaborative, open systems research and development focus, where its members could bring technology for collaborative development. System vendors and software vendors are supposed to come together to use the "prestructured technology" concept to jointly and collaboratively develop a specification and sample implementation of the specification. The guiding idea behind OSF is that, by collaborating, the sponsoring providers work together to develop and bring to market common enabling technology faster and more economically than otherwise possible. While the organization changed, the concept of the hegemony of the Board of Directors, that is, the computing oligarchy, continued, and forms the basis of the merged Open Group.

Before OSF was merged with X/Open to form the Open Group in 1996, they had produced four PST efforts and had more than 380 companies, government agencies, and academic institutions as members.

What Happened

OSF was a consortium that was originally formed by disparate interests to oppose something that each company was not capable of stopping individually. The Open Systems movement, which had been named and marketed by Sun and then subtly changed by the DEC and IBM standardization efforts in the 1987 timeframe, had come full circle, attacking the sponsors who had created it. The market wanted the UNIX-like attributes which were ubiquitous computing. The technologists took over this definition and provided that of POSIX 1003.0, which is worth repeating here:

> A system that implements sufficient open specifications for interfaces, services, and supporting formats to enable properly engineered applications software to be ported across a wide range of systems with minimal changes, to interoperate with other applications on local and remote systems, and to interact with users in a style which facilitates user portability."[1]

The desire for the users was not for the technology but for the attributes of the technology that were described. (See Chapter 6, Evolution and Revolution in Open Systems.) The OSF vendors did not understand that because they were too busy peddling technology and trying to use consortia and standardization to stop the spread of something that they could not market against.

OSF was what was described as an, "Application consortia . . . devoted to taking some aspect of open systems and repackaging it in such a way that it is acceptable to a larger share of the market. They are committed to 'using' standards and 'helping the standards process'. . . ."[2] It tried to use standardization as a tactical tool to stop the spread of a rival technology. This attempt to stop a technology was fundamentally wrong. A wise lawyer (one of a very few of the species left) once told me that, "Marketing strategy based on a legal defense is at best shaky." The same can be applied to a marketing campaign that is based upon gathering a group to tether to oppose something. The type of organization that results from a strategy such as this is one which predicates its existence not upon creation, but rather upon destruction. It's easier, but it doesn't last.

X/OPEN COMPANY, LIMITED

X/Open Company Ltd. is included here for historical reasons, since it was merged into the Open Group with OSF on Valentine's Day, 1996. However, since the nature of this merger is not at all clear as this is being written, a description of this component of the Open Group is necessary so that those reading about the Open Group can understand the history of one of its major components.

Background

The original purpose of X/Open was to create an environment that would allow application portability among user applications. X/Open was originally conceived as an organization to embrace and promote UNIX, to stop the incursion of IBM as a dominant Information Technology (IT) provider in Europe, and to provide European Computer manufacturers a chance at survival. Just as OSI was an attempt to stop the advance of SNA across Europe, X/Open (derived from, according to popular lore, the "X" from UNIX and the idea that the organization could make UNIX open) was an attempt by the Europeans to balance the market in their favor.

What it is Supposed to do Today

Needless to say, the consortium has undergone numerous focus changes in the last ten years. Originally, Olivetti, Honey-Bull, ICL (the British company, not the subsidiary of a Japanese company), and Siemens and Nixdorf were all members, emphasizing its heavy European influence. Today, only Siemens/Nixdorf remains as a viable participant. Other members of the board of Directors (the primary guidance unit of X/Open) are DEC, ICL, Fujitsu, HP, Hitachi, IBM, AT&T (formerly AT&T GIS and before that, NCR) NEC, Novell, and Sun. The oligarchy of X/Open is based upon the payment of dues; that is, the right to help govern is based upon the ability to pay. Included in the Board of Directors (BoD) are members of the User Council, the ISV council, and X/Open management. The BoD and the companies that it represented were the central focus of X/Open.

X/Open saw itself in its publicity release and its charter, as, "a not-for-profit, vendor-independent, international consortium which is dedicated to the advancement of open systems throughout the world. It has become the integrator of standards within the industry, bringing together users, vendors and standards bodies working towards the proliferation of open systems." The question was whether or not the BoD members shared this vision. There is reason to believe that they shared part of it, but not the entirety.

The BoD was the dominant direction provider for X/Open and was the vehicle by which X/Open was merged with OSF to create the Open Group. Because in many cases, the same organizations had seats on both boards, there was the ability to merge the directions of the two organizations into the Open Group. A similar situation exists in the SDOs, where most of the national body and regional representatives to ISO are "members of the BoD of their country organizations" and the same situation is repeated. When ISO wants something, it convinces a majority of its national body representatives that the proposal would be "good," and the majorities' acquiescence is taken as proof that the system works.

Over the past several years, following a user revolt in 1991 at their Rome meeting, X/Open had been making steps to ensure that users and ISV members had a larger voice in the organization. X/Open had created "User Council" and an "ISV Council," as well as a complex operating structure, to allow the users to influence the direction that the providers were taking in their creation of technology. Fundamentally, the users were supposed to come together to create technology and user requirements for the vendors, and were supposed to present these needs to the Open Systems Requirements board, who in turn would eventually pass them to the X/Open Technical Managers, who were usually creatures of the BoD companies.

The User Council includes government and commercial organizations with a vested interest in procuring or implementing open systems. The ISV Council consists of independent software vendors who have committed to developing open applications. The third group is the System Vendor Council. Each of these councils is represented by one vote on the Board of Directors. (This particular seat was added following Rome, and was the direct outcome of Rome, which saw the publication of the Wilmott Manifesto, named after Rob Wilmott, one of the founders of X/Open in 1984.)

Shareholder and council members also participate, through representatives, on X/Open technical working groups and Requirements Topic Groups. The technical working groups provide a forum for the specification and testing of the Common Applications Environment. In addition, there are Requirements Topic Groups that address specific issues of relevance.

Ultimately, the following classes of memberships would be offered in an attempt to snare as many paying customers as possible:

Shareholder Membership (BoD seat, usually $500K or more)

User Council Membership (depended upon company size)

ISV Council Membership (depended upon company size)

System Vendor Council Membership (depended upon company size)

Specification Membership (participate directly in one of X/Open's Technical Development Groups, which, on occasion, varied from year to year)

Technical Buy-out Membership (Expensive, but a right to play on the Technical Manager's committee)

The Technical Managers, who were senior technologists from the vendor companies, were supposed to then put the user requirements into the X/Open pantheon of the

Common Applications Environment (CAE), and then strive to make the CAE real by creating products to the CAE specifications which they hammered out in committee. As a multivolume reference work, the CAE was seen by X/Open as an evolving portfolio of application programming interfaces (APIs), protocols, and specifications. The mature CAE specifications were to be supported with an extensive set of stringent conformance tests and a distinct trademark (the X/Open Brand) carried only on those products that would comply with X/Open portability definitions. The providers would all agree to brand their operating systems and other parts of their computing environment to the CAE to ensure platform portability. The current edition of the CAE is published in a collection of volumes known as XPG4, which is the basis of X/Open's open systems procurement efforts. As of this writing, over $15 billion in procurements have referenced some X/Open specification.

The test suite is a reasonably good test suite. As mentioned above, one of the things that hurt COS was the failure of a viable testing program. The X/Open verification suite, VSX4, contains more than 7,000 conformance tests and is maintained and improved with every major release or change in the CAE. Additionally, X/Open has been very aggressive in protecting the use of the X/Open brand, which is strictly controlled by a comprehensive licensing agreement based on international trademark law. As part of this agreement, many of the board member developers are committed to ensuring that all future versions of their currently branded products will conform to the specifications published in the XPG.

What Happened

There was a curious dichotomy between what the sponsors of X/Open wanted and what X/Open wanted for itself. X/Open saw its job as convincing the senior IT professional from the Open Systems community, to attend the Council meetings to gain a unique understanding of, and up to the minute information on, X/Open developments that they could use in their jobs to gain a competitive edge. They saw X/Open-managed efforts, such as the X/Open Branding program and other activities (such as an attempt to become the Open Systems provider to the United Nations) as providing further incentive for developers to continue to invest in open systems, and provide users a way to more quickly identify and adopt systems that are interoperable and which ultimately made the CIO or equivalent personages realize a quicker revenue gain and return on their investment. Fundamentally, I believe that X/Open management saw itself as peers of the organizations that they were to serve; they were, after all, a British Limited Partnership, staffed with British executives, who were there to save the organizations from themselves. After all, the executives at the subscribing companies couldn't very well have managed this show without X/Open, or else they wouldn't have funded X/Open, now don't you reakon? While they were pushing this theory to the sponsoring organizations (those who paid in excess of $500K per year) they were also trying to convince the users that they were there to serve them by bending the major sponsors to the will of the users through use of the organization. The problem was that the sponsors saw themselves, not as clients of the X/Open company, but as owners, for whom the X/Open management worked. While this was implicit in their thoughts about X/Open, it was never clear in their actual dealing with X/Open. X/Open was not treated as a standardization organization; rather, it had a very confusing status as a cross between a consultant and a technology contractor.

While the management approach may have been faulty, I believe that the technical approach was excellent. The technical program, under X/Open's Chief Technical Officer, Michael Lambert, was probably the only thing that kept the sponsors participating seriously in X/Open, and kept X/Open from enjoying the fate of COS or UI. The rigor that the CTO was able to maintain in specification, testing, and branding are a marked difference to the failures in the same areas that most other programs enjoyed. The only comparable program is the compiler language testing programs run by the National Institute of Standards and Technology (NIST) in the United States. However, the NIST tests are only spot point tests. Lambert managed to persuade vendors not only to brand initially, but also to maintain the brand over time and revisions to product. Finally, the use of the NIST brand is necessary to sell to the U.S. Government; Lambert did what he did by creating and maintaining a value to the brand without any mandated procurement agencies working for him. It was something that has not been done before in any consortium of which I am aware.

The Future

The position of X/Open in the Open Group is not clear. Ideally, the sponsors should probably try to hold on to two of X/Open's most valuable commodities: the ability to determine and focus user requirements and the ability to provide brands identifying interoperating systems. These two abilities, when coupled with the abilities of OSF in the PST process (to collaboratively develop specifications and create sample implementations), would seem to provide the complementary match necessary to meet the demands for a "full service consortium."

UNIX INTERNATIONAL (UI)

UNIX International has ceased to exist. It is included here because it was a major consortium that did have an impact on the development of the consortia, and because not including it would leave a gap in the path that has lead to much of the current thinking about consortia.

History

Some of the background of UNIX International was alluded to in the description of the Open Software Foundation. However, the story really starts with the success of Sun Microsystems and its rise as a workstation vendor in the mid 1980s. Sun used a variant of UNIX based on the work done at Berkeley Software Development, named 4BSD UNIX, which supported TCP/IP. By the mid 1980s, UNIX had become a growing phenomenon, and had spread from universities to technology computing users. (Success in the commercial environment was still reasonably far away.) However, the success of UNIX was enough to threaten main stream systems vendors such as Digital and Hewlett Packard, who were heavily into the technical computing arena. For that matter, HP acquired Apollo Computer just as Apollo began losing market share to Sun.

This set the stage for the next act of the drama. In 1987, AT&T was searching for a partner to help it move its "new UNIX." Realizing that Sun was a powerful UNIX vendor, AT&T offered to throw its support behind Sun if Sun would switch to AT&T's new revision of UNIX. Sun agreed, and set the stage for the UNIX wars. OSF was created to oppose the Sun-AT&T alliance.[3] While OSF represented one form of threat, there was another, more insidious threat to the success of UNIX; the mistrust of AT&T as the owner of UNIX. The licensees of UNIX were legion, and AT&T alone knew what was in the various contracts, including the fee schedules, the terms and conditions, the royalties, and the technology cross-licensing agreements.

To allay this doubt, AT&T created UNIX Systems Laboratories, Inc. to manage all aspects of its UNIX business. To ensure an arm's length relationship, AT&T sold equity in USL to eleven major systems vendors who became the dominant members in the consortium that USL created to act as the customer interface. The intent of UNIX International was to provide a common forum for the warring UNIX factions so that UNIX could continue to be regarded as a viable Open Systems offering, rather than a proprietary AT&T offering. The rationale for the creation was to demonstrate to the users that the concept of a "singular" kernel UNIX, to which others could add value, was viable. UI helped to legitimize SVR4 and to make this a stable platform for the ISVs and users.

What Happened

While a subsidiary that had equity funding, USL nonetheless wanted to make money, since this is how its management would be judged by its parent company. Since USL owned the UNIX technology, they began to crate a "future path" for the technology, and then to give this plan and scheme to UI as their "contribution." This caused UI to begin to expand its goals from SVR4 respectability to programs such as enhanced I18N, Modified Systems Administration, a movement towards OSI, and consideration of Object Management, which many felt was UI's attempt to regain technical ownership and leadership in the UNIX market.

And then the situation became nasty; USL began to interject itself into the picture more and more strongly, and UI began to modify the SVR4 code into SVR4.2 code, which broke the binary migration paths of many of the UI members. Suppliers of clean (that is, reasonably bug free and independently written SVR4 code) began to desert the UI banner, and controversy became heated. The OSF-UI battles became legendary, as did the UI/USL and UI member battles. The situation was becoming very heated when AT&T sold UNIX and USL to Novell.

Within the year, UI retrenched, and retrenched again. Because it had no products to sell into the market, it was entirely dependent upon its sponsors for money, and its sponsors were in no mood to continue the wars with OSF and the other vendors. Then St. Patrick's Day, 1993, arrived, and UI's mission of moving everyone to SVR4-based UNIX, died. And so did UI. It was a victim of its own excesses and an inability to use a consortium's negotiating power to shape an industry through cooperation.

OBJECT MANAGEMENT GROUP (OMG)

History

There are two stories that characterize the Object Management Group as a slightly "different" type of consortia. Both revolve around its leader, Chris Stone, who, more than anyone else, exemplifies the brashness that the formal SDOs have come to associate with consortia.

The first occurred in 1991, when, in response to a question of why he had chosen to form a consortium when there was a perfectly good standards committee available, Chris Stone responded that, "I want to get something out before I die."[4] The second is his most recent statement: "OMG is now the world's largest software development consortium. With over 660 member companies (OSF has 145 and X/Open has 45), OMG is setting the agenda for distributed object computing, which is what client-server computing should have been called originally. . . . To run an industry consortium, you have to be a master facilitator, have a good idea, and keep them interested. Herein lies the rub."[5]

In both cases, the founder of OMG was right. The object committee of X3 (X3H7) continues to move along at a snail's pace, while OMG has managed to create a reference model and actually get companies to commit money to product development and marketing. The trade show "Object World," where companies come and demonstrate their latest OMG-based object technologies (and which was, coincidentally, partially owned by OMG), continues to grow. And finally, OMG is growing at the rate of about two members per week; a growth rate that ANSI, representing all of U.S. industry, wishes it could match.

This is pretty heady stuff for standards and for a consortium. But, OMG is probably the most solvent of all consortia and definitely one of the most important. However, unlike the other consortia in this chapter, OMG has succeeded because it has succeeded. While this may sound trivial, Stone has forced the success because he keeps OMG focused on one thing and one thing only: the success of object paradigm. While it is probably a misuse of psychological terms to say that he is obsessed with the success of the objects, Stone is driven to succeed—and to make the OMG succeed because he believes in the technology and the vital mission that this technology has in creating a "new world order" in computing. He has managed to keep OMG focused on the goal, and recently (1996) reorganized OMG to focus on the vertical applications that are necessary to make OMG's base technologies the driver in the market.

The OMG process is a multi-stage process that tends to work reasonably well, but has not managed to avoid all of the politics of standardization. The first stage in the process was the creation of the "Object Management Architecture Guide (OMA)," which defined the nature of the job to be handled. The centrality of this architectural guide cannot be overstated, since all that follows is built upon it. To safeguard the Guide, the OMG created the Technical Committee. With the guide and guardian in place, the remainder of the process could begin.

The first step in the OMG process was the creation (by the TC) of a task force to look at a particular piece of the OMA to determine the need for standardization. The TC then charters a Task Force (TF) to go away and take care of the problem. The TF normally begins the process with a Request for Information (RFI), to analyze the nature of the industry and the problems that the TF might encounter. Everyone can and at times, it seems like everyone did, respond to the RFI. The TF, after considering the responses contained in the RFI, initiates the Request for Technology (RFT). To respond to an RFT, there are several conditions. Firstly, you must be a Contributing Member of OMG, something that runs between $6,000 and $60,000 per year. Secondly, you must sign a Letter of Intent to Respond (LOI). The LOI fundamentally commits the contributing organization not only to respond to the RFT, but also to implement the technology in the RFT. This precludes the creation of "productless specifications."

The initial phase of the evaluation continues and then usually does not come to a conclusion because the organizations involved suddenly become aware that a competitor may have a better idea. As they evaluate one another's technology, various camps form to advocate a particular solution. This is where the "the rub comes," since it is up to OMG staff to successfully arbitrate and facilitate a discussion among opposing forces in these instances. Finally, the negotiation process is closed, a vote taken, and a decision made.

On the other side of the coin are the users of OMGs base technologies that the Platform Technology Committee develops. In 1995, OMG realized that, while it was succeeding in responding to the base technology requirements, it was leaving the potential application users little room for participation. The reorganization accepted the idea that vertical (or stovepipe) applications might want to join OMG and thereby expand the base and acceptance of OMG technology. To this end, the "Domain Technology Committee" was created to manage the technical activities of these domains with regard to their contributions to the OMGs mission. There was also the growing realization that the various providers of base technologies were spending a lot of time providing base technologies that no one was using, which made the corporations sponsoring Object Technology just a little unnerved. The creation of the Domain-specific technologies such as finance, medical, manufacturing, or multimedia, will serve to "kick start" the development of object-based implementations which both use OMGs technology and which prove to the market that the object paradigm is viable in reality, as well as in theory.

However, because the advent of multiple (and hopefully expanding domains) will begin to tax the bounds of the OMG architecture, OMG has created an "Architecture Board" to maintain the technical correctness of the domain solutions. One of the problems in past consortia is that the applications have relied upon "just a few extensions" each. The advent of "just a few extensions" in an interoperability model would be disastrous. So, the function of the architecture board is to ensure that the applicants to the fundamental model do not break the model.

The Future

The whole success of OMG now rides on the ability of OMG—and Chris Stone—to actually deploy object-based applications based on OMG specifications. If OMG has been right, then the computing universe, including major commercial organizations, should begin a migration to object-based technologies and concepts in increasing numbers during the last few years of this millennium. If OMG and its charismatic Chair are wrong, another paradigm will be chosen as the core technology for computing in the year 2000 and the vision that OMG has of technology-based interoperability will fail. Fundamentally, OMG must continue to proselytize its vision, and must change the way that the users, academics, and providers believe about software philosophy, creation, deployment, and use. It is not an easy task but then, if it was, I tend to think that Christopher Stone and the OMG would be somewhere doing something else that was challenging and exciting.

CONCLUSION

This moral from this chapter is unclear. Of the four major consortia covered, three are either merged or gone as victims of a changing market and attitude towards consortia. OMG continues to survive and adapt, but the proof of its success will be the acceptance of its computing philosophy and paradigm by the market.

It would be too easy to say, as some have done, that the day of consortia has passed. Rather, I believe that it would be safe to say that the day of the large, ill-defined organization has passed, whether in industry, standards, or government. The nature of competition has changed, and this fundamental fact has influenced all of standards and standardization. When a standards committee dies, it passes away in a cold little room, usually unnoticed and unmourned. When a consortium dies, many people attend the wake. The difference is not in the mortality rate, but how the two are treated in dying.

The same can be said, incidentally, of success. When a standards committee succeeds, it has a quiet party to which the few faithful are invited. When a consortium succeeds, it throws a gala bash, to which the industry comes. I believe that ultimately, the successes will outnumber the failures in both environments. But, tracing the evolution of these organizations shows that the market has little time for remembrance of things past. Rather, it seems to ask, "What have you done for me lately?" This is what keeps the discipline of both standardization and of Information Technology fresh and exciting.

NOTES

[1]POSIX 1003.0, Draft 17.

[2]Weiss, Martin and Cargill, Carl. "Consortia in the Standards Development Process," *Journal of the American Society for Information Science,* September 1992, Volume 43, Number 8, p. 561.

[3]There were some engineers at Sun who suggested that OSF really stood for "Oppose Sun Forever."

[4]"Is X3 broken," Jeff Moag, Datamation, June 1991.

[5]Stone, Christopher. "Software Standardization—How the Object Management Group Changed the Model," *StandardView,* September 1995, Volume 3, Number 3, p. 85.

Chapter 17

Regional Standards Bodies

"What dull men are those who tarry at home,
When abroad they might wantonly roam,
And gain such experience, and spy too,
Such countries and wonders, as I do!"

—Abraham Cowley, *Cheer Up, My Mates*

INTRODUCTION

Originally, the regional standardization group was seen as an intermediary between the international organization (such as ISO and IEC with their global presence and focus) and the national organizations with their more intense, but narrower, concerns. Also, the regional organization was seen as a convenient place for a national body to gain information about area concerns that the other national bodies had. Finally, regional organizations, by acting as an information conduit, could ameliorate some of the processing time for standards by serving as a "preprocessing unit" for the international organizations.

All of this was good theory but poor practice. Europe was the only area that employed the concept of "regional standards bodies." Their implementation of this concept brought about a storm of protest in one case and willing acceptance in another. I believe that the continuing saga of "regionals" in Europe provides an interesting story with a highly appropriate moral; it's just that the moral you derive depends, unfortunately, largely upon where you sit. Its ultimate resolution is not clear, but it bears watching because it is either as a "harbinger of things to come" or the "final act in a seriocomic play."

ECMA

ECMA, (formerly the European Computer Manufacturers Association, but now just ECMA) is probably the oldest, and from my point of view, one of the more successful regional standardization entities in the regional movement. As its former full name would suggest, it was an organization that was focused on Europe, and had, as its primary clients, the computer manufacturers of Europe. It was founded with the idea that the creation of regional voluntary standards for the European Information Technology community could balance the power, and possibly increase the influence, of the European Information Technology manufacturers.

History

ECMA was initiated formally in 1960, when several major computer vendors invited all known computer manufacturers in the European area to participate in a meeting to be held in April of that year. This meeting, which took place in Brussels, concluded with the recommendation that an association known as the European Computer Manufacturers Association was to be created, and formed a committee to draw up the necessary by-laws for the creation of ECMA.

The dynamics of ECMA's formation are interesting from a historical perspective. The three major information processing standards groups (ISO's TC 97, ANSI's X3, and ECMA) were formed at about the same time (1960-1961), and within this same timeframe data processing (later know as Information Technology) first began to understand some of its capabilities and some of its problems. The capabilities were variously perceived, but it was becoming rapidly apparent that data processing was extending its boundaries beyond the accounting department and moving into prominence in both corporate and academic environments. Additionally, governments were growing interested in the capabilities of data processing, from both a technical and legislative point of view. It was the realization of this potential, coupled with the understanding that the potential would diminish if some form of standardization were not put in place, that lead to the creation of these standardization organizations. ECMA especially, gained from this new found interest, since it was a regional, as opposed to purely nationalistic, organization.

The ostensible rationale for standardization was to help the users save resources (money and people) by providing a limited degree of interoperability for their system's interfaces such as input/output codes and programming languages. Further, the use of standardization would allow the users to become more familiar with the capabilities of computers, thereby making them less frightening. However, since standards grow from some larger economic rationale, ECMA clearly was responding to the needs of the manufacturers that composed its user (or client) base. ECMA's goals were to ensure survival of the European point of view in data processing, including the specialized needs of the various manufacturers, to see that the market expanded at a rate that would guarantee financial success for the efficient members, and to defend against any structuring of the market that would preclude substantial participation by European manufacturers. Assuring a consensus among European manufacturers through the production of standards that reflected the community of interests made it more certain that the European perspective would be heard.

In addition, ECMA was founded to act as a group that would speak for all the European manufacturers to the European nations. National governments had begun to evolve separate standards that they believed would serve their separate national interests, and could effectively function as nontariff trade barriers. The establishment of such national standards would have fragmented the European market, destroying any possibility of market potential for non-national manufacturers and severely limiting the potential gain for national manufacturers. To prevent this, manufacturers needed to create a supranational body that retained a distinctly European cast.

There was not a need to create similar standards, merely standards that were not incompatible. It is possible to write a standard with multiple subsets to satisfy different national requirements. Such standards can sometimes be expensive to implement completely, but far less so than implementing a different product for each country. The solution seemed to be regional standards, which would allow a company to pick its markets by careful implementation of a standard, or parts of a standard. The company would not necessarily have to fear being closed out of a market because it forgot something.

ECMA was fairly well-defined by December of 1960. Because it was believed that the organization could complement the activities of ISO and the IEC, the new organization was located in Geneva, Switzerland. ECMA came into being and began to carry out its tasks in May of 1961. Even prior to official registration, however, ECMA already had achieved an impressive victory when it was asked, by ISO and the IEC, to join a round-table conference to discuss standardization in the computer industry. The ultimate outcome of this discussion was the creation of the TC 97 (now JTC 1) and the request that ECMA act as a liaison member to that committee.

ECMA: Membership and Organization

I have included a reasonably lengthy section on the rules, membership, and structure of ECMA for two reasons. First, it is probably as precise a set of rules as you will find in the entire standardization universe. The rules are simple, clean, and clear, and subject to a minimum of debate and second-guessing. Second, the rules are this way because ECMA, while one of the smaller standardization organizations, is also one of the more forward thinking. Because it has no dominant "master," it can usually act as a "nearly completely" independent agency, driven only by the requirement to "do what is correct." The current Secretary General, Jan van-den-Beld, carries on the tradition of his predecessor, Dara Hekimi, who emphasized the idea of, "preciseness in procedure and clarity in creation."

The membership of ECMA is open to any company in Europe that develops, manufactures, and markets data processing machines or machines used to process digital information. The definition is written is such a way that any major manufacturer of information processing equipment with a subsidiary in Europe is eligible for membership. To avoid potential conflict, however, it was necessary to limit each company to a single vote, otherwise a company with multiple European subsidiaries could have overwhelmed the organization. As a result, there is a statement in the by-laws that effectively prevents multiple subsidiaries from becoming members.

At present there are two types of memberships: ordinary members and associate members. Ordinary members are full members, with voting rights and the right to attend any and all Technical Working Committees (TC), which are the groups that actually compose standards. Associate members, on the other hand, join to provide expertise to a Technical Working Committee or Committees, who may take part in the discussions of the General Assembly, but who have no voting right in the General Assembly. There are currently twenty-six ordinary (voting) members and fifteen associate (nonvoting) members. New members are accorded their appropriate membership status upon acceptance by two-thirds of the current ordinary members.

The General Assembly is the highest authority of ECMA. It meets a minimum of two times a year, and votes upon the standards that have been developed in the TCs. Only ordinary members are allowed to vote on these proposed standards in the General Assembly. Because the General Assembly is a large group, legal and operational responsibilities are delegated to three officers who are elected from the General Assembly ordinary members: a President and Vice President (elected on a yearly basis, and permitted to serve any number of terms, as long as no more than two terms are consecutive), and a Treasurer, also elected from the General Assembly, but without the time limitations of the two other officers. These officers are responsible for the management of ECMA. They can commit to contracts for the organization and have the right to bind ECMA to a course of action.

The Coordinating Committee is composed of six ordinary members who are elected by the General Assembly for one year terms to advise it on Technical Committees. The Coordinating Committee is charged by the General Assembly with determining when a new TC is needed and what the scope of its work should be, with nominating a provisional chairperson for the TC upon its formation, and with reviewing the progress of the TCs every six months.

As with all standards organizations, there is the Secretariat. The ECMA Secretariat, appointed by the General Assembly, is responsible for managing the ECMA budget, which is based upon membership fees from the ordinary and associate members, and for ensuring that the TCs function correctly. Upon the recommendation of the Coordinating Committee, the General Assembly can vote (by simple majority) to establish a new TC, and the Secretary General of the Secretariat will call the first meeting of the TC. The Secretariat acts as the secretary for all TC meetings, helps to create the TC's agenda, publishes minutes of the meetings, and aids in preparing the activity reports that the TC chairperson provides the Secretary General and the Coordinating Committee every six months.

TCs are the foundation of ECMA. They are composed of volunteers from the member companies and operate under modified consensus rules. Membership in the TCs is open to both associate and ordinary members, who, if present, may vote on technical issues regardless of their membership status. The provisional officers appointed by the Coordinating Committee are responsible for getting the TC going and can be replaced after six months and the first three meetings. Once the TC has established itself and the requisite number of meetings have been held, the TC votes in its own leadership (Chair and Vice-Chair), which can be elected for up to three consecutive terms. The TC Chair is responsible for maintaining the TC focus and calendar target, and prepares semi-annual reports to the Secretary General and the General Assembly. In 1996, there are thirteen active Technical Working Committees and twenty-five other committees that are in the "work completed" stage. Retired committee numbers are not reassigned. A TC has the ability to create Technical Groups (TGs) that are responsible to it for accomplishing a part of the scope of the TC. The TGs are composed of a minimum of two TC members and report on their activities at each meeting of the TC. They operate along the lines of a TC.

Purpose Now

ECMA's role has changed in the past several years. The name change in 1994 was especially significant; it recognized that the native European computer industry was largely gone. (ICL, one of the founders, is now ICL/Fujitsu; Olivetti was gone; Bull was missing, Siemens had merged with Nixdorf, and so on.)

At the same time, ECMA was hurt by the creation of governmentally backed regional organizations, such as CEN, CENELEC, and ETSI, all of which sprang from the fertile mind of the EU in Brussels. (More on them later in the chapter.) By 1992, there was a question of whether or not ECMA would survive. However, ECMA realized, long before other organizations, that information technology and information processing were no longer separate entities, and began to prepare for their merger by encouraging a growth of membership from telecommunications providers. By providing a place for the IT and telecommunications organizations to meet and discuss technologies, outside of both normal industry and governmental channels, ECMA provides a valuable service to the growing community of interest between these two similar, but disparate, disciplines. Also, taking advantage of their special position within the IT community as a class A liaison with ISO's JTC 1, ECMA began to look at how it could respond to consortia requests for help in the field of standardization.

Finally, ECMA had the courage to do what few other committees do. It closed down TCs that were no longer germane to the general population of the IT community, or which had, in the view of the group, outlived their productive lives. As an example, in 1988, the field of workstation and computer ergonomics was seen as the next major area of growth and significance. By 1993, there was a feeling that it was, ". . . better to concentrate our innovation on how the components are put together, on higher level composite user interfaces, on designing the complete environment,...and on building services that enable users to better communicate and collaborate with each other. In other words, stop arguing about track gauge so we can build a railroad."[1] ECMA closed down their committees on ergonomics and interfaces (TC28 and TC35).

The Future

ECMA's survival is by no means assured. Unlike other standardization organizations, it must survive on its ability to capture and execute on interesting and viable programs. It has no large group of providers who *must* participate because ECMA is a national entity, or because "everyone else does," or because it has tacit or explicit governmental support. ECMA survives only as long as it provides a real service to a larger segment of the industry. The price of freedom to "do what is right" can be expensive but is a dearly cherished practice. In this unique approach, it is the prototypical SDO of the future and should be the model for more and more organizations engaged in standardization. SDOs have, in the past, been allowed to survive because they had always been there. ECMA is proving that mere historical presence isn't enough. There must also be a commitment to respond to users: both participants and to their customers. If ECMA succeeds, it may be the harbinger of things to come (responsive SDOs).

FORMAL EUROPEAN REGIONALS: CEN, CENELEC, AND ETSI

Background

Europe is unusual because of the voluntary union called the European Union (EU) and the European Free Trade Area (EFTA). Of these, the EU is probably better organized and has a much greater impact on standardization. The original six members of the EU have grown to fifteen today. It has created a government based in Brussels, and has a Parliament, Council of Ministers to approve legislation, and the necessary civil service called the European Commission (EC) to implement its decisions. It is also embarked on an ambitious program to unify Europe—not as single cultural entity, but rather as a single economic entity. To do this, the EC needs to use standards and standardization, if for nothing else than to heal centuries of local traditions of "doing things uniquely." The EC, which is the bureaucratic extension of the Council, is charged with the thankless job of being the change agent for this at times undesired change.

The EC has over twenty governmental departments, called the Directorates General (DGs). The groups of highest interest to the IT community are DG III, which deals with procurement of information technology and telecommunications equipment. DG XIII deals with standardization of these areas. Basically, DG III sets procurement based on standards for which they (DG III) are responsible, while DG XIII funds and ensures planning in Information and Communications Technologies (ICT). The Fourth Framework Program, due to run from 1994 to 1998, covers the areas of information technologies, advanced communications, telematics applications, and industrial technologies.

The EU has long known that one of the major obstacles to a successful European Union were trade barriers. The technical harmonization required is enormous; just imagine what it would be like if the level of standardization in Europe was as high as the standardization that occurs among the various types of electrical outlets. The standardization of standards (also known as technical harmonization) became one of the first orders of business upon the signing of the Treaty of Rome.

As you may have guessed, the creation of the EU, with governmental powers, and the need to standardize on a pan-European scale has lead to some interesting results. To begin, it was necessary for the EU to recognize and respect the sovereignty of each nation's standardization organization, until a way to preempt them could be found. Secondly, the EU had to do something about the problems of harmonization. This is where CEN, CENELEC, and ETSI come in.

COMITÉ EUROPÉEN DE NORMALISATION (CEN) AND COMITÉ EUROPÉEN DE NORMALISATION ELECTROTECHNIQUE (CENELEC)

Comité Européen de Normalisation (CEN), formed in 1961, is the European regional equivalent of ISO. Although the present organization dates from 1971, the idea of CEN originated in 1957 when the EU was merely a possibility. The Comité Européen de Normalisation Electrotechnique (CENELEC), formed in 1973, was the equivalent of the IEC. CEN and CENELEC, like ISO and IEC, work closely together and have developed common rules for the preparation of European Standards and other related publications. Their membership is open to the respective national standards bodies and electrotechnical committees of the countries belonging to the European Union (EU) and to the European Free Trade Area (EFTA). They nearly ceased to have a role in the world in the early 1980s, suffering through a prolonged period of drought during which time the formal organizations of ISO and the IEC had their heyday. However, with the advent of the "EC 92" initiative, the two organizations became important to European and to worldwide standardization.

This revitalization grew out of the feeling which started in the late 1980s that the European national standardization bodies (DIN, AFNOR, BSI, and so on) were not well-run, pan-European activities were not well-coordinated, and that these various bodies were taking far too long to accomplish what they accomplished. In the IT arena, each country was individually challenging the hegemony of the U.S. in X3 and in the JTC1 arena, and they were not doing well. Very few of the standards were ready to be published and there were still hundreds of work items and drafts floating about in the multiple national committees. With the European Economic Community Single Market due to come into existence on 1 January 1993 (which was a year's slippage from the January 1, 1992 date that gave "EC 92" its name), the EC set about improving its chances, since many of the fundamental concepts of the EU unity depended upon the standards being in place. (The standards were not just for the IT community; rather, the IT community was reasonably low on the list of "high priority items." The chief items from what I saw were toys, which have the greatest appeal to the least educated portion of society. I believe that this was largely the correct approach. Children, who cannot protect themselves, deserve attention. Business people who can protect themselves, but do not can wait.)

In late 1990, the European Commission issued a Green Paper that looked at the development of European standardization. It focused on systems improvement, including ways to speed up the process. It also proposed a single standardization organization for Europe. To use a quaint American phrase, "the fat hit the frying pan about that time." To say that the proposed solutions were not well received by the standardization community in Europe and in the U.S. would be a severe understatement. There was a tremendous brouhaha. The European nations did not want to give up their national bodies and the U.S. did not want to give them up either.

The reason for this possibly surprising second viewpoint lay in the basic nature of the multinational company. The major vendors of everything from computers to cars to tractors to copy machines are heavily weighted with U.S. and Asian-based multinational companies. Many of them had medium to large European subsidiaries (sales, manufacturing, and research), nearly all of which participated in the European standardization process in one way or the other. This had the effect of allowing the larger multinational companies to "vote" multiple times in the standardization arena: once in their national body (where they resided) and once in each European country in which their subsidiaries had active and substantive standards participation. The possibility of losing this ability for multiple votes, as well as losing their entrances into the European standardization mechanism, gave impetus, especially to the U.S.-based companies, to oppose the proposal. The nationalistic viewpoint succeeded; the Green Paper was withdrawn. The movement towards unification in standardization was slowed. It is noteworthy that while there was the indirect requirement that the national bodies remain, there was no concomitant commitment of resources on the part of the vendors. When the economy turned bad, they pulled standardization representation quickly and, in many cases, completely.

CEN then reassessed its organizational structure and introduced a policy of "sectorialization," which allowed the technical work to be arranged into separate areas (sectors), allowing CEN to plan, coordinate, and manage its various work programs more completely. The CEN Administrative and Technical Boards created a number of Technical Sector Boards (BTSs) to manage these various sectors. BTS7 had responsibility for IT standardization. Simultaneously, CENELEC developed an information technology strategy plan, indicating the relationship of CENELEC to other European organizations and activities. CENELEC also described its technical and operational directions, and then specified its major programs of work.

To ensure harmonization with ISO, CEN signed an agreement with ISO (called the Vienna Agreement) allowing the simultaneous adoption of the same standards at international and European levels, through parallel processing. IEC and CENELEC did the same. While the two were pretty much similar, the two were not entirely the same. This nonharmonized state of affairs did not bother most standardization committees; there was only one committee with a real problem. This was with sole ISO/IEC committee—ISO/IEC JTC1, which rested on the cusps of both organizations. To make matters more difficult, JTC 1 had modified the standardization processes to speed up its work—and was reluctant to give up these process improvements that it needed. As a result of these problems, Vienna Agreement was delayed for nearly a year before it could be implemented in the IT area.

The basic function of CEN and CENELEC is to prepare European Standards (Norms), which is the basis of the "EN" prefix that one sees cropping up more often in European procurements. European standards have to be published in three languages (English, French, and German) and adopted in all the CEN and CENELEC member countries. When voting formally on European Standards, each CEN or CENELEC member country has a weighted vote ranging from ten (eg, UK and Germany), to one (Iceland). CEN and CENELEC members are *required to accept* European standards within their countries. To ensure that there is harmony within a country, and to make sure that differing national standards do not exist, any preexisting and conflicting national or international standard adopted nationally must be withdrawn and the European Standard adopted nationally in its place.

While this does not really sound too traumatic, consider the case of the English manufacturer of tripe. (While this story sounds a little strange, I assure you that it is based upon fact. On one of my trips to England, I spent about three days being fascinated on the press and television reports of this instance.) The tripe factory has always run according to the time-honored tradition of English tripe makers. The market is not that big, but it has been a good market. The equipment for making tripe apparently hadn't changed in the past several decades, and the factory was up to snuff as far as British expectations and standards for hygiene went. The came the EU, followed by the imposition of new European standards for food preparation factories. The tripe business is not, from what I could gather, an especially lucrative business, and the factory in question, while "healthy" financially, could not afford to bring its physical plant (including buying new tripe making machinery) up to regulation. As a result, the plant, and company, was forced to close. In the larger scheme of things, it was not earth shattering. In the scheme of things of the people who worked there, and the people who bought the tripe, it was catastrophic.

The EC then decided that there was a need to make international standards into European standards to ensure that the procurements were handled by European standards. As a result, a series of "transpositions" began, which were to bring ISO and IEC standards into conformance with EU requirements. There were, of course, the problems of choosing which ones would be transposed, and then choosing who would do it, and then choosing what other work was to be given up by the national bodies who would actually be doing the transposition. Needless to say, this slowed the progress of national body participation in standardization even more. Even worse, the entire question of whether an international standard is good enough for procurement has been brought into question. On the whole, international standards are the standards of choice and are acceptable on a world-wide basis. Europe seemed to be the only region that seemed to cast doubt on this concept. One could almost believe that there was a bit of xenophobia appearing here.

Then, to complicate matters even more, the EC issued a "standstill" order (Directive 83/189/EEC), effectively preventing any European national body from developing standards where there was an emerging international or European regional standard. The rationale was that such standardization was possibly contributing to the nontariff trade barrier problem; a more cynical view would be that the EC was going to bring the Green Paper into force one way or the other.

As part of the "help" that is available to the EC to force these decisions, the EC provides standardization funding for national bodies. To coordinate this work and to ensure that national bodies really do not overlap or waste resources in the ICT arena, the EC has appointed two committees: SOGITS, the Senior Officials Group for Information Technology Standardization, and SOGT, the Senior Officials Group for Telecommunications. These groups approve the proposals for funding work. In some areas the level of funding has been extremely high. While appropriate for ensuring that standards called for in legislation are forthcoming, it could be construed as industrial policy if the SOGITS chose to fund standards in an area where there were no standards but a perfectly good market solution was available. This could become a major problem if the EC was seen to be funding standardization in an area where a major corporation, who already had a solution, refused to participate in the social or environmental activities that the EC deemed appropriate.

ETSI

The European Telecommunications Standardization Institute (ETSI) has not been mentioned thus far because it was not really in existence while much of this was happening. It is the newest of the regional standardization entities in Europe. It is also one of the most radical or most progressive, depending upon the country, organization, and background of the person with whom you are speaking. While CEN and CENELEC are reasonably restrained, ETSI, possibly because it is the youngest and because it has the free spirits (or at least as far as standards people get to being free spirits), has a varied and interesting series of activities to this date. Some have been successful, while others have been less so.

ETSI was established in 1988 based upon recommendations contained in a 1987 Green Paper on telecommunications.[2] ETSI was created by the European Conference of Postal and Telecommunications Administration (CEPT) and fundamentally succeeded. Because it both allows and encourages participation by non-European national firms and organizations in its technical committees, it is considered to be a more open organization than either CEN or CENELEC, neither of which permit non-European organizations to participate. Also, ETSI was charged with producing telecommunications standards for Europe reasonably quickly. This put it into a "race" (or read competition) with the ITU-T. Not surprisingly, this had the effect of generating unspoken, but non-the-less real, hostility between the two organizations when ETSI first was started. However, because it had the EU blessing and the EC funding, and because the formal standards produced by ETSI are European Telecommunications Standards, ETSI was equipped to give ITU-T a run for its money. By 1992, ETSI had created 140 ETSs and interim ETSs (I-ETS). Many, but not all, are derived from the ITU-T or ITU-R recommendations. Its reach extends from Iceland to Turkey, which is not bad for an organization that did not exist ten years ago. Even the ITU mentioned competition from "regional bodies" in its rationale for changing its organizational structure.

The second major external "consciousness raising event" began in 1991, when ETSI announced that it was planning on limiting the rights of IPR holders. It saw its actions as necessary to change the IPR policies of standardization organizations, which is an area that has become increasingly contentious, especially because of the growth of embedded firmware and chip technologies. The IPR problems spring from the inability of standardization committees to cause a holder of an IPR who has participated in a standardization activity to license the IPR on "fair, nondiscriminatory, and reasonable" terms. (The IPR debate is not limited to ETSI and Europe. It is fought in economic journal articles and in the courts in the United States. Suits such as Lotus versus Borland, Computer Associates versus Atari, and Apple versus Microsoft are symptomatic of a growing crisis in this area.)

However, ETSI decided to act, not to go to court. As a result, ETSI proposed to require the holder of an IPR to either license the technology or to "opt out" of the committee. Although reasonable on the surface, two significant problems arose: one based upon technological and knowledge problems, and one based upon philosophical concerns. The first problem (the technical and knowledge problem) lay with the inability of a committee to go through a proposed specification and do a comprehensive patent search on all aspects of the technologies being employed. If the committee did not do this, then any organization that might have had a viable patent in the area subject to standardization had to do a patent search on the proposed work of the committee before the committee began serious work. With a patent search costing about $15,000 to $25,000, this could quickly become prohibitively expensive for many companies. The rule was that tacit approval was anticipated if there was no active "opt out." On the philosophical side, the argument advanced was that each organization with a patent preferred to negotiate with other users, since cross-licensing or patents, rather than cash payments, were often accepted.

On 1 April of 1993, the policy went into force, having been accepted by the ETSI General Assembly on 18 March 1993. It won provisional approval for this undertaking in March of 1993, when ETSI published its Intellectual Property Rights Undertaking. Short of announcing that it was going to nationalize all physical property owned by major multinational industrial businesses in Europe, ETSI could have chosen no other activity that would create such a furor.

"[T]he proposals met with strong resistance from large IPR holders, such as the major IT and consumer electronics firms. Led notably by IBM, Digital Equipment, and Motorola from the United States, and by the Dutch giant Philips, a major campaign was mounted to block the proposed ETSI reforms."[3] There was a great deal of controversy over the proposal, especially in the United States. The Computer and Business Equipment Manufacturer's Association (CBEMA, now the Information Technology Institute, or ITI), which is an association of the major IT hardware systems vendors (but few software vendors), lead the charge. Fundamentally, the leading opponents of the undertaking were companies with extensive communications patent portfolios, and they stood at significant risk in having their portfolios reduced in value if the ETSI proposal succeeded. Eventually, CBEMA filed a complaint with the EC about the policy. After much debate, "ETSI was forced in August 1994 to abandon the main elements of its [IPR] reforms. A deciding factor proved to be the continued and sustained opposition from many (notably U.S.) IPR holders and from the U.S. government."[4] The EC retreated; ETSI will continue its work in other areas.

The Future

In November 1994, in Genval, Belgium, the EC organized a global workshop on ICT standardization. The conference was timed to follow the "Bangemann Report" on European competitiveness in a global market. DGIII and DG XIII were well represented, as were nearly every other business user, client, consortia, or standardization organization in Europe and most of the civilized world. The topics covered were broad and global—but tended to be set pieces. Conclusions drawn included recommendations such as those listed here:[5]

- More R&D liaison is needed.
- International, rather than national, standards are needed.
- The role on the national bodies needs rethinking.
- The GII will require more standards.
- Standards need to be business driven, with more business like goals.
- The Publicly Available Specification (PAS) process was encouraged, with caution.

Fundamentally, the conference confirmed what almost everyone there knew. The EC would have to do something to the way that standards are done in Europe, at least within the remit that they control. And the remit that they control seems to be increasingly constrained by their ability to manage the externalities (a magnificent economic weasel term if I've ever heard one) that impact standardization. And this ability seems to be less and less significant every year, as multinational companies, multinational organizations, and multinational needs grow and the market changes to meet the needs of the industry (the users and the providers and the government) rather than merely the government. The thrashing caused by the EC in these organizations may be the "final act in a seriocomic play," just before the curtain rings down for the last time on a play that no one attends.

CONCLUSION

I believe that the conclusion is reasonably simple to this chapter. Two forms of regional organization have been identified. ECMA has adapted and adopted the things necessary to stay alive in the reasonably competitive arena of European standardization. While not pandering to the provider clients, ECMA has changed its operating procedures and structure to meet its users' demands. As with many organizations, it has downsized, by chopping committees that were no longer productive or necessary.

On the other hand, CEN, CENELEC, and ETSI, while trying to "do good," appear hamstrung by government regulations and requirements. Part technologist, part market analyst, part sales organization, and part economic provider, these groups seem to be blown over the map at the whim of the Brussels bureaucrats. The Genval conference pointed out again that listening to and responding to the needs of the market was necessary because if you fail the market, it will assuredly desert you. It will be interesting to see over the next several years how the situation plays itself out.

NOTES

[1]Brown, Lin. "Human-Computer Interaction and Standardization," *StandardView,* Volume 1, Number 1, September 1993, p. 8.

[2]Communication of the Commission, Towards a Dynamic European Economy, Green Paper on the Development of the Common Market for Telecommunications and Equipment, COM (87)290 of 30/6/1987.

[3]Shurmer, Mark and Lea, Gary. "Telecommunications Standardization and Intellectual Property Rights: A Fundamental Dilemma?" *StandardView,* Volume 3, Number 2, June 1995, p. 57.

[4]Ibid., p. 56.

[5]For an interesting and sometimes conflicting description of what happened at the meeting, see David Arnold's report on the conference in the March 1995 StandardView (Volume 3, Number 1) pp. 23–28, and David Wood's article on the ICT as part of a European policy on standardization in the September 1995 *StandardView* (Volume 3, Number 3), pp. 112–116.

Chapter 18

The National Standards Organization

"Happy the man, whose wish and care
A few paternal acres bound,
Content to breathe his native air
In his own ground."

—Alexander Pope, *Solitude*

INTRODUCTION

The focus of the first part of this chapter is on the Standards Developing Organization that is the head of the federated system of U.S. standardization bodies. This organization is the American National Standards Institute (ANSI). The reason for this focus is two-fold. First, ANSI is unique among the organizations that I have observed in the world of standardization in that it creates no standards under its own aegis; other national organizations cannot, to the best of my knowledge, make this claim. ANSI must use agents to create standards and this, not standardization creation, is how it adds value to the U.S. system of standardization. Second, the very nature of standards is mirrored by an organization like ANSI which could become an exemplar of how standardization is supposed to work if it is allowed to pursue a set of goals and objectives downward, instead of upward.

The second part of this chapter is a speculative look at national standardization organizations as a whole and follows on to the topics in Chapter 17, which asked if national standards bodies were really necessary. This impacts the Information technology arenas of all standardization bodies from Germany's DIN to SANZ (the Standards Association of New Zealand) because, as the IT SDOs are finding out, being a unique standardization organization is similar to being a unique telephone; you look real nice, but you do not interoperate well at all. And the interoperation is what the whole movement is about.

THE AMERICAN NATIONAL STANDARDS INSTITUTE (ANSI)

The American National Standards Institute (ANSI) coordinates the myriad of standards activities in the United States in areas that range from film size to screw threads, from automobiles to computers. It was organized in 1918 in response to a perceived crisis. The industrialization of the United States was based upon the commonality of interchangeable parts over distance, and the use of "nonstandard" standards was becoming a major problem due to a proliferation of standards, each advocated by only a handful of manufacturers. As was pointed out in Chapter 2, this was bothering the war effort. To counter this situation, five leading United States engineering societies joined forces to create the American Engineering Standards Committee. The purpose of the new group was to make sure that enough commonality existed in the standards of the various disciplines to retain (or create) a set of understood and shared terms among engineers. Codifying this body of knowledge and procedures had a major impact on the rapidly increasing industrialization of the United States. This activity was by no means limited to the United States. Industrialized nations throughout the world were undergoing similar standardization activities. The U.S. organization was unique, however, disdaining official governmental approval, preferring to have the government as a client, rather than as a sponsor. Organizational and name changes occurred in the 1920s, 1960s, and in the 1980s; in the last several years, the mission seems to have begun emphasizing an outward looking international focus, rather than a national focus.

The following statements of purpose are extracted from ANSI's new constitution:[1]

1. To serve as the national coordinating institution for voluntary standards, certification, and related activities in the United States of America through which organizations concerned with such activities may cooperate in establishing, improving, and recognizing standards, based on a consensus of parties-at-interest, and certification programs to the end that such activities remain dynamically responsive to national needs; that duplication of work is avoided; and that individual enterprise and initiative are encouraged;

2. To represent the interests of the United states of America in international non-treaty standards. . .

3. To further voluntary standards and certification activities as a means of . . . facilitating domestic and international trade. . .

4. To ensure that the interests of the public have appropriate protection. . .

5. To provide a means for determining the need for new standards and certification programs;

6. To establish, promulgate, and administer procedures and criteria for recognition and approval of standards;

7. To establish, promulgate, and administer procedures and criteria for recognition and approval of certification programs;

8. To cooperate (with the government);

9. To promote knowledge and use of . . . standards;

10. To serve as an information clearinghouse.

I have always tended to believe that a numbered list denotes priority, unless there is a specific disclaimer or a statement about alphabetizing. Given that neither exist in this case, and further given that I cannot conceive of ANSI's Board just deciding to put up a random list, I would make the assumption that the ordering bears a significance.

Basically, the priorities on the list are that ANSI has hegemony and is the leader (1), that everyone has to follow the leader internationally (2), that the reason we're following the leader is for economic reasons (3), but making sure that everyone is taken care of (4), while making it possible for more and more people to play in the game (5,6,7,8), and teach people the rules of the games (9), and where to get the information (10). A simple word count analysis shows that 46% of the words of the purpose are devoted to "promotion, promulgation, common usage, or cooperation" of external entities with ANSI. About 4% are focused on promoting knowledge and use of standards. About 6% look at making sure that public interest is safeguarded. The approach may be simplistic, but I believe that, while the categories can be manipulated easily and analyzed at length, a quick analysis based on this description is instructive for several reasons.

If these statements reflect the opinion of the Board (which I would assume that they do), then the Board sees the primary function of ANSI not as standardization, but on promotion and growth of ANSI. The lion's share of the statements relate not to ANSI's mission, which one would hope relates to the growth and use of standardization as a discipline, but rather on how to make ANSI as ANSI (and not ANSI as the leader of standardization) more important. The intent of any organization such as ANSI which is a cooperative of all of its members is to grow the common good for its members, rather than trying to grow itself. The Board focused on "growing the organizations that do standards" rather than on "growing standards." Or at least that is my observation. Logically, the response should be, "How do you do standards sans organization?" I do not believe that I am advocating doing away with ANSI, necessarily. What I am advocating is that possibly the directors should be less concerned with preserving an organization and more concerned with creating a discipline. Unfortunately, there are very few people on the board of ANSI who are not somehow related to the current standardization regime and so have a vested interest in preserving the status quo. The question is whether or not ANSI can improve this by bringing on to the Board people from outside the current standardization process to act as change agents, to preserve the formal process in the United States.

Within the United States and increasingly within the international formal standardization arena, ANSI is also the recognized representative to ISO and the IEC, the two major international nontreaty standards organizations. It funds the Secretariat and several Sub-Committees of JTC 1, the ISO committee for information technology. ANSI's position as the United States sole representative to these organizations derives, in large part, upon the international view that ANSI is the most representative standards organization in the United States, as shown by the first statement of purpose.

ANSI does not itself develop standards,[2] but it manages and coordinates private-sector standards activities to ensure that the United States has a strong standards effort that serves the national interest. A nonprofit organization, ANSI is supposed to serve all industries and users in the United States; indeed, its ultimate client is the nation. ANSI "supervises the voluntary efforts of nongovernmental bodies to create standards that serve the sponsoring industries and user organizations." The groups that sponsor and develop these standards range from professional societies to technical groups, trade associations, and various other interested groups.

ANSI encourages these groups to submit their proposed standards for approval as American National Standards, an endorsement that only ANSI can give. If a group chooses not to submit a standard, ANSI has no recourse. However, a standard that is not endorsed by ANSI usually receives little market acceptance over the longer term. One of ANSI's most important attributes is this ability to designate standards as national consensus standards. Approval by the Institute indicates that a standards-writing group used a process that provided everyone who was directly and materially affected by a standard with an opportunity to participate in its development. The right to withhold or bestow this approval, and the economic power that it confers, allows ANSI to exercise a control over the standards process that would not exist in a free market setting. The perceived ability of ANSI to impose a standard is not an accurate reflection of the ephemeral power that ANSI actually possesses. It is the consensus review by all impacted parties, from providers, through users, to the government, that is the key feature of the ANSI standards process. Under consensus, acceptance of a standard occurs when there is no compelling reason not to allow it (to phrase it another way, adoption is only possible when all parties agree that no interests are compromised by the standard). The system is highly dependent upon shared understandings and expectations, both within the community of ANSI and the society as a whole.

However, for the past several years, there has been a growing discontent among standardization groups over the role that they see for themselves and for ANSI.[3] Organizations such as the ASTM have decided that they do not necessarily need to submit their standards for the American National Standard imprimatur. Rather, they feel that their "ASTM" or "IEEE" label is satisfactory for the world, who should recognize this as the "seal of approval" from a "highly knowledgeable" group of Americans who are skilled in doing something. On the face of it, it is a valid argument, for the late 1950s. However, given the reality of the industrialized world, I find it ludicrous that an organization within the United States would suggest that they could go it alone at this time.[4]

If one were cynical, one might suggest that the fight is not so much about giving up the right to be seen as an independent and important organization in one's own right as much as it is about who owns the royalty rights that accrue to the holder of the copyright of the standards document itself. If there is an ANSI imprimatur on the document, then ANSI has a share of the royalties. If, however, you do not have to get that "ANSII" designation, then you do not have to share royalties. I would be loath to believe, however, that any organization would be willing to sacrifice a national standardization program for its own publishing revenue. An activity of this nature would be, the one thing that could be used to justify governmental intervention and take-over of the process, since it clearly indicates that the current participants do not have the ability or desire to manage standardization as a public trust.

As a voluntary consensus standards organization, ANSI realizes that it will fail if it does not achieve consensus in its standards activities. Thus, one of its primary concerns is ensuring that a viable consensus process is followed. As a basic rule, it will not list as a national standard any standard that has not been through its established mechanism for obtaining consensus. This includes using the concept of due process, which allows any interested or impacted party the opportunity to help create or to challenge a standard. It also provides an appeals process that contributes to legitimizing the entire procedure.

This dependence upon consensus, as a community of interest, is a major strength but is also the single largest problem with which ANSI must deal. The problem, however, is part of the legacy of ANSI's creation. By refusing to seek governmental status, or even endorsement, ANSI placed itself in the position of having to depend upon its ability to satisfy any legitimate organization that wanted to become a member. Initially, ANSI's clients were primarily engineers, seeking a commonality in their technology and metrics. Over time, there was an increasing emphasis on the commonality of the parts and pieces and the materials that composed a physical system. Again, leadership was given to the groups or companies that received the greatest good from such standards: the capital-intensive manufacturing and utility companies. These companies long have been the leading proponents of standards, and because of the magnitude and nature of their investments, they tend to move slowly, since a misadvised standard can be catastrophically expensive. However, the evolution in basic industrial makeup of the United States has been transformed over the past two decades: The industrial base is moving from capital-intensive high-volume manufacturing to a service economy, and this service economy, growing at a rapid rate, is predicated upon change and the encouragement of change, as well as the needs of the current and future market, which seem transient to organizations that measure stability in decades. As long as the dominant force in the economy was the main-line manufacturing companies, hegemony in ANSI was theirs. Now, with the increasing economic power of the service and high technology industries, this hegemony is no longer clear cut. This conflict between the new brash high change industries and the more stable older industries is one of the important challenges facing ANSI as an organization, and with no means to enforce its approach to standards except by consensus.

The President of ANSI, Sergio Mazza, identified several challenges to the ANSI standards process in 1995. "The five principal ones are the globalization of markets, regulatory reform, the accelerating speed and impact of technology (even on sectors traditionally not considered technology-driven), the drive for value in the global economy, and electronic publishing."[5] The statements are not new; business has been aware of them for several years. ANSI is aware of them. The organizations that would brake away and go out on their own forget that the reason they have the credibility that they do is because ANSI has spent over seventy years building the "technology infrastructure" to allow their products to be accepted. While there are certain things in the ANSI process to which many people can and do object (often with justification), the fundamental constraint that everyone operates under is that it is needed and there is no replacement for it that is globally acceptable. It is like the superhighway system; it is ugly, expensive, and inconvenient (especially when it runs through your neighborhood), but it is absolutely necessary to the way of life that we have. The replacement would either be chaos or even uglier, more expensive, and more inconvenient, or both.

The last of ANSI statements of purpose had to do with acting as a clearing house for voluntary standards from all major worldwide sources, including ISO, the IEC, and most of the other major national standards bodies. ANSI provides a centralized source of information on these standards for many export-minded companies when they realize that non-U.S. standards must be implemented. While this observation may sound negative, it reflects an unfortunate and rather widespread phenomenon: Providers in the United States tend to produce for a domestic market.

Many U.S. firms (approximately 80%) have never had to go outside the country to sell their products. As a result, they do not understand that they must take international standards into account when they begin to design products and services for export. As the internationalization of trade and business accelerates, and as U.S. companies recognize that other countries have valid reasons for doing things differently (that is, their way), demand for these international standards will grow. Clearly, there must be a mechanism to insure that U.S. companies are aware of international standardization activities, and to disseminate information on international standards, since the availability of a standard serves no purpose if its existence is unknown.

Perhaps the most worrisome fact is that most U.S. companies are neither aware of nor care what ANSI does. Of the several tens of thousands of U.S. companies, only about 1300 are company members of ANSI. To gain a larger base of support, ANSI must promote understanding of its role in the standardization process, as well as the role of standards and standardization in general. This important task will likely be hindered by the ongoing conflict between mature/stable industries and young/evolving industries, as well as by the conflict between old line standardization proponents and the more opportunistic emerging disciplines. Yet, with the minimal educational service that ANSI is able to provide, primarily because its supporting companies do not really participate in the marketing of standards, it will be difficult for ANSI to act in this most necessary field.

I believe that the ultimate question is not whether ANSI will be able to create a better method for dispensing standards or cut standardization time from four to two years but rather whether or not the organization known as ANSI and the consensus standards method that it champions will survive into the next decade.

The thing that is of great importance in this whole discussion is that the members of ANSI are ANSI. In Chapter 9, when dealing with standardization organizations generally, I made the comment that, "It is just much easier to believe that standards are created and given to the industry than to believe that a portion of the industry helped (or could have helped) in their creation. Mysterious benefactors (and malefactors) have always fascinated people." The members of ANSI who have permitted standardization to become less important, who have failed to actively participate, who are content to sit back and "just pay money" to absolve themselves of the need for action, are the major contributors to the enfeebled ANSI. They are also the organizations that probably have the most to lose, because, by their inattention, they have probably not understood the impact and power that standardization can have on business, especially on their business.

ANSI: Membership and Organization

The organization of ANSI resembles that of many other standards groups, such as ISO. It displays some unique characteristics, however, the result of the legislative branch of the U.S. government's occasional investigation of the structural problems in American industry and attempts to "fix" them. Because of this, ANSI has an apparent surfeit of checks and balances, which have served to make it a true consensus standards group, but one which is very slow, in most cases.

ANSI's membership includes over 250 private industry and governmental organizations and over 1300 companies, represented by the ANSI Board of Directors, the governing and policy making body. The Board of Directors are drawn from many of the major industries and user groups that constitute the industrial strength of the United States. The Board must insure that equity is maintained among the members, and pains are taken to avoid overloading a single functional area. While the Board provides general guidance to the activities of ANSI, the Executive and Finance Committees, which act for the Board of Directors when the Board is not in session, are basically the power positions for determining the future of ANSI.

There are multiple other committees and boards, all charged with a series of activities that might have an impact on standardization. However, the largest challenge to all of the committees and boards can be reduced to a single major question, which the Board has, to my perception, been unable to address. The question fundamentally is, "How does ANSI become mainstream when it is the leader of a weak federation?" The board wants standards to be important when they help the board member's bias. As a result, the board members who represent SDOs that make a great deal of money publishing want one thing, the user members and their boards want another, the government another, and the provider participants yet another. And this litany of needs and desires comes from just those members who attend. Those that do not attend probably have even farther ranging opinions and desires. This is the powder keg upon which ANSI currently occupies a tenuous position.

To complicate the matter even further, the unique structure of ANSI makes the entire process more difficult. As noted earlier, ANSI does not develop standards, but rather relies upon groups of accredited standards developing organizations to do so. These organizations usually publicly accept terms and conditions of formal development including the consensus methodology, an openness, and a commitment to participate in the ANSI process, which also means that they will publish American National Standards. This is where the rub comes in, since there are publishing revenues associated with the ANSI ANS designation. However, this is not the major problem associated with this venture. ANSI relies upon these organizations for revenue and for membership. And these various organizations vie for hegemony; one with another, with ANSI separately, and as a group against ANSI. In the past, when the leaders of ANSI tended to favor, or at least appear to favor, one class of member over another, the neglected organizations or groups or coalitions acted as ignored children act, by threatening to run away from home. At the same time, the number of children continued to grow. ANSI, with its various boards, had never learned to say no to a group that appeared and was willing to swear to "the rules" if it could become an SDO. My favorites are the two "screening" associations who are separated by some arcane definition so that they "really are different."[6] The federated system works as long as there are players who are there to take the whole thing seriously, and not merely their role in the larger structure. Again, the idea that one must cooperate before you can compete rears its head.

The Future for ANSI

ANSI will continue as an organization. It has too long a history to fail completely. However, there are several things that I believe that it could do to begin to move itself into more of a mainstream position in the industry. To accomplish these, however, it must be willing to take a chance, because it will have to change not only the way that it thinks but also the way that many of its members think.

One of the boldest initiatives that is currently underway is the "Strategic Standardization Management (SSM) Initiative," driven largely by the ANSI Company Member Council Executive Committee (CMCEC).[7] The SSM initiative is not about standards; rather, it is about using standards to leverage organizational strengths in any discipline, whether service, manufacturing, or R&D. Fundamentally, SSM is about making standardization work for the company, and recognizing standardization as a management tool that has a degree of power.[8] While this specific initiative is being developed in ANSI, there is no guarantee that it is the "right" initiative. However, it is a first step to making standardization more than merely "talking about standards."

This is the core of the problem with the current structure of ANSI and one that is recognized by ANSI's management. Standardization is not about standards and the process of standards creation. Rather, standardization is about the use and utility of standards as a management tool. At the last CMCEC, there was a prolonged discussion on the floor of how to deal with consortia; one of the ideas advocated was a recognition of a standard that was developed without having full consensus because full consensus was not necessary. (The argument was aimed at IT and other fast-moving standardization areas, which really do not need full consensus, but rather consensus of producers who wish to productize something.) The idea was that the new process would encourage organizations to work inside the process, and the result would be a "junior standard." The idea went down in flaming defeat because the majority of people on the committee believed that the market really wanted the ANS standard. The success of the consortia has proven that this is not so, and consortia are now a much larger business in standardization than is ANSI. And yet many of the participants at the CMCEC refused to admit the legitimacy of the consortia's product.

This emphasis must be switched from a consideration of the process to a consideration of the outcome. One of the questions that was not answered was the worth of the "ANS" brand. Groups such as the ASTM and the IEEE seem to believe that they can do well without it; the question is whether they could do well without the standardization infrastructure that ANSI provides.

A leading requirement for ANSI is to place a value on the standards infrastructure—and then to use this value as a lever back into the market. But the lever must be an inclusionary lever, used to encourage cooperation, not competition. If everyone would play, it would be a lot better place for everyone. If everyone is going to play inside their little castle, we will all be separate, and easy prey for the first large army that comes along.

OTHER NATIONAL BODIES

If ANSI, as the standardization organization of the United States, and a powerful and wealthy nation, has this many problems, what does this mean for the rest of the national organizations? Within the IT arena, it paradoxically means very little in the short term, but a tremendous amount in the long term. This paradox derives from the problems of ANSI and the success of the multinational corporation.

The SDOs in Europe have survived two attacks by the EC so far. Each time, the water rises a little higher, and each time the SDOs have to fight harder and harder to maintain their existence. If you look at who is fighting to maintain the separate existence of the SDOs, you will, I believe, find that it comes primarily from two sources.

The first, as is expected, is the actual members of the organizations that are being threatened with dissolution. Nothing quite sharpens your appreciation of the great job that you have been doing as much as the possibility that you may go away. While data is scarce, I believe that a study of the work programs undertaken by the European SDOs in the area of IT has, over the past several years, suffered a precipitous decline. (While this is due in part to Directive 83/189/EEC, the standstill directive), it is also a reflection of the fact that new and fun projects are not being sent to the SDOs for standardization in the IT arena.

This, of course, presents a "chicken and egg" situation. If there are no really interesting programs or projects being offered to the European SDOs (or to other SDOs as well), how do the SDOs create interest and maintain membership so that they can garner the interesting programs? Basically, the concept is that "success breeds success, and failure, failure." To permit their programs to survive, the SDOs have indicted a willingness to undertake programs dealing with standardization for committed prior funding. Some of this funding comes, of course, from the EU, the very organization that is trying to lessen the influence of the SDOs. Needless to say, there is a certain confusion in this arena by all the participants.

What these organizations are really seeking, however, is a way to make their services necessary to an expanding Europe. However, there is a large and growing problem with this; successful European national firms in the IT arena are few and far between. Each country has a major and dominant national body participant; companies the size of an Olivetti, a Bull, an ICL/Fujitsu, or Siemens-Nixdorf. This may appear to be goodness but, in standardization, has exactly the opposite effect. Who will challenge Siemens-Nixdorf's might in Germany? Who is there to challenge ICL/Fujitsu in the United Kingdom? The problem is that standards are made to operate in an environment where there are multiple large participants who can neither dominate nor submit to their opponents. In this arena, standards provide a mechanism for these firms to establish a viable method of dealing with the market. Smaller firms will tend to follow the larger firm, which can afford the extensive research and development necessary to survive in the IT field. Maverick participants will either succeed or fail, but a maverick participant usually does not normally want to use standards, since the whole idea of being a maverick is to buck the common (and standardized) trends. Similarly, the users will use those systems which are the most common and also probably the least expensive. Again, economies of scale work in favor the larger participants.

The need for standardization within Europe, then, appears to be a need for a pan-European standardization that would help to create a larger and more unified market. The objections by the various national bodies to being merged or "rightsized," are natural, but should not, themselves, have kept the national bodies alive. If the central funding authority supports the dissolution of these activities, and this is supported by the government (either implicitly or explicitly), then the organizations should be disappearing. They have not.

Therefore, there must be at least one more piece to the puzzle. The first of these missing pieces is the national manufacturer and the national government. Neither want to see the current market situation disrupted. The creation of national standards is ideal for this purpose. This is, of course, the thing that the EU fears most about standards; their use by a national member to create a nontariff trade barrier. A major question is the ". . . role of the government relative to protecting national interests. There are numerous occasions, both in IT and other areas, where nations (governments, local companies, etc. in some mix) have taken positions and actions related to competition between nation states. HDTV seems an obvious example; there are similar efforts in the areas of cables and wiring. While the IT industry has generally been free from this type of interference, there is no guarantee of noninterference."[9]

The thing that mitigates against this in IT is that a single nation, acting alone, usually cannot force the changes necessary to cause all of the other nations to accept the requested or, in the worst case, mandated, change. The Japanese, in 1995, attempted to force a software quality registration scheme on the software being imported into Japan. After discussions with the USTR, they withdrew their proposal. If there is little chance of a nation using a standardization organization in the IT arena to change the rest of the world, or to force a change in the way that IT is done, why do national IT bodies, as opposed to regional or international bodies, continue to exist? I believe that the reason for this is that IT is glamorous, and that it is considered necessary for prestige. However, prestige costs money, and the follow on question is one of who supports the participants in these bodies?

In a large part, these SDOs are filled with employees of multinational corporations, who participate and keep alive the national activities. As noted in an earlier section, the multinationals tend to commit people to participate in national bodies where they have a large national presence. The reason is simple. The suppliers have a vested interest in maintaining a reasonably planned "change environment," as well as staying abreast of what is happening with their competition. Standards provides a good place to do both of these. The participation in the IT arena allows these players to migrate to the higher administrative positions within the national bodies and thereby influence, within reason, national policies dealing with standardization. And, as part of the national SDO's hierarchy and management, there is the possibility of influencing the management of either ISO or of CEN/CENELEC. This, by the way, is not true only of the multinational corporations, it is also one of the reasons that national organizations participate.

Multinationals, however, do this all over Europe. The rationale for participation is due, I believe, in large part because the multinational corporations are responding to national body pressures to participate and maintain a certain aura of high technology prestige and glamour. This is aided by the multinationals, who do not wish to be seen as adversarial or even opposing the national position of the country in which they are resident. This, however, has had an interesting effect. The major multinationals who participate are the mainline systems vendors that participate in ISO/IEC's JTC 1 technical subcommittees. The problem with ISO is, as noted above, that no new and exciting activities are scheduled for standardization. New and exciting ventures are being taken to other venues, and these other venues have a multinational cast themselves.

This puts the national organizations in Europe in a double bind. They are not getting the "fun" programs because their sponsors either are not creating the fun things or else because the new opportunities are going to other, nontraditional, venues. As the migration to nontraditional venues continues, the national SDOs will lose new members and rationale for existence in the IT arena, which strengthens the hand of the central authorities (CEN/CENELEC). There was an attempt to specialize each of the European SDOs some years ago (that is, the British would take computing, the Germans manufacturing, and so on), but the drive for this seems to have failed, since each organization jealously guarded its ability to participate across the board.

Meanwhile, on the Pacific Rim, the national body SDOs seem to be reasonably healthy due, I believe, in part to the idea that the use of standards can be attractive to developing economies. Japan has, over the past decade, been actively exporting its standardization expertise and structure (not to mention its standards) to Pacific Rim developing nations, while the "Young Tigers" have been using standardization as a method of technology sharing. (There is very little participation by countries other than Japan in ISO /IEC JTC 1.) The idea behind standardization is to permit and encourage the spread of technology so that all may share in its benefits. The Pacific Rim countries have done just that; the majority of standards that are written and published are written describing the market requirements of the Western countries. These are the countries that provide a market for many products produced in developing countries. As an example, the use of the standardized QWERTY keyboard is a great help to providers in Taiwan, as are the standardized interfaces on most equipment. If the standards do not benefit the population of these exporting countries, at least they give them access to the markets for their exported goods.

In these cases, the national body is not so much acting as a standardizing agent for the country, as acting as a conduit for the information that the worldwide standardization organizations provide. There is no real attempt to use the standards imported by these organizations for standardizing national activities (the home market), except as they impact the ability of these nations to export goods and services. As an example, IEC 950 is an international safety standard, to which the electrical appliances exported to Europe must apply. The question is whether the electrical appliances made for use inside a major exporting country are also required to meet IEC 950, or whether the requirement is an "export only" requirement. If the requirement applies to all of the products, import and export, then the organization is acting as a traditional standardization body. If, on the other hand, the organization is a conduit for foreign market requirements and does not impact the domestic economy, then the SDO can be seen as an "export focused" standardization body, using standards to help its export industry while not opening its national markets to competition.

CONCLUSION

The national body organizations—both the Federated (ANSI) and the Unitary models are under severe strain. In Europe, in areas such as regulation and safety, they are gradually being overtaken by regional or international standards. In both the United States and Europe, in areas such as IT, they are being overtaken by consortia and alliances. These groups do, in fact, allow products to be produced more quickly to something that looks like a standard. In Asia, the "export SDOs," with tacit government sponsorship, are doing well in the areas in which they are active; that is, providing the standards for their manufacturers to permit them to compete internationally.

This activity coupled with the ability of a national government to set the agenda of a standardization organization casts doubt upon the validity of the state financed national body model. Within the high technology community, the multinationals, and now the industry as a whole is becoming pan-national, ignoring borders and other geographical distinctions. The growth of the Internet, which is an application of new and evolving technologies to create a new mode of expression and communication, will have an extreme impact on the way that "technology is done" in the next millennia. And, I am afraid, will completely leave out the state managed or supported SDOs.

The ANSI federated model of subordinated specialized SDOs has the potential to work both in Europe and within the United States if the participants forget about being unique and admit that they are competing for mind share and not for publishing rights. The idea of competition is fundamentally good. It encourages responsiveness to the market. The idea of competing standards has been cited as dangerous; "Too many standards are as bad as no standards." And yet, in areas where the market deems it necessary to have standards, it seems to settle on one. The public is not really that easily swayed by SDO and provider claims.

However, if the SDOs and consortia that exist continue to squabble amongst themselves, or if the governments continue to want to use IT standardization as a tool to limit and constrain, they will find that they and the groups that they represent are left behind. The interesting thing about information technology is that it moves and does not seem to have time to wait for standardization groups to settle on treaties, establish Memorandums of Agreement, or create other lofty and noble power sharing documents between themselves. Fundamentally, IT moves where it will, creating the standardization that it needs as it moves. The national body SDOs appear to be unable to lead the movement, because they are loaded with complex structures and oligarchic perceptual leftovers. If they wish to lead, or at least move to the forefront of the movement, they must change. And, within the IT arena, they have very little time left to make these changes, because much of the industry has already embarked upon an exodus from national body standardization.

NOTES

[1]American National Standards Institute Constitution and Bylaws (revised and approved March 22, 1995), Section 1.02, ANSI, New York, pp. 1–2.

[2]This is specifically prohibited by Section 1.03 Limitation of the American National Standards Institute Constitution and Bylaws, which states, "In seeking to fulfill the purposes set forth in Section 1.02 of these Bylaws, the Institute itself shall neither develop standards nor conduct certification programs."

[3]See U.S. Congress, Office of Technology Assessment: *Global Standards: Building Blocks for the Future,* TCT-512, March 1992. Linda Garcia's analysis of the situation between ANSI and its subordinate organizations is well described on pages 13 and 14. The use of the term "subordinate" in this note is bound to cause some problems; ASME, ASTM and the IEEE all seem to view themselves as peers to ANSI, and ANSI is merely "one

among equals." Unfortunately, these organizations have displayed no leadership or tolerance for ideas that seem to develop outside their narrow range. ANSI does not have the luxury that these organizations do—to care for a few lucrative standardization efforts. ANSI, by charter and design, serves all the United States, not merely a subset of participants who agree with its views.

[4]The IEEE at one time was even mounting a major campaign to have itself referred to as a "transnational organization," which is the height of absurdity. While the IEEE, the organization that trains professionals in the fields of electrical and electronic engineering, is a huge organization with branches throughout the world, the IEEE standardization organization receives its credibility from being an ANSI "Accredited Organization." Even worse, neither ISO nor any other standardization organization of which I'm aware have a category for that is called "transnational organization." I believed for a while that there was a direct connection between the transnational concept and the toxic waste dumps near Piscataway, New Jersey, where the IEEE has its headquarters.

[5]Mazza, Sergio. "The Future of ANSI," *StandardView,* December 1995, Volume 3, Number 4, pp. 140–142.

[6]One screens insects, the other is focused on wire woven screening. It is one of the things that sometimes enlivens an otherwise dull afternoon of research.

[7]The CMCEC was lead, when the initiative was proposed, by Francis "Tex" Criqui of General Motors Office of Standardization. Tex Criqui took a reasonably moribund council of ANSI and gave it a new direction and vitality. At the same time, the new President of ANSI, Sergio Mazza, was working from the ANSI side to make ANSI more receptive, especially to comments from ANSI's largest stakeholders, U.S. industry.

[8]See "The Evolution of Strategic Standardization Management," by Diego Betancourt and Robert Walsh in *StandardView,* Volume 3, Number 3, September 1995, pp. 117–126.

[9]Spring, Michael; O'Donnell, Jon; Rutkowski, Anthony; Oksala, Steven. "The Structure of IT Standardization," *StandardView,* Volume 4, Number 2, June 1996.

Chapter 19

The Internet

"Just for a handful of silver he left us,
Just for a riband to stick in his coat—
Found the one gift of which fortune bereft us,
Lost all the others she lets us devote;"

—Robert Browning, *The Lost Leader*

INTRODUCTION

The wonderful thing about the Internet from a standardization point of view are the people in it. While many of the people in other standardization organizations are often filled with self doubt, the hard core members of the Internet are certain that, "[t]he Internet standards development process is the best in the business. More than just a standards process, it is a distributed collaboration and innovation engine that has produced a thriving new field of electronic communication and a ten-billion-dollar global market place growing faster than any communications technology yet devised."[1] It is extremely difficult to argue with people who firmly believe "*Deus Vult*" (God wills it), which, I believe, was the rallying cry of the First Crusade.

The reason that this chapter is entitled "The Internet" is because the Internet has come to mean many things to as many people. Since the Internet is what one might describe as a fluid organization, I find it helpful to lump all the things associated with the Internet in one convenient chapter. Finally, the phrase that members of the group that claim standardization rights to the Internet chant as a mantra is, "We reject kings, presidents, and voting. We believe in rough consensus and running code."[2] This chapter will look at the idea of "rough consensus and running code" and the organization that prides itself on these virtues.

255

IN THE BEGINNING . . .

In the mid 1960s, the U.S. government began to develop the Internet through the Defense Advanced Research Project Agency (DARPA). The ARPAnet effort was focused on research on the basic issues of packet switching. Its original intent was to create a communications schema that the military could use in the event of a nuclear war, hence the emphasis on packets. The activity was initiated, appropriately enough, among the academic community who were actually doing the fundamental research; the ARPAnet let them try out their ideas by implementing them. If they failed, they (the ideas and the implementations, not the researchers) were removed and reworked. If they worked, people used them. The original specifications were the result of "champions" working on something to get it out; they did not care too much about consensus, since the process, if it existed at all, was reasonably informal.

Over time, there came the need to do more than just casually act. The "Request for Comments" (RFC) came into being about 1969. Basically, the RFC was just that. Someone put an idea out and asked for comments. People commented. If it looked good, a protocol resulted. If the protocol met someone's needs, it was implemented. If it did not break anything, it stayed and was proliferated. The academicians were having a good time creating a communications system with the government's money.

In 1981, in an attempt to provide more results from the money being spent, the Internet Configuration Control Board was put into place to advise the DARPA program manager on what was happening. The ICCB became the Internet Activities Board in 1984. And then, in 1986, the National Science Foundation decided to make practical use of the Internet to hook up researchers on a national basis. By 1989, the IAB had run out of bandwidth and created two committees: the Internet Engineering Task Force (IETF) and the Internet Research Task Force (IRTF). The Internet, now lead by the IETF, began to move more aggressively off campuses to commercial research facilities and then to international research facilities and then to companies and other organizations. Meanwhile, the IAB continued to view the Internet as a kind of specialized R&D activity. As time went on, the IETF picked up more and more of the running of the Internet, including the standardization programs.

In the early 1990s, the slowdown and eventual cessation of funding by the government was announced. It became clear to the members of the IAB that the commercial sector would win undue influence unless something was found to replace the governmental funding. To this end, they began to contemplate the formation of an "institutional home and funding support" for the Internet. The funds were to be obtained from industry and other sources. So, the Internet Society (ISOC) was created in January of 1992. The ISOC was to be the legal entity that acted as the umbrella organization for the amorphous IETF. However, the IETF itself is not part of the ISOC; the IETF is a "loosely self-organized group of people who make technical and other contributions to the engineering and evolution of the Internet and its technologies."[3]

Then, in mid 1992, a crisis shook the Internet. Because the Internet growth had been so phenomenal, it appeared that the Internet was running out of address space, and new users would not be able to connect. The IAB came to the rescue, and mandated acceptance of a JTC 1/ ITU-T Open Systems Interconnect (OSI) addressing scheme. For the general membership of the IETF, this was rank heresy. Ever since the Internet had been started, they had fought the ITU and ISO, and OSI was seen as the result of a bureaucratic structure loaded with the minions of industry.

A rebellion ensued. At a meeting in Boston, over 700 members of the IETF met and protested to the ISOC the actions of the IAB, and demanded that the IAB's decision be revoked. In Kobe, the IAB was placed under the direction of the ISOC, was renamed the Internet Architecture Board, and had all standardization stripped and given to the IETF. The role of the IAB, the part of the Internet driven by Vint Cerf and other researchers, was reduced to an advisory role and to solving disputes brought to it by the IETF when they could not be solved by the IETF. The kings had fallen.

THE INTERNET NOW

There are several major components to the Internet standardization activities. I would like to review them piece by piece, since all of these players have a role to play in maintaining an intricate system of checks and balances.

The Internet Society is the international organization charged with coordinating the activities of the Internet and its networking technologies and applications. Anyone can join and meetings are free and open (but require payment of a meeting fee). The rationale for ISOC's existence is to maintain and grow the Internet both as a technical challenge and because the Internet has potentials that the ISOC wants to see realized. Its specific goals and purposes include creating and maintaining the standards that the Internet depends upon, archiving and harmonizing the standards within the IETF, promoting and educating people, groups, and countries about the Internet, evolving the architecture and planning the Internet's growth, administration, and liaison with other organizations. It is also the source of funds for some of the Internet's work since it does hold conferences and seminars and so on.

The Internet Engineering Task Force (IETF) is the protocol engineering and development arm of the Internet. Open to anyone, the IETF has grown from forty people in 1987 to nearly 1200 in 1995. These people participate in work groups that define the fundamental technologies of the Internet and make it work. The IETF meets three times a year, but the Internet is used for much of the work of committees. Because of the size of the work groups now (approaching 200 people in some areas), a self-nominated and appointed "design team" now does the core work, and then submits it to the larger committee for approval. The original ideas for work come from a birds of a feather session, in which the various needs and initial agreement is reached for forwarding to a work group.

The fundamental process is in four stages. The first stage is basic development, which lasts until the specification is stabilized and has a known constituency. At this time, it may become a Proposed Standard, where it must remain for six months while at least two implementations are tested and verified. After this, it advances to Draft Standard for a minimum of four months while everyone pokes and prods it to see if they like it. After this, it can become an Internet Standard. (An Internet Standard carries the added descriptor "STD" as well as an RFC appellation.)

Internal IETF management is handled by the area directors, who, with the Chair of the IETF, form the Internet Engineering Steering Group (IESG). The IESG does the operational management of the Internet standards process for the Internet Society. Finally, the Internet Assigned Numbers Authority (IANA) is the central coordinator for the assignment of unique parameter values for Internet protocols.

The Corporation for National Research Initiatives (CNRI) runs the IETF Secretariat, which is responsible for running the thrice yearly meetings, managing teleconferences, and generally doing the administrative legwork that is needed to keep the organization running. CNRI is funded by agencies of the U.S. government and the Internet Society. The ISOC provides the IETF with about $250,000 per year; the remainder of the budget must come from the government.

CURRENT ACTIVITIES AND PROBLEMS

The success of the Internet has contributed to some of the problems that it now faces. Among these problems are commercialization (with its attendant baggage) and the increasing awareness of the Internet and its derivative works, such as the World Wide Web as morally neutral (but powerful tools in spread of all ideas).

Commercialization can be traced to the activities of the IETF when it first began to differ from the IAB. The competition to the success of the Internet came from the OSI model, and the OSI model was built for business. The awareness of a competing technology focused on the commercial side spurred the IETF to compete in the commercial environment and the IETF succeeded. Internet growth is substantial and continuing. It is as though the growth of the world's telephone network occupied only a decade instead of a century.

However, the measured growth of the telephone system allowed some form of controls to be put in place. The unparalleled growth of the Internet has allowed none of the "social" controls to be created in a planning mode. The very nature of the Internet was one of "just in time engineering," in which a problem would appear and a fix to the problem would be applied. It was very much a reactive, academic type of exercise, which rewarded brilliant suggestions but not necessarily good planning. (However, in fairness, there is very little in the way of viable planning that could be ascribed to this entire area, and the ebullient nature of the participants, who dared to think differently, may have been much more constrained had they been forced to work within a plan.)

The problem with this approach, however, is that it does not take into account the peripheral impacts of the technology. There was always a restriction against commercial use of the Internet, that is, you could not go out and solicit business. The code of conduct that everyone was supposed to adhere to prevented this. The reality was that nothing legally prevented this, and if a user was willing to face the wrath of the other members, then she or he was free to utilize the commercial aspects of the Internet. As one might expect, the first to challenge the "good taste and code of conduct" caveats were lawyers, who decided that the Internet was a good way to attract potential clients. (It was easier than actually having to chase ambulances.) This was followed by marketing opportunities on the Internet. Today I received a study entitled "Customer Buying Behavior and the

Channel Dynamics in the Internet Market." I can learn, if I wish to purchase this study, how to trap addresses of the people who visit my WEB site and respond to them person- ally with advertisement, thinly disguised as "product information" or "requested informa- tion." Anyone in business today cannot fail to be impressed by the number of offers that are flooding the market to make "Internet marketing" a reality.

However, the commercialization has made the Internet a much less democratic place than it used to be. Most major firms in the IT and telecommunications business have at least one participant in the IETF to defend their position. The real problem is that the participant is there to make sure that an idea that her or his organization owns is not im- pacted badly by the IETF, or, if possible, that the idea is adopted by the IETF so that the company proposing the idea can make money. Since many of the companies are small start-ups, the personal involvement may amount to a tremendous stock option package. These are the type of things for which many participants are willing to fight furiously.

At the same time, the growing importance of the Internet, coupled with its growing need for technology to continue its growth, has made it necessary for firms who partici- pate and who wish to grow the Internet to share intellectual property. When the IETF was dealing in the academic community, there was not such a problem. However in 1994, at the request of the IETF, ISOC transferred responsibility for further evolution of the ONC, RPC, and the XDR technical specifications from Sun Microsystems to the IETF. The agreement referred to licensing arrangements for implementors of this technology and was a rather tortuous path for the IETF and ISOC. As a result, the IPR provisions of RFC 1602 are being reviewed.

The problem stems from the fact that the commercial arena has a lot of patents. Mo- torola holds quite a few patents in areas of telecommunications, as does IBM. In Chapter 17, there was a reference to the ETSI IPR undertaking. While the IETF was not as ambi- tious, it made the assumption that large firms would act the way that small firms acted; that is, to license the technology on a single set of terms and conditions.[4] This assumption is, of course, not necessarily correct. A firm will negotiate with each user to obtain the best terms and conditions possible.

This approach surprised the IETF. It had not occurred to them that their IPR policy might be questionable. At the 1995 meeting in Stockholm, "Ole Jacobson, a long time IETFer, [stated] 'Nowadays, what I hear at IETF meetings is people worrying about patents and lawsuits and all sorts of crap we never used to have to deal with.'"[5] The fear of lawsuits, of course, stems from the possibility that the IETF may have to deal with something like the Addamax lawsuit against OSF, in which Addamax claimed that, by choosing a certain technology, OSF hurt Addamax economically. The ISOC has also pur- chased liability insurance for board members, because while the IETF cannot be sued since it doesn't really exist, members who help make the decisions can.

Within more formal bodies that do not "reject kings, presidents, and voting," the rules protect the participants from suit, because everyone gets a chance to play and be rec- ognized. The gratuitous rejection by the IETF of the trappings of organization, while fos- tering a proud and independent spirit, makes each member vulnerable to lawsuit in an an- titrust action. And with billions of dollars at risk, the possibility of a lawsuit grows.

However, if the IETF slows down because of the possibility of lawsuits, there is the waiting "new organization" that will take its place. The World Wide Web Consortia (W^3C)

is a consortium like the IETF and ISOC and is already signing members up to do "web things." Modeled vaguely on the principles of the X-Consortium, the W^{3}C is growing as members of the IETF seek faster ways of getting specifications out and settled upon. And the W^{3}C is only one of a whole group of potential challengers. Consortia, for the founders, can be a money making business, especially when they satisfy a major market need.

The second challenge mentioned above, that of moral neutrality, is of more concern in the social and political environment. The Telecommunications Act of 1996 bans certain types of transmissions as immoral or censorious. The first challenges, of course, appeared as the Act was being signed. However, the very fact that the legislative arm of the United States passed the Act, and that the Executive arm signed it, would give one pause for at least a moment. If the majority of the members of Congress and the President believe in this concept well enough to publicly admit it, then they must be sure that the majority of Americans do as well (1996 is, after all, an election year). The idea of censorship, which seems to astonish most members of the IETF, is not viewed as germane to their task. However, the deployment of a technology carries with it a certain implicit responsibility for the capabilities of that technology. The members of the ISOC and the IETF are about to find out that the technology, despite the best claims to the contrary, does not come without the moral responsibilities. The attitude of many IETFers was expressed by the chapter's quote that the Internet was, "[m]ore than just a standards process, it is a distributed collaboration and innovation engine that has produced a thriving new field of electronic communication and a ten-billion-dollar global marketplace." To take credit for creation is also to take some responsibility for the implications of the net. So far, the governments of Germany, France, China, and the United States have all weighed in on the side of censorship, as has a goodly percentage of the U.S. population. The question is now one of how the IETF will respond to this pressure, since respond it must. Its options seem to be either to accept a level of responsibility and try to work in some way, with the governments in practical forms of permitting them to limit access and information on the Internet, or to ignore the governments and claim that the Internet knows no bounds.

This, of course, brings up a serious question that the IETF has been avoiding. The question is one of, "Where does one man's freedom become another man's anarchy?" In 1946, Justice Felix Frankfurter stated, "If one man can be allowed to determine for himself what is law, every man can. That means first chaos, then tyranny. Legal process is an essential part of the democratic process."[6] While I do not believe that it is fair to saddle the IETF with the problem of the solution, I believe that they must recognize that if they claim that they've done something (as they have) people who don't know any better are going to believe these claims and blame them when something goes wrong.

CONCLUSION

I tend to believe that the future of the IETF, as the old traditional IETF, is bleak. There are too many pressures that will be brought to bear on the structure and organization for it to continue to exist as it has in the past. The old guard of independent participants has been heavily supplemented by "organizational participants," who owe allegiance to their sponsors as well as to the discipline and the IETF. The allegiance to the sponsors in many organizations is always seen as diminishing the participation. It has been my case that most competent engineers work for an organization in which they believe, and whose aims and goals they support. It is extremely rare among highly skilled professionals to find one that has prostituted him or herself to a company. If these participants exist, there is a tendency for them to be found out quickly, and their opinions dismissed.

I believe that the biggest challenge for the IETF will not be in continuing (standardization groups are hard to close down) but in remaining relevant if it fails to change and adopt different methods of operation. While it is nice to believe in the myth of, "We reject kings, presidents, and voting. We believe in rough consensus and running code," the reality is that the rest of the world does, and like it or not, the IETF and the Internet are now part of the mainstream culture, subject to the same stresses and shocks to which every other organization is subject. If the organization can change from being "special and apart" to being one of the many organizations focusing on changing society, and change to being inclusive rather than exclusive, it will succeed. Otherwise, it will find out about another facet of the commercial environment called obsolescence.

NOTES

[1]Rutkowski, Anthony M. "Today's Cooperative Competitive Standards Environment and the Internet Standards-Making Model," Kahin, Brian and Abbate, Janet (editors) Standards Policy for Information Infrastructure; MIT Press: Cambridge, MA, 1995, p. 597.

[2]IETF Credo, ascribed to Dave Clark (1992).

[3]Network Working Group, Internet Architecture Board and Internet Engineering Steering Group *Request for Comments: 1602;* Section 1.2, March 1994.

[4]Network Working Group, Internet Architecture Board and Internet Engineering Steering Group *Request for Comments: 1602,* March 1994; Section 5.4.2. "Standards Track Dcouments" states that:

> (A) ISOC will not propose, adopt, or continue to maintain any standards, including but not limited to standards labeled Proposed, Draft, or Internet Standards, which can only be practiced using technology or works that are subject to known copyrights, patents, or patent applications, or other rights, except with the prior written assurance of the owner of rights that:
>
> 1. ISOC may, without cost, freely implement and use the technology or works in its standards work;
> 2. Upon adoption and during maintenance of an Internet Standard, any party will be able to obtain the right to implement and use the technology or works under specified, reasonable, nondiscriminatory terms.

[5]Abate, Thomas. "Internet Infighting," *Upside,* October 1995, p. 86.

[6]United States vs. Mine Workers, 330 U.S. 312 (1946), Justice Felix Frankfurter, concurring. Felix Frankfurter was an associate justice of the U.S. Supreme Court from 1939 until 1962. A profound supporter of civil liberties, he founded the American Civil Liberties Union (ACLU).

Chapter 20

The Working Standards Developing Organization

"But oh! I backward cast my e'e
On prospects drear!
An' forward tho' I canna see,
I guess an' fear!"

—Robert Burns, *To a Mouse*

INTRODUCTION

This chapter looks at two working SDOs—an Accredited Standards Committee (ASC) and an Accredited Organization (AO)—operating under the aegis of the American National Standards Institute. Both are major SDOs in the area of Information Technology, and both are confronting significant problems in their standardization arenas. I believe that their problems are mirrored by most of the IT-focused SDOs around the world. The problems that these archetype organizations are suffering are due, in large part, to the inability to adapt to the changes that have marked the Information Technology over the past five years and to reinvent themselves to be relevant to the problems that are of real significance to the industry.

ASC X3: ACCREDITED STANDARDS COMMITTEE FOR INFORMATION PROCESSING SYSTEMS

History

X3 was formed in 1960, at the same time as ISO TC 97 and ECMA. After nearly a decade of rapid growth in the data processing industry, X3 reorganized in 1969, establishing the structures that it now has. In 1980, the X4 Committee (Office Machines and Supplies) was merged with X3, and X3 was given the charter for, "Standardization in the areas of computers and information processing and peripheral equipment, devices, and media related thereto; standardization of the functional characteristics of office machines, particularly in those areas that influence the operators of such machines." This has remained the charter. It recognizes that information processing is the key, no matter how it is done. Modifications to it are attempts to modify the charter to so that it resonates more clearly with the industry at large.

For many years (at least since 1960, when X3 was created) ASC X3 and CBEMA were considered to be linked. The reality was a little more complex. A formal SDO such as X3 needs to have a Secretariat to manage its administration; this requires money. Since an ASC is a legal fiction, it also needs a real organization to act as its sponsor. Basically, the Secretariat of X3 was sponsored by the Computer and Business Equipment Manufacturers Association (CBEMA), which assumed responsibility for legal and financial backing for the Secretariat.

It is worth examining CBEMA which is now the Information Technology Industry Council (ITIC) and is a Washington-based trade association that represents members of the information processing, communications, and business products sectors. CBEMA (ITIC) was founded as the National Association of Office Appliance Manufacturers in 1916 in Washington to act as the trade association of the business equipment industry. After several moves and name changes, it settled in Washington and became the Computer and Business Equipment Manufacturers Association. In 1994, it changed its name to the ITIC in an effort to reach a broader base for membership, since the traditional systems vendors had fallen on hard times and many new organizations (big software firms, midrange systems vendors, and so on) were not about to join a "business manufacturing lobbying firm." Membership in the Council is open to all who engage in the engineering, manufacture, finance, sale, and support of all types of office equipment, computer systems and peripheral devices, telecommunications, services, and business equipment. (That this sounds suspiciously like the charter of X3 is, I am certain, no accident.) ITIC's primary function is to provide a viable arena forum where companies identify and discuss issues of like concern and lobby the legislative, administrative, and executive branches of government. As an example of the leadership that the ITIC provides its members, the opposition to the ETSI IPR undertaking (Chapter 17) was lead by CBEMA/ITIC. Also, ITIC provides the chair for the ANSI National Information Infrastructure (NII), reflecting the mainstream opinion of its members in this charge.

Because it had been around for some time, and because it was seen as a stable platform with a certain financially responsible track record, ITIC was asked, in 1960, to sponsor X3. The acceptance of this activity is not completely altruistic. It served to reinforce ITIC's position as the dominant lobbying association within the Washington arena for high technology companies. Since the X3 committee served as a forum where many of the providers met with users, government, and academia (that is, the industry as a whole), the mission of ITIC was well-served because X3 provided another place where opinions could be merged for use in their lobbying. As long as ITIC was "king of the hill," this was not a bad thing. However, with the growth of the industry in both sophistication and wealth, and with the advent of particular lobbying bodies and research consortia, the ability of ITIC to retain its position as the dominant lobbying body has come into question. And with this question has come the additional question of the benefit that ITIC derives from maintenance of the Secretariat, which, while supposedly self-funding, can become a resource sink.

What It Is Supposed To Do

ASC X3 is the Accredited Standards Committee for Information Processing Systems operating under the procedures of the American National Standards Institute (ANSI). All standards developing organizations accredited by ANSI are required to operate according to strict procedures; both ANSI's procedures and the SDO's ANSI-approved procedures. As noted earlier, one of the roles of the Secretariat is to protect the accreditation of the SDO by ensuring the organization's compliance to due process procedures. X3's Secretariat is probably the best and most thorough in the industry.[1] This is important to X3 because X3 has no other mission in life but to create IT standards.

Fundamentally, ASC X3 has the right to standardize (under the terms of its charter from ANSI) anything in the field of information technology to include storage, processing, transfer, display, management, organization, and retrieval of information. (One would suspect that this charter gives X3 the right to print encyclopedia's as well.) As with any organization in the standardization arena, X3's charter or scope is much broader than it can ever hope to accomplish, even if it had the willing cooperation of all members of the IT community. However, with this charter, X3 has the right to accept any "preconceptualization" scheme that arrives. (Chapter 11 identified a multistage model of standardization, where one of the stages involved finding a home for an idea after it looked like the market might accept it.) The reason that the SDOs such as X3 have these overarching charters is to provide a safe haven for ideas that might help them build membership. While this is an admittedly sarcastic viewpoint, there is no other way to justify a charter such as the one contained above.

With this charter or scope, one would suppose that the mission statement is equally broad and generous. This proves to be the case. X3's mission is to develop, maintain, and promote the use of IT standards; to provide an efficient process to develop national standards and participate in international standardization; and to provide a viable and effective national body. By expansion, this mission statement allows X3 to engage in multiple activities, from education in colleges to creation of a national database on standardization, and so on. However, the focus is on IT standardization, and not upon the organization, which is a good sign. The ANSI "statement of purpose" in Chapter 18 made reference to several things that were to ensure ANSI's continued existence. X3 is more focused on "doing standards" while preserving X3 as the organizing body.

How It Works

Membership in X3 is open to all organizations that believe that they are directly or materially affected by the development or use of standards-based information technology products and services. This membership requirement, like the charter and the mission statements, is hopelessly broad. It fundamentally states that *anyone* can join, because there is not a person or organization in the United States not materially affected by standards-based IT products and services.

There are three classes of membership: producers, consumers, and general interest. Membership must be balanced among these groups, so that there is no preponderant group who can sway the voting or unbalance the committee. (The Supreme Court has ruled that packing a committee is a violation of the Sherman Act, and in the Allied Tube case[2] permitted treble anti-trust damages, worth $11.4 million dollars.) Representation is by a U.S. domiciled organization only, since X3 is the U.S. committee on information processing. The current X3 membership represents computer systems providers, middleware companies, data base providers, consultants, semiconductor manufacturers, communications carriers, systems integrators, software publishers, other SDOs, user groups, academia, and government agencies. It is important to note here that voting membership in X3 and all of its subgroups is by organization, not individual. It was long ago decided that individual representation merely left the system open to abuse, since large organizations could flood a meeting with delegates, while a poor organization could probably afford only a single participant. By setting everyone equal at voting time, the large and small are equal, at least in the number of ballots that can be cast directly.

Standards work in X3 occurs in three management committees, forty-six technical committees, and twenty-seven formal subgroups under the technical committees. These committees meet as often as six times a year, working on over a thousand national and international standards projects. Membership in X3 subgroups (Technical Committees and Task Groups) is open to anyone whose organization is affected by the scope and project(s) of a particular subgroup and who has technical expertise. Organizations can send as many people as they like to these meetings (as long as "as many" does not exceed two), and invited experts can attend to present a particular piece of technology. The work is advanced in the meetings, which are planned with specific events, and deals with national or international standardization activities. X3's subgroup officers are appointed by the Operational Management Committee (OMC) and they are required to know the procedures to run a group properly. Failure to attend training can, and has, resulted in an officer recall.

There are several options to attending a committee, depending upon how serious a participant wishes to be. Participant, or "P" status, provides the privilege of having voting rights on action items (letter ballots, contributions, motions) and of voting in the committee. Participants also receive all documents that the committee produces. To stay in the good graces of the management, you must pay your dues (usually a small amount), return all the letter ballots on time, and attend two out of three consecutive meetings in a row.

Two of these three conditions are very important. The dues part is minor; if the organization that sponsors the activity believes that the activity is important, then the fees are insignificant. However, the next two conditions are important. If members do not read, understand, and return the letter ballots, or do not attend the committee meetings, they are considered to be nonparticipatory members and therefore not part of the standardization effort. While this sounds like a good condition, there is a problem with it. It is very easy to mark a ballot "Yes" and return it without taking the time to read it thoroughly. It is assumed that members of these committees do (and I would tend to believe that, at the Technical committee level, they do) a good job. However, this is an area that is subject to considerable questions at the Senior or X3 committee level.

There is another level of membership, called the observer status. Fees are the same; documents are minimal, consisting of only the meeting notices, agendas, and minutes. You do not get to vote, but then you do not have to attend meetings. It is an ideal membership for anyone who just wants to keep track of what is happening in a committee.

There was mention made of three committees of X3. In reality, there are really only two active committees: the Operational Management Committee (OMC) referred to earlier, and the Policy and Procedures Committee (PPC).

The Long Range Planning Committee was established as the Strategic Planning Committee in 1988, partially in response to a push from the British for a standardization planning function, and partially in the hope that organizations would commit senior people (Chief Scientist, VP of R&D and so on) to the process to help define where the IT industry was going. While the idea was good, it did not happen that way, and what the committee ended up with was a split of technical and organizational people. After several years of meetings, the LRPC produced a strategic plan that overviewed what was interesting technically and could conceivably be interesting for standardization, and a reasonably good definition of the process as the formal SDOs knew it. When the membership in the Long Range Planning Committee dropped below five in 1992, it was closed due to lack of interest. Since I was Chair of the Committee when it finally became moribund, I feel strongly about its demise. I believe that its greatest failure lay in the inability of the committee to understand and work with consortia and to expand the definition of standardization outside the bounds of what X3 knew. The reason for this failure derived from the inability of the committee either to posit anything interesting to the consortia or to influence X3 to look at consortia positively. In 1989 I wrote that, "SPC also has a responsibility to define the role of IT standards in the industry, to look at methods of improving the consensus process, at the rationale for some of the standards activities, ..." In these activities, the LRPC could not carry off its charter.

The real power in X3 is really vested in the Operational Management Committee (OMC). It has a wide range of functions, centered on the functional and economic aspects of standards. Part of this responsibility involves the evaluation of proposed standards projects to see how they fit within the scope of X3. This review ensures that few jurisdictional disputes occur among the SDOs that help create standards for IT and related industries. Once a decision on jurisdiction is made, OMC helps to initiate the standards process by verifying that the objectives for the standard are valid; that is, that no potential technical solution is negated by the requirements and that the requirements reflect the need that the standard is projected to fill, both functionally and economically. Finally, OMC acts as X3's project management team, monitoring and tracking the progress of the standard through the consensus standards process.

The interesting thing about OMC is that it defines its scope as considering, ". . . the functional and economic, rather than the detailed technical aspects of standardization."[3] While this is made clear in the scope section of the document, there is no mention made of economic evaluation in the section entitled "3.2.2 Program of Work." Of the twenty-two items carried under "3.3.2," none of them relate to the economic criteria that will be used.

Even stranger, if one looks at the makeup of the OMC, I believe that you will find that the majority of the members are technologists, not economists or business people. Additionally, you will also, I believe, find that most, if not all, of the people are mid-range technical managers within their companies. If the organizations that comprise X3 were serious about the goal and mission of X3, it would seem appropriate that they would send their more strategic business planning people to sit on this committee, which, after all, does consider the economic aspects of standardization. But, they do not and the OMC continues to review and comment on the activities of X3 as it proceeds along the same path.

The Policy and Procedures Committee (PPC) is responsible for, "all matters pertaining to the X3 and subgroup procedural documentation."[4] This is the group that spends time not in writing standards but writing standards about how to write standards. And it is one of the two active management groups within X3.

Problems and Opportunities

Both the OMC and the PPC are staffed by members who are doing the right thing. They believe in the process as it exists and wish to preserve it. However, with their focus on the current running of X3, they have lost the ability to look outside of X3 and see what is happening. In the 1993 to 1995 timeframe, X3 lost about a third of its participating members. Membership in X3 Technical Committees declined from a high of about 3300 people to less than 2000 before the membership stabilized. At the same time, membership in the parent committee declined as well, and recruitment of major new players in the IT arena has been slow. At the same time, participation in and funding of consortia in the industry continued. X3's entire budget of approximately $700,000 is just about equal to the payment that a "Sponsoring Organization" makes to X/Open on a yearly basis.

More importantly, new programs are not coming to X3 for assignment to the Technical Committees. Just as ISO is not getting the exciting new technologies internationally, X3 TCs are not getting the exciting new technologies domestically. The trend began, in large part, with the creation of the Object Management Group (OMG) (see Chapter 16). X3 had an object group that started simultaneously with OMG; OMG has captured the market with its approach. It started its program in fair competition with X3's object Technical Committee (X3H7). In 1991, the rationale for this activity was that, "consortia [would] attempt to create a *de facto* standard if they [could] not find a comparable *de jure* standard to implement."[5] The situation has changed substantially now. In 1996, it is more common for a group wishing to standardize technology to create a consortium if they can not find an extant consortium that is acceptable. The best example of this is the creation, by companies and organizations involved in the World Wide Web, of the World Wide Web Consortium (W^3C), rather than using X3. No consideration was given to using the formal organizations, even though browser technology can be seen as closely related to much of what X3 is doing (Languages, security, GUI).

The reason for the lack of success by X3 in these areas is twofold. The first reason is one that X3 has hesitated to address for a long time; the problem of "X who?" While the people in X3 are proud of their work, X3 is a little known committee except among the cognoscenti in standardization. It is usually referred to as "ANSI" in press releases. This problem is not unknown to X3; it is just that they can not seem to agree on how to correct it. The original idea of the LRPC (Vice Presidents and Chief Scientists) might have helped, but to a generation growing up on the IETF, OMG, the IEEE, and X/Open, the awareness of yet another standardization committee called X3 probably has little significance.

The second reason centers on the oft-repeated litany of, "We cannot wait for the formal system." With respect to the Web browsers, the "formal system" was the IETF and the W3C. With its mandatory ten month minimum standardization cycle, the IETF is seen as too slow. The important thing in the statement above is not that the process is seen as too slow; it is just that the process is not viewed as relevant to what the companies in the arena are trying to do. This has significant implications for X3.

Basically, it says that even if X3 was to get its cycle time down to less than 18 months, it would still be out of the running as the arena of choice. The majority of organizations entering the standardization arena are looking for a quick tool to legitimize a market event, such as the creation of a "new computing paradigm" (which they all seem to be), and to allow the market to proceed beyond that point, building upon what was previously offered. The case in point is that the Web was built upon the Internet, and the browsers were built on the Web, and the interactive languages that are coming (Java and Inferno [recently promised by AT&T's hardware division]) are built upon a stable browser technology. All of this has occurred in less than two years. The providers are trying to build the techno-infrastructure on the fly, and do not have the time or patience to have their technology modified by a committee of what are generally perceived to be "noncurrent technicians" in the arena.

The Future

The process of standardization should be focused on creating a standard that meets user needs and requirements, not upon meeting the needs of an organization. Unfortunately, the fundamentals of X3 include the enforcement of the concepts of consensus and due process. This makes for a slow turnaround in an industry that is increasingly driven by rapid and constant changes.

The TCs, when they get the chance to work, do turn out solid, competent, technical work. However, when they become involved in politics, they turn into horror shows that serve to drag all the committees down. One of the more unusual activities occurred within a small committee called X3T6, which was looking at trying to standardize Radio Frequency Identification Tags (RFID). The committee, realizing that the discipline and technology were too immature to standardize, decided to create a user-defined test that would serve as the basis for a standard. The test was defined in about three years, but seemed to be what a majority of the users on the committee wanted. However, the vendors on the committee split, and managed to tie the committee up in parliamentary maneuvering for about an additional two years. While there was obviously more to it than I have indicated, the result was that the user participants in the committee who were stymied fundamentally had no recourse by to create their own "de facto" standard.

The management skills of the OMC were not up to handling this type of dispute. Under the terms and conditions of how the OMC and its predecessor organization,

SPARC, worked, situations like these were necessarily overlooked and eventually, a standard would appear. However, the "old days" are long gone; the management style associated with them should be as well. If OMC is responsible for the "economic and functional" aspects of standardization, it should have the capability to interject itself into a process and ensure that the process runs. One of the major problems with the standardization process is, I believe, a complete lack of accountability for results. OMC does not keep committees to schedule; it has no real power to cause the volunteers to produce to schedule. Failure to produce to schedule would result, in an organization with fiduciary responsibility, in the termination of the committee members. Yet, in the OMC, the same people keep coming back, year after year. And their management continues to sponsor them.

This would lead one to conclude that their collective managements are either willing to accept the laxity in the output of X3 or frankly do not really care. The members of the OMC come from some of the largest IT companies in the world. These are the same companies that are funding consortia and creating alliances to create *de facto* standards to compete with the processes and output of X3. It is this, more than anything else, that makes the work of X3 suspect.

The process through which X3 has to guarantee consensus is legitimate and appropriate. The key for X3's survival will lie in its ability to attract and retain managers who can manage to the new reality of the IT world and manage to schedule, to program, and to deliver. The senior committee of X3 continues to be driven by technologists, not by business people. If standards are to be viable, they must be treated as a business tool with a technological cast, and managed as a business. The current management structure of X3 discourages this. And this, in turn, permits business management of IT organizations to discourage participation in X3.

U.S. JOINT TECHNICAL COMMITTEE 1
TECHNICAL ADVISORY GROUP (U.S. JTC 1 TAG)

The ISO/IEC Joint Technical Committee 1 (JTC 1) has been described elsewhere (Chapter 15). Because JTC 1 is an ISO committee, it needs to have a national body vote for each national that attends. For the United States, ANSI is the national body that casts the vote in ISO/IEC. The problem is that since ANSI is not very knowledgeable on how to vote on these issues. Since they do not do standards, but rather have an administrative bias, they turn to a "Technical Advisory Group (TAG)" for instructions on how to vote. In the U.S., the TAG for JTC 1 is called, appropriately, the U.S. JTC 1 TAG. Similar structures exist in other countries, where national body organizations provide advice to the national body voting member.

Membership in the TAG is open to members of X3 and U.S. SDOs that are impacted by the regime of international IT standardization. The TAG's function is to ensure that U.S. positions on the international work items are valid U.S. positions, and then to ensure that these positions are carried forward to JTC 1. The question of whether or not the TAG is a "value added" organization, or merely forwards the opinions of its constituants has, I believe, been decided on the side of the activists; the TAG attempts to add value to the U.S. positions that are carried to it.

Since the TAG is largely composed of the same people who populate X3, it might be safe to say that the problems that plague X3 are the same that plague the TAG. I do not believe this to be entirely false, but would offer another problem that needs to be confronted.

When the TAG forwards its opinion to ANSI, it represents that opinion as representative of U.S. industry. The problems with this scheme is that it assumes that the organizations that the TAG contains compose the sum total of all opinions in the United States; a case that is manifestly untrue. The more valid phrase would be that the opinions that the TAG carries forth are the sum total of the standardization groups in the United States and represent the opinions of those groups. The classic rejoinder to the idea that there may be more opinions than are represented is, "Everyone has a chance to join the organizations." This is a true statement, but it is absolutely meaningless in this context. Many companies make a trade-off and determine that participation in the formal standardization arena is not a valuable way to spend resources. The U.S. JTC 1 TAG is obviously under no requirement to seek opinions from organizations that choose not to participate, yet I can not help but think that the forty or so organizations that sit on the TAG wonder why there are not more participants. It would seem to me that they would be actively recruiting more members; the problem, I suppose, is in offering some form of payback to these potential members. Obviously, if people believed that their needs were not being satisfied, they would seek some method of satisfying these needs. Failure of more people to participate indicates that they either are unaware that they have these needs or that they do not, in fact, have unsatisfied needs. In either case, the TAG loses.

The TAG is only as effective as its members. As with X3, the TAG needs to learn to reflect basic business disciplines in their approach to standardization. Part of the business discipline is telling people that you have a product in a way that makes people want to acquire it. The old maxim attributed to Emerson of, "If a man can write a better book, preach a better sermon, or make a better mousetrap than his neighbor, though he builds his house in the woods, the world will make a beaten path to his door"[6] is valid, as long as there is a market for books, sermons, or mousetraps. The thing that the TAG must do and the thing that all TAGs must do, is to validate that there is still a market for the goods that they are peddling, and if there is not, then either find new goods to sell that people want or rekindle the need for the goods that they have.

THE INSTITUTE FOR ELECTRICAL
AND ELECTRONICS ENGINEERS (IEEE)

Background

The Institute of Electrical and Electronics Engineers (IEEE), one of the largest professional organizations in the world, has as a fundamental goal the advancement of the theory and practice of electrical and electronics engineering. Members are admitted upon the recommendation of a current member, and are required to pay dues to the organization. There are other qualifications for entrance, primarily, that the member must be technically qualified in an electrical/electronics, computer, communications, or associated technical discipline. The organization is broken into societies which are distinct and identifiable groups representing either a technical discipline or an industry. Each society has its own structure and form.

The Process and What It Does

IEEE standards are usually written in the Society with a dominant interest in the area. A Society that wants a standard created must first agree to sponsor the standard, and then must submit a Project Authorization Request (PAR) to the New Standards Committee (NesCom), which examines it for completeness, applicability by/to IEEE, and verifies that the proper organization in IEEE is acting. If it approves, the NesCom then forwards this request to the Standards Board. If the Standards Board approves the PAR, the Society responsible for creation of the standard is charged with creating an interest list of possible members, coordinating the activities of the standards committee within the IEEE, and generally ensuring that the concept of consensus, as required by ANSI rules, is followed. When the standard has been completed, it returns to the Standards Board through the Standards Review Committee (RevCom) for final review, approval, and publication as an IEEE standard.

Because the IEEE is recognized as an Accredited Organization, it MAY submit its standards directly to the ANSI Board of Standards Review for adoption as American National Standards. Again, consensus must be observed and all parties impacted by the proposed standard must have a chance to vote on it as it is being processed.

The Standards Board is the ultimate IEEE authority on matters relating to standards. The chairperson of the Standards Board is elected by the Assembly and holds the title of Director, Standards Activities. The Standards Board itself consists of between eighteen and twenty-four members, who vote on proposed IEEE standards. Part of the role of the various groups in the IEEE is to provide experience in the ways of the standards world to first-time standardization efforts. As the IEEE Standards Companion states, "The IEEE Standards Board is your final pool of expertise on which to draw. Much of their experience is reflected in the published documents of the Board, to which you should refer frequently. They are also the overseers of process and procedure in the IEEE. It is their job to ensure that the imperative principles of standardization are followed, that the rules and procedures they decide upon are obeyed, and that the work of IEEE standards meets the rules of consensus standards-developing organization."[7]

Problems

One of the more "hotly contested" issues in the IEEE is the nature of representation of the members. Because the IEEE regards itself primarily as a "professional society of peer engineers," it uses individual representation as the basis of all of its activities. There are few organizational sponsors. Basically, everyone is there to represent her or himself. In so far as I am aware, this is a unique approach. It denies the power of the major organizations to influence the process directly. That is, a major systems vendor cannot vote its power while allowing that same systems vendor to send ten engineers to a program, each of who could vote in accordance with their sponsoring organization's wishes. X3 has opted for sponsoring organization vote to preclude the possibility of individuals flooding a committee.

In the chapter on the Internet (Chapter 19), I made the comment that it is extremely rare for a professional in this area to act as their employer's agent and ignore their professional discipline. In the few times that I have seen this happen at the IEEE meetings, the people who acted in this fashion were quickly found out. After the discovery that they were operating in a vendetta mode, they came to be regarded as nuisances or, in the worst case, a temperamental demagogue, who did extensive damage to their company. Because their actions were so extreme, their own organizational colleagues distanced themselves from the agreed to corporate position, effectively isolating the individual and the organization they were representing within the IEEE.

The use of the practice of individual representation, like that in the IETF, always invites comments and requires constant vigilance to ensure that it is not abused. It is a recognition that the activities of the AO are representative of the beliefs of the IEEE as a whole; the belief in the individual's discipline and professional competence. This introduces a larger problem, however. Because it is a professional society, and because it has obligations to ensure that its members become better professional engineers, the IEEE tends to look at standards as a technical issue and as a method of ensuring "good engineering practice."

This phrase "good engineering practice" occurs throughout the IEEE's references to standards work. The emphasis in IEEE standards is on the validity of the technical solution, rather than upon the practicality of the standard as a solution to a business or economic need. This technical discipline and focus to the exclusion, in a large part, of the economic focus, is one of the strengths of the IEEE, as well as one of the major weaknesses. This penchant for leading into new fields of technology has paid handsome dividends at times, and at other times has lead to nonimplementable standards. In the first instance, there is the work done by the IEEE 802 Committee on Local Area Networks (LANs). This work was in the van of technology and it created a new industry. The IEEE undertook the standardization project because no other SDO was willing to do so, and there appeared to be no market for the standard. Indeed, the IEEE has undertaken projects that other committees would not touch, such as IEEE 1003's creation of the POSIX standard. The success or failure of POSIX is a question that will remain debated for some time.[8] However, because it was responding to technical need, the IEEE believed that it was worthwhile.

However, within the IT industry, attendance at IEEE standards committees is following the same path that other SDOs are experiencing; falling membership in its mainline SDO activities, and a paucity of new programs or projects. Some of this is blamed upon the collapse of the economic slowdown that occurred in the 1992–1995 timeframe; however, during this time the IETF grew by several thousand percent. I believe that the IEEE has also proven too slow and too cumbersome to deal with the complexities of the current market. The IEEE Standards Companion, cited earlier in this chapter, is a seventy-six page document that describes in partial detail how to "do" an IEEE standard. "It's meant to be a companion to the official rules and policies of IEEE Standards, both to try to explain them in less 'legal' terms and to offer practical examples from people who have worked with standards for years."[9] If the informal rules guide takes seventy-six pages, the full set of rules must really be something and would, of course, be required reading for anyone in a small company who wanted to standardize a new program or product. I believe that this focus on the "proper route" to ensure a proper process has had a severe and deleterious effect on the IEEE as a standardization body.

Future

Associations tend to be led by the last generation, since leadership is often a function of age and experience. The belief that the past should serve as a guide to the future and that evolution, not revolution is important, is the hallmark of many professional associations. This idea worked well in a static environment. However, the most significant feature of the IT industry is the rapid rate of technological change. Technology is now a competitive weapon in the quest for market share. The association, which is structured to permit and even encourage gradual, proven change with a minimal impact upon its client groups cannot keep pace with IT, where professional lifespans are approximately seven years, unless the professional continuously updates the technical base upon which their education is built. Experience has been devalued in favor of education; all the experience in the world in Local Area Network connectors will not help someone understand the nature of the Java programming language or the intricacies of data base management.

To complicate the situation even further, advancement in a Society is based, not upon technical or managerial competence, but rather upon seniority, a form of experience. This places all associations, including the IEEE, in an interesting position within the IT community. Is the rational for election to leadership technical competence, managerial competence, or seniority? Within a corporation, the trade-off is less important, since it is expected that a person with a technical ability either will be educated further or will learn the discipline of management. Within a society devoted to professionalism in a discipline, it is expertise in that discipline that counts and most often, it is the younger engineers, who have the benefit of a more current education, who are the most technically competent, and, by implication, the most professional in the discipline.

Yet, if one reads the IEEE Standards Companion, one senses the reverence that the IEEE has for "experience." Yet, the experience gained is focused on the way that things used to be done, not on how things should be done in the future. ("Future experience" is somewhat of an oxymoron.) The success in dealing with the particular method of standardizing hardware (the 802 LANs were the IEEE's claim to fame) did not transfer directly to standardization of software. The two are distinct; with perfect hindsight, it is now obvious that the POSIX effort was probably correct, but the rules that the IEEE tried to use were based upon its experience in building hardware and components, and were inappropriate for a subject as complex and subjective as software, which is heavily based on cognitive psychology and is application dependent.

CONCLUSION

John Stuart Mill once stated that, "A great statesman is he who knows when to depart from traditions, as well as when to adhere to them." The problem faced by the standardization effort in the IEEE is that the tradition to which they are heir may no longer be appropriate. While the best of the past can serve to illuminate the future, the "best" of the past must be chosen. The best, in the case of the IEEE, is not embodied in its rules and experience in standardization. The best was embodied in its willingness to take a chance, to try something new. It succeeded in this for a while and then decided that the best was in the process, not in the individual. The process does not make good standards, any more than the process makes good engineers. While the best that the process can do is to ensure that no one is disadvantaged, the worst that the process can do is to ensure that no one is allowed to be better or to win. The current mind set of the IEEE is to use the process to equally disadvantage all participants. This seems to be antithetical to the goals of a professional society that wishes to advance of the theory and practice of electrical and electronics engineering.

NOTES

[1]For a very good description of the activities of a Secretariat, see Kate McMillan's article "The Secretariat in Formal Standards Development," *StandardView,* Volume 2, Number 1, March 1994, pp. 14–17.

[2]Allied Tube and Conduit Corporation v. Indian Head, Inc., No. 87–157, argued February 24, 1987, decided June 13, 1987. The Supreme Court voted by a 7–2 margin, that the petitioner, Allied Tube, had been guilty of anti-trust by packing a meeting of the National Fire Protection Association and voting down a proposal to let Indian Head's plastic conduit be accepted by the National Electrical Code. The case was decided upon appeal, and the major thrust of the court was that even if the arguments of Allied were correct, it was still illegal to pack an association meeting.

[3]X3 SD2, *Organization, Rules, and Procedures of X3.* Paragraph 3.2.1. Available from X3 Secretariat.

[4]Ibid, Paragraph 3.4.1.

[5]Cargill, Carl F. "Standards" In: Ralson, Anthony D. and Reilly, Edwin D., (eds), *Encyclopedia of Computer Science,* (Third Edition), Van Nostrand Reinhold: New York, 1993, p. 1280.

[6]Attributed to Ralph Waldo Emerson by Sarah B. Yule, *Borrowings,* 1889, p. 138. Cited in *Respectfully Quoted, A Dictionary of Quotations from the Library of Congress,* ed. Suzy Platt, Congressional Research Service, Washington D.C. 1992; p. 335.

[7]IEEE. *The IEEE Standards Companion,* IEEE: Piscataway, N.J., 1995, p. 41–42.

[8]For a good overview of the POSIX experience, see Hal Jespersen's and Stephen Walli's articles on POSIX in the March 1995 *StandardView,* Volume 3, Number 1. Hal, now Distinguished Engineer at Sun Microsystems, was one of the longtime chairs and editors and participants in POSIX, having been involved in the IEEE 1003 effort from its inception. Stephen Walli, now a Vice President of R&D at Softway, Inc. spent four years in the POSIX committees and is now instrumental in making POSIX valuable as a portability tool. Their conclusions in their articles are similar: POSIX was a great idea, well implemented at first, that eventually was overcome by its own success, and ultimately, became a victim of that success.

[9]*IEEE Standards Companion,* op. cit. p 1.

Chapter 21

The Model Consortia

"Honour and shame from no condition rise;
Act well your part, for there all the honour lies."

. . .

—Alexander Pope, *An Essay on Man*

INTRODUCTION

This chapter looks at five consortia chosen as "model" consortium. The ingredient that they all have in common is that they all deal with a component of Information Technology and they all illustrate a different aspect of consortium theory and practice. They are not necessarily successful; in several cases, they have been reorganized to change with the changes in the industries that spawned them. However, all five are significant in that they help to show the extent and variety of consortium organization, focus, mission, activities, and self perception. They are neither the terrors of the IT industry, not the great hope. They are organizations of people who usually strive to do good, but occasionally foolish, things. In this, they have succeeded.

PETROTECHNICAL OPEN SOFTWARE CORPORATION (POSC)

Purpose

The Petrotechnical Open Software Corporation (POSC) can be seen as an industry-led response to a financial crisis that was threatening the health of a major segment of the world's economy. "The oil and gas industry need[ed] to dramatically improve its overall efficiency because generally low and volatile oil processes are in a long-term downturn after spectacular increases in the late 1970s and early 1980s. . . . [O]il companies must streamline their operating costs, and may have to move to regions of the world where production costs are low."[1]

The description belies the complexity in the petrochemical industry. The oil companies are making significant long-term investments (up to eighty years) based upon their ability to analyze data. The old days, in which success was based upon oil seepage on the surface (Pennsylvania), or wildcat strikes (Texas), or easy explorations (Arabian peninsula), are gone. The oil company now must first test the land, analyze the tests, buy the land (or at least the rights to the oil), choose where to drill and the type of equipment with which to drill (towers and off-shore platforms), choose the transportation routes for moving the oil, deal with environmental impact studies, and also keep track of what is happening underground. (Everyone has heard the mythical story of the oil company that closed down a site after drilling a series of dry holes, only to have a rival company move in and drill a "gusher.") Imagine doing all of this for thirty years in a row.

The problem is that, in the global economy, where a platform can cost $500 million, a mistake can ruin a company. Now, imagine trying to use proprietary geophysical data captured and stored in unique formats by an obsolete and unsupported application originally intended for use in 1960 on a pre-open systems processor in a format that is no longer supported by any known company for an oil field that is drying up prematurely, after your company has invested $600 million in new production facilities. To really complicate the matter, some of the field data was recorded on word processors from the Exxon corporation, and all are archived in multiple places throughout the world in nearly every piece of media (except punched paper tape). The CIO, in this case, normally goes mad. It is this problem that POSC was created to overcome in the future.

History

POSC is a not-for-profit corporation that was a creation of five (now six) of the major oil producing companies in the world. Beginning in 1989, the POSC jumpstart team began to create its scope by analyzing five projects that were required if POSC was to succeed. The analysis of needs and technology took some time. Once the needs were analyzed, however, POSC did something that other consortia do not do. They took some time to analyze other standardization group's and consortia's operating practices and procedures. "The formal standards process was not perceived to be timely or highly consumer focused. Further, there was little hope that organizations with generic scopes would have enough interest or sufficient knowledge to define an industry-specific data model. However, the value of these organizations is that they provide legitimacy to generic standards and serve as a foundation to build upon."[2] Ultimately, POSC adopted a model based upon OSF's model, and this was validated by the major participants. In 1990, POSC was launched.

The major participants in the consortia are the six oil companies. Other participants join at various levels to play a role in the activities that the major oil players need filled. The key thing about POSC is that POSC was dedicated to making the exploration and production (E&P) segment of the international petroleum industry more productive and/or less expensive. It is not there to help create Open Systems—unless the open systems serve the good of the oil and gas E&P market. To achieve this end, POSC developed and delivered specifications for a software integration platform for E&P technical applications. The basics of this platform are a set of standard interfaces between petrochemical software applications, database management systems, workstations, and the users. The problems that POSC deals with include the use of disparate data formats, different database systems, in-house developed and purchased applications that do not communicate with each other, and diverse workstations that have specialized capabilities but differing operational requirements and application interfaces. POSC is now focused on the development of interface specifications, prototype implementations, and test suites that allow verification of compliance with a particular specification. POSC is also initiating a program to certify compliance and to foster trust between buyers and suppliers.

Future and Implications

POSC is a significant consortium in the fact that it is focused upon solving a user problem in the use of IT rather than solving an IT provider problem. As was noted in Chapter 6, the "empowered user" has the ability to look at IT products as tools to help sole business problems. Usually, industry groups form to solve problems within the industry's sphere of expertise. Normally, organizations like the "Seven Sisters" oil companies have their own standardization groups such as the American Petroleum Institute (API), which is an ANSI Accredited Organization (AO) and has the right to develop standards which relate to the oil and gas industry. However, the API has no expertise in IT standards and relies, in the formal process, upon something like X3 or the IEEE within the U.S.

POSC violates the fundamental separation that standardization organizations have managed to impose on the industry. Basically, it seems to say that since the IT vendors cannot successfully service an industry, and make their minds up on how to interoperate and cooperate, we, the oil and gas companies, will create our own group to do it for us. As noted, POSC looked at the formal organizations and found them too generic.

The need is there. The petrochemical industry is one of the largest users of geospatial data in the world. It is one of the biggest consumers of IT equipment in terms of raw purchasing power that exists. It is an important industry to the IT providers, and yet it felt that its needs were being ignored by the majority of vendors. If the petrochemical industry felt this way (and it felt this way enough to create and fund a separate organization), imagine how other, less powerful organizations feel. The U.S. Government has set up the Defense Information Systems Agency (DISA) for some of the same reasons, and the EC has created DGIII. All of these groups are struggling with the same problem of how to make the providers responsive to the needs of the users. These organizations have been reasonably close in their thinking, fortunately.

If the POSC model of consortia succeeds, however, the real problem for the IT industry may only be starting. If POSC succeeds in reducing the E&P costs for oil and gas, and the success is widely heralded, this should encourage other organizations to do the

same. The automotive industry, for example, is big enough and powerful enough economically to set up a "Computing for Automotive Requirement Systems" (CARS) consortium, or the pharmaceutical companies could set up the "Desired Requirements for Universal Generic Solutions" (DRUGS). The list of industries that are capable of setting up
their own consortia does not exceed a dozen—but those dozen industries would influence
thousands of their subordinate suppliers, and so on down the supply chain. This is something that the IT industry should see and something with which the IT industry will be
forced to deal.

There are several scenarios that result from the success and growth of the POSC
model. The first is outlined above, in which all the various industries require industry specific solutions. Following this to a logical (although possibly absurd) conclusion, the
worst case scenario is that the pharmaceutical, automotive, petrochemical, and aircraft industries mandate solutions that are architecturally incompatible, requiring each major
vendor to choose to support a single industry. This is a threat on the "ubiquitous architecture" approach which most standardization organizations tend to try to provide. I believe
that this problem is less severe now than it was ten years ago, when most standards looked
at hardware and the wrong standards could obviate an architecture.

The second scenario that this provokes is the creation of the commodity "one software package does all" approach. This approach would see a single package being designed well enough to satisfy all possible users. This likelihood of this scenario coming to
fruition is also small, since a global package that was that complete is unlikely.

The third scenario is one that forces a reengineering of the information activities in
many organizations and causes them to determine where there are bottlenecks caused by
poor information flow practices. With the redesigned processes in place, the members of
the consortium can then proceed to go forth and change their information handling structure to be whatever they want and force vendors to supply whatever they need. This idea
is good for an emerging coherent and tightly organized industry, and none of the major industries listed above suffer from these syndromes.

As with most things in business, the outcome will be a little of all three possibilities.
What POSC has proven is that if an industry feels strongly enough about a problem as an
industry, it can merge its economic power to create a somewhat unified position. However, once it specifies that solution, it has to carry through and implement that solution.
The major danger that POSC faces in its quest to make things better for E&P is not the
failure of the vendors to provide solutions to the necessary standards; this is an economic
decision, and as the industry becomes ever more competitive, it will meet the users' demands. The real problem for POSC is whether or not it can convince the major companies
that created it to accept a solution that took nearly five years to work out, and whether or
not the problem that was being solved in 1991 is the same problem that confronts the oil
and gas industries in 1998. The danger is not from the IT vendors. It is from their own
sponsors who may reject the solution because it tramples the fiefdoms within the companies. Open systems is an opportunity if you are on the outside looking in. It can be
a real danger if you are one of the insiders being opened up. This is the problem that
faces POSC.

X CONSORTIUM

Original Purpose

The X Consortium was the follow-on to the "Project Athena" started at the Massachusetts Institute of Technology. The original goal of the group was to standardize the technology underlying X Windows and the follow-on improvements to the X Windows system. At one time, the X Consortium was part of the GUI wars, but evaded that trap very quickly and became an independent observer. The original X Windows system was accepted as a Federal Information Process Standard (FIPS) and required governmental procurements. In the early 1990s, the X Consortium was preparing to shut down its MIT activities and become a "marketing cum technology consortium" under new leadership. It reversed itself in the mid 1990s, and once again focused on doing the latest version of Windows. In 1996, it shut down and joined the Open Group.

Purpose Now

The X Consortium was an independent, not-for-profit membership corporation formed in 1993 as successor to the MIT X Consortium. The Consortium was a highly participative body with representation from hardware and software vendors, as well as users and other consortium. Standardization was only part of the program. X Consortium was also involved in the design, coding, and testing of sample implementations of the specifications that it created. It supported itself with membership fees and for hire program and project management. There are no license fees associated with the use of X Window System standards or code developed by the X Consortium.

The rationale for membership lay in the ability to help set direction for the X Consortium and to participate in the working groups of the consortium. These working groups were the heart of the consortium, and allowed a good deal of idea sharing among members. Additionally, members received snapshots of the code as it was being developed, so that they could begin to plan around use of the code, understanding where it fits in and how the code works in their environment. Each member appoints a representative to the Advisory Board, which is involved in the general direction setting of the consortium.

Process

Proposals for a new standard were generated by either the members or staff of the X Consortium. As a group was formed, an "Architect" is appointed as chair, and a working group is created to do the technical work and evolve the proposal to specification stage. Most of the work of the group is done via electronic means, and all the messages relating to a particular effort are archived. After a working group has voted to accept a draft specification, the Advisory Board was polled for ratification. (The Advisory Board is composed of member representatives (one per member). They are expected to provide advice to the management of the X Consortium, and to act as a sounding board for ideas generated by the staff and other areas.)

While the specification was being reviewed, there was usually an effort underway to produce a sample implementation of the standard. As a minimum, the sample implementation is designed to serve as a "proof of concept," to ensure that the design can be implemented, and to provide members of the working group information on how well they did with respect to creation of the standard. It also provides the vendor providers a good bit of code that they can use in implementation, to help them productize the standard, since most vendors are interested in "running code," rather than specifications for running code.

Future

The initial reports of the death of the X consortium in 1993 proved unfounded. The key to the X Consortium and to its continued viability rested largely with its president and founder, Robert W. Scheifler. His responsibilities read a lot like the charter of X3; impossibly broad. He was charged with the day-to-day administration and operation of the X Consortium, as well as the strategy, business, and administrative issues. The really frightening thing is that he did all of this extremely well. Scheifler once described his role as the "gentle tyrant," whose function is to ensure that the consortium goes about its business professionally and correctly. Over the years, he managed to maintain the highest professional standards and produce exceptional code, with no trace of partisan politics.

Even more impressive was that he has maintained the X Consortium's focus on areas where it has competence, rather than letting it go off and expand its charter, attack areas with which it is unfamiliar, or even expand beyond its ability to survive. Finally, he managed to evolve the work of the consortium so that it remains germane to the industry. I do not believe that there is another standardization group leader (consortium or SDO) who can make the same claim, other than Christopher Stone of OMG.

THE UNICODE CONSORTIUM

History

In the late 1980s, ISO/IEC Joint Technical Committee 1, Sub-Committee 2, Working Group 2 (JTC 1, SC 2, WG 2), circulated a first draft of a standard that they had been working on for several years (now ISO/IEC 10646). The standard was designed to augment the then current methods of representing character and code sets, based on U.S. technologies and U.S. needs (since most international standards began in the U.S., especially in the pre-1985 period). The need that WG 2 was trying to address was the ability of various national bodies to represent their national languages in a single common specification, rather than forcing every nation or every dialect to create, embrace, and maintain a separate standard.

Since this was to be an international standard, it was decided that the encoding scheme would encompass the sum of all the possibilities in the world. This idea made its way through the committee, gaining adherents and detractors as it was created. Finally, in 1990, the first international draft was readied for publication. The MOC was a compromise between what was needed and what was required by all the national bodies in JTC 1. It contained substantially more capability than the standards that it was enhancing, and insured that every nation could uniquely encode its national language. (There are approximately 119,000 characters in Asian derivations of Han. Of these, only about 21,000 are different characters; the rest are duplicated characters that have different meaning, depending upon the nation using them. For example, the Han character for "hot water" in Korean and Japanese means "soup" in Chinese.) To achieve this flexibility, however, the MOC expanded to four 8-bit octets, which could be used in varied grouping (between one and four octets).

In the early 1990s, a group of U.S. companies, led by Microsoft, Xerox, and Apple, began to look for a method of achieving the flexibility promised by the MOC but did not break any known operating system, as well as a way to limit the memory and cycle usage requirements of the multi-octet solution. In January of 1991, the Unicode Consortium was born to find a technical solution to what they saw as an unnecessarily complex problem. The Unicode Consortium members looked at what ISO 10646 was attempting to accomplish, and determined that it was possible to reduce the unique national character sets to a size that could be accommodated by a single 16-bit fixed-length character set. They did this by encoding the Han characters that are found in many Asian languages, ignoring the different national meanings for the same character, assuming that a printed Han character in a Korean text would be read as a Korean Han character, not as a Chinese Han character. Additionally, Unicode deliberately limited what it would encode, stating that Unicode is not aimed at standardizing ". . . rare, obsolete, idiosyncratic, personal, novel, rarely exchanged, or private use characters." Characters omitted are rare in IT arenas, but may be common in personal names or addresses or proprietary (company-unique) encoding.

Members of SC2, WG 2 (as well as their national standards bodies) took immediate offense, and a dispute began between the two approaches. The two organizations fought for several months, and then began to work towards a compromise led by the JTC1 Project Editor, Masami Hasagawa, that would satisfy both sides in the discussion. The Unicode argument was probably technically correct, but the national bodies were offended that a U.S. consortium would tell them that their characters "were all the same." So, after much discussion and pain on both sides, a compromise was reached. Unicode was accepted as a 16-bit subset of what was being attempted in ISO/IEC 10646. The Unicode Consortium agreed to some changes in their specification and WG 2 agreed to include Unicode Version 1.1 in the larger ISO/IEC standard. Unicode 1.1 now forms the basic plane of the 10646 standard. It is large enough to include a vast majority of characters necessary for the Information Technology industry to continue to grow. The basic plane holds approximately 65,000 characters, all uniquely identified in the Unicode 1.1 specification and the ISO 10646 standard. Of these 65,000+ character sets, over 20,000 are still available. ISO 10646, however, is multiplanar; that is, there are substantially more planes available to the user of full 10646 than to the user of Unicode 1.1.

The Problem

The complicating factor is, of course, national politics and human nature. Many countries are very proud of their language's uniqueness, both written and spoken, and want this uniqueness to be recognized and savored. While there may be no technical reason to differentiate between two Han characters, there may be ephemeral, but real, reasons of national pride, chauvinism, or mere reluctance to change. For this reason, the ISO 10646 permits the use of multiple planes to express national character encoding.

At the same time, the creators of Unicode forgot that their solution was also unacceptable to a large contingent of UNIX providers, who could not deal with the embedded characters in the Unicode variant. As a result of this, these UNIX providers have gone to X/Open and asked the X/Open Internationalization group, run in conjunction with UniForum, to come up with another scheme to allow what 10646 was attempting to do without breaking the UNIX language. Eventually, this solution will sort itself out.

The Future

One would assume that since the Unicode Consortium had accomplished what it set out to do, that is, modify the international standard and have the modifications accepted, the Consortium would fold its tents and go away. This is not quite what happened. The Unicode Consortium decided that it would continue existence but as a consortium now focusing on localization and internationalization. It continues to limp along, supported by the few members of companies who can convince their management that the consortium is necessary. In the interim, the industry has moved on.

UNIFORUM CONSORTIUM

History

UniForum really is a consortium, and not just a trade show for UNIX vendors and suppliers. The consortium began in 1980, with a small group of UNIX hackers called */usr/group* joined to create what they wanted to be the standards for UNIX. The */usr/group* Standards Committee had worked for several years to create a set of UNIX standards that would allow multitasking and open architecture. These standards were proposed for ANSI standardization. They were not quite ready for ANSI primetime, so the POSIX effort was started to rewrite them according to ANSI process and procedure rules. This was the beginning of POSIX, the standardization effort.

At the same time that the standardization effort was happening in */usr/group*, the same people began a trade show event at which UNIX providers could display the latest UNIX things. As the reputation of the trade show grew, more and more users began to come to the show. What the users came for is important. There was no single place in the mid to late 1980s where users could get unbiased information on UNIX; the AT&T and Sun alliance was just beginning, and the SVR4 announcements and competing Berkeley UNIX developments and announcements were dividing the market. At the same time, there were (and still are) skills associated with UNIX that are arcane, and more of a "magic" than a science.

To help solve this "magic versus science" conundrum, several members of */usr/group* proposed creating a consortium of users who wanted to "get together" at a conference but who could somehow keep in touch formally and "do things" with one another.

It is important to remember that this time frame (the late 1980s) was the high water mark of the big corporate user groups (such as DECUS and CUBE and GUIDE), each of which had a big trade show at which the supporting vendor demonstrated the latest hardware, talked limited futures, and at which the users traded stories about how their equipment worked. Since there was no big vendor called UNIX, Incorporated, it fell to UniForum to fill the gap. It was a user's society that was funded by member dues and aided by vendor participation. It did not have a single corporate sponsor. It had about eighty corporate sponsors who each paid a share of the show's cost. The users came to listen to events that were focused on user needs and tricks of making UNIX work.

Fundamentally, UniForum is a throwback to the days when the large systems vendors operated in a homogeneous environment and the user groups got together to discuss how to manage homogeneous computing environments. The interesting thing about UniForum is that it survived when all of the other organizations did not. The reason for this success seems to be rooted in the fundamental nature of UNIX.

The other user groups were used to operating in an environment that was truly homogeneous. For a DEC user, VMS was VMS. DEC had ensured source-level compatibility on its operating system, and when they broke compatibility, they were punished economically. On the other hand, UNIX users were not that lucky. UNIX was sometimes UNIX and sometimes not. However, the fundamentals between Sun UNIX and HP UX were closer than the fundamentals between DEC's VMS and IBM's MVS. The UNIX users learned quickly what the true nature of open systems meant. When the users at the other user groups were confronted with noninteroperating heterogeneous systems, they had trouble dealing with the problem, and began the migration to Microsoft. On the other hand, the UniForum participants expected things to "mostly interoperate," so they were prepared to 'tinker' with obdurate systems.

This is the atmosphere that UniForum has striven to maintain. In 1994, UniForum hosted a special show at which multiple UNIX vendors announced that they were cooperating on the development and deployment of a new common desktop GUI. At the 1995 show, Microsoft presented details of the NT operating system for the UNIX audience, and the Unified UNIX branding program was launched. At the 1996 show, vendors in the UNIX community announced a way to make NT look like UNIX so that UNIX applications could run on NT. The show has maintained a user focus by looking at ways to make the users of UNIX more capable of surviving in the heterogeneous networked environment.

Future

I have included UniForum because I believe that it can play a significant role, although I am not sure whether it represents the last of the old way of doing things (along the Guide and DECUS models), or whether it represents a new wave of user driven consortium. If it is the last of the old wave of DECUS type activities, then it will fail, although it may take a little longer than other organizations of this ilk. On the other hand, if it's really a new way of joining users, then it has a way to go, since it must begin to understand a new method of determining a unifying factor other than UNIX.

UniForum has, in my opinion, begun to make this move to establishing a more common ground, describing itself as a consortium for "open systems professionals" rather than a consortium for "UNIX professionals." There is still a heavy technical bias within the organization, but the management of UniForum seems to be trying to move towards a greater business focus. At the same time, there is an increasing emphasis on acting as a broker for cooperative industry ventures, such as joint publishing ventures and other things that encourage vendor and user cooperation. If UniForum can succeed in attracting and holding a sufficient number of users who actually buy things, and who are willing to reward cooperating vendors, UniForum will succeed. But, the "if" remains a major hurdle.

THE OBJECT DATABASE MANAGEMENT GROUP (ODMG)

The Object Database Management Group (ODMG) is a consortium that is the ideal technical consortium; it is focused on a single program, is composed of interested and knowledgeable participants, runs under a very tight time schedule, and has a clear deliverable. It is included here because it is one of the best examples of a successful consortium of which I am aware.[3]

History

In the late 1980s, object-oriented programming was beginning to become more and more widely accepted. With the appearance of the object paradigm, it became apparent to technologists who specialized in databases that the standard relational databases would not be adequate for use with objected-oriented programming, and that a new model was needed. By 1991, the principles that would drive this new form of database were reasonably well-documented. However, there was something that the object database management systems (ODBMS) needed before it was ready to change the market.

The missing ingredient was the same one that propelled the relational databases to success a decade before: the creation of a standard. In the case of relational databases, the standard was the Standard Query Language (SQL) from IBM. While not actually achieving much in the way of true interoperability, the SQL standard provided the market with the assurance that there would be a second source for any relational database. The actual standard for SQL was the result of the work of X3H2. The success of the standard as an implementable piece of technology can be traced to the efforts of the SQL Access Group (SAG), which actually took the standard, cleaned it up, and provided implementation details for companies who would use it.

As the market for object DBMS began to take off, it was recognized that a standard was necessary if the growth was to continue. However, little action was undertaken. OMG formed an SIG to look at the problem, but the group eventually ceased. Special task groups were formed under X3, but little happened. X3H2 sponsored a committee to do object extensions to SQL, but this was not what the Object DBMS vendors needed.

ARPA started a program, but then stopped work when it became clear that these efforts were not producing a standard.

What fundamentally was happening was that there was no precedent for the standard, and creation of a standard from ground zero in a committee is nearly impossible. Finally, in desperation, five object DBMS vendors met in the fall of 1991 to craft the standard. Each vendor committed one person for one week per month over a two-year period. The group worked madly, and within a year, a draft standard was ready for publication. Within two years, ODMG-93 was published for use and implementation by the industry. There was a commitment from seven major vendors (the ODMG had grown) to implement the standard in 1995.

The consortium is now beginning to work with other consortium (primarily Object Management Group), and with SDOs X3 J16 (C++), and X3H2 (Databases) to ensure that the work on the OBMG-93 is made available to a larger audience for study, review, and implementation.

The Future and Implications

Whether or not the consortium has succeeded in making object DBMSs successful is beyond the scope of this work. However, if it does hand off its work and quietly go away, it will have succeeded where few other consortia ever have; in successfully and gracefully concluding a standardization effort and then going "peacefully into the night."

More importantly, it is significant to look at how the ODMG succeeded in creating its standard and relating them to the multistage model described earlier in the book (Chapter 11). The preconceptualization stage was accomplished when OOP began to become popular; it was apparent that some form of object DBMS would be necessary. The concept was shopped around, and no one bought it. Finally, in desperation, a group of vendors opted to do it themselves, since they needed a common specification that they could implement. At the first meeting, the group decided how to operate and what was needed. This marks the conceptualization and discussion phases. The writing phase was very constrained, with each member being assigned a section to produce and then having that section merged with the others.[4] Membership was limited to vendors who had an object DBMS who needed the standard to succeed, and each member was required to commit a high level of energy and participation to stay on the committee. Failure to meet that level of commitment was cause for removal.

These actions violate the "open process" model that most consortia and SDOs have; they are very reminiscent of a business approach to a problem. They recognize the importance of building a standardized specification that can coalesce an industry. In this view, improvements to the specification and the open standardization process and all that this implies can come after the market is established. Until the market is established and people have something with which to deal, there can be no standard and no improvement. While an approach that is sure to alarm the traditionalists, it seems to have worked, and seems to be a viable alternative to the appearance of the sole provider *de facto* standard.

THE OPEN GEOSPATIAL INFORMATION
SYSTEMS CONSORTIUM (OGC)

The Open Geospatial Information Systems Consortium (OGC) is included because it represents a new way of looking at consortium trying to standardize a broad technical arena. It represents an innovative and different approach to structuring a standardization organization.

History

The OGC is a relatively new consortium, having been founded in 1995. The initial problem that it set for itself was creating a viable interface layer for geospatial data, which was saved in multiple formats by multiple organizations. While this does not seem to be too much of a problem, it rapidly becomes complicated with the advent of computerized databases. While each separate entity that saves information may use a consistent method of data storage (that is, the electrical company may know where all the power poles are because they have a consistent recording methodology, and the cable company may know where all the poles that it uses are), there is no way of ensuring that the same information in each database can be correlated. This becomes expensive when the telephone, cable, and electrical company try to coordinate the impact of a change from poles to buried cables, but it becomes tragic when there is an earthquake, hurricane, or tornado or other disaster and the various databases have to be manually compared before coordinated action can be taken. Add to this confusion the geospatial data for the transportation infrastructure, the water and sewage data, and the population data. These service providers each have their own separate databases and none of them necessarily can be computer integrated.[5]

This was the initial problem upon which OGC focused. However, the sum of spatial data is not necessarily encompassed by the needs of the geospatial market. The initial solution was focused on solving the incompatible database problem; the next step in the problem of spatial data might be representation of nontraditional spatial imaging (such as cartographic photogrammetry) or other activities, such as defining methodologies for assigning spatial attributes to data that does not fit into the traditional spatial data paradigm.

The question that faced the creators of OGC was how to create an organization that focused on a single issue of pressing importance, yet allowed them to accept other related areas under their aegis. It should be noted that there is an ISO committee (ISO TC 211 Geographic Information/Geomatics) that is dealing with the first problem from an international point of view, but which is more concerned with moving towards a global model of geographic information than geospatial information. Therefore, the ISO model provided little help to OGC.

OGC's solution to the problem was to write into their structure a possibility for creating several separate "tracks" or technical disciplines, while retaining an overarching Board structure. The various tracks were, in effect, miniature "spot point" consortium that could use the OGC administrative and financial umbrella to accomplish their standardization activities, and then could go out of existence without fearing that they would lose

what they had gained. The OGC board and the management layer (both technical and administrative) would solve the problem of consortium longevity by providing a single place for the group memory, while at the same time overcoming the need for the technologists to do the marketing and other activities.

Future

OGC's model is a viable solution to the problem of a consortium that is starting out in a new arena, possibly unbounded, requiring standardization. OGC has no idea where it may go with its activities; it cannot pursue all of them endlessly, nor can it afford to pursue a limited subset without having to fight constant turf battles. The solution that OGC has chosen is a viable solution to several problems in standardization. This solves the "elegance creep" problem that has infected many groups. "Elegance creep" occurs when a standardization group tries to include "just one more feature" in its specification or standard. It results in late, global, large, and useless standards. By defining each group precisely, OGC can declare victory when it has concluded a specific task and then shift work to another track, which may have already been under operation. There is no need to unnecessarily prolong the standardization effort.

At the same time, declaring victory and walking away from something is difficult for many consortia, because it tends to spell the end of their useful life. With multiple tracks, OGC can separate the efforts to make them independent of one another, as far as the members of each group are concerned. There is the hope that the work will be somehow related and will build upon itself, but the larger hope is that a series of programs will be completed with some measure of constancy and discipline.

NOTES

[1]Kowalski, Vincent J, and Karcher, Bruno. "Industry Consortia in Open Systems," *StandardView,* Volume 2, Number 1, March 1994, p. 34.

[2]Ibid., p. 36.

[3]Much of the following description is derived from Dr. Rick Cattell's account of the activities of the ODMG, contained in "Experience with the ODMG Standard," *StandardView,* Volume 3, Number 3, September 1995, pp. 90–95.

[4]Conversations with Dr. Rick Cattell, who lead the effort, are instructive on this last point. The members had their final "merge" meeting scheduled for two weeks in the Caribbean. Apparently, they finished the work in seven straight solid twelve-hour days. The lures of being able to go outside into the warmth and relax (the meeting was in January) was apparently a great incentive for accurate work and lessened argument.

[5]For a more complete description of the problems that are confronting geospatial information systems in standardization, and for a good description of the organizations that are active in the arena, see the September 1994 *StandardView,* Volume 2, Number 3, which was entirely focused on geospatial information systems.

Chapter 22

Governmental and Other Accredited Standards Bodies

> "I might get up to-morrow to my work
> Cheerful, and fresh as ever. Let us try.
> To-morrow, how you shall be glad for this!"
>
> —Robert Browning, *Andrea Del Sarto,*
> *Called 'The Faultless Painter'*

INTRODUCTION

This chapter looks at several standards bodies who, like the organizations in the previous chapter, serve as exemplars for some aspect of standards organizations. All exist (as of this writing) and all perform some function in the formal standards arena. The single government organization in this book is NIST, and specifically the CSL group, where much of the technology infrastructure that is necessary to the United States is either created or validated. Much of the work is thankless drudgery that the private sector should, but does not, do. The other organizations cover a gamut of activities, but all serve to illustrate a particular point about the evolution of standardization.

GOVERNMENTAL ORGANIZATIONS

NATIONAL INSTITUTE FOR STANDARDS AND TECHNOLOGY (NIST)

The National Institute for Standards and Technology (NIST) is the current name for the organization that was the National Bureau of Standards (NBS). The name change occurred in 1988, following passage of the Omnibus Trade and Competitiveness Act of 1988. All the old functions of the National Bureau of Standards remain intact, and additionally, NIST was given new functions including helping insure that technology transfer occurred, that small business could use this technology, and that technological competitiveness was retained. Funding, at one time substantially increased, is again under fire as the republican Congress looks for ways to save money.

History

NIST's predecessor organization, NBS, was created by an act of Congress in 1901. NIST is the most important of the government organizations involved in standardization. The function of the Institute is to help remove barriers to trade and new technologies, as well as to provide a national laboratory for use by academic, business, and governmental interests. Its major rationale lies not in its standards activities, per se, but rather in its ability to help the academic, private, and governmental sectors better utilize technology and technological advances.

Much of the standards activity by NIST is in the voluntary consensus standards area, where NIST personnel attend standards meetings and act to disperse their findings to this arena. A great deal of the effort is aimed at non-IT activities, since NIST serves the entire U.S. effort, as ANSI does. However, one section of NIST does specialize in IT matters: the Computer Systems Laboratory (CSL), formerly the Institute for Computer Sciences and Technology (ICST). This organization was formed in 1966, in response to the Brooks Act of 1965. The Brooks Act was essentially a procurement act to resolve the problem of incompatibility in computer systems within the federal government, an issue complicated by the fact that there were no clear specifications on what to buy. With the Brooks Act, the federal government was given a mandate to standardize its procurement practices.

To meet this mandate, the CSL (ICST) developed Federal Information Processing Standards (FIPS), federal government procurement standards quoted in procurements for ADP equipment for the government. Several hundred FIPS are currently in effect, covering everything from languages to peripheral interfaces to X Windows to Geospatial Information Systems. The ultimate purpose of the FIPS is to decrease the cost to the government of computers, both in terms of procurement and of the manpower used to operate them.

CSL has understood that a federal standard is largely useless if it is not backed by the IT industry and users. Simply mandating federal standards would be counterproductive and would not serve the government, the user, or the producer. With this realization, the CSL began to encourage its employees to participate in the industry IT standardization process. Because of their high degree of technical expertise, CSL members are welcome at SDO meetings, whereas participants they can often provide information about developments in the NIST laboratories, as well as gathering industry information for consideration by the government. Additionally, CSL members have also begun to help consortium and other standardization organizations in their standardization activities.

Current Situation

The CSL is largely out of the standards-creating business now. As more and more standards were developed by the consensus process, CSL recommended adding them to the list of FIPS, rather than creating new standards. However, when the government needs a standard, and when the industry and its standards groups show no response to this need, the CSL has the ability to develop its own FIPS; a procedure that it normally avoids but has the technical competence to achieve. Because it always has this option, and because the government is the largest single purchaser of IT equipment in the world, CSL sits in a position of influence. But this position is precarious: If the CSL chooses to use its power to create a standard, its influence may be diminished by the ensuing political backlash. If it chooses not to exercise its authority as the government's standards maker even though a standard is clearly needed, then it risks losing the goodwill of its client, the U.S. government.

The CSL is currently emphasizing activities in several areas that have strategic importance to the United States. The National Information Infrastructure, which CSL hopes will be based on standards, is being developed in close cooperation with the American National Standards Institute. As envisioned by ANSI and NIST, the NII is an "information superhighway" that will be supported by scaleable high-performance computers, advanced high-speed communications networks, and advanced software. Much of the development of these components is, however, occurring outside of the normal IT standardization arena in which either CSL or ANSI plays a part. Another major arena for CSL is the venue of "Electronic Commerce," which has the potential to transform the way that the United Sates does business. Again, much of the work on "Electronic Commerce" is occurring in places such as the World Wide Web Consortium and other newly founded consortia that are evolving from the Internet. An area where the CSL has participated is in the security arena, where they have proposed a public key escrow methodology.

The Future

The larger problem is the assured funding for NIST and the CSL. The Republican Congress that was elected in 1994 has had an effect on the funding that NIST previously enjoyed under the Democratic controlled Congress. As the budget talks have continued, it appears that NIST, as a centralized organization, will be spared, as will the Department of Commerce. However, there is no guarantee that the efforts of the CSL will continue; as noted above, the continued existence of NIST depends upon its continued perception of utility by its primary client, the U.S. Government. As with any business, if the CEO and the Board of Directors are feuding, any organization that finds itself interjected into the fray can be diminished. Within the U.S. government, the Legislative and Executive offices are looking for ways to lessen spending by getting rid of redundant organizations. If there is consensus that NIST, and particularly the CSL, are merely governmental agencies that are mimicking the private sector, they could be in trouble. And if NIST, and particularly the CSL are deleted, the entire IT industry could be in trouble, since the CSL does fund much of the techno-infrastructure that is important to the U.S. competitiveness.

OTHER STANDARDIZATION ORGANIZATIONS

ASC T1: ACCREDITED STANDARDS COMMITTEE FOR TELECOMMUNICATIONS

ASC T1 deals with standards for the telecommunications industry in the United States and plays an increasingly important part in the activities of IT standards programs. X3 and T1 are inextricably linked: Telecommunications are essential to modern information technology, and IT is an integral component of telecommunications. Yet the two differ fundamentally on a very important point. Competition among IT manufacturers is based upon technical advantage, which goes to a firm that exploits and manipulates technology the most quickly; change is a marketing weapon. In the telephony industry, the premium is on stable, proven technology built on the tremendous installed base that made change increasingly difficult. Backward compatibility as well as stable, problem-free technological advances are critical to the health of the industry, since competition is based, not on technological change, but on nearly flawless service. This basic philosophical disagreement about the nature of technology is, and will remain, a major stumbling block in relations between the IT and telecommunications standards groups. Whether it can be overcome in the United States depends in large measure on the success of the telephony operators engaging in competition based on technological advantage. The international challenge is much broader.

History

While many ASCs were created to help unify a market and champion a single standard set for an industry, T1 was formed in response to the disappearance of an industry's de facto standards maker, American Telephone and Telegraph. The dismemberment of this company produced a vacuum the telephony industry within the United States; a vacuum that needed to be filled, and quickly. With the appearance of the "Baby Bells" and the growth of the telephone service companies, a reasonably stable environment was threatened with a potential disaster. While the restructuring of the industry promised to increase competition and therefore lessen the economic burden to the ultimate consumer, the disappearance of the unofficial standards-making body promised to make the industry disintegrate into a chaotic maze of competing, noncomplementary products. While in the information technology arena this would be perceived as "goodness," in the telecommunications industry it would destroy the very basis of the market. It is this point that is critical to understanding T1: It serves a client base that wishes to standardize because the very survival of the industry depends on a standardized interconnect capability. There is no place in the public telephony network for a proprietary solution. If such a solution were to be offered, it would either fail because of lack of market acceptance, or it would succeed and destroy the remainder of the system.

To ensure that there was some centralized standards-setting body, on August 1, 1983, the industry formed the Exchange Carriers Standards Association (ECSA), with the two-fold purpose of providing a public forum and representing exchange carrier interests in the standards process and the technology that fed these standards and of acting as a secretariat to telecommunications ASC. Earlier, when the Federal Communications Commission had suggested that an existing regulatory committee be expanded to manage the standards process, both ECSA and ANSI indicated that they felt that the private sector could manage the process more efficiently. As a result, when ECSA informed the FCC that it was prepared to support the secretariat to a standards committee that would operate under the concept of ANSI consensus, the FCC welcomed the proposal. The call for participation in the ASC was announced in November 1983, and in February 1984, T1 became the

ASC for telecommunications within the United States, with ECSA acting as the legal and financial entity responsible for the T1 Secretariat, in much the same manner that ITIC does for X3. Like CBEMA, ECSA underwent a name change in 1993. It is now called the Alliance for Telecommunications Industry Solution (ATIS).[1]

Purpose Now

Committee T1 develops technical standards and reports regarding interconnection and interoperability of telecommunications networks at interfaces with end user systems, carriers, information and enhanced-service providers, and customer premises equipment (CPE). Fundamentally, the purpose of T1 is to maintain "the systemness" of the telecommunications systems within the United States. T1 also monitors the activities of the ITU-T and formulates positions that reflect the U.S. view on telephony interconnects, which it forwards to the U.S. National Committee, run under the auspices of the State Department, as well as the ITU Telecommunication Standardization Advisory Group (also under the control of the U.S. government). Finally, T1 produces reports that provide the industry's diverse constituents with an understanding of the potential directions and thoughts of the industry as a whole. The reports usually are produced by subcommittees, and their publication may or may not signal the imminent initiation of standards writing activity.

T1: Membership and Organization.   Membership and participation in Committee T1 are open to all parties with a direct and material interest in the T1 process and activities. It currently has over 1200 participants working on 140 individual projects. (This broad criterion for membership, which is shared by X3, is key to the U.S. voluntary standards program, since it denies no one the opportunity to be heard, and gives T1 the overarching charter for all activities that even vaguely resemble what it does.)

Committee T1 has six technical subcommittees that are advised and managed by the T1 Advisory Group (T1AG). Each technical subcommittee develops draft standards and technical reports for consideration and acceptance by T1. These committees are focused on functions and characteristics associated with interconnection and interoperability of telecommunications networks at interfaces with end user systems, carriers, and information and enhanced service providers including switching, signaling, transmission, performance, operation, administration, and maintenance aspects. These committees or their predecessors are developing about fifty standards or technical reports a year. (In 1992, approxmately 100 Standards/Technical Reports [TR] were created; 1994 saw about 200 standards or TRs completed. So, there seems to be geometric growth in this arena.) Technical subcommittees and their areas of expertise are listed here:

T1A1—Performance and signal processing

T1E1—Interfaces, power, and protection of networks

T1M1—Internetwork operations, administration, maintenance, and provisioning

T1P1—Systems engineering, standards planning, and program management

T1S1—Services, architectures, and signaling

T1X1—Digital hierarchy and synchronization

T1 has eight major focus areas in which it is trying to establish itself:

- Digital Access Technologies, including narrowband and broadband ISDN (including ATM), frame relay, and others
- Multimedia capabilities
- Synchronous Optical NETwork (SONet)
- Personal Communications (to improve personal productivity)
- Intelligent Network
- Common Channel Signaling (SS7)
- Network Survivability
- Network Management

While these activities are not necessarily encompassed by the technical committees, T1 has another area that makes it germane to the telecommunications arena as a whole. This is the planning exercises in which T1 engages. Unlike ASC X3 which gave up its active Long-Range Planning Group, T1 created their own planning group, borrowed some of X3's ideas (such as the standards life-cycle concept), and made planning a viable organizational function and requirement. T1 operates to a five year strategic plan, complete with an implementation plan.

As part of this plan, T1 has identified that if, ". . . standards development is to be effective and if standards are to be implemented, development cannot be viewed as an isolated process. Standards bodies must communicate with other interested parties in the process."[2] This means that T1 recognizes that consortia (which they define as user groups) really exist and should be actively included in the planning cycle for T1 standardization. While these groups, which include the IETF, ISDN User Forum, the ATM Forum, Frame Relay Forum, and the Network Management Forum, may not realize that T1 is including them in its work, the key here is that T1 has recognized that consortia standardization efforts are just as important as its own efforts in the standardization arena.

The Future

Complete deregulation of the telephone companies and IT companies and cable companies, coupled with the increasing confusion between a "communicating computer" and a "computing telephone" will result in T1 facing ever greater and more severe challenges in the next decade. The proliferation of consortia, and the increasingly "free market nature" of the Internet all promise to make not only T1, but also the ITU-T, possibly redundant in the upper (or fun) reaches of telecommunications. One survival tactic for T1 is to retreat to the fundamentals; that is, to keep the technical infrastructure viable. It's boring, but necessary, work, and it's an area that is reasonably free from competition.

ELECTRONIC DATA INTERCHANGE: ASC X12 AND EDIFACT

The field of Electronic Data Interchange, the fundamental language syntax for business computers, touches upon the problems of the formal organizations in developing time sensitive application-based standards. It shows what happens when a group, concerned with making business happen quickly, meets a similar group, intent on making sure that business happens correctly.

History

The EDI saga starts in the 1960s, when the United Nations Economic Commission for Europe (UN/ECE) created Working Party 4 on the Facilitation of International Trade Procedures. The charter of this group was to develop rules that, "comprise a set of internationally agreed standards, directories, and guidelines for the electronic exchange of structured data, and in particular that related to trade. . . ." The group started working and by 1972 had developed UN standard data elements, which became part of ISO 7372. By 1974, the U.K. had managed to have its EDI syntax standard (TDI) accepted as the basis of the UN/ECE guidelines for trade data interchange, which was published in 1981. The fundamental approach that EDIFACT uses is to design general universal rules, which are then used to design more specific rules.

While the U.N. committee was busy creating an overarching framework, a U.S. transportation industry consortium published an EDI standard that was put into practice by rail, motor, ocean, air carriers, and most other shippers. The standard is in widespread use. In 1979, ANSI chartered the Accredited Standards Committee (ASC) X12 to develop uniform standards for interindustry electronic interchange of business transactions. They did, and the first standards from X12 were punished in 1984.

In 1985, the UN/ECE realized that its theory work was being displaced by practical reality. They called a meeting with X12 to merge the two standardization efforts and have a single standard. The meetings continued and continued. Eventually, X12 and EDIFACT (the name that the UN gave the effort in 1986) came to an agreement that the merger would occur in 1995, on newly developed specifications. The U.S. Customs Commissioner has moved to accept EDIFACT, another indication that X12 may be slowing down.

Present

X12 standards are in heavy use in North America, where EDI penetration appears to have achieved less than 10% in this market. At the same time, EDIFACT has fifty-three members, but has not really managed to produce any national or sectoral implementations of its work. If one considers that the United States is Europe's largest trading partner, and that the Europeans have not really taken to the EDIFACT standard, you begin to sense the nature of the problem that confronts EDIFACT and the EDI industry as a whole. The EDIFACT theory is good, but X12 standards are used. The pragmatic X12 approach is probably not optimized, but it works. The question of long-term viability for the X12 approach, however, is probably valid, since the X12 approach is predicated upon spot point, rather than systematic, standardization.

Future

The advent of the Internet, with its enhanced communications capabilities, may make the whole argument moot. EDI was initiated in the 1960s when there were no Internet browser enabled PCs with a gigabit of memory each. The solution that EDI is proposing is the transmission of common data elements to describe trading activities, including bills of ladling, invoices, customs documents and more. This may be able to be made into a simple applications package for a memory chip, or may be part of a RFID tag that travels with the goods.

However, the EDI issue is a very instructive one for standardization developers. The X12 approach was to march forward and deploy a solution, while the UN/ECE decision was to develop an overarching concept. The ASC X12 solution seemed to have worked, but it was eventually overtaken by events in the world. As it is now, there is an X12 legacy that will continue to exist for possibly several decades, with another set of standards in the process of coming into being, just as new technologies which may obsolete the entire effort begin to make their appearance.

VME BUS/FUTUREBUS+ EXTENDED ARCHITECTURE INTERNATIONAL TRADE ASSOCIATION (VITA)

VITA and its associated SDO, the VITA Standards Organization, are included in our discussion because they represent a "nontraditional" approach to standardization that has had an impact on the formal standardization arena. Ray Alderman, the head of VITA, is an experienced standardization professional who knew what he was doing and how to do what needed to be done when he initiated the process to have VITA made into an SDO.

History

VITA started life as the VME Bus/Futurebus+ Extended Architecture International Trade Association in 1984, led by Ray Alderman.[3] VME bus is a computer bus architecture standard in which Ray firmly believed; he proselytized it for several years in the IEEE, introducing it as a program and standardization initiative. Because VITA was also seen as a manufacturer's association for the VMEbus and Futurebus, the good faith standardization efforts of VITA were suspect. However, the program was on its way to completion when it ran into a series of blocking objections. The VITA representatives tried to get around the block as best they could, but were unable to change the opinions of the blocking committees and organizations.

Present

In late 1992, fed up with what were considered to be blocking tactics by other providers and other associations in the IEEE, VITA applied to ANSI for accreditation as an SDO, bypassing the groups and organizations that were halting progress on the standards effort. After Ray appeared before ANSI and demonstrated what he believed to be a valid case for accreditation, VITA was accredited as an ANS in June of 1993. VITA received accreditation as a canvass method organization.

To ensure the legitimacy of the standardization effort, VITA assumed the role of the secretariat to the VITA Standards Organization (VSO). Because VSO is a canvass method SDO, it has a duty to find all interested parties who might want to comment on a VSO proposed standard. Standards activities of VSO begin in study groups, which may be initiated by any member who wishes to build consensus for a specific standard. When consensus is reached for the need for a standard, a task group may be formed by the study group to actually create the standard. The formation of a task group requires the support of three VITA members. Once a group is started, it is the responsibility of the task group chair to progress the standard.

Because VITA's management felt that they were delayed in the IEEE by individuals who were working different agenda items, they are very conscious of the power of an individual in making or breaking a standards effort. They have attempted to limit the amount of power that one person can have in their organization.

The Future

The activities of the VSO in becoming accredited were successful for two reasons. First, they had a good technical staff supporting a lead delegate. Because the technology was neutral (or at least available from multiple vendors), the charge of prejudicial standardization was avoided. Second, the escalation process that ANSI advertised was used to work the program; nothing that VITA did was either unethical or illegal. It may have violated unspoken "we don't do that" rules, but ANSI's Information Systems Standards Board—would have condoned neither unethical nor illegal behavior in granting VITA its right to form an SDO.

Most importantly, VITA had the time to create an alternate path to a standard. If this had been some other program, such as embedded software or communications activities, VSO would not have worked because it would have run out of time. Busses, however, have a longer lifespan than does software, and as such, VSO had the luxury of pursuing an alternate path.

This is another factor in dealing with the complexities in the standardization arenas. Because the parliamentary blocking can be used to slow a program in the name of due process, there are fewer and fewer companies willing to actually commit to a formal standardization path. VITA is an example of an organization, which, when it was stymied in one organization, had the time and skill to create another path. Yet if this had been a small manufacturer, or if it had been a less experienced association, it could not have done what VITA, an association of manufacturer's, could do. The lesson was not lost on the industry as a whole.

NOTES

[1]The rationale for the name change stems from a decision by the Exchange Charriers Standards association began to include all telecommunications service providers who also have a plant or infrastructure investment. Cellular providers, cable tv operators, alternate access providers, and even the interexchange providers were thus drawn into the ACIS web.

[2]Reilly, Arthur T. "Defining the Network of the Future," Kahin and Abbate, op. cit., p. 584.

[3]See Alderman's article in *StandardView,* December 1995, Volume 3, Number 4, on the topic of "Rejuvenating A Technical Consortia" for his views of how to make a technical consortium work as it should. By understanding his VITA experience, the article takes on a different meaning than if it was merely read as a bland prescription.

Chapter 23

The Cyclical Nature of Open Systems

"Not, I'll not, carrion comfort, Despair, feast on thee;
Not untwist—slack they may be—these last strands of man
In me or, most weary, cry I can no more. I can."

—Gerard Manley Hopkins, *Carrion Comfort*

INTRODUCTION

This concluding essay, for that is what it is, is the result of a series of lectures that I gave at places as diverse as Stanford University and Rotorua, New Zealand. It provides a slightly different twist to the idea of standardization and open systems and makes the claim that standardization is cyclical.[1] Basically, the completion of a cycle defines the start of a new challenge. With each iteration, we have gotten closer to achieving something memorable; we are now at the point where we are about to launch into a wonderful and daring adventure.

The Cycles

Although this is probably anathema to many in the IT industry which prides itself on innovations and a disregard for the past, the thing that the IT dreamers and planners and visionaries forgot is that the entire IT industry is *based on standards and standardization.* And they forgot that standards and standardization take time and patience, go through cycles, and have to be assimilated and treated just as any other business cycle. As with any change agent—and standards are a change agent—it takes time for the critical mass to be achieved and time for the market to respond to the changes that are happening.

With this as background, I'd like to turn to the central character of this play—the humble standard and show how the definition of open systems and standardization have changed and continue to change. And, how, within this definition, there is a great deal of hope for the future of "open systems".

Standardization—in its broadest sense—looks at "open" versus "closed" solutions. Basically, the market moves towards open solutions and moves away from closed solutions. This is intuitively obvious; what is not so apparent is what is "open" and what is "closed". All too often, the vendors equate "proprietary" and "closed". This is one of the greater fallacies of the standardization industry. **Only in the last 10 years has the association of closed and proprietary been firmly—and in my feeling, incorrectly—cemented.**

In the "beginning" (not more than 50 years ago), everything connected with computing was new, and, because it was being invented, usually closed and proprietary. Mainframes—by definition—were the complete product of a single provider. Over time, peripheral devices—such as keyboards, printers, card readers, and disks became standardized—but it was a touch and go battle for a long time, involving, among other things, an extended Department of Justice monopoly suit against IBM. Ultimately, the market became more open; companies cross-licensed patents, made business arrangements, and sometimes, even violated IPR rules to "open up" peripheral sub-systems. Usually, the most popular way of doing things was imitated in standardization. (ASCII and EBCDEC are classic examples of things that went right and things that went wrong.) COBOL and Fortran were created, peripheral connectors were standardized, and the mainframe market grew.

However, there was a movement growing to use mini-computers. The use of minis brought about a whole new standardization challenge—including the challenge to standardized data flow between the minis. This wasn't a problem with mainframes—they were complete into themselves and usually talked to themselves of their clone kin. Minis posed a different problem, however. They were dispersed, talked funny operating systems (PrimeOS, RT11, VMS, RMS, WangOS, and whatever DG's OS was called), and were largely heterogeneous. (However, they did accept the standards from the mainframe era, and built on them.) The question of how to cross communicate data became a problem—and was solved by, among other things, the initiation of the Open Systems Interconnect (OSI) model. This idea ultimately blew up—but not before it had redefined the nature of computing so that the Local Area Network and Wide Area Network and Metropolitan Area Network were accepted, and the idea of a networked system came into being. Just as the "openness" that marked the mainframe was in peripheral connectors, the "openness" that marked the mini-computer era was in the idea of interconnects and cross communications. The problem with the minicomputer was that their era was over before the solution—which was TCP/IP and the Internet—became obvious. However, this does not deny the essential contribution of the mini market—which made communication between disparate computers a necessity and eventually lead to a standard way of cross communication.

The "open versus closed" argument continued with winners and losers. DECNet was a loser because, even though it was based on standards, it was seen as a proprietary solution. OSI lost—because although it was completely standards based, there were few "open" implementations of it. Rather, the providers (those that existed) decided that they would be standard while still retaining a proprietary overlay. The reason for the success of TCP/IP rested upon the impression that it was open—as open was defined by the market in the late 1980s. OSI was seen as an invention of a group of large vendors, and therefore, closed. Again, the market chose to reject the perception of the OSI solution as "closed", even though it was "open" according to the definitions of the time. The end of the creative time in this era occurred in the mid to late 1980s—about the time that consortia began to appear.

The next era—which followed the "mini" era—is what I call the PC/Workstation era. This era, which has lasted approximately a decade, is just ending now. It was in this time that the split which had begun in the preceding era came to a bifurcated conclusion. The conclusion has tremendous implications for the concept of Open Systems—and the future of the formal standardization movement.

The concept of "Open and Standards" became closely aligned here—driven by the activities of the two sides in the Graphical User Interface (GUI) wars, which saw Sun opposing the remainder of the industry, lead primarily by DEC. Sun initiated the activity, claiming to be a "standards" company, and by implication, "open". The standards were UNIX (AT&T's proprietary operating system), Open Look (Sun's proprietary GUI), and the SPARC chip (owned by SPARC International, a consortium.), and TCP/IP. On the other side, there was OSF 1, (a proprietary consortium owned OS), MOTIF and DCE (licensable but proprietary technology) and proprietary chip sets as well. Some of these struggles were legacy battles from the previous standardization activities—and quite frankly, the market didn't really take them too much into account after about 1992.

The rationale for this lack of concern was that the market had already begun to move in another direction—that of sharing data. There were two approaches to this problem—and this lead to the dual solutions. The first solution was driven by the hardware systems vendors who had an installed base of systems. The solution was contained in the POSIX 1003.0 definition of how to achieve this data sharing. The definition is as follows:

> "A system that implements sufficient open specifications for interfaces, services, and supporting formats to enable properly engineered applications software to be ported across a wide range of systems with minimal changes, to interoperate with other applications on local and remote systems, and to interact with users in a style which facilitates user portability". (POSIX 1003.0, Draft 17)

This definition led most of the workstation vendors on their quest for open systems in the 1985-1995 time frame. It was, according to all that they'd done before, the correct path to pursue. It was well phrased in terms of the necessary architectural constraints, and defined a user problem in terms such that it could be solved by the vendors in a standardized fashion.

While this made sense to the systems vendors, the users were discovering a different solution. Microsoft defined the "data sharing" problem within its own construct. Since Microsoft was not a major player in the standardization flora and fauna, it needed to come up with a different solution. And it did—the solution I call "ubiquitous, inexpensive, computing". By standardizing upon a single chip set (Intel), and by stabilizing many (if not all of its interfaces), Microsoft provided a new definition of "open"—which corresponds to the user view of "letting everyone participate in areas that the user considers important." To a majority of users, the ability to buy any of half a hundred platforms and over 10,000 application packages was important because this allowed them to share data. True, sneaker net was sometimes involved, but if spreadsheets produced the same result, and a user could integrate and modify someone else's data easily, then the goal of shared data had been achieved. Less important was the fact that the Microsoft was a single source for its software; this was seen as a positive benefit, since the other options were multiple shades of UNIX available from multiple vendors or a closed operating system (VMS). The user saw that, for less than US $200, he or she could choose from multiple platforms and thousands of applications. And while the OS wasn't perfect, it was "good enough".

The standardization wars in the "data sharing" arena are largely over. There are still battles to be fought, of course—battles about how to connect servers and clients, battles about how to store and retrieve information, the attributes of the OS (multi-threading, real time, administration) and so on. But the war in open systems has shifted—and now the question is "How do we share information?"

The real contribution of the PC/Workstation standardization activity was to change the emphasis from vendor driven technical solution as exemplified by the POSIX definition above to a user definition of "how to do collaborative computing". After all, the intent of standards based open systems computing was to "allow users to be better at what they were good at and to make things more efficient, better, more responsive, and faster." It was not to allow them to have faster computers, better displays, or anything else. These were attributes of computer systems—not open systems.

So, what is the future of "Open Systems"? Basically, a period of revolution is about to start—again. The revolution should be centered on increasing the ability to share information. This time, it will be the users who lead—and the vendors will be running to catch up. The key to success will be an understanding of the nature of the information that is being shared. The popularity of the World Wide Web shows that people—nations, companies, individuals—want an audience and want to share "information". The next movement in open systems is going to be focused on answering the question of "What is Information" in the context of the provider and the user of the information. The process by which the information is shared will probably be related to computers and computing—but will not be limited by the providing vendors.

CONCLUSION

The wars in standardization that we've just finished fighting—whose OS, whose GUI, whose processor, whose network—will all go away. They will be replaced by the questions of "Whose information" and "How to incorporate it?" and "Is it valid?" What has occurred before in the "Open systems" arena has merely been but prelude to the main act, which is now opening—the free sharing of information, and eventually, one hopes, knowledge. And this is the legacy of the standardization and "Open Systems" movement.

NOTE

[1]The genesis of this idea was a conversation with Gary Robinson, in which he stated that he and Joe DeBlasi, formerly of IBM and now Executive Director of the ACM, had been looking at the nature of standards, and among other things, detected a cyclical nature. The explication is mine, but the original idea is based upon the Gary and Joe conversation. The idea was developed and critiqued at Uniforum in New Zealand in 1996. I have found Uniforum N2 an ideal place to expose new ideas. They receive an audience, and I receive valid and thoughtful criticism and encouragement.

Epilogue

"Were I so tall to reach the pole
Or grasp the ocean with my span,
I must be measured by my soul
The mind's the standard of the man."

—Isaac Watts, *True Greatness*

Had I completed this book two years earlier, I believe that I would have used the Donne poem "A Valediction Forbidding Mourning" as the poetry heading for the chapter. When I began my research for the second edition of my original work, I became depressed and put the work aside for about a year. The picture was too bleak and too discouraging. There was little good news in the Information Technology standardization arena, and there was no indication that the situation would improve.

Fortunately, life continued, and I began to detect a new "interest" in standards. The companies that had previously rejected standards (or who had appeared to reject standards) began to pay more than lip service to the concept. Additionally, the government began to rationalize its participation, and there were significant organizational and structural changes in the IT industry, as well as in the supporting infrastructure of industry. Change began to occur, slowly, and usually when no one was looking. However, this change proceeded, and, despite the many attempts that failed, it wrought more change. The pace of change began to increase, very slowly.

This change, slow and uneven at times, was the focus of this book. The organization of the book, as explained in the introduction, looks at the various areas of standardization, from the theory and application of standardization in the IT arena, to standards generally, to the placement of and use of standards, to the organizations that create these standards. The book tries to point out where there is change, either in the organization or in the environment that supports or requires it. I have tried to be reasonably honest in this examination; where I have found a fault, I have been quick to point it out. Similarly, where I have found something that is good, I believe that I have been just as quick to compliment and praise. I have also offered observations on how to fix what I believe to be broken, since a fundamental rule of standardization is that you cannot just complain, you must counter-propose to make things better.

During the time that I wrote both books, I had managed to be an embedded and largely neutral participant within the process, which allowed me to participate in and understand the process as an involved, and in most cases, concerned player. Because I have been employed by a large corporation for most of my career in standards, I have also been empowered, allowing me to help make decisions that would help cause things to happen in standardization. (How often does a theorist actually get to implement theory?) Additionally, I have been granted the luxury of being able to try to understand and improve the process, both for my employer and for the industry, over a lengthy period of time. This book was intended to make the discipline of standardization more of a discipline and hence more understandable and manageable for a larger number of people.

One of the compelling reasons for writing this book is my hope that people will use the information in it to understand more completely the utility and benefits, as well as the pitfalls, of standardization. With this understanding will come the increased ability to participate, either directly or by proxy. It is the participation by more people that makes the standardization arena viable.

It is also the genius of the standardization system. Standardization is an act of people both giving up and accepting something; the willing trading of options and freedoms for what is perceived to be an increased gain of other options and freedoms. The trade-off is sometimes based upon economics, sometimes based upon trust, or any of a hundred other factors. As an example, implementing the standards for Heating, Ventilating, and Air Conditioning (HVAC) probably add significantly to the cost of a heating system. However, there is a corresponding increase in safety when the standard is adhered to by providers. The state, using its "public good" authority, made a decision that saving lives and preventing fires was worth the incremental product cost for everyone. Similarly, a decision was made for automobiles when seat belts were first introduced.

In most cases, the trade-offs on accepting or rejecting a standard are made by the individual consumer, usually hundreds of times a day. These range from clothing customs to food choice to computing choice.[1] What is important to recognize is that, as I stated in the opening sentences of the book, standardization is the measure of an industrialized society. The greater the industrialization, the greater the amount of interdependence required for the elements of society to interoperate. As all aspects of life, from necessities through absolute luxuries, become more intertwined and interconnected, the number of relations of one thing to another that a person must remember increases geometrically.[2] If there were no standards, the maintenance of all of these relationships would drive us stark, raving mad.

The same is true with the IT industry. As more and more "things" have to be remembered, more and more standards will be necessary to ensure that these things do not need to be remembered, they will just work. This is what standardization is all about; making things "just work" so that people can move on to other things.

Ultimately, then, standards and standardization are invisible change agents. They act to continuously raise the level of things that people expect to be the same, or to interoperate. With the ability to forget these relationships because they have been subsumed into the infrastructure, there is the ability to create new and better things. Standards enable change because they provide a common from which to begin change.

Without this structured change, the industry will not continue to grow in a coherent fashion. Robert Browning once noted:

> Ah, that a man's reach should exceed his grasp
> Or what's a heaven for?

The standardization process and standards put things within the industry's grasp, so that the reach can be extended to help the industry to keep moving, to keep wanting, to keep achieving, to keep changing. This, more than anything else, is the ultimate rationale for standards.

NOTES

[1] As an example, while claiming no experience in the subject what-so-ever, it would appear that high heels are a clothing choice dictated by custom, not utility. And yet I've had some incredible arguments with women wearing high heels who have told me that they find standards completely archaic and no longer germane to their life. Since I have a healthy respect for my wellbeing, I've never had the courage to make this observation in the conversation.

[2] The derivation of this belief is based on work by V. A. Graicunas, a French management consultant who did some initial work in determination of span of control. If someone manages only noninteracting people or things, then a large span of control is possible. However, if the people and things being managed interact, they assume characteristics based upon the interaction that also must be remembered. To illustrate, if A and B are managed, then the relations of the manager to A and B must be remembered. If, however, A and B interact, the manager must remember the relationship to A when both A and B are present, and what the relationship to B is when A is present, and what the relationship to A is when B isn't there, and so on. Graicunas expressed the relationship mathematically (where n is the number of objects/things/people managed) as

$$\text{Total possible relationships} = n \left(\frac{2n + n - 1}{2} \right)$$

Appendix A:

Committee Lists

The following is a list of Technical Committees of the International Organization for Standardization (ISO) as of January 1996:

ISO/IEC JTC 1 Information technology
TC 1 Screw threads
TC 2 Fasteners
TC 3 Limits and fits
TC 4 Rolling bearings
TC 5 Ferrous metal pipes and metallic fittings
TC 6 Paper, board, and pulps
TC 8 Ships and marine technology
TC 10 Technical drawings, product definition, and related documentation
TC 11 Boilers and pressure vessels
TC 12 Quantities, units, symbols, conversion factors
TC 14 Shafts for machinery and accessories
TC 17 Steel

TC 19 Preferred numbers
TC 20 Aircraft and space vehicles
TC 21 Equipment for fire protection and fire fighting
TC 22 Road vehicles
TC 23 Tractors and machinery for agriculture and forestry
TC 24 Sieves, sieving, and other sizing methods
TC 25 Cast iron and pig iron
TC 26 Copper and copper alloys
TC 27 Solid mineral fuels
TC 28 Petroleum products and lubricants
TC 29 Small tools
TC 30 Measurement of fluid flow in closed conduits

TC 31 Tyres, rims, and valves

TC 33 Refractories

TC 34 Agricultural food products

TC 35 Paints and varnishes

TC 36 Cinematography

TC 37 Terminology (principles and co-ordination)

TC 38 Textiles

TC 39 Machine tools

TC 41 Pulleys and belts (including vee-belts)

TC 42 Photography

TC 43 Acoustics

TC 44 Welding and allied processes

TC 45 Rubber and rubber products

TC 46 Information and documentation

TC 47 Chemistry

TC 48 Laboratory glassware and related apparatus

TC 51 Pallets for unit load method of materials handling

TC 52 Light gauge metal containers

TC 54 Essential oils

TC 55 Sawn timber and sawlogs

TC 57 Metrology and properties of surfaces

TC 58 Gas cylinders

TC 59 Building construction

TC 60 Gears

TC 61 Plastics

TC 65 Manganese and chromium ores

TC 67 Materials, equipment, and off shore structures for petroleum and natural gas industries

TC 68 Banking and related financial services

TC 69 Applications of statistical methods

TC 70 Internal combustion engines

TC 71 Concrete, reinforced concrete, and pre-stressed concrete

TC 72 Textile machinery and allied machinery and accessories

TC 74 Cement and lime

TC 76 Transfusion, infusion, and injection equipment for medical use

TC 77 Products in fibre reinforced cement

TC 79 Light metals and their alloys

TC 81 Common names for pesticides and other agrochemicals

TC 82 Mining

TC 83 Sports and recreational equipment

TC 84 Medical devices for injections

TC 85 Nuclear energy

TC 86 Refrigeration

TC 87 Cork

TC 89 Wood-based panels

TC 91 Surface active agents

TC 92 Fire safety

TC 93 Starch (including derivatives and byproducts)

TC 94 Personal safety—Protective clothing and equipment

TC 96 Cranes

TC 98 Bases for design of structures

TC 99 Semimanufactures of timber

TC 100 Chains and chain wheels for power transmission and conveyors

TC 101 Continuous mechanical handling equipment

TC 102 Iron ores

TC 104 Freight containers

TC 105 Steel wire ropes

TC 106 Dentistry

TC 107 Metallic and other inorganic coatings

TC 108 Mechanical vibration and shock

TC 110 Industrial trucks

TC 111 Round steel link chains, chain slings, components, and accessories

TC 112 Vacuum technology

TC 113 Hydrometric determinations

TC 114 Horology

TC 115 Pumps

TC 116 Space heating appliances

TC 117 Industrial fans

TC 118 Compressors, pneumatic tools, and pneumatic machines

TC 119 Powder metallurgy

TC 120 Leather

TC 121 Anaesthetic and respiratory equipment

TC 122 Packaging

TC 123 Plain bearings

TC 126 Tobacco and tobacco products

TC 127 Earth-moving machinery

TC 130 Graphic technology

TC 131 Fluid power systems

TC 132 Ferroalloys

TC 133 Sizing systems and designations for clothes

TC 134 Fertilizers and soil conditioners

TC 135 Nondestructive testing

TC 136 Furniture

TC 137 Sizing system, designations, and marking for boots and shoes

TC 138 Plastics pipes, fittings, and valves for the transport of fluids

TC 145 Graphical symbols

TC 146 Air quality

TC 147 Water quality

TC 148 Sewing machines

TC 149 Cycles

TC 150 Implants for surgery

TC 153 Valves

TC 154 Documents and data elements in administration, commerce, and industry

TC 155 Nickel and nickel alloys

TC 156 Corrosion of metals and alloys

TC 157 Mechanical contraceptives

TC 158 Analysis of gases

TC 159 Ergonomics

TC 160 Glass in building

TC 161 Control and safety devices for nonindustrial gas-fired appliances and systems

TC 162 Doors and windows

TC 163 Thermal insulation

TC 164 Mechanical testing of metals

TC 165 Timber structures

TC 166 Ceramic ware, glassware and glass ceramic ware in contact with food

TC 167 Steel and aluminium structures

TC 168 Prosthetics and orthotics

TC 170 Surgical instruments

TC 171 Document imaging applications

TC 172 Optics and optical instruments

TC 173 Technical systems and aids for disabled or handicapped persons

TC 174 Jewelry

TC 175 Fluorspar

TC 176 Quality management and quality assurance

TC 177 Caravans

TC 178 Lifts, escalators, passenger conveyors

TC 179 Masonry

TC 180 Solar energy

TC 181 Safety of toys

TC 182 Geotechnics

TC 183 Copper, lead and zinc ores, and concentrates

TC 184 Industrial automation systems and integration

TC 185 Safety devices for protection against excessive pressure

TC 186 Cutlery and table and decorative metal hollow-ware

TC 187 Color notations

TC 188 Small craft

TC 189 Ceramic tile

TC 190 Soil quality

TC 191 Animal (mammal) traps

TC 192 Gas turbines

TC 193 Natural gas

TC 194 Biological evaluation of medical devices

TC 195 Building construction machinery and equipment

TC 196 Natural stone

TC 197 Hydrogen energy technologies

TC 198 Sterilization of health care products
TC 199 Safety of machinery
TC 200 Solid wastes
TC 201 Surface chemical analysis
TC 202 Microbeam analysis
TC 203 Technical energy systems
TC 204 Transport information and control
   systems
TC 205 Building environment design
TC 206 Fine ceramics
TC 207 Environmental management

TC 208 Thermal turbines for industrial application (steam turbines, gas expansion
   turbines)
TC 209 Cleanrooms and associated controlled
   environments
TC 210 Quality management and corresponding general aspects for medical devices
TC 211 Geographic information/Geomatics
TC 212 Clinical laboratory testing and in vitro
   diagnostic test systems

Appendix B:

List of IEC Committees

TC stands for Technical Committee, SC for Subcommittee.

TC1: Terminology

TC2: Rotating machinery

TC3: Documentation and graphical symbols

TC4: Hydraulic turbines

TC5: Steam turbines

TC7: Bare aluminium conductors

TC8: Standard voltages, current ratings, and frequencies

TC9: Electric traction equipment

TC10: Fluids for electrotechnical applications

TC11: Overhead lines

TC12: Radiocommunications

TC13: Equipment for electrical energy measurement and load control

TC14: Power transformers

TC15: Insulating materials

TC16: Terminal markings and other identifications

TC17: Switchgear and controlgear

TC18: Electrical installations of ships and of mobile and fixed offshore units

TC20: Electric cables

TC21: Secondary cells and batteries

TC22: Power electronics

TC23: Electrical accessories

TC25: Quantities and units, and their letter symbols

TC26: Electric welding

TC27: Industrial electroheating equipment

TC28: Insulation coordination

TC29: Electroacoustics

TC31: Electrical apparatus for explosive atmospheres

TC32: Fuses

TC33: Power capacitors

TC34: Lamps and related equipment

TC35: Primary cells and batteries

TC36: Insulators

TC37: Surge arresters

TC38: Instrument transformers

TC39: Electronic tubes

TC40: Capacitors and resistors for electronic equipment

TC42: High-voltage testing techniques

TC44: Safety of machinery; Electrotechnical aspects

TC45: Nuclear instrumentation

TC46: Cables, wires, waveguides, r.f. connectors, and accessories for communication and signalling

TC47: Semiconductor devices

TC48: Electromechanical components and mechanical structures for electronic equipments

TC49: Piezoelectric and dielectric devices for frequency control and selection

TC50: Environmental testing

TC51: Magnetic components and ferrite materials

TC52: Printed circuits

TC55: Winding wires

TC56: Dependability

TC57: Power system control and associated communications

TC59: Performance of household electrical appliances

TC60: Recording; Restructured as SC 100B

TC61: Safety of household and similar electrical appliances

TC62: Electrical equipment in medical practice

TC64: Electrical installations of buildings

TC66: Safety of measuring, control, and laboratory equipment

TC68: Magnetic alloys and steels

TC69: Electric road vehicles and electric industrial trucks

TC70: Degrees of protection by enclosures

TC71: Electrical installations for outdoor sites under heavy conditions (including open-cast mines and quarries)

TC72: Automatic controls for household use

TC73: Short-circuit currents

TC74: Safety of information technology equipment including electrical business equipment and telecommunication equipment

TC75: Classification of environmental conditions

TC76: Laser equipment

TC77: Electromagnetic compatibility

TC78: Tools for live working

TC79: Alarm systems

TC80: Maritime navigation and radiocommunication equipment and systems

TC81: Lightning protection

TC82: Solar photovoltaic energy systems

TC84: Equipment and systems in the field of audio, video, and audiovisual engineering; Restructured as SC 100C

TC85: Measuring equipment for electromagnetic quantities

TC86: Fibre optics

TC87: Ultrasonics

TC88: Windturbine generator systems

TC89: Fire hazard testing

TC90: Superconductivity

TC91: Surface mounting technology

TC92: Safety of audio, video, and similar electronic equipment

TC93: Design automation

TC94: All-or-nothing electrical relays

TC95: Measuring relays and protection equipment

TC96: Small power transformers and reactors and special transformers and reactors

TC97: Electrical installations for the lighting and beaconing of aerodromes

TC98: Electrical insulation systems (EIS)

TC99: System engineering and erection of electrical power installations in systems with nominal voltages above 1 kV A.C., particularly considering safety aspects

TC100: Sound, vision and multimedia systems and equipment

CISPR:International Special Committee on Radio Interference (C.I.S.P.R.)

CIS/A:C.I.S.P.R. Sub-Committee A: Radio interference measurements and statistical methods

CIS/B:C.I.S.P.R. Sub-Committee B: Interference relating to industrial, scientific and medical radio-frequency apparatus

CIS/C:C.I.S.P.R. Sub-Committee C: Interference relating to overhead power lines, high voltage equipment and electric traction systems

CIS/D:C.I.S.P.R. Sub-Committee D: Interference relating to motor vehicles and internal-combustion engines

CIS/E:C.I.S.P.R. Sub-Committee E: Interference relating to radio receivers

CIS/F:C.I.S.P.R. Sub-Committee F: Interference relating to household appliances, tools, lighting equipment, and similar apparatus

CIS/G:C.I.S.P.R. Sub-Committee G: Interference relating to information technology equipment

Appendix C:

List of SDO Addresses

Australia: Standards Australia (SAA)
P.O. Box 1055
Strathfield NSW 2135
Telephone: +61 2 746 4700
Fax: +61 2 746 8450
Telex: 2 65 14 astan aa

Austria: Osterreichisches Normungsinstitut
Heinestrasse 38
Postfach 130 A-1021 Wien
Telephone: +43 1 21 30 00
Fax: +43 1 21 30 06 50
Telex: 11 59 60 norm a

Belgium: Institut Belge de Normalisation
Av. de la Brabanconne 29
B-1040 Bruxelles
Telephone: +32 2 734 92 05
Fax: +32 2 733 42 64
Telex: 2 38 77 benor b

Brazil: Associacao Brasileira de Normass T'cnicas
Av. 13 de Maio n 13-27 andar
Caixa Postal 1680
CEP: 20, 003 Rio de Janeiro-RJ
Telephone: +55 21 210 31 22
Fax: +55 21 240 82 49
Telex: 213 43 33 abnt br

Canada: Standards Council of Canada
45 O'Connor Street, Suite 1200
Ottowa, Ontario K1P 6N7
Telephone: +1 613 238 32 22
Fax: +1 613 995 45 64
Telex: 053 44 03 stancan ott

China: China State Bureau of Technical Supervision
4, Zhi Chun Road
Haidian District
P.O. Box 8010
Beijing 100088
Telephone: +86 1 203.24.24
Fax: +86 1 203.10.10

Czech Republic:
Czech Office for Standards, Metrology,
and Testing (COSMT)
Vaclavske namesti 19
113 47 Praha 1
Telephone: +42 2 24 22 47 34
Fax: +42 2 24 22 47 26

Denmark: Dansk Standard (DS)
Baunegaardsvej 73
DK-2900 Hellerup
Telephone: +45 39 77.01.01
Fax: +45 39 77.02.02

Egypt, Arab Republic of:
Egyptian Organization for Standardization
and Quality Control
2 Latin America Street
Garden City, Cairo
Telephone: +20 2 354 97 20
Fax: +20 2 355 78 41

**Finland: Finnish Standards Association
SFS**
P.O. Box 116
FIN-00231 Helsinki
Telephone: +358 0 149.93.31
Fax: +358 0 146.49.25

**France: Association Francaise de
Normalisation (AFNOR)**
Tour Europe
Cedex 7
F-92049 Paris La D'fense
Telephone: +331 42 91 55 55
Fax: +331 42 91 56 56
Telex: 61 19 74 afnor f

**Germany: Deutsches Institut fur Normung
(DIN)**
D-10772 Berlin
Telephone: +49 30 26.01-0
Fax: +49 30 26.01.12.31

**Ireland: National Standards Authority
of Ireland**
Glasnevin Dublin-9
Telephone: +353 1 837.01.01
Fax: +353 1 836.98.21

**Italy: Ente Nazionale Italiano di
Unificazione**
Via Battistotti Sassi 11
I-20133 Milano
Telephone: +39 2 70.02.41
Fax: +39 2 70.10.61.06

**Japan: Japanese Industrial Standards
Committee**
c/o Standards Department
Agency of Industrial Science and
Technology
Ministry of International Trade and
Industry
1-3-1 Kasumigaseki, Chiyoda-ku
Tokyo 100
Telephone: +81 3 35.01.92.95/6
Fax: +81 3 35.80.14.18

Korea, Republic of:
Bureau of Standards
Industrial Advancement Administration
2, Chungang-dong, Kwachon-city
Kyonggi-do 427-010
Telephone: +82 2 503 79 28
Fax: +82 2 503 79 41
Telex: 2 84 56 fincen k

**Morocco: Service de Normalisation
Industrielle Marocaine (SNIMA)**
1, Place Sefrou (Tour Hassan)
Rabat
Telephone: +212 7 72.16.78
Fax: +212 7 76.0675

**Netherlands: Nederlands Normalisatie-
    instituut**
  Kalfjeslaan 2
  P.O. Box 5059
  NL-2600 GF Delft
  Telephone: +31 15 69 03 90
  Fax: +31 15 69 01 90
  Telex: 3 81 44 nni ni

**Norway: Norges Standardiserings-
    forbund**
  Hegdehaugsveien 31
  Postboks 7020 Homansbyen
  N-0306 Oslo 3
  Telephone: +47 22 46.60.94
  Fax: +47 22 46.44.57

**Romania: Institutul Roman de
    Standardizare (IRS)**
  Str. Jean-Louis Calderon Nr. 13
  Cod 70201
  Bucuresti 2
  Telephone: +40 1 611.40.43
  Fax: +40 1 312.08.23

**Russia: Committee of the Russian
    Federation for Standardization,
    Metrology, and Certification (GOST R)**
  Leninsky Prospekt 9
  Moskva 117049
  Telephone: +7 095 236.40.44
  Fax: +7 095 237.60.32

**Slovenia: Standards and Metrology
    Institute (SMIS)**
  Ministry of Science and Technology
  Kotnikova 6
  SI-61000 Ljubljana
  Telephone: +386 61 131.23.22
  Fax: +386 61 31.48.82

**Sweden: ITS, Information Technology
    Standardization**
  Electrum 235
  S-16440 Kista
  Telephone: +46 8 793 9000
  Fax: +46 8 751 5653

**Switzerland: Swiss Association for
    Standardization (SNV)**
  Muhlebachstrasse 54
  CH-8008 Zurich
  Telephone: +41 1 254.54.54
  Fax: +41 1 254 54.74

**Ukraine: State Committee of Ukraine
    for Standardization, Metrology,
    and Certification (DSTU)**
  174 Gorkiy Street
  252006 Kiev-06
  Telephone: +7 044 226.29.71
  Fax: +7 044 226.29.70

**United Kingdom: British Standards
    Institution (BSI)**
  389 Chiswick High Road
  GB-London W4 4AJ
  Telephone: +44 181 996.90.00
  Fax: +44 181 996.74.00

**United States of America:
    American National Standards
    Institute (ANSI)**
  11 West 42nd Street
  New York, NY 10036
  Telephone: +1 212 642-4900
  Fax: +1 212 398-0023
  Telex: 42 42 96 ansi ui

Index